MESSALINA

Honor Cargill-Martin is an author, classicist, and art historian from London. She read Classical Archaeology and Ancient History at Oxford, winning a scholarship and graduating with a first-class degree in 2019. She has masters degrees in Greek and Roman history and Italian Renaissance Art. She is currently studying for a doctorate focusing on political sex scandals in Ancient Rome at Christ Church, Oxford. She has published a number of children's fiction titles. Her biography of Messalina is her first non-fiction title.

MESSALINA

EMPRESS, ADULTERESS, LIBERTINE

*The Story of the Most Notorious
Woman of the Roman World*

HONOR CARGILL-MARTIN

PEGASUS BOOKS
NEW YORK LONDON

MESSALINA

Pegasus Books, Ltd.
148 West 37th Street, 13th Floor
New York, NY 10018

First Pegasus Books cloth edition June 2023

ISBN: 978-1-63936-395-7

10 9 8 7 6 5 4 3 2 1

Printed in the United States of America
Distributed by Simon & Schuster
www.pegasusbooks.com

*To my mother, Perdita, who taught me how
to write and how to think.*

Contents

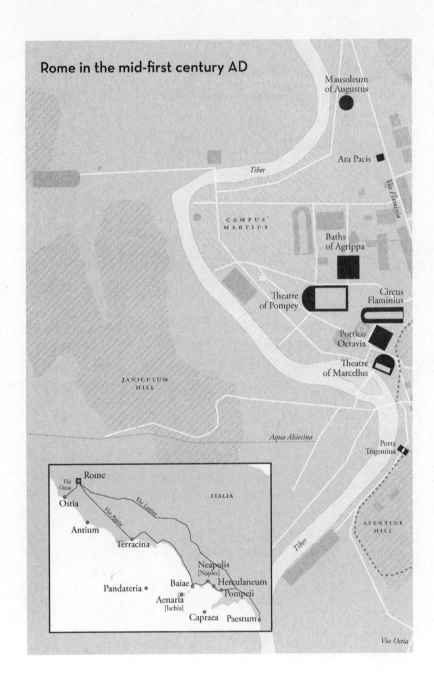

Rome in the mid-first century AD

Mausoleum
of Augustus

Ara Pacis

Tiber

Via Flaminia

CAMPUS
MARTIUS

Baths
of Agrippa

Theatre
of Pompey

Circus
Flaminius

Portico
Octavia

Theatre
of Marcellus

JANICULUM
HILL

Aqua Alsietina

Porta
Trigemina

AVENTINE
HILL

Tiber

*Via
Ostia*
Rome

Ostia

ITALIA

Antium

Via Appia

Via Latina

Terracina

Neapolis
[Naples]

Pandateria

Baiae

Herculaneum

Pompeii

Aenaria
[Ischia]

Capraea

Paestum

Via Ostia

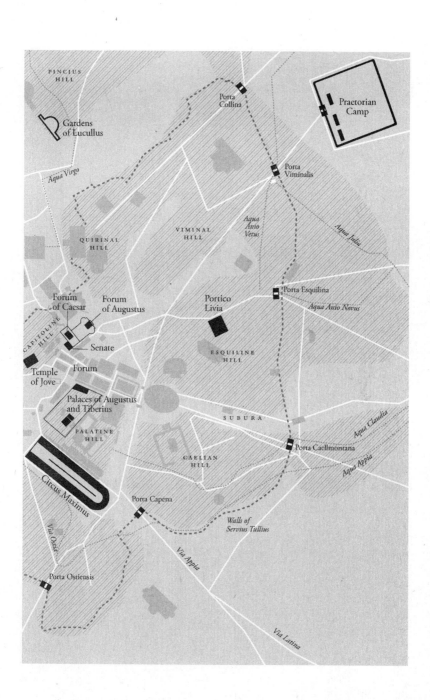

PINCIUS
HILL

Gardens
of Lucullus

Porta
Collina

Praetorian
Camp

Aqua Virgo

Porta
Viminalis

*Aqua
Anio
Verus*

VIMINAL
HILL

Aqua Julia

QUIRINAL
HILL

Forum
of Caesar

Forum
of Augustus

Portico
Livia

Porta Esquilina

Aqua Anio Novus

CAPITOLINE
HILL

Senate

ESQUILINE
HILL

Temple
of Jove

Forum

Palaces of Augustus
and Tiberius

SUBURA

Aqua Claudia

PALATINE
HILL

Porta Caellmontana

Aqua Appia

CAELIAN
HILL

Circus Maximus

Porta Capena

Walls of
Servius Tullius

Via Ostia

Via Appia

Porta Ostiensis

Via Latina

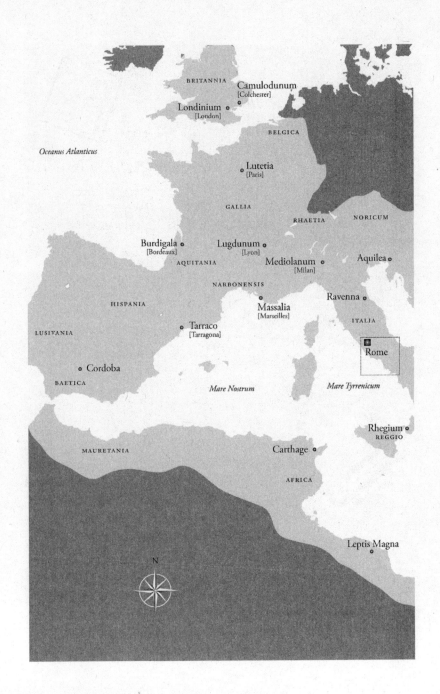

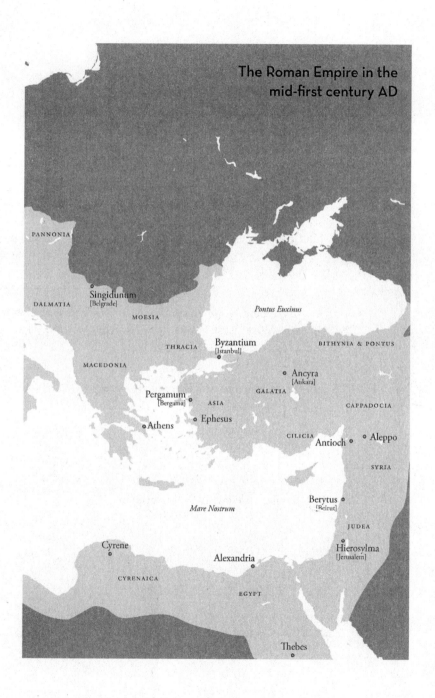

The Roman Empire in the mid-first century AD

PANNONIA

DALMATIA

Singidunum
[Belgrade]

MOESIA

Pontus Euxinus

THRACIA

Byzantium
[Istanbul]

BITHYNIA & PONTUS

MACEDONIA

Ancyra
[Ankara]

GALATIA

Pergamum
[Bergama]

ASIA

CAPPADOCIA

Athens

Ephesus

CILICIA

Antioch

Aleppo

SYRIA

Mare Nostrum

Berytus
[Beirut]

JUDEA

Cyrene

Hierosylma
[Jerusalem]

Alexandria

CYRENAICA

EGYPT

Thebes

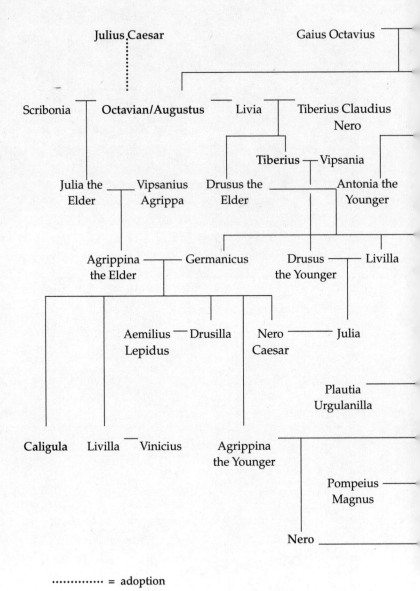

Julius Caesar

Gaius Octavius

Scribonia   Octavian/Augustus   Livia   Tiberius Claudius Nero

Tiberius — Vipsania

Julia the Elder —— Vipsanius Agrippa   Drusus the Elder —— Antonia the Younger

Agrippina the Elder —— Germanicus   Drusus the Younger — Livilla

Aemilius Lepidus — Drusilla   Nero Caesar —— Julia

Plautia Urgulanilla

Caligula   Livilla — Vinicius   Agrippina the Younger

Pompeius Magnus

Nero

.... = adoption
– – – – – = betrothed

The Julio-Claudian dynasty

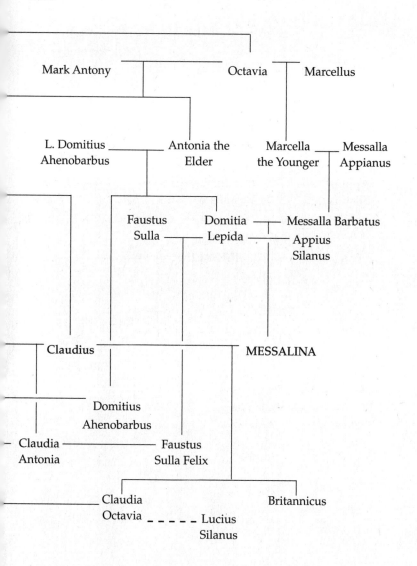

Attia

Mark Antony   Octavia   Marcellus

L. Domitius _____ Antonia the   Marcella ____ Messalla
Ahenobarbus   Elder   the Younger | Appianus

Faustus   Domitia ——┬── Messalla Barbatus
Sulla ——— Lepida ———├── Appius
                              Silanus

Claudius   MESSALINA

Domitius
Ahenobarbus

Claudia ————————— Faustus
Antonia   Sulla Felix

Claudia   Britannicus
Octavia _ _ _ _ _ Lucius
                    Silanus

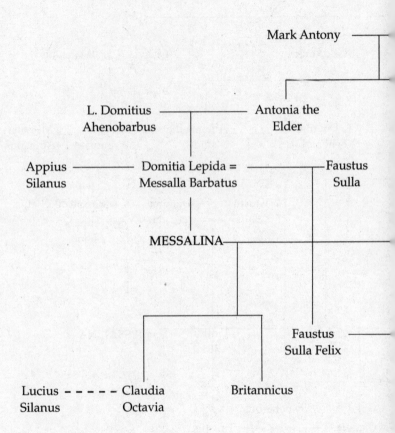

Mark Antony ———

L. Domitius ——————— Antonia the
Ahenobarbus   Elder

Appius ————— Domitia Lepida = ————————— Faustus
Silanus   Messalla Barbatus   Sulla

MESSALINA

Faustus
Sulla Felix

Lucius – – – – – Claudia   Britannicus
Silanus   Octavia

The family of Messalina and Claudius

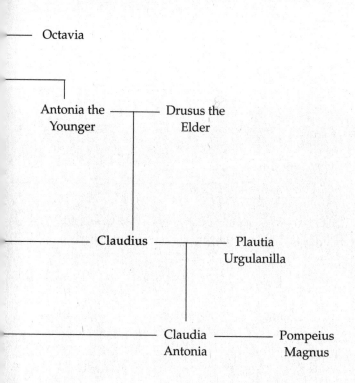

Octavia

Antonia the — Drusus the
Younger   Elder

Claudius — Plautia
Urgulanilla

Claudia — Pompeius
Antonia   Magnus

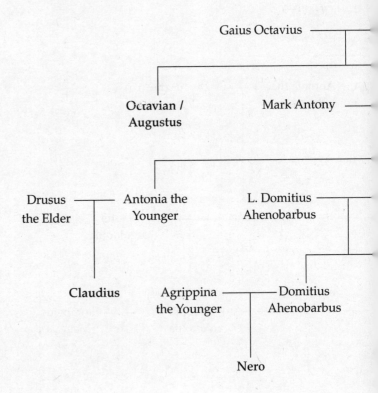

The Family of Augustus and Claudius

Gaius Octavius

Octavian / Augustus   Mark Antony

Drusus   Antonia the   L. Domitius
the Elder   Younger   Ahenobarbus

        Claudius   Agrippina   Domitius
                          the Younger   Ahenobarbus

                        Nero

Messalina's family connections
at the time of her marriage

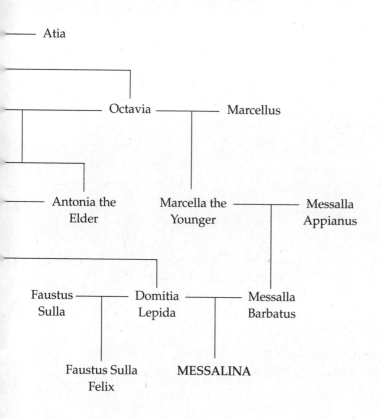

Atia

Octavia ——— Marcellus

Antonia the
Elder

Marcella the ——— Messalla
Younger   Appianus

Faustus ——— Domitia ——— Messalla
Sulla   Lepida   Barbatus

Faustus Sulla   **MESSALINA**
Felix

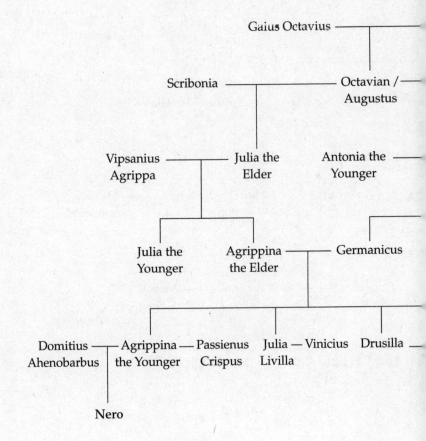

Gaius Octavius

Scribonia ———— Octavian /
Augustus

Vipsanius ———— Julia the   Antonia the
Agrippa   Elder   Younger

Julia the   Agrippina ——— Germanicus
Younger   the Elder

Domitius ——— Agrippina — Passienus   Julia — Vinicius   Drusilla
Ahenobarbus   the Younger   Crispus   Livilla

Nero

The imperial princesses and their husbands

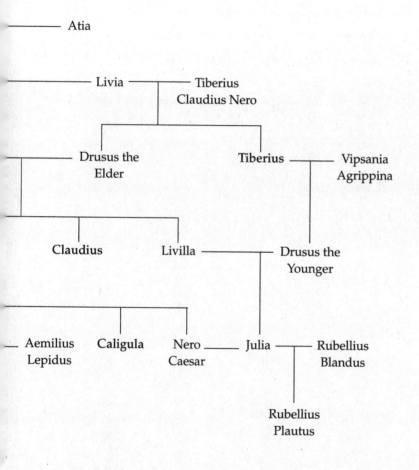

Atia

Livia ——— Tiberius Claudius Nero

Drusus the Elder

Tiberius ——— Vipsania Agrippina

Claudius

Livilla ——— Drusus the Younger

Aemilius Lepidus

Caligula

Nero Caesar

Julia ——— Rubellius Blandus

Rubellius Plautus

The eyes of Messalina drag
The best, most beautiful, of all Patrician men
Towards the very wretchedest of ends.

— Juvenal, Satires, 10.331-333

Dramatis Personae

Messalina's Family

Domitia Lepida: Messalina's mother.

Messalla Barbatus: Messalina's father. Died when she was very young.

Faustus Sulla: The second husband of Domitia Lepida. Messalina's step-father.

Faustus Sulla Felix: Messalina's half-brother. Later married to her step-daughter Claudia Antonia.

Claudius: Messalina's husband. Emperor of Rome.

Claudia Octavia: Messalina and Claudius' daughter. Later the wife of the emperor Nero.

Britannicus: Messalina and Claudius' son.

Claudius' Family

Antonia the Younger: Claudius' difficult mother.

Drusus the Elder: Claudius' dead father.

Germanicus: Claudius' golden boy brother. Died in mysterious circumstances. Married to Agrippina the Elder, and father to the emperor Caligula and his sisters.

MESSALINA

Livilla: Claudius' sister. Accused of helping her lover Sejanus to murder her husband Drusus.

Plautia Urgulanilla: Claudius' first wife. Divorced amid a scandal involving allegations of incest and murder.

Claudius Drusus: Claudius' son by his first wife. Died in a pear-throwing accident as a teenager.

Aelia Paetina: Claudius' second wife. Divorced for minor reasons.

Claudia Antonia: Claudius' daughter by his second wife. Messalina's step-daughter.

The Court of Augustus

Octavian/Augustus: the first emperor of Rome. Named Octavian until he took the honorific name of Augustus in 27 BC.

Octavia: Augustus' beloved and powerful sister. Messalina's direct ancestress.

Livia: the wife of Augustus. Held unprecedented power and prestige as Rome's first real 'empress'. Mother of Augustus' successor Tiberius.

Julia the Elder: Augustus' daughter. Tiberius' second wife. Exiled on scandalous adultery charges.

Julia the Younger: Julia the Elder's daughter. Augustus' granddaughter. Later followed her mother into exile on matching adultery charges.

The Court of Tiberius

Tiberius: Livia's son. Augustus' step-son. The second emperor of Rome.

Sejanus: powerful Prefect of the Praetorian Guard under Tiberius. The archetypal sinister advisor.

Drusus: Tiberius' son. Later believed to have been poisoned by his wife Livilla and Sejanus.

Agrippina the Elder: the wife of Claudius' brother Germanicus and the mother of Caligula and his sisters. Became a rallying point for opposition to Tiberius and was exiled.

The Court of Caligula

Caligula: the young and famously volatile third emperor of Rome. Claudius' nephew.

Drusilla: Caligula's favourite sister and rumoured lover. Worshipped as a goddess after her death.

Aemilius Lepidus: husband of Drusilla. Allegedly conducted affairs with all three of his wife's siblings: Caligula, Julia Livilla and Agrippina. Executed on charges of conspiracy and adultery.

Gaetulicus: Governor of Upper Germany. Was executed for his part in an alleged conspiracy against Caligula.

Livia Orestilla: Caligula's second wife, whom he married during her wedding to another man.

Lollia Paulina: Caligula's wealthy third wife.

Milonia Caesonia: Caligula's fourth wife and the mother of his daughter. Murdered alongside her husband and baby.

The Praetorians

Cassius Chaerea: a distinguished Praetorian officer with Republican convictions. One of the leaders of the plot against Caligula.

Cornelius Sabinus: a high-ranking Praetorian officer involved in the plot against Caligula.

Catonius Justus: Praetorian Prefect during the early years of Claudius' reign. Executed, allegedly on the orders of Messalina.

Rufrius Crispinus: Praetorian Prefect. A loyal supporter of Messalina.

Lusius Geta: Praetorian Prefect. Spoke against Messalina during her fall, but was later deemed too loyal to Messalina's memory and removed.

The Palatine Court in the time of Messalina

Freedmen, Slaves and Servants

Narcissus: a powerful freedman, in charge of the emperor's correspondence. Messalina's closest ally turned mortal enemy.

Callistus and Pallas: two powerful freedmen at Claudius' court.

Calpurnia and Cleopatra: two of the emperor's mistresses.

Sosibus: Britannicus' tutor and an ally of Messalina.

The Extended Imperial Family at Claudius' Court

Julia Livilla: one of the sisters of Caligula. Recalled after Claudius' accession. Accused of adultery with Seneca and exiled allegedly at Messalina's instigation.

Marcus Vinicius: the husband of Julia Livilla. Later rumours accuse Messalina of having him poisoned.

Julia Livia: daughter of Livilla and Drusus. Allegedly killed at Messalina's instigation.

Pompeius Magnus: married to Messalina's step-daughter Claudia Antonia in AD 41 but later executed.

Lucius Silanus: betrothed to Messalina's baby daughter Claudia Octavia. Forced to commit suicide by Agrippina.

Appius Silanus: the third husband of Messalina's mother Domitia Lepida. Executed, allegedly on the basis of a fake dream devised by Messalina and Narcissus.

Agrippina the Younger: one of the sisters of Caligula. Mother of the emperor Nero. Married her uncle Claudius after Messalina's fall and was accused of arranging his murder.

Passienus Crispus: Agrippina the Younger's second husband. A famed wit and reliably loyal to Claudius' regime.

Women of the Court

Poppaea Sabina the Elder: a famed beauty. Allegedly Messalina's rival for the affection of the dancer Mnester. Forced to suicide over her alleged affair with Valerius Asiaticus. Her namesake daughter replaced Octavia as the wife of Nero.

Arria: a close friend of Messalina's. Committed suicide alongside her beloved husband Caecina Paetus.

Pomponia Graecina: the wife of Claudius' general Plautius. Wore mourning for the rest of her life in protest at Messalina's treatment of Julia Livia.

Junia Silana: Gaius Silius' noble and blameless wife. Divorced, apparently on account of his affair with Messalina.

Junia Calvina: the beautiful sister of Lucius Silanus. Accusations of incest led to her brother's suicide and her (temporary) exile.

Senators

Publius Suillius: skilled orator and notorious prosecutor. Long-time ally of Messalina.

Lucius Vitellius: senatorial ally of Messalina for most of her reign. His namesake son was later briefly emperor.

Seneca: courtier and stoic philosopher. Accused of adultery with Julia Livilla and exiled, allegedly on Messalina's instigation. Later tutor to Nero.

Camillus Scribonianus: Governor of Dalmatia. Mounted a short-lived rebellion against Claudius and died by suicide or assassination.

Caecina Paetus: forced to commit suicide for his involvement in Scribonianus' revolt. Joined by his devoted wife Arria.

Aulus Plautius: Claudius' most prominent general. The mastermind behind the British campaign.

Valerius Asiaticus: a vastly wealthy and eminent senator from Gaul. Forced to suicide after being convicted of conspiracy and sexual misbehaviour, allegedly on Messalina's instigation.

Messalina's Alleged Lovers and Associates

Gaius Silius: the most handsome young aristocrat in Rome. Allegedly Messalina's lover, bigamous husband, and co-conspirator.

Mnester: an irresistible pantomime star. Allegedly the lover of Caligula and later Messalina.

Polybius: a powerful freedman, Claudius' literary advisor. Allegedly one of Messalina's lovers and killed on her orders.

Traulus Montanus: a strikingly beautiful and innocent young equestrian. Said to have been summoned, slept with, and dumped by Messalina in the course of a single night.

Vettius Valens: a renowned doctor. Allegedly one of the empress' lovers.

Titius Proculus, Pompeius Urbicus, Saufeius Trogus, Juncus Vergilianus, Sulpicius Rufius, Decrius Calpurnianus: more of Messalina's alleged lovers and associates.

Helvia, Cotta and Fabius: three more men who may also have fallen alongside Messalina.

Plautius Laternaus: the nephew of Claudius' most powerful general. Accused alongside Messalina but pardoned.

Suillius Caesonius: the son of the feared prosecutor Publius Suillius. Accused alongside Messalina but pardoned.

The Women of Nero

Claudia Acte: a freedwoman with whom Nero conducted a passionate affair.

Poppaea Sabina the Younger: a lover of Nero and the daughter of Messalina's old rival Poppaea Sabina the Elder. Nero divorced Octavia in order to marry her.

Introduction

In 1798, a Parisian publisher by the name of Pierre Didot decided to branch out into porn. He commissioned sixteen luxuriant engravings depicting positions ranging from the basic to the impressively athletic. To keep things classy, he cloaked the whole project in two layers of historical respectability.* The title laid (erroneous) claim to descent from the most notorious of Renaissance erotic works: *I Modi*, or, *The Positions*. This collection of sixteen engravings and sixteen sonnets had been deemed so dangerously explicit by the Catholic Church that two entire print runs were seized and destroyed, leaving the work to survive only in unsatisfactory fragments and scandalous reputation.[1] Didot also provided each of his positions with a classical title drawn from Greco-Roman myth or history and a few pages of quasi-intellectual historical explanation; in Plate VI Hercules puts his famous strength to good use by lifting Deianira entirely off the ground, Plate X depicts Bacchus making love to a head-standing Ariadne, and in Plate XVII, we catch Aeneas fingering a kneeling Dido from behind.

Position XIV is called 'the Messalina'. We are in a Roman brothel and Messalina – empress of the known world, wife of the emperor Claudius – is lying back on a lion-footed bed,

---

* The book was published under the name *L'Arétin d'Augustin Carrache, ou recueil de postures érotiques* with engravings by the artist Jacques-Joseph Coiny.

masquerading as a common prostitute. We can hardly see the face of the anonymous, muscled client preparing to penetrate her but it doesn't matter. Messalina's leg is on his shoulder and her hand is on his back, pulling him towards her. The plate illustrates a famous passage from the poet Juvenal's early second-century AD *Sixth Satire* in which he claims the empress, desperate to feed her insatiable sex drive, would wait for her husband to fall asleep before disguising herself with a blonde wig and a cloak and slipping from the luxury of the Palatine palace, through the dark streets of Rome, to a seedy brothel.[2] There she'd take a room, stuffy and stinking, strip off and put herself on sale under the fake name 'Lycisca' – 'Little-She-Wolf'. She'd flirt and fuck for a few coins a go and it was only in the morning, when the sun was rising and the pimp was getting tetchy, that she'd finally, reluctantly, agree to leave. She'd return to the palace dirty – the sweat of her lovers and the soot of the cheap oil lamps on her skin – and happier but, Juvenal claims, still not entirely satisfied.

The text that accompanies Plate XIV describes its subject's prodigious sex life. Messalina, we are told, slept with every officer in her husband's palace; in fact, there was hardly a man in Rome who could not boast that he'd had the empress. It claims she blithely murdered men who, over-exerted by her endless demands, no longer had the stamina or skill to satisfy her. It ends with the assertion that Messalina's name would never die; it would live on, down through the centuries, as a label for any woman unrestrained in her sexual appetites and unsurpassed in her reputation for debauchery.[3]

In this respect, at least, Didot wasn't wrong. In the centuries following Messalina's execution in AD 48 her name became a metonym for the nymphomaniac, the *femme fatale*, the woman who dared express sexual desire. In an illuminated manuscript from medieval France, we encounter a remarkably relaxed-looking Messalina burning in the eternal flames of damnation, engaged in a furious debate with the emperors Tiberius and Caligula over which of them had sinned the most. French revolutionary pamphleteers decried Marie Antoinette as a new Messalina, while her sister, the powerful Queen of Naples, Maria Carolina, was described by one observer as combining 'all the lubricity of a Messalina and the unorthodox tastes of a Sappho'.[4] In 1920s British suburbia, a woman convicted of driving her lover to murder her husband was immortalised as the 'Messalina of the Suburbs', and in the 1930s the Player's Cigarette company produced cigarette cards (as part of a series on 'famous beauties') showing a red-lipsticked Messalina draped across a couch, dress slipping off one shoulder, her arrogance and self-possession palpable as she empties her wine glass onto the floor. The theatrical release poster of the 1977 film *Messalina, Messalina!* shows the titular empress in a backless tunic cut all the way down to the top of her thighs; its slogan promises viewers 'the varied amorous adventures of the most insatiable devourer of men'. Messalina had become the archetypal 'bad woman', a monstrous personification of the intersection between male fantasy and male fear.

Messalina's legacy in Western cultural consciousness is hardly surprising given her treatment in the ancient sources. Following her execution the empress suffered *damnatio memoriae*; her name was chiselled off monuments, her statues were destroyed and her reputation was rendered unprotected. Left to do their worst, male historians, poets, even scientists, had a field day, accusing Messalina of adultery, greed, prostitution, bigamy and murder and working through anxieties about women's morality and power in the process.

The combined destruction and bastardisation of her history make the reconstruction of an accurate 'factual' account of Messalina's life difficult. Much is disputable; even the most basic facts are subject to debate. To take just one example:

estimates of Messalina's date of birth range from AD 17 to as late as AD 26. For a woman who most likely never saw her thirtieth birthday, the difference of nearly a decade is crucial. If you take AD 17 as the year of Messalina's birth, she was around twenty-one years old when she married Claudius in AD 38, and around thirty-one when she died in AD 48. If, however, you contend that she was born in AD 26, she was only thirteen at the time of her marriage and only twenty-two at the time of her death. This has obvious consequences for our analysis of the woman and her actions. Was she a virgin married to a man more than three times her age? A teenager exploring her sexuality? A girl far out of her depth in a court teeming with political intrigue that she could not understand? Or was she a young woman well aware of her sexual power and perfectly capable of plotting with the best of them?

*

So is Messalina a lost cause for the historian? Perhaps I'm biased, but I would argue that she is not.

By the standards of the ancient world, Messalina lived in a place and time about which we possess a huge amount of information. The hundred years or so that lie to either side of her birth are perhaps the best-documented age of Western history before the Renaissance. Roman society in this period was immensely, overtly, ostentatiously literate. Its people inhabited an urban landscape saturated with writing: laws and decrees were inscribed on stone or bronze; eulogies to the deceased were carved onto the tombs that lined the roads; plaques named the subjects of public statues and enumerated their achievements; painted graffiti covering every spare wall told you whom to avoid, whom to vote for – and whom to fuck.

The educated could read and write, both in Latin and in Greek. They knew a whole oeuvre of literature off by heart – the epics of

4

Homer, the tragedies of Aeschylus, the speeches of Demosthenes – and they peppered quotations with a smug familiarity through the letters they exchanged. And the exchange was constant. Letters formed the backbone of the administrative empire; it was the new imperial postal service (the *cursus publicus*), established by Augustus to carry directives and reports across the length and breadth of the empire, that made the vast expanse of Roman dominion centrally governable. At the same time, epistolatory writing began to be held up as an art form as Cicero and Pliny the Younger collated and published vast volumes of private correspondence. On the Capitol, senatorial archives preserved minutes, judgements and decrees for future reference.

Latin literature thrived too: in his *Aeneid*, Virgil finally gave Rome an epic to rival those of the Greeks; Catullus and Ovid poured out elegiac longings for forbidden lovers; Horace, Persius and Juvenal perfected the acerbic and peculiarly Roman new genre of satire. Soon recognised as a literary golden age, the texts of the first centuries BC and AD would be preserved for posterity in abbey libraries through the centuries of the Christian Middle Ages, as copies of copies of copies by monks who respected their literary importance or needed teaching aids for 'proper classical Latin'.

Messalina's time left a no less indelible trace on the physical than on the literary landscape. The imperial elite built monuments designed to withstand the ravages of time. Many were later reworked into the fabric of the Eternal City of the Catholic Church; temples of the old gods became churches to the new, arches and columns were repurposed to adorn noble palazzos. Elsewhere, the preservation of the landscape of Messalina's Italy was more fortuitous. The eruption of Vesuvius in AD 79, while unfortunate for the Pompeians, froze a time capsule of the everyday life of Roman cities and villas as it really *was* – rather than as it was designed and parcelled for commemoration – in the mid-first century AD.

From these disparate sources we can create a remarkably rich tapestry of the world Messalina inhabited; its laws, social norms, political institutions and familial networks, its economy, appearance, ideals and anxieties. Once we understand the environment in which Messalina lived – and in which the first histories of her life were written – we can work backwards, asking whether the stories we are told are plausible and, where they are not, examining the prejudices and ulterior motives that might have driven their creation.

This process is pernickety but it is also profitable. Sometimes, the fictions a society concocts about itself tell us just as much about that society as the facts. Perhaps they might even tell us more. Events might occur by chance but, in a world in which oral history abounded and writing materials were expensive, the creation of a story demanded a concerted effort – conscious or unconscious – of invention and selection.

The stories told about Messalina are as cracking as they come. She takes down one of the richest and most powerful men in Rome because she likes his garden; murders men who refuse to sleep with her; challenges the most notorious prostitute in Rome to a twenty-four-hour competition of sexual stamina – and wins; plots a coup to overthrow the emperor and publicly *marries* her lover while her husband is out of town.

In contrast to the character of 'the Messalina' – the woman defined entirely by her sexuality – that develops later in the Western cultural tradition, the real Messalina was a political, as well as a sexual, force. The empress' alleged intrigues, her sudden downfall and the hyper-effective process of character assassination that occurs after her death reveal a great deal about the inner workings of the new court politics that emerged as Rome moved from Republic to empire – a process of development in which, I will argue, Messalina played a pivotal role. It was a change that terrified contemporary historians hailing from the old senatorial class. Politics was now beyond their control: an obscure and slippery thing that occurred behind closed doors, defined by personal rivalries and internal factionalism, played out through suspected poisonings and false accusations rather than public assemblies and debates.

It is a process that concerns us no less today. The election of Donald Trump in 2016 should put flight to the myth – so fashionable in the twentieth century – that history can be explained systemically, entirely without recourse to the individual, the irrational and the emotional. In Trump's White House, character, ego and personal relationships all undoubtedly shifted the course of the presidency. I will not attempt to make some glib point about how the Classics remain vitally relevant to our understanding of modern politics – they are not vitally relevant, they are interesting (which is better), and, in the main, the novel global problems which we face today demand novel solutions. Rather, our experience of the contemporary politics of personality should remind us not to underestimate the power of personal temperament, love, lust, family ties, jealousy, prejudice and hatred as drivers of real historical change. Scholars, most of them male, have long overlooked Messalina as a subject of serious study, dismissing historical accounts of her life as unreliable and the woman herself as a vacuous slut. But I would argue that her story is central to, and inextricable from, the story of her time; it forces us to confront all the unquantifiable irrationalities that define this period of Roman political history.

The problems we encounter in trying to understand Messalina should be recognised as part of her story, and part of the story of ancient womanhood in general. As rich as the literary corpus that survives from the classical world is, it includes almost no female voices. There are the fragments of the poets Sappho and Sulpicia but by and large the 'words' of the great women of ancient history and myth – formidable, powerful women like Helen, Medea, Antigone, Penthesilea, Artemisia, Lucretia, Cleopatra, Livia, Boudicca – are written by men. Medea's bitter lament that 'of all creatures that can feel and think, we women are the worst-treated things alive' came from the pen of Euripides; Boudicca's call to arms was composed by Tacitus.[5] Again and again we find these female characters transformed into either paragons or nightmares of femininity in service of the male author's message.

It is a tendency that we have not entirely grown out of over the past two thousand years – our culture still seems to find it difficult to confront female complexity. Modern female characters still tend, much more than their male counterparts, towards the black and white; there is still less space in the cultural consciousness for the complex heroine than the complex hero.

The women who have words written for them by male authors are the exceptions; more commonly, the women of ancient history do not speak, and are not spoken of, at all. The feminine ideal in the ancient world was quiet, unassuming and private; in the Greek courts merely *naming* a woman in a public speech was tantamount to calling her a whore.[6] In the early first century AD, the following was inscribed on the grave of a woman named Murdia:

> the praise of all good women tends to be simple and similar, because their natural good qualities [...] do not demand any great variety of description. Doing those same things that every good woman does ought to be enough to win her a worthy reputation. It is harder, after all, for women to win new praises when their lives are upset by so little variation. So, we must celebrate their common virtues...my dearest mother merited the greatest praise of all because in modesty, honesty, chastity, obedience, wool-working, diligence and faithfulness she was the equal and indeed the picture of every other upstanding woman.[7]

The 'good' woman, busied with her duties in the home, was simply not of interest to most Greek and Roman writers – and so they simply did not mention her. This silence redoubles beyond the world of the elite. We are left to reconstruct the lives of poorer women – whether slave girls, artisans' wives or prostitutes – from broken pottery, worn spindle whorls, burn marks left in ancient floors by hearth fires, and snippets of offensive graffiti.

The fact that we know so little of Messalina's life prior to her marriage that we are unable even to date her birth with total confidence is not an anomalous accident of historical oversight, it is indicative of a cultural assumption; that women were simply not interesting until their lives intersected, in earnest, with those of men. This assumption was so deep-seated that it was woven into the language: neither Ancient Greek nor Latin has a distinct term for the unmarried adult woman. The obscurity and voicelessness of the '*real* Messalina' – who, in all the accounts of her life, is never given a moment of direct speech – reflects the obscurity and voicelessness of the vast majority of ancient women.

Messalina's vilification is the best introduction you can get to the dangers of navigating womanhood within the misogynistic patriarchy that we call the birthplace of Western civilisation, rationality and liberty. But the anxieties about a powerful woman – worse, a *young* powerful woman, worse yet, a young powerful *sexual* woman – that seep, palpably, from every sentence written about Messalina, are more than just a good introduction to the realities of ancient prejudice. They remain recognisable to the modern reader. Familiar too are the knee-jerk responses these anxieties provoke; sexual scandal, slut-shaming, the presentation of the woman as emotionally irrational. The history of Messalina – so far as we can reconstruct it – is in some ways a very modern one: it is the history of a woman daring to wield power in a man's world and suffering the consequences of that choice.

More important than any relevance Messalina might have to the modern world is the restoration of her proper place in the historical narrative. Her story is no parable of wronged womanhood; Messalina is not simply the innocent female victim in a misogynistic narrative. She was shaped by, worked within, and sometimes perpetuated, the brutal patriarchy in which she lived.

Her story is, in some ways, the story of the consolidation of imperial power in the mid-first century AD and the constitutional transformation of Rome from a Republic to what was a monarchy in all but name. Augustus had established an autocracy and sowed the seeds of a dynastic system – but his real masterstroke was to moderate the speed of this transformation and its revelation. Things were still in flux when Messalina and Claudius came to power in AD 41, some twenty-five years after the death of the first emperor, Augustus. As empress, Messalina would become an active participant in the slow revolution of the Roman political landscape, pioneering new ways of exerting power that exploited or circumvented the old all-male institutions of Roman public life. She created new models for female power, ones that would be used by her successors and that would help to define Roman ideas about what it meant to be 'empress'.

Messalina, I will contend, was a crucial figure in the history of imperial Rome's first century. Our obsession with her sex life has obscured this to the detriment not only of *her* memory, but also of *our* understanding of the period.

Prelude

Messalina's Ancient Chroniclers

Most of what we know about Messalina's life comes from a series of written sources composed in Latin and Greek in the centuries that followed her death: primary among them, Tacitus' *Annals*, Suetonius' *Lives of the Caesars*, and Cassius Dio's *Roman History*. Tacitus and Suetonius were near contemporaries around the turn of the second century AD; Dio was writing about a century later, around the turn of the third. Each work is written in a different format and each author had biases of his own, which we need to understand before we begin to unpick their presentations of Messalina. There are other sources that mention Messalina too, of course, but these will be introduced as and when they become relevant.

Publius Cornelius Tacitus was born just a few years after Messalina's death in the mid 50s AD. His origins are somewhat obscure but he appears to have come from a family of provincial nobility in what is now northern Italy or southern France; they were certainly rich and well connected enough to give their son the best of educations in the city of Rome itself. Tacitus showed promise and quickly embarked upon a public career under the emperor Vespasian, making an advantageous marriage, winning magisterial offices and probably entering the Senate during the reign of the emperor Titus in the early 80s AD. He rose through the ranks steadily – his career unimpeded by the tyranny of Vespasian – and was consul in AD 97.

Like many of his fellow senators, Tacitus had long dabbled in literary pursuits, but after his consulship he turned his mind seriously to history. His first work, the *Historiae*, covered the period between the fall of two tyrants: Nero in AD 69, and Domitian in AD 96. In the introduction to this work, Tacitus had promised that his next would deal with the more contemporary history of the reigns of Nerva and Trajan, but when it came down to it he changed direction, instead casting his attention further back still to write what remains the best account of the Julio-Claudians, Rome's first and most notorious dynasty.

The *Annals*, as this work was called, was composed after Tacitus' stint as governor of the province of Asia, perhaps in the late 110s and early 120s AD. When it was complete, its sixteen or eighteen books presented an unbroken narrative of the period between Tiberius' accession and Nero's fall. In his introduction, Tacitus acknowledged that 'the histories of Tiberius, Caligula, Claudius, and Nero were falsified on account of fear while they flourished, and in all the heat of recent hatred after they had fallen'. Now, Tacitus claimed, he would write the history of those times 'without anger or zealous partiality – I keep any cause for either at a distance'.[2]

Tacitus' aspiration to be even-handed was admirable, but impossible to adhere to. By the time he sat down to compose the *Annals*, Tacitus had been a senator for nigh on forty years, well over half his life. His senatorial status was central to his identity, particularly as this was a status that he had won for *himself* as a *novus homo* (a new man) from a family of provincial equestrians. He had had his own experiences of tyranny too, under the despotism of Domitian; yet it was to this emperor that Tacitus owed the greatest advancements of his career, a fact which he had to acknowledge and which must have played, guiltily, on his mind. The story of the Julio-Claudians was the story of the transformation of Rome from a senatorial Republic into an autocracy – there was no way that Tacitus could be neutral.

Tacitus' themes of tyranny, dynasty and constitutional corruption are woven into the very structure of the *Annals*. Tacitus begins his narrative not with the reign of Augustus, but with the accession of his successor Tiberius – the moment at which it becomes clear, beyond all doubt, that Augustus had created not only a personal domination but a quasi-monarchical dynasty. The same theme presents itself in the contrast between Tacitus' content and his structure. The *Annals* is written, as its name suggests, in the annalistic format, with the narrative broken into years introduced by the names of the presiding consuls. This was the most traditional form of Roman history writing, one designed for a time when the elected senatorial magistrates controlled the events of the year. In using this structure to tell a story increasingly dominated by personal whims and court politics, Tacitus draws our attention, again and again, to the lies and hypocrisies of the early empire.

Tacitus had a point to prove, and Messalina's story had the potential to be very useful to him. Her power as empress (an entirely unconstitutional position with no Republican precedents) demonstrates how close Rome was to monarchy and how far it had come from senatorial rule. The rumours that she had used that power to gratify her own greed, caprice and sexual insatiability were perfect examples of the dangerous instability and corruption of the new court politics. Messalina's tale was simply too tempting a case study for Tacitus to tell it impartially.

There is a more practical impediment too to our use of Tacitus as a source: only part of the *Annals* survives, and books 7–10, which cover the whole of Caligula's reign and the beginning of Claudius', are lost completely. Tacitus leaves us no insight into

Messalina's rise; we meet her, in what survives of his narrative, just before her fall.

Suetonius was most likely born into an equestrian family that seem to have hailed from Hippo Regius (in modern day Algeria) around AD 70. He was just a generation younger than Tacitus – and, as a protégé of his friend Pliny the Younger, may even have known him – but their careers, and their literary outputs, developed on quite different trajectories. Rather than embarking upon a public senatorial career, Suetonius joined the imperial administration, serving as a literary advisor, librarian and a correspondence secretary to the emperors Trajan and Hadrian before being dismissed (for some unknown infraction) from imperial service in the AD 120s.

Suetonius' intellectual interests were wide-ranging and he composed monographs as diverse as 'On Famous Courtesans' and 'On Names of Winds'. His primary interest, however, was biography, and it is his *Lives of the Caesars* – twelve biographies of the emperors from Julius Caesar to Domitian – that concerns us here. Then, perhaps even more than now, biography was a distinct genre of history writing; these tales of famous men, both good and awful, served didactic purposes, and their telling was governed by long-established and proscriptive structural conventions.

As a biographer, Suetonius' primary interest lay with his subjects. He possessed a famous nose for anecdote and his *Lives* are character studies as much as historical accounts. Their content is defined, too, by ancient ideas about what made a man, and women appear only when they directly affect or reveal the development of the emperor at hand. While Tacitus is interested in Messalina for how she reflects the moral and political conditions of her time, Suetonius is interested primarily in how she reflects the morality and personality of her husband.

Although the senatorial Tacitus and the equestrian imperial secretary Suetonius must have conceived of their identities, allegiances and literary aims quite differently, both men were writing against a similar background. They moved in the same social circles – with connections to Pliny the Younger and the imperial courts of Trajan and Hadrian – during the early second century AD – an era when discourse about tyranny and good rulership was rife as the new ruling dynasty actively sought to define itself in opposition to the despotism and instability of its predecessors.

Our third main source, Cassius Dio, was writing in a different context entirely. Born in the middle of the 160s AD in Nicaea (in the north-west of modern-day Turkey), he did not begin writing his *Roman History* until early in the third century. He lived in less stable times than those that had afforded Tacitus and Suetonius space for scholarship: they had seen the start of Rome's run of its famous 'Five Good Emperors'; Dio saw its end with the death of Marcus Aurelius in AD 180.[*] The years that followed were marked by a succession of tyrannies, civil wars and provincial crises and for much of this period Dio's career kept him at the heart of the action.

Although he came from a powerful Bithynian family, Dio (like his father before him) carved out a prominent senatorial career in Rome, serving as a military general, a provincial governor, and holding the consulship twice before returning to his home province of Bithynia and Pontus for his retirement in AD 229. The complexity of Dio's cultural identity is reflected in the nature of his work: this is a history of Rome – often driven by senatorial concerns about constitution, freedom and tyranny – written in the language and literary tradition of classical Greek.

Unlike Tacitus and Suetonius, Dio did not pick a sub-genre of history writing (annalistic, biographical, etc.) that would place

---

[*] The 'Five Good Emperors' comprised Nerva, Trajan, Hadrian, Antoninus Pius and Marcus Aurelius.

constraints on his purview or structure. Instead, he set out to write a history of Rome from the legendary Aeneas' arrival in Italy right up until his own retirement at the end of the third decade of the third century AD. The work – which would number eighty books in total – took him some twenty-two years: ten for research, twelve for writing. The structure is broadly chronological, but Dio afforded himself more flexibility than Tacitus – introducing undated anecdotes when they are most useful to character development arcs, or combining narrative threads that run over multiple years into a single section in the interests of concision and clarity.

Not all of Dio's *Roman History* is extant. That part of the work that covers the period 69 BC to AD 46 (and thus includes most of Messalina's reign) survives in Dio's own words – preserved in a tradition of continually copied manuscripts. The rest exists only partially in quotes and summaries made by later authors.

Not one of our three main historians was Messalina's direct contemporary, and their accounts of her exploits are obviously not first hand. Instead, these writers relied on a network of lost sources to which they make explicit reference rarely and with a wild inconsistency. Some of these were official: the *acta diurna*, for instance, which constituted a day-to-day record of official engagements as well as lawsuits and speeches; and the *acta senatus*, an archive of the minutes of senatorial meetings that would have been available to Tacitus and Dio on account of their status as senators. The equestrian Suetonius might not have had direct access to the *acta senatus* but he did have another advantage: he was a secretary and archivist to the emperors Trajan and Hadrian, a job which afforded him privileged access to private imperial notes and correspondence which, on occasion, he quotes directly. All three would also have made use of contemporary written accounts – transcribed speeches, recent histories and autobiographies – and of oral traditions.* When relating the story of Messalina's fall, Tacitus, for example, declares: 'truly I impart only that which was said or written by my elders'.[3]

Finally, it is important to note that the Roman view of history itself differed fundamentally from our own. The writing of history in the ancient world was expected to be an exercise in literary creation as much as in the reconstruction of historical reality, and these are texts unashamedly concerned with character, narrative, setting, genre, rhetoric and textual allusion. Female characters were particularly susceptible to these processes of narrative manipulation. Their lives were generally less well documented than those of men – their actions were not often the kind to appear in official records like the *acta* and their power was almost always exerted through private channels of influence – and so their stories were more twistable. The creative element of Roman historical writing has much to offer the modern historian – when properly analysed, historians' literary choices tell us a great deal about their ideas and their biases – but it can be dangerously misleading if its inventiveness goes unacknowledged.

---

* Messalina's successor Agrippina, for example, wrote an autobiography. Now lost to us, it must have made for fascinating (if somewhat biased) reading.

I

A Wedding and a Funeral

'And so the House of the Princeps had shuddered...'

Tacitus, *Annals*, 11.28

The story of Messalina's fall, as Tacitus tells it, goes something like this.[1]

The wedding procession, winding its way through the imperial palace on the Palatine, was in full swing. The year AD 48 had already reached early autumn but evenings in the city of Rome were still balmy enough for outdoor celebration. The bride was wearing the traditional yellow-red veil, choruses of men and women sang songs to Hymen, the god of marriage, the witnesses were assembled, the guests were fêted and feasted. No expense was spared; this was a wedding party for the ages.

It was unfortunate, then, that the bride was already married. And it was particularly unfortunate that the man she was already married to was the supreme ruler of the vast majority of the known world. Entwined with the handsome young noble and consul-elect, Gaius Silius, on the garlanded marital couch, lay Messalina, empress of Rome and the lawful wife of Claudius, emperor of a territory stretching from the island of Britain to the deserts of Syria.

Messalina and Silius had hardly been subtle in celebrating their love, and this in a city where, as Tacitus puts it, 'everything was known and nothing was kept silent'.² Nowhere was this inborn Roman impulse towards gossip more pronounced than in the sprawling, opulent and ruthlessly competitive imperial court where, since its inception some eighty years before, rumour and scandal had always been matters of life and death. And already, as Messalina and Silius slept off the wine and the sex, messengers were riding out of the Porta Trigemina, taking the Via Ostiensis south-west heading for Ostia.

In the mid-first century AD, it was the port city of Ostia that kept Rome running. About fifteen miles south-west of the capital, it was here that every day legions of workers unloaded the cargoes that had arrived from across the Mediterranean and beyond, packing them high on barges headed up the Tiber towards the thronging city and its 1 million consumers. It was through Ostia that rich Romans got their hands on pearls from the Gulf of Persia, Spanish silver, perfumes from Egypt, spices from India and Chinese silks. These luxuries had made the city and its merchants incredibly rich, but there was a more important trade at work too – one on which the emperor's crown, his life even, might depend.

It was concern for the corn supply – arriving via the great trade route that allowed a million Romans to feed off the flood plains of Egypt – that brought Claudius to the port city this particular autumn. He was to review the logistical arrangements and preside over sacrifices designed to ensure the safety of the ships leaving Alexandria laden with the cargoes of Nile Delta grain that would keep the urban populace adequately fed and politically amenable over the winter. Rather than appear by her husband's side as First Lady, the empress Messalina had pleaded illness and remained in Rome.

The messengers arriving at the gates of Ostia carrying news of Messalina and Silius' 'wedding' did not dare approach the emperor himself. 'Don't kill the messenger', after all, becomes more of an entreaty than an idiom when the recipient controls the greatest army on earth and the message is that his wife is in the process of marrying someone else. Instead, the messengers went straight to his advisors, Callistus, Narcissus and Pallas. Former slaves of the emperor who had risen meteorically to become Claudius' closest and most powerful political confidants, they were among the most successful players of the game of court politics Rome had ever seen.

The news presented the imperial freedmen with a serious problem. If Messalina had celebrated a marriage so flagrantly, the freedmen agreed, there could be no doubt as to her next move; the lovers had shown their hand to such an extent that this could only be the beginning of a coup. Gaius Silius was the kind of man who *could* be emperor. He was as blue-blooded as they came, with charisma and noble good looks and an intelligence honed by the best education money could buy. The political game was one Silius could and would play: he had already been selected to hold the consulship the very next year. Messalina, they guessed, planned to overthrow Claudius, have Silius adopt her son Britannicus, and install her lover on the imperial throne. This was no mere affair; it was a conspiracy to overthrow the emperor – if Claudius was to be saved, Messalina would have to go.

But how could the news be broken to the emperor? Claudius' advisors knew Messalina had a hold over him; everyone did. The ageing emperor was quite evidently as infatuated with his young wife as his young wife was with Gaius Silius. If he saw her, the game was up; Claudius could on *no* account be allowed to hear his wife out. The more the advisors discussed the issue, the clearer it became to them that, however strong the case against Messalina, her downfall was not guaranteed. Pallas excused himself, Callistus counselled caution and delay, which amounted to much the same thing. So the task of devising a way to inform Claudius of his wife's betrayal fell to Narcissus. He had to act fast. Messalina, he decided, could receive no forewarning of the accusations against her. But from whom were those accusations to come in the first instance? Not from him, of course – he had far too much to lose.

Instead, Narcissus recruited two of Claudius' favourite mistresses, Calpurnia and Cleopatra. (Love for his wife had, perhaps unsurprisingly, done nothing to induce the world's most powerful man into monogamy.) Hearing the rumours of his wife's treachery from two of his mistresses would, Narcissus hoped, soften the blow to the emperor's pride. Having Calpurnia and Cleopatra make the first move would also buy the freedman precious time to gauge Claudius' reaction before he got his own hands dirty. In return, Narcissus suggested, the women need only think of the gifts, the opportunities, the influence, the power and position even, that they might have to gain from the fall of their lover's wife. The irony of using two of a husband's mistresses to accuse his wife of adultery, Narcissus safely assumed, would be lost on Claudius.

Calpurnia and Cleopatra had little difficulty wangling a private audience with the emperor. As soon as the three were alone, Calpurnia threw herself crying at Claudius' feet, and declared that Messalina had married Silius in Rome. The emperor turned in disbelief to Cleopatra, who nodded and told him, as arranged, to call for Narcissus. The freedman was shown in and confirmed that the rumours were true. He told Claudius that everyone had witnessed his wife's wedding – the people, the Senate, the soldiers – and that unless he moved quickly his wife's new husband would hold the city.

Claudius summoned his advisors. The council descended into chaos as courtiers – each with competing interests and significant amounts to lose – shouted over each other. It quickly became clear, however, that the council was seriously concerned about the situation and deemed the threat to Claudius' rule to be potentially existential. They agreed there was no time to waste and that the emperor should go straight to the army. His position with the elite Praetorian cohorts was crucial – as the only soldiers encamped within the city bounds of Rome they maintained order and had the power to make and unmake emperors. Personal revenge could come later, when the loyalty of the army was certain and Claudius' position was secure.

Claudius was overcome with panic. He is said to have asked again and again if Silius was still his subject and if he was still in control of his empire.

Back in Rome, Messalina and Silius were still partying. Autumn had reached its mellow height and they were celebrating with a new level of extravagance and debauchery. The palace was filled with wine presses, each churning out steady streams of wine, replenishing the overflowing vats faster than the empress' guests could empty them. The attendees had come dressed as bacchantes – the wild followers of Bacchus, god of wine – in vine garlands and animal pelts. And they were behaving like bacchantes too, out of control, performing ecstatic dances and leading raucous choruses of rhythmic chants.

Messalina appeared as their ringleader, her dark hair flowing down over her shoulders, with Silius by her side, wreathed in ivy and wearing the laced buskin boots worn by actors in ancient tragedies. This addition to his costume was an apposite one considering the turn that events were about to take.

The wine, the drink and the late autumn heat must have been a heady mixture; at one point during the night Vettius Valens, a famous doctor and one of the empress' ex-lovers, climbed out of the throng and up into a tall tree. The city of Rome and its surrounding hills and countryside stretched out below him, all the way to the coast. As he clung to the upper branches, the crowd below clamoured to know what he could see. It was funny, he said, but it looked like there was a terrible storm brewing over Ostia.

It was not long before the nature of that storm revealed itself. Despite Narcissus' orders that the empress should hear nothing of the charges against her, messengers began to arrive from Ostia carrying reports that Claudius knew everything, that he was already on his way, that he was bent on retribution. The party broke up; the guests were falling over each other to leave, to distance themselves as much as they still could from the confrontation that was about to occur. Messalina and Silius departed too: he went straight to the forum to attend to his public duties and show his face as though nothing were wrong; she sought solace in the so-called Gardens of Lucullus on the Pincian Hill, which had recently come into her possession.

Centurions, meanwhile, had arrived at the palace and any party guests who had lingered or tried to hide were arrested. When the news that her associates were being rounded up reached Messalina, she sprang into a frenzy of action. She sent word that her children by Claudius – Claudia Octavia, aged about nine, and Britannicus, nearly eight – should go straight to their father. She also recruited the Vestal Vibidia – the most senior of the virgin priestesses who tended to the symbolic hearth fire of the empire and enjoyed extraordinary powers of legal intercession – to plead her case with Claudius.

Finally, Messalina herself set out on foot across the city, accompanied by just three loyal attendants, suddenly isolated among the teeming urban crowds. She was certain that if she could just see her husband – or, perhaps, if her husband could just see *her* – the situation would be resolved. Reaching the city gate, the empress hitched a ride on the only vehicle that would take her and set out for Ostia on the back of a cart of garden rubbish.

The mood in Claudius' carriage, as it made its way along the road from Ostia to Rome, was tense. The emperor was conflicted. One moment he'd be ranting about Messalina's profligacy and

24

denouncing her infidelity; the next he'd dwell on memories of their wedding, their relationship, their two young children. And now, just as Narcissus had feared, Messalina came into view. There, in the middle of the Via Ostiensis, she stood, crying and shouting, begging her husband – in the name of Britannicus and Octavia – to hear her out.

Narcissus shouted over her; enumerating her crimes, naming Silius, describing the sordid details of their affair and their wedding. All the while, he passed Claudius document after document recounting his wife's alleged debaucheries. He knew that, with Messalina in view, it was not just Claudius' mind, but also his eyes that needed distraction. Through all of this the emperor was strangely silent. He saw his wife, he took Narcissus' dossier, but he said nothing.

The cavalcade continued towards Rome. As it neared the gates, Britannicus and Octavia attempted to reach their father. Narcissus simply had them removed. The Vestal Vibidia was less easily got rid of. She demanded that Messalina be afforded a trial and defence, refusing to leave until she received assurances to that effect. Narcissus promised that the emperor would, of course, hear his wife out – there would be an opportunity for her to rebut the charges, if such a thing were possible, on the morrow. In the meantime, Vibidia was ordered to return to the temple and attend to her religious duties.

Once in the city, Narcissus took Claudius straight to Silius' house and treated him to a guided tour. In the vestibule, hanging among the other portraits of his ancestors, was an effigy of Silius' father – the same father who had been arraigned for plotting rebellion against the emperor Tiberius.[*] In the face of certain conviction, Silius' father had committed suicide and the Senate had confiscated much of his property and ordered

---

[*] The charges are generally acknowledged in the ancient sources to have been false and trumped up for political reasons.

the destruction of his images. His son's display of his portrait was without a doubt a direct contravention of senatorial decree, but it might also be interpreted as a statement of revolutionary intent. The tour continued. Narcissus showed Claudius pieces of furniture that had once stood in *his* palace and heirlooms inherited from *his* ancestors, the Drusii and the Nerones: stolen gifts that could only have been given to Silius by Claudius' wife.

The heat of Claudius' anger, which had been simmering in his silence, now boiled over, erupting into threats and curses against his wife and her lover. Narcissus escorted the emperor straight to the Praetorian Camp. The soldiers were already there, massed and readied for the meeting that Narcissus had arranged. The accused men were there too – captured, shackled and awaiting judgement. Claudius did not make one of his usual lengthy and digressive speeches: on this occasion he spoke only a few words, carefully weighed, and concealed his emotions as best he could.

The response of the Praetorian cohorts did not match the measured tone of Claudius' speech. A great clamour rose from the ranks; in waves of angry shouting they demanded to know the names of those involved and to see their proper punishment.

Silius was up first. The charges against him were read and he made no attempt to refute them. Like his father, he knew that to be accused of a crime against the emperor could mean only one thing and the case, he rightly judged as he looked out over the crowd of baying soldiers, was already decided. He asked only for a quick death. It was a request that was readily and immediately granted.

The killing of Silius was the first in an efficient stream of summary executions. A number of wealthy and illustrious equestrians followed Silius' example, accepting their execution with fortitude. First came Titius Proculus, then Vettius Valens, the storm he'd seen over Ostia had finally caught up with him. Both confessed and both were executed directly. Then came one

Traulus Montanus; he was young, perhaps little more than a teenager, modest, and devastatingly handsome. He'd spent only one night in the empress' bed but that won Traulus no mercy from the emperor. Then there was Pompeius Urbicus; Saufeius Trogus; the senator Juncus Vergilianus; Sulpicius Rufus, procurator of a gladiatorial school; and Decrius Calpurnianus, prefect of the night watchmen. The ground was littered with the dead bodies of Messalina's exes.

Now an actor took to the stage. Mnester was the brightest star of his time; Caligula had been such a super-fan that he'd had anyone who talked during Mnester's performances dragged from their seats and flogged. For this, his last show, Mnester gave his audience the theatrics that they wanted. He did not deny that he had slept with Messalina; to the contrary, he made the scandalous claim that she had coerced him – pointing out that unlike his powerful co-defendants, he had been in no position to refuse the empress. To underline his point, he tore the clothing from his body and showed the crowd the lash scars of slavery that criss-crossed his back. Claudius hesitated for the first time that afternoon, but Narcissus urged him on – pointing out that Mnester had still slept with Messalina, whether he'd fancied her or not. So Mnester was killed too and the emperor's entourage repaired to the palace for dinner.

Across the city from the Praetorian Camp, back in the Gardens of Lucullus, Messalina was preparing her defence. The empress did not share the despair that had driven Silius to ask only for a quick execution; she was sure that if her husband could hear her, could *see* her, he would not be able to order her execution. Messalina was confident that if she begged and pleaded and denied, her husband would forgive and forget. She was so confident, in fact, that her fear was already beginning to mutate into anger and her anger into plans; plans directed most of all against Narcissus.

Messalina's confidence was not entirely misplaced. It was halfway through dinner at the imperial palace; the wine had been flowing and Claudius had reached that stage of drunkenness when you think getting back with your ex is a good idea. He called over an attendant and ordered him to send word to 'that poor woman' that she should come to him the next morning and plead her case. Narcissus started to panic. He could see that Claudius' resolve was already weakening and he knew the emperor would soon finish dinner and repair to his bedroom; a bedroom that would be filled, in the soft light of the night, with all Claudius' most pleasant memories of his wife. Narcissus slipped from the banqueting hall and took a guard to one side. Messalina's execution was to go ahead tonight, he said. Claudius' orders. There was no time to waste.

A group of soldiers set off from the Palatine at once, crossing the city and beginning to search the gardens. Messalina was with her mother, Domitia Lepida; the two had not been close, but now, in her daughter's ultimate crisis, she was there. As the soldiers advanced, Lepida urged her daughter not to wait but to take matters into her own hands and kill herself to avoid the indignity and dishonour of an execution. The game was up, she said; the only thing Messalina could do now was to show courage in facing death. But Messalina could do nothing but lie prostrate on the ground, crying and lamenting.

This was how the soldiers found her. The tribune approached the empress in silence, but as the freedman sent by Narcissus to see the thing through shouted coarse abuse, the true reality of her predicament finally dawned on Messalina. She took up the sword with trembling hands, she held it to her throat, then to her chest, then back to her throat, but she could not bring herself to do it. In the end it was the tribune, tired of watching her dither, who had to finish her off.

Claudius was still at dinner when he was brought the news of his wife's death. The messenger didn't specify whether it had been suicide or murder and Claudius didn't ask. He betrayed not a flicker of emotion – no sadness or joy, no anger or pity. He moved only to beckon over an attendant and ask for another glass of wine.

II

A Marble Stage

'Look what the Capitol is now; look what it was of old,
You'd swear that these were temples built to different Joves.'

Ovid, *Ars Amatoria*, 3.115–116

When the future empress Messalina was born, most likely
in the early 20s AD, Rome was the greatest city of the
greatest empire the world had ever seen. The Roman empire was
a vast network of provinces stretching from the Rhine to the
Euphrates, encircled by a thick buffer zone of client kingdoms,
and it had made the city at its centre exceedingly rich.

Spread over its seven famous hills, Rome had been founded
(as a result of fratricide and divine intervention, if you believed
the legends of its mythical founder Romulus) in the mid-eighth
century BC, but the Rome of the first century AD would have
been unrecognisable from the city of even a century before.
The small brick and tufa temples, raised by the competing
aristocrats of the late Republic, had been replaced by huge
complexes designed for politics, commerce, worship and
play and clad in shining polished marble, that proved the
magnificence and munificence of the emperor alone. Messalina
was born during Tiberius' reign, but she was born into a city
that had been created by his predecessor Augustus. This was
a place of unimaginable opulence – a living monument to the

imperial power of Rome and, more subtly, to the dynastic power of its imperial family. It was a city that could not help but shape its children.

In the late first century BC Augustus had raised a whole new forum, now known as the Forum of Augustus. While old Rome with its ancient Forum Romanum had grown slowly and organically into an irregularly shaped melting-pot of different styles and materials, the Forum of Augustus was designed and constructed in one go, built from the ground up on an area of flattened slum.[1] The complex was cohesive in style but also in theme: every detail was calculated to broadcast the message of Augustus' domination.

A vast court of polished marble spread itself out, prostrate before the Temple of Mars Ultor, which rose on a podium at the forum's north-east end. Octavian (the future emperor who would, from 27 BC on, be known as Augustus) had vowed to build this sanctuary to 'Mars the Avenger' in 42 BC after the Battle of Philippi when he'd finally defeated the forces led by Brutus and Cassius, the assassins of his adoptive father Julius Caesar.[2] Raised colonnades stretched out along either side, concealing shaded walkways, punctured by semi-circular exedrae. Statues of the *summi viri*, 'the great men', of Roman history lined the colonnades, and representations of her mythical founders nestled in the exedrae. To the west you would find a triumphant Romulus, carrying the armour of a vanquished enemy. To the east, Aeneas – ancestor both of Romulus and, it was claimed, Augustus' adoptive family, the Julians – fleeing the flames of Troy with his aged father on his back and his young son at his side, headed for Italy. Finally there was a statue of Augustus himself, driving a four-horse chariot – the natural heir to all Rome's past heroes.

The young emperor also remodelled the ancient Forum Romanum which abutted his new complex.[3] A new Senate House, begun by Julius Caesar, was finally completed, and a new Rostra – the raised platform from which speeches were made – was decorated with the prows of Mark Antony and Cleopatra's ships, captured at Actium in 31 BC, and topped by the equestrian statue of a nineteen-year-old Octavian that had been commissioned by the Senate in 43 BC.[4] As a woman, Messalina would never speak for herself in the House or from the Rostra, but she would come first to influence, and then to be the subject of, the speeches and debates they hosted. If a speaker on the Rostra looked straight out over the crowd of listeners, he would have seen a new temple rising at the south-eastern end of the forum. This was the Temple of Divus Julius, built by Octavian in honour of Julius Caesar (made a god by decree of the Senate in 42 BC). Its dedication upon Octavian's triumphant return to Rome in 29 BC heralded a new age in which the Roman people would be expected to worship men, at first strictly in death but, over time, increasingly in life too.[5]

Not everything was new. Augustus was careful to preserve the great antiquities of the old Forum Romanum in their original positions.[6] Here was the black stone, said to mark an ancient cult site or even the burial place of Romulus. And there the *umbilicus Romae* – the 'navel' of Rome – said to be the spot where Romulus' plough first cut into Roman soil and still the point from which all distances to and from Rome were measured. He pursued programmes of restoration too and almost all the great Republican structures were given glittering new imperial robes.

No expense was spared. The floors of Augustus' buildings were paved with geometric patterns of coloured marble. Purple porphyry from Egypt, grey-green cipollino from the Aegean, and golden giallo antico from North African Numidia.[7] This was a geography of stone that invited each Roman to walk across Augustus' conquered world without ever leaving the centre of his native city.

These building projects were political statements, but they were also public gifts. Strolling through the Forum of Augustus, the Roman plebeian could taste something of the life of an aristocrat. He had access to the material luxury – the pillars and exotic materials and bold colours – that adorned elite domestic spaces. He could take pride too in the statues of the great heroes of early Rome. These were common forefathers and role-models for the Roman people – they stood in for the generations of ancestral portraits that decorated the atria of aristocratic homes.

Such exalted surroundings could hardly have been more different from those the mass of Romans experienced at home. The city had hit a population of 1 million – a level reached by London only in 1810 and by New York not until 1875 – and the rapidity and unexpectedness of Rome's urbanisation showed.[8] The ground plans of the new cities built across the Mediterranean world under Roman direction were famously regular, stringently gridded and zoned (features that would come to be regarded as representative of Roman rationality and practicality), but the mother city herself was a warren. Space was at a premium; the slum landlords built upwards, and tenement blocks – known as 'insulae' or 'islands' – reached five storeys high. Fire was a constant danger, as was disease, despite the relatively good public health infrastructure of sewers, aqueducts and baths. Streets in these parts of the city, darkened by the shadows of the monolithic 'islands' that lined them, were cramped and heady places: shops and stalls encroached on what pavement space was available, smells of cooking emanated from the corner takeaways. The noise too – of commerce, crime and family life – must have been incessant and inescapable. It was the perfect environment for the spreading of rumours.

Messalina and her family occupied the opposite end of the spectrum. The prospect of imperial gold that had enticed so many of the new urban poor to live in city squalor had enabled the urban elite to enjoy previously unknown levels of domestic luxury. In 78 BC, when Marcus Lepidus had built a new home for himself, to what was then an unprecedentedly luxurious specification, observers agreed that it was the finest in Rome.* By 45 BC, not thirty-five years later, it was said not to have numbered in the first hundred.[9] Marcus Lepidus had been much criticised in 78 BC for his use of blood-red, purple-veined Numidian marble for the thresholds of his doorways; twenty years later, in 58 BC, the millionaire Marcus Aemilius Scaurus would furnish his atrium with solid columns of shining black Melian marble soaring nearly forty feet high.[10] In the 40s BC Mamurra, a self-made man who had been Caesar's chief military engineer during his Gallic campaigns, went further still; he clad every inch of wall in marble and there was not a single column in his house that was not fashioned from solid Cararran or Carystian stone.[11]

If you found wall-to-ceiling marble cold, tacky, or just prohibitively expensive, there was a wealth of other decorative options. Frescoes were a classic choice. Great vistas wrapping around entire rooms immersed the visitor in other worlds: a luxurious seaside villa perhaps; or a lush Italian garden; or even the exotic landscape of recently conquered Egypt, where hippos and crocodiles and reed boats appeared and disappeared in the waters of the Nile and people attended banquets and orgies between the temples that lined its banks. Later, fashions shifted, and narrative mythological scenes were set against backdrops of red, ochre yellow or lacquered black, framed by spindly columns decorated with garlands or Egyptianising lotus motifs. The subjects were often related by

---

* This is the Marcus Lepidus who was consul in AD 78, father of the Lepidus who joined Octavian and Mark Antony to form the Second Triumvirate during the civil wars that followed the assassination of Julius Caesar.

obscure thematic or genealogical threads, showing your guests that you were *au fait* not just with the latest fashions but also with the Homeric epics and the complex web of Greco-Roman mythology.

The halls of the rich, already resplendent with frescoes or exotic marbles, were, then as now, filled with collections of ruinously expensive antique art. The Romans knew their illustrious ancestors had really been uncultured militaristic thugs, and they were chippy about it. For art, you simply had to go to Greece. And go to Greece they did. From the end of the third century BC, the Romans bought, plundered or extorted Greek masterpieces on an extraordinary scale. Boatload after boatload of priceless marbles, bronzes and panel paintings was shipped from the centres of Greek culture to the centre of Roman wealth.

In the city, rich men bought up and flattened whole neighbourhoods to create personal pleasure gardens. In these vast urban parks and on their expansive country estates away from the heat and dirt of the city, they attempted to outdo nature, building mountains, excavating caves, creating fake rivers which they called 'the Nile' or 'the Euphrates'.* It was amid this wave of competitive garden building that Lucullus laid out his terraced park on the Pincian Hill; the property that Messalina, it was alleged, would later kill to acquire – and the place where she would herself be killed.

On the face of it, at least, Messalina chose a good time to be born into the Roman elite. And yet the Roman aristocracy were still in recovery from the hundred years of civil dissent and fifty years of civil war that had afflicted the Republic until the ascension of Augustus to sole rule.

---

* The extravagant pleasure gardens were ironically called *horti*, or 'vegetable gardens'.

In the year 146 BC, Rome had become the undisputed ruler of the Mediterranean world. The hotch-potch of city-states that then made up Greece had capitulated in their entirety following the capture and sack of Corinth. The spring of the same year saw the total destruction of Carthage – for so long Rome's definitive rival for naval supremacy. But even as Carthage burnt, the victorious Roman general Scipio Aemilianus mused on the potential consequences for Rome of uncontested domination; 'A glorious moment, Polybius,' he is claimed to have remarked, 'but I have a dread foreboding that someday the same doom will be pronounced on my own country'.[12] His comments were remarkably prescient.

The rewards of political success were now very different from those that the sixth-century BC aristocrats had had in mind when they designed the Republican system of power sharing. Then, the holding of public office was valued for the respect and honour the candidate gained in the community. Now a magistracy at Rome was automatically followed by a 'pro-magistracy' abroad.[13] This put its holder in command of an army and allowed him to exercise summary power, with his decisions subject to retroactive senatorial oversight only after his year was up.[14] He could wage wars of conquest that enriched his troops and made him a god to the public back home. And, if he was only willing to countenance a little corruption, there was *big* money to be made. As the stakes rose exponentially, the checks and balances designed to constrain individual ambition broke under the strain. Powerful politicians began to assemble personal armies and to refuse to relinquish office. Alliances were made and broken and factional disputes driven by individual egos were fought out on battlefields across the Mediterranean world.

It was onto this scene that the future emperor Augustus burst in 44 BC. Then known as Octavian, he was nineteen and, he claimed, the rightful heir to both the fortune and the political position of his murdered great-uncle and lately adoptive father, Julius Caesar. When Caesar was stabbed on the Ides of March by the group of senators led by Cassius and Brutus, Octavian was undergoing military training in Apollonia, a city in the area of the Balkans then known as Illyria (in what is now Albania). When the news of Caesar's assassination reached Octavian, he sailed straight for Italy.

It is not at his birth in 63 BC, but rather at this moment, that the *Res Gestae* – Augustus' own account of his life and achievements – begins, with these remarkable words: 'At the age of nineteen I raised an army at my personal decision, and at my own expense, and with it I liberated the state, which had been oppressed by a dominant faction'.[15] Exactly who this 'dominant faction' was appears to have changed according to Octavian's personal interest at any given time.

First Octavian was allied with Cicero's senatorial faction, fighting against Mark Antony on behalf of the '*res publica*'. Within months, however, he and Mark Antony had joined forces as part of the Second Triumvirate and declared Cicero and the other 'Republicans' enemies of the state. Eventually every faction, 'dominant' or otherwise, that could possibly challenge Octavian's power was gone. Any real 'Republican' resistance was crushed with the defeat of Brutus and Cassius at Philippi in October of 42 BC. Then, after a decade of alternating between civil war and uncivil alliance, Octavian finally crushed Antony and Cleopatra's forces at Alexandria in August of 30 BC.

With every viable enemy safely dead, Octavian now set about establishing himself as a paragon of peace, prosperity and stability. He closed the gates to the temple of the double-headed god Janus in 29 BC for the first time in over two hundred years, an act which declared worldwide peace on land and sea.[16] The great gates had been shut only twice before in all of Rome's long history; Augustus would shut them three times in the course of his forty-one-year reign.[17] The Senate played their own part in this rebranding. In 13 BC they decreed that an altar should be raised in Augustus' honour on the Campus Martius.[18] Standing next to an obelisk that the emperor had installed to commemorate his bloody military victories in Egypt, it was to be known as the *Ara Pacis Augustae* – the Altar of Augustan Peace.[19] The name was apposite: this was without a doubt a peculiarly Augustan vision of peace. The interior walls of the altar's precinct were carved with heavy swags of ripe and verdant foliage – the fruit of peaceful prosperity. On the exterior an image of the personified goddess Roma seated comfortably on the arms of her vanquished enemies was placed by the entrance, and a procession including members of Augustus' extended family – accompanied for the first time ever on a state monument by their wives and their children – was carved along the sides. Messalina's grandparents on both sides have been identified among the crowd, as has Octavia, the sister of Augustus, Messalina's great-grandmother on both her mother and her father's sides, and the grandmother of her future husband Claudius. Messalina's parents Domitia Lepida and Messalla Barbatus may be among the children who stare around at the spectacle or tug at their parents' togas.[20] The monument connected the fate of Rome to that of Augustus' family, and Messalina only had to walk past the *Ara Pacis* to visualise her place in this great dynastic project.

Octavian also set to work overhauling his official position in the state. Between 28 and 27 BC, he declared an end to the temporary constitutional arrangements of civil war, giving up the unlimited authority that he had wielded over every province and every army and the stranglehold he had exerted on political institutions in the city.[21] He would later declare that, in doing so, he had restored the Republic, and there does appear to have been some return to the institutions and appearances of Republican politics; elections were held for the old magistracies and the courts and the Senate could deliberate again without overt threats of military force.

In reality, however, Octavian was not giving up power but rather reconstituting his sole rule in a more sustainable form – moving away from exceptional and unconstitutional commands towards a wide collection of honours, titles and powers, both official and unofficial, that gave him supreme and legitimate peacetime authority.

The Senate agreed that Octavian would retain control of a number of 'imperial provinces' and the troops that were stationed there. Octavian's allies argued in the Senate that these provinces – including Egypt, Gaul, Spain and Syria – were harder to handle, more complex, in need of the kind of leadership that only Octavian could provide.[22] These unstable border provinces required large numbers of troops to defend them; so, by retaining his hold on the provinces, Octavian also retained control over the majority of Rome's legions.

On 16 January 27 BC, the Senate made Octavian *princeps senatus*, the 'leader of the Senate', and bestowed upon him the honorific name by which he would henceforth be known – 'Augustus'.* Then, when Augustus ceased to hold continuous consulships in 23 BC the Senate granted him *tribunicia potestas* ('tribunician power') and *imperium maius* ('greater power').[23] These new powers gave him, respectively, the right to introduce or veto legislation, and to take command of any army in any province or unilaterally override the orders of any other

---

* 'Augustus' is difficult to translate directly. It derives from an adjective meaning 'majestic', 'venerable' or 'worthy of honour'. Its original uses were religious and may have had connections with augury. After its adoption by Octavian it became the ultimate signifier of imperial status and honour.

magistrate. These extraordinary powers were to be held for life – connected not to a transient and transferable office, but to one man. The principate had well and truly begun.

Still further honours followed: in 12 BC Augustus became *pontifex maximus*, the highest priest of Roman state religion, and in 2 BC, he was named *Pater Patriae* – 'Father of the Fatherland'.

The Republican dream of power sharing was over. Yet all Augustus' posts and honours had been officially voted to him by the Senate and the assemblies, ostensibly on their own initiative. Some among the Roman aristocracy would whisper that they had made a deal with the devil. They'd gained stability, to be sure, but at what price? What would their ancestors, the ones who had expelled Rome's kings, have thought to see them now, beholden once again to a monarchy in all but name? But if there were men among the political elite that thought this way, there were more – the pragmatic or perhaps the more distracted among them – who did not.

By 27 BC the Roman aristocracy were tired. They had endured fifty years of intermittent civil war; great lineages had been all but wiped out and fortunes confiscated or lost in bids for supremacy or survival. They deserved a break, a bit of luxury, and a return, at least nominally, to the predictable hierarchy of magistracies that had always provided them with a steady flow of public honours. A number of the great Roman families also worked out that a ruling dynasty could provide them with more specific benefits. Cosying up to a ruler was an easier route to prestigious office, however stripped of real power it might be, than canvassing an uncouth public, and both Messalina's grandfathers would gain the consulship through Augustan favour.* Nor did it take long

---

* Messalina's maternal grandfather, L. Domitius Ahenobarbus, was consul in 16 BC; her paternal grandfather, M. Appianus, was consul in 12 BC.

for families like Messalina's to recognise that dynastic politics could provide new routes to power altogether; by the time of Messalina's birth, her branch of the *gens Valeria* was tied, by marriage and blood, to the House of Augustus.

The survival of the Augustan settlement depended on a complicated network of bargains and conventional lies. The balance was theoretically awkward and fundamentally hypocritical but it was also unprecedentedly effective. By the time Augustus died peacefully in his bed in AD 14 at the age of seventy-six, he had been at the centre of Rome's political fray for nearly sixty years and its sole emperor for over forty.

Augustus' death threw the true nature of his new system starkly into the spotlight. His assorted powers, carefully collected and collated over half a century of rule, passed wholesale to his adopted heir, his step-son and erstwhile son-in-law, Tiberius. While Augustus lived, people could tell themselves that this was the personal primacy of one exceptional man; the smooth accession of his heir made it difficult to deny that the new order looked very like a monarchy.

On his deathbed, Augustus is said to have turned to his friends and asked whether he had performed well in the comedy of life.[24] The answer was clear: Augustus had performed the protagonist's part to perfection. But more than that, he had constructed anew the stage, the set and the auditorium. Born some six years after the great autocrat's death, Messalina, and everyone she knew, still acted upon Augustus' stage. In public and in private they inhabited Augustan architectural spaces, constructed in the enduring new styles he popularised. Their lives were constrained (or not) by the moral boundaries and the social categories he delineated, and their fortunes rose and fell within the dynastic system he created. By the time Messalina came of age, the actors might have changed, but the stage set remained Augustus'.

III

An Education

'Don't let her know the whole of history –
Let there be something in the books that she
Cannot quite understand as well as me'

Juvenal, *Satires*, 6.450–451

Messalina's pedigree was of the highest quality that Rome
had to offer. The heritage of her family – the *gens Valeria*
– stretched back to the very earliest days of Roman history:
Valerius Poplicola had been among the men who had overthrown
the monarchy and established the Republic following the rape
of Lucretia, and in 509 BC he had been one of the two men
selected to serve as the first consuls of the new state.[1]

Since then, the family's prominence had hardly waned.
Messalina's parents, Marcus Valerius Messalla Barbatus and
Domitia Lepida the Younger, were extremely well connected.
Both their fathers had held the consulship; their mothers were
half-sisters, and both nieces of Augustus through their mother,
the emperor's beloved and influential sister Octavia.[2] By virtue
of their descent, Messalina's parents occupied the highest circle
of Augustan society: they were members of the old Roman
aristocracy and of the new imperial family.

Messalina would never have been allowed to forget that she
had a long and illustrious heritage to live up to. The rooms

42

she inhabited were filled with heirlooms and military trophies and the *imagines* of her ancestors stared down at her every morning from the *atria* walls. These realistic wax masks of the faces of those men in the family who had won election to high office were taken from life and worn by impersonators to recreate long processions of the (successful) dead at family funerals. When not in use they were kept, carefully labelled with epithets extolling their achievements, in the most public part of the house to remind occupants and visitors of the family's long lineage of public glories.[3]

Familial identity was also woven into every syllable of a Roman girl's name. Unlike boys, girls were not given *praenomina*, what we might today understand as 'first names', but were identified instead using feminised versions of their father's surnames, his *nomen* and sometimes his *cognomen*, the first of which identified his clan and the second the more particular branch of the family to which he belonged. A daughter of Marcus Valerius Messalla Barbatus was thus always going to have been called Valeria Messalina.* Had our subject had a sister she would have been Valeria Messalina too, distinguished only (if at all) by the epithet *maior* if she were older, or *minor* if she were younger. That this would prove a nightmare for the historian seeking to trace the narratives of individual women (it is sometimes, for example, very difficult to distinguish between Messalina's mother, Domitia Lepida, and her elder sister, Domitia Lepida) was of no concern to Roman parents, who could hardly have wanted their daughters

---

* These conventions were just starting to shift at the time of Messalina's birth. Her own daughter, Claudia Octavia, would be named not only for Claudius but also for Octavia – her shared paternal grandmother and maternal great-grandmother. It can hardly be a coincidence that upper-class women begin to be afforded personal names only as their social and political power begins to expand within the dynastic system of empire.

43

to do anything distinctive enough to earn them column inches in the annals of history.* While stubbornly unhelpful for the identification of individual women, these names did send one message clearly and effectively – that it was her family that defined the status and the identity of a Roman woman. It was a message that the young Messalina cannot have failed to grasp.

Despite the prominence of her family, none of the sources felt it necessary to preserve the precise date of Messalina's birth. Such an omission was not unusual; Roman women, even those born into the greatest and most distinguished families, generally only enter the historical record when they contract a politically significant marriage. The birthdates of Roman women are usually calculated by working backwards from the date of their marriage, subtracting the thirteen or fourteen years that constituted the conventional age of first marriage for the elite Roman maiden. In Messalina's case, this formula would produce a birthdate of around AD 24 or 25.

Unfortunately, by AD 23, Messalina's father appears to have been dead – a circumstance that would have rendered her conception tricky. Messalla Barbatus' father Messalla Appianus is known to have died early in the course of his consulship in 12 BC, making this the latest possible date for his son's birth. Given his connections to the imperial house, Messalla Barbatus would have expected to hold a consulship of his own by AD 23 (when he would have been at least thirty-five) – his failure to do so suggests he was already dead.[4]

These circumstances are confirmed by the fact that Messalina had a half-brother, Faustus Sulla Felix, by her mother's second marriage. He held the consulship in AD 52, which – given that he

---

* Messalina's mother seems more often to be referred to as Lepida and her sister as Domitia in the sources, but both are also referred to at other times by their full, and identical, names.

was likely granted dispensation to hold it five years early when he married the imperial princess Claudia Antonia – suggests a birthdate no later than AD 23.[5]

We must imagine that Messalina's marriage to Claudius in AD 38 was her first: given the sources' obsession with Messalina's sexual and romantic relationships it seems impossible that a prior marriage would have gone unmentioned. In her late teens, Messalina was already old to be marrying for the first time so we should probably place Messalina's birth just before, or perhaps even just after, her father's death, and as close as possible to her mother's remarriage and the birth of her step-brother.[6] If Domitia Lepida remarried and bore her son in the early years of the 20s AD, that places Messalina's birth around the start of the new decade. From this point on, I will take AD 20 as the 'best guess' for the date of Messalina's birth.

When Messalla Barbatus died, he left Lepida a young widow and Messalina a fatherless baby. Messalina's mother – then perhaps twenty, beautiful, rich, and of proven fertility – quite naturally wasted no time in remarrying.[7]

As her second husband, she chose Faustus Cornelius Sulla, the great-great-grandson of the bloodthirsty dictator Lucius Cornelius Sulla who had given the Roman Republic its first real taste of autocracy in the 80s BC. We possess little information about Faustus Sulla's own character and none at all about his relationship with Messalina. Divorce and sudden death were both so common in Rome that blended families were not something to be commented on. Besides, Faustus may have been dead before Messalina was a teenager – we hear nothing of him after his consulship in AD 31.

In the first years of the 20s AD, Domitia Lepida presented her new husband with a son and Messalina with a half-brother, Faustus Cornelius Sulla Felix. Messalina and her half-brother were close in age and their relationship appears to have been good. When Messalina married Faustus Sulla Felix to her step-daughter Claudia Antonia in AD 46 or 47 it was a gesture of both honour and of trust.[8]

Domitia Lepida now had two young children to contend with – although it is unlikely that she nursed either of them herself; Messalina and her brother were probably raised by wet-nurses during the earliest, most vulnerable years of their lives. The relationships between children and their nurses could be close and life-long, but the practice may also have impeded children's bonding with their mother. In his account of Messalina's death, Tacitus makes a throwaway comment that Domitia Lepida was at her side 'although the two had never got on while her daughter thrived'.[9] This rupture in relations may have occurred during the early years of Messalina's reign – perhaps over the murder of Domitia Lepida's third husband Appius Silanus (of which more later) – but its seeds may have been sown earlier.

Tacitus (not a fan of her daughter and never disposed to be kind to imperial women) describes Domitia Lepida as 'immodest, infamous, and forceful', a woman as inured to vice as she was favoured by fortune.[10] When Messalina was grown up and married, Domitia Lepida would, for a time, be given custody of her nephew, the future emperor Nero. She is said to have spoiled the young boy rotten, lavishing him in attention and gifts.[11] History does not recall whether she had taken a similar approach in raising Messalina.

If Messalina's mother was difficult she was, at least, fabulously wealthy. Domitia Lepida held, in her own right, sprawling agricultural estates at Fundi, a town sitting halfway along the Appian Way, the vital artery connecting Rome with the south, and in Calabria, right down in the toe of Italy. The damp and sheltered plains of Fundi produced cellars of Caecuban wine – a strong and long-aged vintage, this full-bodied wine was judged by many connoisseurs to be the best Italy had to offer; the rich soil of the Calabrian estates bred heavy harvests of citrus and olives.[12] Domitia Lepida eked out every last drop of this natural abundance; after her daughter's death she would be accused of failing to properly discipline the huge gangs of agricultural slaves that worked her Calabrian estates.[13] Her investments were diversified too; she owned plots of land by the harbour in Puteoli – the great commercial port of the Bay of Naples. She leased these out to an investor for the construction of rentable warehouses that would skim profits both from the incoming cargoes of Alexandrian grain and the outgoing consignments of sweet Pompeiian wine.[14]

Messalina was a trust-fund baby with the real estate to prove it. Faustus and Domitia Lepida must have kept a house on one or other of Rome's more fashionable hills. Here the rich lived above the forum with its commercial hustle and constant building work and away from the unwholesome smog of the Suburra slums that nestled in the damp dip between the southern slope of the Viminal and the western slope of the Esquiline.

Behind the high windowless walls and heavy doors that were a necessity in the city, a wide atrium, well decorated with inlays of coloured marble and lined with those images of illustrious ancestors, would have received family friends and political associates, business agents and old retainers, waiting to be led on to Faustus Sulla's scroll-lined office, or to one of the impressive halls or galleries he used for receptions. If they were lucky, they might pass through a succession of shaded and well-watered courtyards to network and negotiate over dinner. Grand and luxurious though they were, the townhouses of the Roman nobility were designed for *negotium* – the business of doing politics and preserving one's property. Vitruvius, a successful first-century architect who authored an architectural treatise that remains influential to this day, reminds his reader that the houses of nobles

who bear honours and magistracies, and who must commit themselves to the duties of the state, should be furnished with high-ceilinged regal vestibules, vast atria and colonnaded courtyards [...] all finished to a standard which becomes the dignity of their position. There should be libraries too, and basilicas, in a style no far cry from the magnificence of equivalent civic buildings, because public councils as well as private trials and arbitrations are often conducted in the homes of these men.[15]

In the country, away from the fast pace of politics and the demands of his clients, the aristocrat could afford to relax a little. The old Republican ideal of a simple rustic retreat, far not only from the stresses but also from the luxuries of urban life, had long given way to a preference for expansively comfortable and luxuriously designed country piles. Just like its owners, the architecture of the Roman house relaxed when it left the city. Porticoes turned outwards to frame country views rather than inwards to enclose courtyards, wide wings spread out on either side of main houses, long corridors led guests into vast private bath complexes or out through the gardens and into the country. These were spaces designed not for *negotium* but for *otium* – a term which translates literally as leisure but which, in Latin, carries more specific overtones of *well-spent* leisure, the improvement of the self through culture, art and contemplation. In the pursuit of such noble aims, villas were furnished with generous libraries, galleries of paintings, Greek sculptures (some original, some copied) and huge peristyle gardens that mimicked and domesticated the *gymnasia*, the distinctive civic exercise and education grounds of Hellenistic cities. Messalina's family would have owned multiple such villas, perhaps on lands abutting Domitia Lepida's agricultural estates, on ancestral holdings of Faustus's family, the Corneliae Sullae, or in the pretty hills of Latium which offered rustic charm yet lay within easy reach of Rome.

Life in Messalina's parents' rural villas might have been pleasantly edifying, but it can hardly have been *exciting*. For excitement, the Roman jet-set headed to the Amalfi Coast. In the first century AD the string of rich resort towns that clustered around the Bay of Naples was the *only* place to summer; anyone who was anyone had a villa here. Domitia Lepida and Faustus were likely among them, and Domitia Lepida's elder sister certainly was; her estates at Baiae were so desirable that the emperor Nero was said to have had her murdered just to get his hands on them.[16] The best villas were perched on the cliffs above the sea, with tiered terraces commanding panoramic views of the bay and steep steps cut into the rock-face leading down to the water.[17]

The summer season here was a social whirl – the great orator Cicero called it 'that mixing-bowl of voluptuous luxury'.[*] The houses were designed for entertaining, with private coves for beach parties, jetties for mooring pleasure boats, and kitchens with the capacity to feed guest lists numbering well into the hundreds. The late first-century AD poet Martial portrayed it as a place that could corrupt a nun:

Chaste Laevina never yields like those Sabine girls of old,
And though her husband is severe, she is twice as cold,
Yet now she to the Lucernine, now the Avernus does
* surrender,*

---

[*] From a letter from Cicero to his friend Atticus dated 16 April 59 BC. The word Cicero uses here – *Cratera* – is a Greek loan word that describes the vast bowls that the more civilised of the ancients used to mix their wine with water, but it was also used, in Latin, to refer to the crater of a volcano. For Cicero, who owned multiple properties in the area, Baiae was a place where distinctions, moral and social, could become dangerously blurred, and here he expresses that linguistically, blending Baiae's hedonistic moral character and the physical character of its round Vesuvian bay until they become indistinguishable. Cicero also gives an evocative description of summer parties on the bay: Cicero, *For Caelius*, 49.

*Now she, down in Baiae, lets the loosening waters warm
  her,*
*Now she falls to fire; leaves her husband for some young
  swain,*
She might arrive Penelope, yet she will leave as Helen.[18]

Growing up in places like these, it is hardly surprising that
Messalina developed something of a taste for luxury. But she
might also have gleaned some understanding of what it *meant*
to be a Roman aristocrat in the Julio-Claudian high noon of the
first century AD. The showy halls and enfilades of her parents'
townhouses revealed the permeability of the line between private
life and public duty; their country houses, filled with books
and art, attested to the significance of cultural capital; and the
sumptuous villas which clustered around the Bay of Naples
reflected an increasing assumption among the upper classes that
pleasure was a Roman birth right.

Whatever lessons Messalina absorbed from her ancestors'
imagines and her parents' luxurious portfolio of real estate, they
were just footnotes to her formal education.

For a society that was unreservedly patriarchal in structure
and often ragingly misogynistic in culture, the ancient Romans
loved educating women. It appears that during the first
centuries BC and AD (our best documented period) a significant
proportion of urban women, even outside the upper echelons
of the elite, were at least partially literate. A number of writers
mention, without any expression of surprise, girls as well as boys
attending the mid-priced elementary schools that taught reading,
writing, arithmetic and sometimes the basics of literature to the
children of the urban upper-middle classes in shaded corners
of town forums across Italy.[19] Fragments of Pompeian graffiti,
scrawled on the walls of the city's public spaces – 'Romula hung
out here with Staphylus', 'Serena hates Isidorus', 'Atimetus got

me pregnant' – suggest that some women even lower down the social scale could at least write names and a few choice phrases.*
And more women still, by virtue of having grown up in urban environments that were so aggressively *written on*, could probably read a few key words that cropped up again and again in formal inscriptions and informal scratchings: the names of the gods, perhaps, or the magistrates, or the most popular of that season's gladiators.

Messalina's education would have gone much further. Unlike the education of an upper-class Roman boy, which was conceived primarily as a systematic preparation for a public career, the education of an upper-class Roman girl had no clearly defined purpose beyond equipping her with the knowledge and accomplishments that befitted her social standing. Perhaps for that reason, it was never written about with any of the methodical clarity of the treatises devoted to the education of boys. Our evidence is patchy and anecdotal, but we can collect enough of it, from the late Republic and early empire, to construct a facsimile of what Messalina's education might have looked like; the facts she might have known, the ways in which she might have been taught to think, the skills with which she would have been equipped to enter the adult world.

With a succession of private tutors, Messalina would have learnt Latin and Greek and possibly the basics of mathematics. She would have read, recited, and sometimes memorised passages of the literary 'greats' – Homer, the Greek tragedians, and the illustrious Augustan poet Virgil. These works formed the backbone of the universe of quotation and allusion with which educated Romans liked to elevate their letters, poems

---

* The first of these is from the House of the Tetrastyle Atrium; the second is from a tomb in the Nocera Necropolis; the third is from the House of C. Vibius on the Vicolo del Panattiere.

and speeches. She might also have been expected to analyse the language of these texts, their grammar and use of poetic meter. Other lessons might have included musical theory, singing and lyre playing. Dance lessons may also have been arranged to teach her how to move beautifully (but not so beautifully as to call into question her respectability). In order to lend her letters a certain rhetorical flourish, she may have participated in the prose-writing exercises that formed the basis of her brother's training in oratory. Some training in philosophy may have been organised too, designed to teach Messalina how to evaluate ideas, think logically and, most importantly, to behave morally.[20]

All in all, Messalina might have been expected to accrue a range of accomplishments similar to those praised in the twenty-one-year-old widow Cornelia Metella, who had married Pompey the Great in 53 BC. 'The young woman', Plutarch tells us, 'had many charms apart from her youthful beauty. She was well versed in literature, in playing the lyre, and in geometry, and had been accustomed to listen to philosophical discourses with profit.'[21]

To some upper-class women in the century or so before Messalina's birth, this remarkably extensive education must have seemed a cruelly liberal preparation for a conservatively constrained adulthood. Plutarch, after all, had followed his praise of Cornelia's education with the crowning assertion that Cornelia 'had a nature which was free from that unpleasant officiousness which such accomplishments are apt to impart to young women'.[22] If she wrote poetry, the Roman lady was expected not to publish it; if she composed clever letters to prominent men it was most likely their replies alone that would be collected and published; if she learnt philosophy, she was expected to use it to find contentment within the limits of her feminine lot.

By the 20s AD, however, these old distinctions between the knowledge a woman might possess and the knowledge she might put into practice were beginning to blur. The upper-class Roman woman had always been expected to use her education to guide her in the raising of sons fit for Republican office. But in a *dynastic* system, in which a boy's illustrious future might be guaranteed from the very moment of his birth, this role took on a whole new potency. And there were other more novel (and, to male observers, more frightening) ways for the imperial woman to put her education to good use. In a world in which matters of law and of state were increasingly being decided not out in the open, in the forum or the Senate, but in private, in the halls, dining rooms or even the bedroom of the emperor, a clever woman had new opportunities. She might use a knowledge of politics or history to offer advice and a knowledge of literature or rhetoric to make that advice beguilingly persuasive.

It was for this role that Messalina's education was preparing her, whether she knew it then or not.

IV

Eavesdropping on Tiberius

'Everything from then on was tearing, pressing despotism...'

Tacitus, *Annals*, 5.3

The wealth of Messalina's parents, their properties, their armies of servants and their proximity to power made for a privileged childhood. But it must also have made for a somewhat unsettled one.

As Messalina entered her teens, she can hardly have been ignorant of a sense of growing political unease suffusing the conversations she overheard in her step-father's corridors. Rome was a city built on social networks, and Domitia Lepida and Faustus' wealth and position would have meant a constant cycle of suppers and meetings, banquets and concerts, lectures and readings, country trips and garden parties – attended by the crème de la crème of Roman society.

It was a social world in which Messalina would, to some extent, have been included. The childhood of noble Roman girls was by no means cloistered. Writing about the death of a friend's thirteen-year-old daughter, Pliny the Younger, an early second-century politician, author and orator, demonstrates the social contact a Roman girl might have with her parents' friends. Pliny clearly knew the girl well: 'I never saw a girl so lively and loveable [...] who had all that wisdom that comes with age, the dignity of womanhood, and yet still had the sweetness of girlhood and the bashful modesty of youth' and he remembers how she would 'cling to her father's neck and embrace us, her father's friends, so lovingly and so modestly'.[1] With parents close to the heart of the Tiberian political elite, the list of family friends Messalina encountered would have read like a who's-who of movers and shakers of the new principate. She might have overheard references, dropped just above her head, to a political environment that was degenerating, increasingly, into crisis; and she might have noticed when one or other previously familiar face suddenly disappeared from her parents' guest lists forever. This would, perhaps, prove the most important education of all.

Tiberius became emperor upon Augustus' death in AD 14. He had not been his step-father's first choice of successor.* It was only after the deaths of a number of potential heirs that Augustus began to promote him as a key player in his dynastic plans, forcing Tiberius to divorce his pregnant wife Vipsania Agrippina and marry Augustus' own daughter Julia the Elder. Tiberius was heartbroken. The first time he saw Vipsania after their divorce, Suetonius tells us, he 'pursued her with eyes so intent and so tearstained' that Augustus saw to it that the two of them never laid eyes on one another again.[2] Unsurprisingly, Tiberius' marriage to Julia the Elder soon disintegrated and in 6 BC he left Rome against the wishes of the imperial family to seek out peace and retirement on the island of Rhodes, leaving his much-resented wife to the delights of the city. In 2 BC a letter arrived informing Tiberius that Julia the Elder had been convicted of adultery and exiled, and that Augustus had

---

* Tiberius was the son of Livia by her first marriage to Tiberius Claudius Nero. Augustus allegedly admitted that he did not view Tiberius as an ideal heir. Suetonius, *Life of Tiberius*, 23.

55

already initiated divorce proceedings on his behalf.[3] Tiberius finally planned to return to Rome in AD 2 on the proviso that he would take no part in public life. That year, however, saw the deaths of both Augustus' heirs, his grandsons, Gaius and Lucius.[4] Tiberius, after a decade of retirement, was now heir to the empire.

Tiberius was a strikingly unwilling autocrat. A sound orator, cool-headed diplomat, and a great general, he had earned both military glory and a reputation as a strict disciplinarian in the course of an illustrious career that had taken him from the rich borders of Parthia in the east to the wild hinterlands of Germany and Pannonia. He was not blessed, however, with an affinity for public relations: he had no feeling for the volatile appetites of a crowd and he was evidently uncomfortable with anything that smacked of pageantry, spectacle or popular fun. With the stiffest of stiff upper lips and a bitter hankering after some shadowy conception of the 'old ways', Tiberius would perhaps have been better suited to a life of middling glory on the battlefield and in the forum during the early days of the Republic. Now, aged fifty-four, he found himself in a role for which he was deeply ill-suited, and in supreme control of a political system utterly incompatible with his personal ideals of aristocratic conservatism.

During the first few years of his reign Tiberius did his best to reconcile his traditional aristocratic ideals of collegiality, liberality, modesty and moderation with the demands of the autocratic role to which he had acceded. He rejected a number of the honours, like the title '*Pater Patriae*', that had defined Augustus' position and attempted to check some of the more outlandish expressions of adulation; the month of September was *not* to be renamed in his honour. Once, when a senator attempted to embrace his knees in an obsequious display of deference, Tiberius retreated so quickly that the suppliant lost his balance and toppled backwards onto the ground.[5]

Even the generally hostile Tacitus has to admit that, during the early years of Tiberius' reign, 'all public business, and the most significant of private cases, were handled in the Senate, and its leading men were afforded the freedom to argue them [...] the offices of consul and of praetor each retained their distinctive honours [...] and if ever there arose some dispute between the princeps and a private citizen, there was recourse to the forum and to justice'.[6]

Increasingly, however, Tiberius' personal ideals proved irreconcilable with the political reality of the system he led. When, in AD 21, Tiberius encouraged the Senate to pick a new governor for Africa – one of the last provinces nominally under senatorial control – the senators, paralysed by fear that their choice might displease, referred the decision immediately to the emperor. Foreign embassies that were directed (constitutionally correctly) to the Senate complained that they were being prevented from fulfilling their missions: they had been sent, they said, to speak to the *emperor*. The lack of enthusiasm the foreign embassies displayed towards the Senate was matched only by the Senate's lack of enthusiasm for foreign embassies. When, in AD 22, a number of delegations brought questions relating to rights of sanctuary in provincial temples before the Senate, its members quickly tired of listening to endless petitions and exhaustive evidence and transferred their powers of investigation and judgement wholesale to the consuls.[7] If Tiberius wished to *force* his senators to behave independently, he was fighting a losing battle. By the end of that year, Tacitus reports, he was wont, upon leaving the Senate House, to mutter that these were 'men primed for slavery'.[8]

Even as Tiberius decried the failings of the Senate, however, he was locked in a stasis of his own, trapped between the self-image of Tiberius the man, and the self-interest of Tiberius the princeps. He wanted his senators to display a freedom of speech, but it was crucial to the survival of the principate that they remain *his* senators; total freedom for the Senate would, necessarily, mean the end of the principate and, indeed, of the princeps. Tiberius understood this, and as much as he felt uncomfortable with the autocratic nature of Augustus' system, he also actively perpetuated it, keeping tight control over the military and violently removing his most serious rivals.*

It was a zero-sum game: Tiberius knew that every action he took to shore up his position as princeps weakened the old moral order he revered, and yet failure to shore up his position meant death – there was, after all, no such thing as an ex-emperor. Tiberius was leading a system he did not create – one with which he did not feel entirely comfortable. He was doing a job he did not ask for, to which he was poorly suited, and which he could not leave except via the slow death of old age or the less than appealing option of violent assassination.

Ancient historians liked to split the reigns of 'bad' rulers into two halves; an initially promising period of apparent liberality and moderation, followed, inevitably, by a descent into tyranny, cruelty and madness. This division provided authors with a useful means of rationalising seemingly contradictory actions and a satisfying structure for biographies that fitted well with the classical conception of human history as essentially degenerative. But for all that this was a literary trope, it might, in the case of Tiberius, have come pretty close to the truth.

Messalina was born just on the cusp of the turn. In AD 19, Germanicus – the brother of Messalina's future husband Claudius, and Tiberius' extremely popular adoptive son and putative successor – died in mysterious circumstances while on imperial business in Syria.[9] His widow Agrippina the Elder

---

* Tacitus calls the murder of Agrippa Postumus 'the first crime of the new regime' and pointedly places it, in his narrative, before the Senate had officially bestowed power on Tiberius: Tacitus, *Annals*, 1.6.

cried murder, claiming that this illness had been too terribly intense to have come on naturally. People spoke of poisoning and even witchcraft, whispering that human remains, burnt embers and lead curse-tablets inscribed with Germanicus' name had been found stashed inside the walls and under the floor of his room. Tiberius was the obvious suspect and the court of public opinion appears to have all but convicted him of the crime.[10] Then, in September AD 23, Tiberius' only son Drusus died after a short, sudden and unexplained illness. No suspicions were raised at the time, but it would later be alleged that this had been a murder too.[11]

Tacitus presents this as a watershed moment in the reign. His analysis, while probably overly simplistic, is perhaps not entirely inaccurate. In the years following Drusus' death, Tiberius appears to have become increasingly withdrawn and paranoid; he attended meetings of the Senate less and less frequently and was increasingly willing to countenance prosecutions, based on scanty evidence, for nebulously defined crimes. The most feared of these charges were those related to the law of *maiestas*, most commonly, although somewhat unsatisfactorily, translated as 'treason'. This set of laws punished actions that were seen to compromise the 'dignity' or 'power' of the state. In the Republic, when 'the state' had meant the Senate and people of Rome, the offences prosecuted under the *lex maiestatis* had generally been the gravest of military transgressions: leading an army against the state, aiding the enemy, abandoning a fortress. Now that 'the state' had come increasingly to mean the emperor, the law was thrown open to interpretation. Anything that might be seen to diminish the dignity of the House of the Caesars was theoretically punishable with exile or death.

By AD 26 the desire for escape that had driven Tiberius to Rhodes three decades earlier had caught up with him once again. This time he chose Capri: a mountainous island of volcanic rock that rose from the waves some five miles out in the Bay of Naples. Tiberius had inherited property there – a villa perched right on the summit that had once belonged to Julius Caesar – and now he intended to use it. The views were beautiful, but Tacitus expresses the belief that 'it was the solitude of the place that most appealed to him, since it is surrounded on all sides by a harbourless sea [...] no one could have landed there without one of the look-outs having knowledge of it'.[12]

Whatever the nature of his attraction to Capri, Tiberius would never return to Rome again. Astrologers had predicted as much upon his initial departure from the city in AD 26 (ostensibly for the dedication of Temples to Jupiter at Capua and Augustus at Nola) and this had been universally interpreted as a signal of his impending death.[13] The idea that a Roman would voluntarily live away from their native city for any length of time was unfathomable. Tiberius would do so for the full eleven years that remained of his life and reign; although, on occasion, he would travel right up to the shadow of Rome's walls, he would never again cross the sacred boundary, the *pomerium*, that defined the official limits of the city.

Absence, it transpired, did not make the heart grow fonder. With Tiberius away from the city, relations between the Senate and its princeps went into free fall. The Senate had always found Tiberius' true intentions hard to read, and now found the task impossible. The emperor sent long letters to be read out in the *curia* and the senators spent hours picking apart the possible double-meanings of his choices of vocabulary. Tiberius, for his part, believed more and more that the Senate hated and resented his leadership – and that they wanted him dead.

One man did particularly well out of this atmosphere of mutual suspicion. Lucius Aelius Sejanus was not a member of the imperial family, he was not even a senator, but he was the prefect (commander) of the Praetorian Guard. A sort of outgrown imperial bodyguard, the Praetorians now numbered some ten thousand men and were, crucially, the only military cohorts authorised to be stationed within the city of Rome itself. The Praetorians owed their allegiance directly to the emperor, and the emperor, in turn, relied upon their support – a decade and a half later, the assassination of Caligula and the accession of Claudius and Messalina would make it clear just how deep this reliance ran. Tiberius trusted Sejanus implicitly and, as he withdrew ever further from his public duties, he found the Praetorian Prefect invariably willing to pick up the slack.

Once the emperor was safely isolated on Capri, Sejanus was free to act the power broker. With the Imperial Post under Praetorian protection and the ear of the emperor increasingly monopolised by the prefect, the senators knew that Sejanus controlled the flow of both information and advice to the emperor – and acted accordingly. The Senate voted for the dedication of altars, decorated with statues of Tiberius and Sejanus, to Clemency and Friendship.[14] Meetings with Sejanus were like gold dust; senators followed him from Rome to Campania and back again, filling the forecourt of his house, desperately trying to win the favour and the patronage of the slaves who guarded his door. One New Year's Day a couch in his atrium collapsed under the sheer weight of his visitors.[15] The situation was such, Dio writes, that it seemed Sejanus was emperor of Rome, and Tiberius, secreted away on Capri, merely the petty lord of an island potentate.[16] These anxieties about sinister, non-senatorial imperial advisors, would return two-fold under Claudius – although this time they would fixate on the influence of the emperor's freedmen, and his wives. The rising tide of *maiestas* prosecutions was attributed to the consolidation of Sejanus' power. One Sabinus, arraigned and executed on treason charges at the start of AD 28, screamed over and over as he was dragged to his death that he was a 'sacrificial victim' to Sejanus 'killed to inaugurate the New Year'.[17]

There was crisis within the imperial family too. There had long been rumours of factionalism and now they broke in spectacular style. In AD 29 Germanicus' clever, popular and ambitious widow, Agrippina the Elder, and her eldest son Nero Caesar were declared public enemies and exiled. Her second son Drusus Caesar followed the next year. By AD 33 all three of them were dead.[18] These were deaths of which Messalina must have been aware. The families were closely connected: Germanicus had been a cousin on both her mother's and father's side and Agrippina's namesake daughter had just been married to Messalina's uncle Domitius Ahenobarbus. A number of prominent aristocrats had already fallen on account of their friendship with Agrippina and her family: among them the renowned general Gaius Silius and his wife Sosia Galla.[19] Faced with false charges of sedition and extortion, Gaius Silius committed suicide and Sosia Galla was exiled – the teenage son the couple left behind was the same Silius who would fall as Messalina's 'husband' in AD 48.[20] Again, the sources lay much of the blame for the family schism at Sejanus' door.

Now comfortably ensconced at the heart of power, the sources claim that Sejanus, although born a mere equestrian, began to aspire to nothing less than the principate itself. At the start of AD 31, it was starting to look like he might get there; on 1 January, he assumed the consulate with none other than Tiberius as his colleague and, Suetonius claims, the emperor implied that a marriage to Livilla, the widow of Tiberius' son Drusus, might be on the cards.[21] Had the year gone to plan, it would have made Sejanus both a senator and a member of the imperial family and, thus, a potential successor to Tiberius' power. As it happened, Sejanus would not live to see AD 32.

It is not entirely clear what precisely precipitated Sejanus' fall from power – the section of Tacitus' work which covered the events of AD 31 is lost, and none of the explanations offered by the other sources is entirely convincing. The most likely reconstruction has a letter written to the emperor by Messalina's future mother-in-law Antonia the Younger, alleging a plot or simply hinting to Tiberius that his loyal favourite was not so unthinkingly loyal as he appeared.[22] Whatever the trigger, the fall, when it happened, was spectacular.[23]

Sometime around May, both Sejanus and Tiberius gave their consulships over to other senators. This was normal; the 'suffect consulship', as it was known, had been developed to give larger numbers of senators a shot at the top job and increase the emperor's opportunities for patronage. The suffect consul who replaced Sejanus that May was none other than Messalina's step-father, Faustus Sulla.*[24] In his new role, Faustus Sulla was expected to preside over meetings of the Senate, but the task was becoming increasingly difficult. As spring turned to summer, Tiberius sent a series of letters to the Senate, each more confusing and contradictory than the last. First Tiberius would write that he was so ill that he was close to death, next that he was quite well and would soon be returning to the city; he would write first to promote some close ally of Sejanus, then to denounce another; he would first praise Sejanus, then castigate him. Faustus Sulla tried to maintain order as the Senate, frantic to discern the emperor's true intentions, argued endlessly over their interpretation.

The senators, led by Faustus Sulla and his co-consul, desperate not to end up on the wrong side, hedged their bets – publicly honouring Sejanus but privately avoiding his company. Messalina's family must have been relieved when October arrived and Faustus was able to relinquish office to yet another set of suffect consuls. Sejanus himself was starting to get jumpy; he felt neither secure enough to pursue his plans, nor scared enough to

---

* Faustus Sulla served from May until October when the consular fasces were handed over to a new set of suffect consuls.

begin considering desperate measures. Pleading that Livilla was unwell, but presumably actually hoping to get a better handle on the situation, he asked Tiberius if he might come to Capri to see them. Tiberius refused. He would, himself, soon be back in Rome, he promised, and he would see Sejanus then.

Neither of those promises would be fulfilled. When Tiberius finally struck in the autumn of AD 31, he did so quickly and without warning. Under cover of night he sent the new Praetorian Prefect, a man called Macro, from Capri to Rome to deliver a letter. Macro announced his arrival to no one except one of the new suffect consuls, Memmius Regulus, and the prefect of the *vigiles*, the night-watch. As the senatorial meeting began the next morning, Macro stationed guards around the building's perimeter and delivered the letter to the consuls. He did not wait to hear it read out.

The contents of the letter came as a surprise to many of the senators – Faustus, perhaps, included – and it surprised Sejanus too. It did not, Dio claims, contain any outright order that Sejanus should be put to death, but it did contain a litany of criticisms and order the execution of two of his closest associates as well as the imprisonment of the man himself.

There was no doubting what would happen next. Sejanus was executed the very same day that he was imprisoned. His body was thrown down a steep flight of stairs, known as the Gemonian Steps, between the prison and the forum. There it lay, broken and abused by the crowds, for some three days before it was finally cast into the Tiber. The bodies piled up as Sejanus' old allies rushed to accuse each other, hoping that they might thereby absolve themselves.

Sejanus' children were executed too. His young daughter Junilla, recently betrothed to an imperial prince (Claudius Drusus, the son of Messalina's future husband Claudius by his first wife Plautia Urgulanilla) and about the same age as Messalina, begged over and over to be told where she was being taken and what crime she had committed and why a 'child's beating' would not suffice for its punishment. It was thought an outrage to execute a virgin and so she was raped before being strangled and thrown, along with the bodies of her siblings, down the Gemonian Steps.[25]

Messalina would have been just old enough to understand something of what was going on. These chaotic and bloody events – including the brutal execution of a girl her own age whom she would have known – must have been her first real introduction to the violent realities of Roman high politics.

There was more to come – this time courtesy of Sejanus' ex-wife Apicata – and it would hit Messalina's family even closer to home. Sejanus and Apicata had divorced in AD 23, presumably on bad terms given that she was not included in the spate of prosecutions and executions that followed Sejanus' downfall. Unable to bear to watch the execution of her children for the crimes of their father, Apicata wrote a final letter to Tiberius and took her own life.

The letter contained a series of extraordinary allegations dating back almost a decade, pertaining to the events surrounding the death of Tiberius' son Drusus in 23 BC. At the time, no one had considered Drusus' death to be suspicious. It had been unexpected and sudden, but there had been no evidence of foul play. Apicata's letter told a different version of events. She claimed her husband had seen Drusus as a rival to his own ambitions of supremacy, and had resolved to get rid of him. Sejanus had tested the water with a number of possible allies and found one more promising than the others – Drusus' wife Livilla.

Livilla was Messalina's first cousin once removed, and her future husband Claudius' sister. Not a pretty child, Livilla had nonetheless grown into one of the great beauties of the age and was, it seems, unhappy in her marriage to the often drunk and sometimes violent Drusus.[26] Sejanus, Apicata claimed, had seduced Livilla with protestations of love and driven her to hope that, were her husband out of the way, they might marry and rule the empire together. Livilla began to feed him details of her husband's secrets, and finally, once he was fully prepared, Sejanus had struck, choosing a poison which 'in creeping on little by little would mimic the course of a natural disease'.[27]

The business done, Sejanus divorced Apicata and wrote to Tiberius asking for the widowed Livilla's hand in marriage, a request that was initially refused and finally acceded to only in the year of his downfall.

In Tacitus' narrative of the affair, Livilla's adultery and her role in her husband's politically motivated murder go hand in hand. 'As if aflame with love', Tacitus tells us, 'Sejanus drew her into adultery, and after that first shameful boundary had been broken (for having lost her virtue, a woman rarely refuses other things), he urged Livilla to dream of marriage, of a share in the rule of the empire, and of the death of her husband.'[28] This connection – the presentation of adultery as a gateway drug to insurrection – is one that the sources would later play on in relation to Messalina herself and her ill-fated, bigamous 'marriage' to Silius.

Of course, we have no way of knowing if Apicata's assertions were true, but the truth hardly matters. Tiberius believed Apicata's final testimony, and so Livilla was executed. She was the first woman to suffer *damnatio memoriae*; the official destruction of all a person's images and inscriptions. Seventeen years later Messalina would be the second. According to Dio, Tiberius did not have Livilla executed directly. Rather, he handed her over to her mother (Messalina's future mother-in-law) Antonia the Younger, who locked her wayward daughter in a room until she starved to death.[29]

Things did not improve, as many of the senators had hoped they would, after Sejanus' death. Tiberius had lost the last man he thought he could trust, his 'partner in toil' as he called him.[30] The emperor maintained his isolation on Capri and his estrangement from the Senate; he exchanged public duties as much as possible for the pursuit of personal pleasures; he gave ever greater rein to his tendency towards mistrust and the gnawing of his paranoia.

Tiberius the emperor was not a happy man; his head lay uneasy under the weight of a crown he'd never wanted. In AD 32, the year after Sejanus' death, Tiberius began a letter to the Senate with these words: 'If I know what to write to you, Conscript Fathers, or how to write it, or what not to write at all at this present moment, may every god and goddess inflict a ruin upon me, worse than this death that I already feel each and every day.'[31]

However much Tiberius might have felt his existence in AD 32 to be a daily death, it would not be until some five years later, in AD 37, that he would encounter the real thing. When Tiberius died in his bed on Capri he had reigned for twenty-two and a half years.* Now his nephew, the young Gaius Caligula, would succeed him as emperor.

It is impossible to understand Messalina, or the stories told about her, without understanding the long and often painful reign of Tiberius.

Messalina was a teenager when Tiberius died: it was in this reign that she was born and raised. It was the intrigues and crises of the Tiberian court in the early 30s AD that provided her with a schooling in Roman dynastic politics; the brutal deaths of Agrippina, Sejanus' young daughter, Junilla, and Livilla showed her the dangers she might face as a woman embroiled in Julio-Claudian politics.

---

* Tiberius probably died of natural causes, although the sources, unsurprisingly, also record rumours that he was murdered by Caligula and the praetorian prefect Macro.

But, perhaps most importantly of all, it was in the environment of seclusion and secrecy that characterised the latter part of Tiberius' reign that the 'genre', as it were, of the salacious imperial rumour began to come into its own. The tales that grew up around the isolated Tiberius influenced the development of what would become a long and venerable tradition of rumour-mongering; one that would affect the course of Messalina's short life and lengthy afterlife.

People said that the once noble-looking emperor had hidden himself away because he'd become physically repulsive, his face covered in spots and ulcers.[32] They also said that those pustules were merely external manifestations of something *internally* corrupt; shameful desires that Tiberius was increasingly unable to control and conceal. They said that he had degenerated into sexual obsession and perversion; that the twelve interconnecting villas he had built on the summit of Capri were filled with erotic paintings and sex manuals; that the gardens' grottoes and terraces were staffed by prostitutes dressed as nymphs and satyrs. They said that he raped young men, chosen as much for their aristocratic pedigree as for their beauty; that he trained little boys to lick his balls in the swimming pool; that he had crack teams of male and female prostitutes – performers, 'inventors of preternatural forms of intercourse' – who 'would defile themselves before him, three at a time, all joined together, that the view might reinvigorate his failing libido'.[33] Tiberius, the erstwhile uptight traditionalist, had created on Capri a depraved wonderland of 'enflamed lusts' and 'mysterious passions'.[34]

Some of this, perhaps, was true. Tiberius would not have been the first powerful man to abuse his power for twisted sexual gratification, and he certainly would not be the last. But much of it, most likely, was not. The remote isolation of Tiberius' later years, coupled with the very visible bloodshed of the early 30s AD, created a petri dish for the popular imagination, one in which connections between debauched sexuality and the dimly lit, private world of imperial politics could grow until they took on a life of their own.

It was Augustus who established the power structure of Roman autocracy, but it was under Tiberius that the new *culture* of autocracy really came into focus. Here are all the secrets, the show-trials, the adulteries, and the perversions with which the House of the Caesars, and the name of Messalina in particular, would soon come to be so indelibly associated.

V

A Bad Year for a Wedding

'The burning torches shake out their locks of golden hair:
Come forth, new bride.'

Catullus, *Wedding Hymn*, 61

The year of Messalina's marriage to Claudius began inauspiciously. On 1 January AD 38 a slave named Machaon climbed up onto the sacred couch of Jupiter Optimus Maximus in the Capitoline temple – the heart of Roman state religion. First, he pronounced 'many dire prophesies'; then he slaughtered a puppy which he had brought with him, presumably for the occasion; and then, finally, he turned his knife on himself.[1]

Neither the wild pronouncements of a slave, nor even the murder of a dog, could put a dampener on the spirits of the aristocracy that January. The old emperor Tiberius had died on Capri the previous March and Rome was enjoying an intense honeymoon period with its new princeps. Caligula was young, fun and saying all the right things – and after twenty-two years of Tiberian severity, the nobility was ready to believe them.

Besides, the plans for Messalina's marriage could hardly be delayed any further. Most aristocratic girls were married at around fourteen – at eighteen or so Messalina was already old to be marrying for the first time. Although a prior marriage would surely have been mentioned in the sources, this may not have been the first time she was engaged. In the mid-30s AD, it was very easy to lose a fiancé – or even two, if one was careless – to disease, military service or the constant crises of Tiberian court politics. It is possible that Messalina had been betrothed before and that the match fell through.

Whatever the reason for delay, in AD 38 Domitia Lepida would finally get to see her daughter in the costume of the bride. As the morning of her wedding day dawned, Messalina would have woken early, her room invaded by her mother and other female relatives, attendants carrying clothes and jewellery, professional hairdressers and old family slaves. She was dressed in the pure white *tunica recta*, its folds gathered around her waist by a girdle, perhaps hanging heavy with pearls and jewels, tied in a convoluted Hercules knot. This knot was designed for her husband alone to untie later that night. Her hair was ritually parted with the tip of a spear – in service of some arcane symbolism that no one could quite recall – and then twisted, braided and bound into the complicated six-sectioned bridal hairstyle known as the *seni crines*. This 'towered crown' was topped with a wreath of verbena leaves, marjoram and flowers which, if Messalina was doing things the traditional way, she would have gathered herself.[2] Her feet were slipped into delicate yellow slippers, necklaces of gold, precious gems and pearls were strung about her neck, bracelets were twisted onto her wrists. Finally, Messalina's head was draped in the *flammeum*. A veil variously described as the colour of 'egg yolk' or 'blood' or 'lightning,' the *flammeum* was the most distinctive marker of the Roman bride.

Dressed in all this finery, Messalina prayed and sacrificed to the gods, offering them incense and a sprinkling of wine or, perhaps, her childhood dolls.[3] The marriage contracts were checked one final time and augurs sought, and accordingly found, favourable omens of marital happiness. Messalina might have been expected to cry as she left her family home, probably just as the sun was setting into evening. The weeping first-time bride was a trope in Latin poetry – in one of his wedding songs the late Republican poet Catullus had written: 'throw open the closures of the door/the maiden comes [...] but natural shame and noble blush delays [...] she weeps, for she must go'.[4]

The procession of family members, illustrious friends and clients must have attracted crowds of spectators as it wound its way through the city streets, lit by flaming torches and singing rhythmic wedding hymns to Hymen: 'io Hymen Hymenaeus io, io Hymen Hymenaeus'.

The destination was Claudius' townhouse, one of Messalina's three new homes, the door of which was garlanded and wreathed and brightly illuminated for the occasion.[*][5] Inside, awaiting the young bride, was a great wedding feast, an adorned marital couch, and a groom: Claudius, Messalina's forty-seven-or-eight-year-old cousin once removed, the uncle of the new emperor, and a man who had so far been unlucky both in life and in love.[6]

Claudius, or Tiberius Claudius Nero if you wanted to be polite, had been born the third and final surviving child of Drusus the Elder and Antonia the Younger in 10 BC, on the first day of the high summer month that would soon be renamed 'August' in honour of the reigning emperor.

Claudius' lineage, in true Julio-Claudian style, was as convoluted as it was exalted. His father Drusus was nominally Augustus' step-son. Livia had been six months pregnant with him when she'd divorced her first husband to become Augustus' third wife, meaning that the boy had been born under the princeps' roof. Livia's ex-husband was legally declared the boy's father but, naturally, rumours swirled that his real parentage

---

* Claudius' private property seems to have included a townhouse, a house with gardens in the suburbs and an estate in Campania.

was more *august*. One contemporary verse noted wryly that 'three month children are born to the blessed'.[7]

Claudius' mother, Antonia the Younger, had a more official, though possibly less direct, blood relationship to the emperor. Antonia the Younger was the daughter of Octavia, Augustus' sister, and Mark Antony, his erstwhile ally turned ultimate enemy. Her elder sister was Messalina's grandmother. The date of Claudius' birth, 1 August, must have hit a bittersweet note for his mother Antonia. It marked twenty years to the day since her uncle Augustus had taken the Egyptian capital of Alexandria, securing control of the empire but also driving his last rivals – her father Mark Antony and Cleopatra, the woman for whom he had left her mother – to suicide.

Claudius' father Drusus the Elder was something of a golden boy. By the time Claudius was born, Drusus had cemented his position as a military hero with a string of successful northern campaigns under his belt and a reputation for personal bravery. Perhaps even more importantly, Drusus, unlike his elder brother, the future emperor Tiberius, was also in possession of the kind of easy manners that added a touch of romantic glamour to reports of his victories.*

In 10 BC, Drusus was sent back to the north-western front. This remained one of the most unstable regions of the empire and the start of the summer campaigning season saw Drusus sallying forth out of Gaul and across the Rhine to face hordes of German barbarians. The heavily pregnant Antonia remained in Gaul at the provincial capital of Lugdunum (modern-day Lyon), and it was here that Claudius was born.[8] Drusus closed the summer campaigning season of 10 BC on a high, and that

---

* For example, Drusus embarked on a dramatic quest for the Spolia Opima (the armour and weapons of an enemy leader, won in hand-to-hand combat, and the most highly prized war trophies in Roman culture): see Rich, 'Drusus and the Spolia Opima', 544–555.

autumn the family, with the newborn Claudius in tow, returned to Rome to witness Drusus' election to the consulship.

The following year would not be so kind. Right from the off, if we believe Dio and his three hundred years of hindsight, the omens were bad; brutal storms battered Rome and the Capitoline Temple of Jupiter was damaged by lightning. But Drusus, omens or no omens, planned to reach the Elbe before the year was out, an expedition that would take him farther north and east into Europe than any Roman had been before. He made it to the banks of that river and then, strangely, instead of attempting to cross it, he turned his troops back towards the Rhine.

Once again, ancient observers perceived dark portents at work. It was said that on the banks of the Elbe, Drusus had met with the apparition of a peculiar, Latin-speaking Barbarian woman 'of superhuman size' who addressed him thus: 'Whither, pray, art thou hastening, insatiable Drusus? It is not fated that thou shalt look upon all these lands. But depart; for the end alike of thy labours and of thy life is already at hand.'[9] Whether Drusus really believed himself to have been visited by such a spirit, or whether the Elbe just looked harder to cross up close than it had seemed from further away, is impossible to say. Either way, he decided to leave the dark forests on its north-eastern bank well alone.

It was a decision that would do him no good. On the long journey back to the army's summer camp Drusus was involved in a serious riding accident that saw one of his legs crushed under the weight of his horse. He made it back to the camp but he was dead within the month.[10] Like Messalina, Claudius had been left a fatherless baby.

Drusus' death triggered an outpouring of public grief. His body was given a hero's welcome, escorted along its route to Rome by a relay of leading citizens, before being cremated on the Campus Martius and interred in the strange and grandiose

Mausoleum of Augustus. The fort where he died became, in the soldiers' parlance, 'the accursed camp'; the army built him a cenotaph on the banks of the Rhine and held yearly, fully-armoured races in his memory. The cities of Gaul vowed annual sacrifices in his memory; the Senate raised an arch decorated with military trophies on the Via Appia, and conferred the honorific name 'Germanicus' upon Drusus and his descendants.

Drusus was that most ideal of politicians – a glamorous and promising leader, dead before he'd ever had a chance to rule badly – and his legacy was to cast a long shadow.

Claudius and his two siblings – a six-year-old brother, now known by his father's honorific 'Germanicus', and the four- or five-year-old Livilla (future wife of Tiberius' son Drusus and the alleged lover of Sejanus) – were left to be raised by their mother.

Despite Augustus' urgings, Antonia would never remarry. Contemporary sources present this as a grand romantic gesture, the action of a woman in perpetual mourning for a lost love.[*] But Antonia may also have enjoyed the status and relative freedom widowhood granted her. There was still a certain cachet attached to the old Roman concept of the *univira* – the 'one-man woman' – and, as the widow of the people's hero, Drusus, the protector of his children and his legacy, Antonia knew that she would never want for public prestige or influence within the court.

Nor was there any financial incentive to remarry. Antonia owned vast and richly productive estates stretching across Italy, Greece and Egypt in her own right, purchased perhaps with the funds Augustus had granted her from the dissolution

---

[*] The writer Valerius Maximus presents both Drusus and Antonia as paragons of marital love and fidelity. He claims that Antonia continued to sleep in her old marital bedroom after Drusus' death. Valerius Maximus, *Memorable Doings and Sayings*, 4.3.3.

of her father Mark Antony's property. Scraps of papyri record her possessions in Egypt: fertile wheat fields, grasslands for the pasturing of flocks of sheep and goats, and palm groves for the cultivation of sweet, heavy dates, perhaps, or for the production of woven rattan baskets.[11] According to new Augustan laws designed to bolster a birth rate that was still lagging after a century of civil war, the birth of Antonia's third child, Claudius, had liberated her from the *tutela mulierum* – the legal and economic guardianship usually exerted over a woman – giving her official control over her own affairs.

Instead of setting her sights on a second husband, the widowed Antonia set about putting together her own household. She collected philosophers, poets, and a remarkable range of foreign princes and princesses – among them Antiochus IV of Commagene, Tigranes V of Armenia, Herod Agrippa of Judea, and Ptolemy of Mauretania – all of whom were sent to Rome to be educated under her auspices.[*] In this, Antonia was to some extent recreating the conditions of her own childhood: her studiously self-sacrificing mother Octavia had raised her ex-husband Mark Antony's three children by Cleopatra (Ptolemy Philadelphos and the twins Alexander Helios and Cleopatra Selene) alongside her own.

Antonia's composite and cosmopolitan household migrated between a section of the rambling warren of interconnected houses that constituted the Augustan palace on the Palatine and a great villa near Baiae, on the bay of Naples, now known as the Cento Camerelle – the house of a hundred rooms. The gardens, running down the cliff to the sea, were landscaped with curved colonnades and ornamental fishponds filled with the moray eels that were fashionable garden accessories for Rome's super-rich.[12] It was said that Antonia adorned her favourite eel with earrings.[13]

---

* Herod Agrippa and Ptolemy were almost exactly the same age as Claudius and would have been brought up alongside him.

Antonia might have doted on her eels, but she was less kind to Claudius. The first signal that something was amiss arrived with Claudius' coming of age in AD 5 or 6. A Roman boy's ascent into manhood was marked by a change of clothes: at fifteen or sixteen, he would put away the child's *toga pretexta*, with its coloured border, exchanging it for the plain white *toga virilis*, the 'toga of manhood'.[14] The event was a cause for celebration. After the toga was exchanged, sacrifices would be offered and the *novus togatus* (the 'new toga-wearer'), accompanied by his father and a procession of attendants, would be led into the public world of the forum. For the boys of the House of Caesar the event had evolved into a long and extravagant series of public ceremonies, designed to introduce the people to their future leaders. Gifts of food and cash were donated to the public, and banquets laid out in the streets as the *novus togatus*, often conducted by Augustus himself, made his way through the forum, up the Capitoline hill to the Temple of Jupiter and on to his bright public future as a leader of men.

Claudius' experience, however, was quite different. There was none of the customary fanfare to mark his coming of age – no public celebration, no procession, no feasts, no commendation from Augustus, no proud display of the young prince to his future people. Instead, he was conveyed to the Capitoline to make the necessary sacrifices in a closed litter in the dead of night. It looked like Claudius was being hidden from public view.[15]

The reason for Claudius' exclusion seems to have lain in a puzzling combination of physical and mental abnormalities that plagued the young prince. Suetonius claims that a series of 'varied and clinging maladies' haunted Claudius' infancy and adolescence and that, over time, this persistent ill health 'blunted his faculties, both of mind and of body'.[16] It was said that his head had a tendency to shake, his knees sometimes buckled beneath him, his right leg dragged slightly, his wrists were limp and his hands quivered. His speech was sometimes slurred and stuttering. Claudius' laugh was uncontrolled and 'indecent', while his displays of anger – which caused snot to run from his nose and saliva to foam at the sides of his mouth – were even more revolting to witness.[17]

Historians' attempts to match Claudius' panoply of symptoms with modern diagnostic criteria have met with little success: some have blamed childhood polio, others a mild form of cerebral palsy. Whatever the real medical source of Claudius' physical infirmities, Antonia's diagnosis was unequivocal: to his mother he was 'a portentous monster of a man, not finished by Mother Nature, only begun'.[18] The Romans were never particularly forgiving of disability; it accorded ill with their ideals of masculinity and ancient thought had long drawn troubling connections between physical malformation and moral degeneracy.

For the imperial family, Claudius' condition also posed a peculiar set of political issues. When Claudius came of age, Augustus' plans to acclimatise the Senate and the People of Rome to the concept of hereditary rule were still very much a work in progress. In a city that, after half a millennium of bitter and deeply rooted ideological opposition to the idea, was only just becoming used to justifying power on the basis of blood, the perception that there was 'bad blood' in the imperial family might threaten everything.

The question of Claudius' future provoked frenzied discussions within the imperial family. In AD 12 Augustus wrote to his wife Livia, seeking to settle the issue once and for all. Claudius was now twenty-two, and if he was ever to embark on a public career there could be no further delay:

I have spoken with Tiberius, as you ordered, my dear Livia [...] and now we both agree that it must be decided, once and for all, what plan we are to pursue in regards to that boy. For if he is sound and, so to say, complete, why would we doubt that he should proceed through those same classes and ranks through which his brother has already advanced? If, however, we feel him to be defective and unsound, in body and mind, such material for the potential derision both of him and of us must not be offered up to the public on a plate.[19]

The eventual verdict of these deliberations was evidently not in Claudius' favour – he received no political offices and was not even, technically, a member of the Senate.

With the death of Augustus and the accession of his uncle Tiberius in AD 14, Claudius saw an opportunity to improve his position. He wrote to the new emperor, asking that he be given the opportunity to prove his abilities in the role of consul. Tiberius tried to fob him off with consular regalia – an empty honour – but Claudius pushed back – he wanted the actual office, with real powers and real responsibilities. The emperor's response was short and brutal: 'I have sent you forty gold coins for the Saturnalia and the Sigillaria.'[20] Tiberius had not even acknowledged Claudius' request; he had sent him pocket money for Christmas presents.

The restrictions placed on Claudius' freedom extended beyond his access to public office. Even after he reached the age of majority, the family kept him under the strict control of a 'tutor'. Later Claudius would complain that the man was a 'barbarian, a former driver of beasts of burden who had been appointed for the sole purpose of punishing him with the utmost ferocity on any pretext whatsoever'.[21] The cold cruelty of Claudius' family and the curbs on his independence would cast a long shadow.

Claudius' position cannot have been eased by the conspicuous success of his older brother Germanicus. He had assumed the honorific cognomen granted posthumously to their father

Drusus and now he was beginning to look like an equally picture-perfect Roman prince. Dashing, brave, single-minded, dramatic and arrogant, he possessed a taste both for the heat of war and the theatre of a triumph. The people loved him, and in AD 4, shortly before Claudius' conspicuously clandestine coming of age, Augustus forced Tiberius to adopt Germanicus as his future successor in the principate. We know Germanicus would never come to rule – he died in mysterious circumstances in the east in AD 19 – but during the first decades of the first century AD, Claudius' shortcomings, and the humiliation of his sidelining, must have been magnified by Germanicus' success.

And yet, despite everything, Claudius showed signs of a capable, even a prodigious, intelligence. At an early age, and with the encouragement of the pre-eminent Roman historian Livy, Claudius had embarked on writing a history. More contemporary than Livy's work, Claudius' narrative was to start with the assassination of Caesar, running through the civil wars and the establishment of Augustus' principate to the present day. The work, apparently, was good – his research would be used as a source a century later by Tacitus – but his choice of subject was misguided. The period Claudius had chosen encompassed all the mess of blood, ideology and civil strife that had defined the beginning of Augustus' principate. Claudius' mother and grandmother intervened, demanding that the history begin *after* Augustus' triumph in the civil wars – the point at which the new princeps, with all his rivals dead, had been able to safely set aside brutality and embark on magnanimity.

For his next subjects, Claudius shied away from the contemporary and the controversial. He produced histories of the Etruscans and the Carthaginians, and, despite his struggles with vocal delivery, he wrote theoretical monographs on oratory. Some of his interests were more niche: feeling that the Latin alphabet was not quite fit for purpose, he invented three entirely new letters and produced a book describing their theory and advocating their use. Later, he would use his position as emperor and censor in AD 47 to enforce the official inclusion of these letters.

Claudius' overlooked intelligence must have made his position unbearable. Indeed, his condition appears to have been partly psychological. His physical difficulties improved as he matured, but worsened with the highs and lows of emotion. His speech was said to be flawed in conversation but clear and commanding when he declaimed a pre-prepared speech.[22] Most strikingly of all, Claudius' disabilities visibly abated upon his accession to the principate – and to all the respect and agency that accompanied it. Suetonius tells us that in the end all that remained was a susceptibility to heartburn.[23] Claudius' maltreatment up until this point – the disregard, disrespect, and insidious lack of expectation – had clearly created a self-fulfilling cycle.

After his accession, Claudius would explain it differently; he claimed that he had been actively playing up his weakness as a means of self-defence.[24] Suetonius states that the emperor's contemporaries found the suggestion risible, but it is undeniable that Claudius did manage to survive the bloodbaths of both Tiberius and Caligula which, between them, had seen the deaths of his brother, mother, sister, sister-in-law and two of his nephews, as well as the exile of two of his nieces. Whether by chance or design, Claudius' apparent incapacity and his concomitant lack of power undoubtedly protected him – it was simply impossible in the 20s and 30s AD to perceive him as a genuine threat.

So, for almost half a century, Claudius lived the life of a private citizen. There were fewer immediate risks to his life but there was endless boredom. He divided his time between a house in the suburbs and a villa in Campania, absorbing himself in his studies. He cultivated less highbrow hobbies too, developing a taste for wine, women and gambling in the company of the poor and the poorly bred.[25]

During this period Claudius was as unlucky in his private life as in his public career: by the time he met Messalina, he already had two failed engagements and two failed marriages under his belt. He had been betrothed for the first time as a teenager to Aemilia Lepida, a great-granddaughter of Augustus, but the match was broken off in AD 8 following the spectacular fall of the bride-to-be's mother, Julia the Younger. Accused of adultery with the senator Decimus Junius Silanus, the pregnant Julia the Younger was exiled to the barren Adriatic island of Tremirus where her child was exposed on a mountainside and she herself died some twenty years later. Decimus, by contrast, entered a leisurely voluntary exile when the scandal broke and returned to Rome following Augustus' death six years later. Aemilia was replaced with a new fiancée, Livia Medullina Camilla – the daughter of the consul of the previous year, Marcus Furius Camillus – who dropped dead of a sudden illness on the very morning of their wedding.

After this run of misfortune, Claudius finally made it to the altar in AD 9 or 10. The bride, on this occasion, was Plautia Urgulanilla. The daughter of a consul of Etruscan descent who'd served with distinction alongside Tiberius and the granddaughter of one of the empress Livia's closest friends, Plautia was a well-connected, though by no means an impressively noble, match. The marriage initially went well and Plautia was soon delivered of a son named Claudius Drusus.[26]

It was during Plautia's second pregnancy that things began to fall apart. In AD 24 Plautia's brother, Plautius Silvanus, hurled his wife to her death from an upper-storey window of their house in Rome. When Silvanus claimed that her fall had been a suicide, the emperor Tiberius attended the scene himself to investigate and found the unmistakable remnants of a violent struggle in the couple's bedroom. A senatorial court was convened for Silvanus' trial. Before it could begin, the defendant was sent a dagger by his grandmother and, taking the hint, swiftly dispatched himself.[27]

Deprived of the catharsis of a trial, the court of public opinion sought new scapegoats. First, Silvanus' ex-wife was accused and acquitted of driving her ex-husband mad with poisons and magic. Suspicion now seems to have turned on Plautia. Rumours swirled of an incestuous relationship between brother and sister, one which, it was suggested, had led to conspiracy to murder. There is no evidence that such hearsay was founded in reality but the reputational damage was irreversible. Plautia, then four months pregnant, was promptly divorced.

Claudius initially accepted the child Plautia bore five months later as his own and planned to raise her within his household. Soon, however, doubts began to fester in his mind regarding her paternity. Eventually Claudius publicly repudiated the baby in the traditional way: leaving the child naked and alone on her mother's doorstep. Perhaps because he believed it to be so, or perhaps because he wished to humiliate Plautia further by suggesting she had taken a low-born lover, Claudius put it about that the baby's real father was his ex-slave, a freedman named Boter.[28]

Claudius and Plautia's first child, their son Claudius Drusus, remained in his father's house (children were the legal property of their fathers and so automatically remained with them in the event of a divorce) until he choked to death in his mid-teens on a piece of pear which he had tossed playfully into his mouth.[29] This untimely death at least spared him the pain of watching the rape and murder of his fiancée Junilla, the daughter of Sejanus, following her father's fall from power in AD 31.

The breakdown of Claudius' next marriage, to Aelia Paetina – once again the daughter of a consul but no great aristocrat – was much less dramatic. The two had married in the mid-20s, and had a daughter, Claudia Antonia, by AD 28 at the latest. Suetonius comments that, in contrast to Plautia's 'shameful lusts and the suspicion of murder', Aelia was divorced for 'trifling offences' and, indeed, a remarriage to his second ex-wife was one of the ideas floated by Claudius' freedmen following Messalina's death.[30] Ironically, it was probably *for* Messalina and her more exalted family connections that Aelia had been divorced in the first place.

As his third wedding day dawned in AD 38, Claudius must have felt that his fortunes were on the rise. The accession of his nephew Caligula in March of the previous year had precipitated a welcome shift in Claudius' position – in July the new emperor had taken him as his colleague in the consulship. Nearly a quarter of a century after he had first written about the matter to Tiberius in AD 14, Claudius' ambition to hold the consulate had been realised. Claudius' appointment also finally made him a senator for the first time at the age of forty-seven.

His marriage to Messalina – a teenage heiress and imperial princess of the first degree – was further evidence of this advancement. Other, less coolly pragmatic, factors may also have recommended the bride. Messalina's portraits reveal a sensuous beauty with a straight nose and pouting, fleshy lips, set within a delicately rounded face. Most striking of all are the large, almond-shaped, heavy-lidded eyes beneath gently sloping brows. Just over half a century after Messalina's death, the poet Juvenal would emphasise the irresistible power of the empress' eyes in his Tenth Satire. He blames them wholesale for the fall of Silius in AD 48: 'the best and most beautiful of the patrician stock', Juvenal claims, 'is being dragged off towards a wretched ending by the eyes of Messalina'.[31] Although we can hardly take his description for fact, in singling out Messalina's eyes, Juvenal may well be playing on an established tradition.

Whether Messalina felt herself quite so fortunate in her match with Claudius is harder to guess. Legally, no Roman girl could be forced to marry against her will and, as her father was dead, Messalina technically had the right to contract a marriage on her own account to a partner of her own choosing.*[32] These rights meant precious little in reality. Culturally, the choice of marriage partner for an elite teenage girl on her first marriage lay with the family – especially if there were dynastic concerns at stake.† In Messalina's case, the marriage to Claudius was probably arranged between her mother Domitia Lepida, Claudius, and the emperor Caligula. For Caligula, the match presented another way of signalling his uncle's promotion while also settling a highly eligible imperial princess in a position that seemed to offer no threat to his own dynastic plans. For Domitia Lepida, the marriage strengthened her branch of the family's ties with the emperor; she may have been thinking of Faustus Sulla Felix's future as much as her daughter's. Messalina's consent may have been required for the signing of the marriage contracts but she was in no position to stand up to her mother and the emperor.

Suetonius presents Claudius as something of a silver fox. 'In body he was tall but not lanky, his looks and his grey hair were handsome, and he had a strong, full neck', all in all, an 'authoritative and dignified appearance' – so long as he remained still and sitting down; standing, moving, speaking or showing emotion apparently aggravated his remaining physical ticks and infirmities.[33] But for Messalina, who would later demonstrate

---

* The death of a girl's father (provided her paternal grandfather was also dead) left her *sui iuris*. Although important decisions regarding the disposal of her property were subject to the consent of an appointed guardian (a *tutor mulierum*), she did not require his consent (or the consent of her mother) to contract a marriage.

† There are instances where we do find evidence for elite Roman women choosing their own spouses, but these tend to be slightly older women who have been married before. Even in these instances we often find the family is also involved (e.g. in the case of Cicero's daughter Tullia, who chooses her third husband in conjunction with her mother while her father is out of Rome), or that the events cause controversy.

such a taste for youth and beauty in her passions for Traulus, Mnester and Silius, the 'authority' and 'dignity' of the middle-aged prince may have held little appeal. Her new husband was more than twice her age and his portraits as emperor, which are more unsparingly lifelike than the idealised images of his dynastic predecessors, reveal a weak-jawed man, with a nose more bulbous than was classically ideal, sinking cheeks and eyes heavily bagged by the sleepless nights of leadership. Still, Messalina must have recognised that the match offered more intangible benefits. Her husband-to-be was not one of the richest members of the imperial family, nor was he one of the most powerful, but marriage to Claudius would guarantee Messalina entry into the inner circle of the Caligulan court – with all the glamour and drama it promised.

We cannot reconstruct Messalina's thoughts as she sat on the garlanded marriage couch after the wedding guests had left, her bridegroom untying the special knot in her bridal girdle. She likely understood something of what was to come; ancient culture did not seek to conceal the realities of sex, and images of love making abounded in Messalina's Rome.[34] Beautiful couples caught in the act were painted onto the walls of elite homes, moulded onto silver tableware, and engraved onto gems or mirror covers.* Whatever hazy knowledge Messalina might have gleaned from her walls or her mirrors, however, must have been outweighed by the unknowns: how it would feel, if he'd be kind, whether she'd get pregnant, whether they'd be happy. We do not know if, in that moment, Messalina found her new husband attractive, whether she enjoyed his company, whether

---

* These images seem incongruous to the modern eye but they were *de rigueur* in elite homes from the Augustan period onwards, where they were prominently displayed in schemes that also included non-erotic images. Their display was probably not intended to arouse the viewer but rather to evoke an atmosphere of luxurious sensuality, emphasising the wealth and leisure enjoyed by the home's owner.

she felt comfortable with him, whether she was scared or excited, whether she trusted him.

We can perhaps come closer to imagining what she thought the next morning. When daylight slipped in between the shutters of the unfamiliar bedroom, Messalina would have awoken to a whole new identity. The Roman man assumed his adult identity independently – shedding the clothes of childhood and donning the toga that denoted adult citizenship automatically upon reaching his mid-teens. This was not the case for a Roman woman. There was no coming-of-age ceremony for the Roman girl that might compare to her brothers' assumption of the *toga virilis*. There was only marriage. It was on the eve of her wedding that the Roman girl dedicated her dolls to Venus and took off the clothes of girlhood for the last time.* The next morning, she would rise in a new house – a house of which she was the mistress – and would dress in a new costume – the long draped dress and mantle of the *matrona*.

Whatever Messalina thought of her bridegroom, she had awoken to a new identity, a new role, a new *life*. The change was entire and irreversible.

---

* The poet Propertius, for example, describes the moment that a girl changed her dress upon her marriage thus: 'now, my girl's dress gave way to the wedding torches/and a different type of headband won out and swept my hair up'. Propertius, 4.11.33–34.

VI

The Bridge Over the Bay

'Malice, craftiness and duplicity are the concomitants of absolute
power; and [...] our patrician families tend for the most part to
be lacking in the feelings of ordinary humanity'

Marcus Aurelius, *Meditations*, 1.11[1]

The court of Gaius Caesar Augustus Germanicus – better
known as Caligula – was a strange place for a teenage bride
to begin her married life. On the eve of Messalina's wedding, the
new reign was still enjoying a golden, heady honeymoon. The
young princeps had come to the throne amid an outpouring of
optimism; his ten-day journey from Tiberius' self-exiled court
at Capri back to the city of Rome was lined with celebratory
sacrifices and half-crazed crowds calling him 'star', 'chick',
their 'boy', their 'foster-child'.[2] The festivities, once he passed
through the city gates, were said to have continued for three
months. One hundred and sixty thousand bulls, sheep and pigs
were sacrificed to the gods and cooked into steaming banquets
for the people.[3]

The twenty-four-year-old princeps certainly had an aura of
tragic glamour about him. The public had never quite got over
the mysterious death of Caligula's father Germanicus (Claudius'
brother) or the execution of his mother and his two brothers.
That Caligula had survived seemed a miracle.

The new emperor had begun life in a series of military camps. His mother had transformed him into a sort of mascot for the troops, dressing the infant in the miniature uniforms that earned Gaius his nickname – Caligula, or 'little boots'.[4] This early introduction to the power of optics was not lost on Caligula: one of his first acts as princeps was to travel in conspicuously stormy weather to the barren islands where his mother and brothers had been executed to retrieve their ashes and re-inter them in the Mausoleum of Augustus in Rome.[5]

Caligula's promotion of Claudius to the office of consul, as his colleague in the summer of AD 37, was part and parcel of this same messaging.[6] In showing deference to the uncle who had been so conclusively sidelined by the last regime, Caligula distanced himself from the unpopular Tiberius and tied himself closer to the revered legacy of his father. Claudius' improved position at court meant that the eighteen-year-old Messalina was thrown in at the deep end of what was already showing itself to be a quite extraordinary milieu.

Messalina's marriage followed the second bout of relentless partying to occur within the first year of Caligula's reign. Throughout the summer and autumn of AD 37, the emperor had presided over celebrations on an unprecedented scale. At the end of August, to mark the long-delayed inauguration of the Temple of the Deified Augustus, Caligula organised sixty horse races in two days, programmes of plays that lasted late into the night, with the stages lit by torches, and games comprising the hunting and slaying of some eight hundred wild animals – half of them bears and the other half exotic beasts imported from the deserts of Libya.[7] On these occasions, Caligula played the participant as much as the patron. Senatorial onlookers commented with horror that the emperor behaved as one of the crowd, openly cheering on his favoured team of charioteers, the Greens, and singing along to the songs of his favourite plays – but the people loved it.[8]

The emperor made it clear during this first summer that under *his* auspices the pursuit of pleasure was to be taken seriously. For the first time, senators were permitted to sit on cushions in the theatre and wear hats to shield them from the sun. These measures signalled that if Caligula was putting on plays that lasted late into the night, he expected his senators to stay seated and watch them late into the night. Unlike the dour Tiberius, who had hated the races and done no more than the bare minimum when it came to the provision of public festivities, it was evident that the new emperor believed that entertaining the court and public was not merely an imperial right but an imperial *duty*. In the scale of these festivities, Caligula displayed a nascent interest in the construction of sensory experiences so overwhelming and exotic that they verged on the surreal.

Even before her marriage to Claudius, Messalina would probably have been present at least at some of the great events that followed Caligula's accession. There were two banquets, likely held in the August of AD 37 – during Claudius' consulship – at which Caligula wined and dined the entirety of the senatorial and equestrian orders, together with their wives and children. Messalina, with her senatorial step-father, would have been among the guests, tasting the vast array of dishes set out on each of the tables and receiving one of the expensive scarves of scarlet and Tyrian purple that Caligula distributed to the women and children as party favours.[9]

If Messalina attended other entertainments that summer – the theatre, races, gladiatorial games, beast fights, and concerts – she might have been struck by the peculiarly prominent position of the emperor's sisters. These three princesses – the twenty-one-year-old Agrippina the Younger, twenty-year-old Drusilla, and nineteen-year-old Julia Livilla – would have been easy for Messalina to observe, sitting as they were in the imperial box alongside their brother. The right to sit in this conspicuous place of distinction was not usually afforded to women; it had been specially granted as part of a slew of honours bestowed upon the three sisters by their brother just after his accession. They also received the extraordinary legal rights of Vestal Virgins and the people were ordered to include them in the oaths of loyalty they swore to the emperor. Even the consuls were to introduce new motions on the Senate floor with the words 'fortune and good luck to Gaius and his sisters'.[10]

Sitting in the garlanded imperial box, Caligula's sisters must have struck Messalina as an extraordinarily glamorous group. Their faces were now world famous. Immediately upon their brother's accession, images of the girls had proliferated across the empire; cities commissioned their portraits in marble and bronze, while Caligula struck coins casting them as divine personifications of 'Security', 'Peace' and 'Prosperity'.[11] Only a few years younger than the imperial sisters and absorbed in the final preparations for her upcoming wedding, Messalina might have watched the swift and dizzying promotion of these three young women, of whose family she would soon be a part, with a singular curiosity.

Caligula's devotion to his sisters went beyond mere show. Suetonius claims that, when he fell gravely ill in the winter of AD 37, it was Drusilla that Caligula named as the heir to his *imperium*. Caligula cannot have hoped that Drusilla would rule in her own name (for all the constitutional contortions that had occurred over the past fifty years, such a thing remained legally inconceivable); instead he may have intended that her husband Aemilius Lepidus – Caligula's favourite and rumoured lover – would govern until such a time as Drusilla's future children could assume the reins of power.[12]

Still, Caligula's decision was an extraordinary one, quite without precedent in Roman history. Rumours soon began to circle about an incestuous relationship between the emperor and his sister. It was even said that their grandmother Antonia the Younger had once caught them *in flagrante* when the two were still minors and living under her roof.[13] This tale was rendered all the juicier by the fact that Antonia (Claudius' mother as well as Caligula's grandmother) had died less than two months into the new emperor's reign and it was said that she had quarrelled with Caligula over some unknown issue just before her death. Suetonius notes contemporary rumours that the emperor had her poisoned, while Dio theorises a forced suicide.[14]

We cannot, of course, rule out the possibility that the relationship between Caligula and his younger sister was sexually abusive. And yet it is also easy to reconstruct the channels through which an unfounded rumour of incest might have taken root. Incest constituted one of the greatest taboos that Roman society had to offer; it was 'nefarious', 'sacrilegious', a violation of nature and of the laws of heaven. In this context, the accusation of incest provided immediate proof of Caligula's tyrannical disregard for the laws and mores of his forefathers. The association between incest and tyranny in Roman thought was intensified by a knowledge of the practice of incestuous marriage in some Eastern royal dynasties, most notably in Egypt where the Ptolemies used brother–sister marriage to 'purify' the bloodline and associate the rulers with the mythologically incestuous gods. Allegations of incest hinted that the emperor harboured a disregard for the most deeply held principles of his own people, and a desire to transform himself into an extravagant and absolutist Eastern king.[15]

Perhaps even more significant in driving the accusations levelled against Caligula and Drusilla was the inextricable connection in the Roman psyche between female power and female sexuality. That Drusilla's extraordinary rise to power should have inspired rumours of a sexual relationship between herself and her brother is not surprising; the Romans simply assumed she must have slept her way to the top. These same anxieties about the connection between sex and power would later dog Messalina herself.

By the January of AD 38 – the year of Messalina's wedding – Caligula had recovered from his illness. The emperor's brush with death broke the unremitting gaiety that had coloured the first eight months of his reign. Either suddenly acutely aware of his own vulnerability or moving to take advantage of the fact that his illness had plunged the court into an atmosphere of confusion and anxiety, Caligula used his recovery as an opportunity for a reshuffle.

First to go was Tiberius Gemellus, the grandson of the last emperor and Caligula's only feasible rival within the House of Caesar. Caligula accused Gemellus of conspiring against him and ordered his suicide. Only eighteen, Gemellus had to ask the presiding centurion where he should stab himself to ensure that the wound would be mortal. As the Jewish philosopher Philo, who was present at the imperial court two years later as part of an embassy from the Alexandrian Jewish community, commented: 'having received this first and last lesson he was forced to become his own murderer, poor boy!'[16] Similar suicides were demanded of the Praetorian Prefect Macro – accused of having boasted of his role in securing Caligula's accession, 'it is I Macro who made Gaius [Caligula], I am his begetter more or not less than his parents' – and Silanus, an erstwhile aristocratic mentor of the emperor.[17]

Suetonius claims that Claudius was implicated too and was 'spared only as a laughing stock'.[18] In reality, Claudius' position was perfectly well protected at the beginning of AD 38. He had enjoyed no power under Tiberius, owed his elevation entirely to Caligula, and, nearing fifty, famously infirm and only recently made a senator, he seemed to pose no real competition to his nephew. If anything, those first volatile months of the year served to confirm Claudius' new position at court, a position further consolidated by his marriage to the highly eligible Messalina later that year.

If Messalina did pick up on any residual anxieties at the imperial court in the months following her wedding, they can hardly have consumed her. She would have been busy, after all, acquainting herself with a new husband and what was, essentially, a new job. Claudius maintained at least three households: a townhouse in Rome, an estate just outside the city, and a villa on the Bay of Naples, each staffed by a significant retinue of slaves. Responsibility for their management would now have fallen upon his teenage bride. Messalina's duties were not purely domestic: she would also have been expected to play socialite and hostess, cultivating the sort of social connections that would bolster her husband's new position at court.

A fresh tragedy later that year would demand more of the newlyweds' attention: on 10 June Drusilla died.[19] Caligula's grief at the loss of his favourite sister was all-consuming. A period of public mourning, requiring the cessation of all public business and private amusements, was declared and enforced with an iron hand. All meetings and trials were adjourned; entertainments were cancelled without exception; the thermal baths were closed; laughing was outlawed. One street trader who sold warm water of the type used for mixing wine was charged with treason and executed.[20]

Caligula heaped unprecedented honours on Drusilla's memory. A lavish, quasi-religious festival with banquets for the Senate and equestrians was to be held each year to mark her birthday. A gold portrait of her was to be installed inside the Senate House, and another statue (equal in height to the cult statue itself) was to be raised in the Temple of Venus Genetrix, the mythological matriarch of the Julian dynasty.

One senator (shrewdly ascertaining the direction of

Caligula's thoughts) declared – under oath and on the lives of his children – that he had seen Drusilla ascend to heaven and speak directly with the gods. The gamble won him a million sesterces and Drusilla was promptly deified, becoming the first woman in Roman history to join the ranks of the immortals.[*] Drusilla was to have a temple, attended by a new college of twenty priests, both male and female, and women were to swear by the deified Drusilla whenever they took an oath. On Caligula's orders, shrines to Drusilla sprang up across the empire, venerating her either as 'the New Aphrodite' or as 'Panthea' – 'the all-goddess'.[21] Egypt went further, renaming a month 'Drusilleios' in her memory.[22]

Prior to AD 38, the most honoured woman in Roman history had been Augustus' wife Livia: an elder stateswoman who had died at eighty-six and a matron of unimpeachable sexual virtue who had made a public show of weaving her husband's togas. That place was now occupied by Drusilla: a woman probably not yet twenty-two, dogged by rumours of adultery and incest. It was a shift that may have been noted by the teenage Messalina.

It may have come as a relief to Messalina and the other courtiers when the grief-stricken Caligula withdrew from the city altogether. He went first to the Alban hills outside Rome and then, when he found his sorrows followed him there, travelled down the coast to the Bay of Naples before crossing the sea to Sicily. The court received worrying reports of his behaviour: he had grown his hair and beard and given himself over entirely to wine and gambling.[23] These reports were not entirely fair; Caligula was in Sicily on official imperial business, inspecting a number of public construction projects.[24] But while the Sicilian cities celebrated the emperor as a civic patron, Rome continued

---

[*] Julius Caesar and Augustus had been deified after their deaths, but the same honour had never before been granted to a woman.

to view the emperor's absence as a sign of selfish, uncontrolled and un-Roman sorrow.

When Caligula returned to Rome in the autumn he plunged himself, and his court, into a life defined more than ever by pleasure, expenditure and the thrill of the outrageous. The dinner parties (to which Messalina would now have been invited) grew more lavish, with guests served 'loaves' and 'joints of meat' cast in solid silver or gold.[25] On one occasion, a single evening's entertainments were said to have cost 10 million sesterces.[26] Pliny the Elder would later recall seeing Lollia Paulina, a famously beautiful heiress whom Caligula had married in the summer of that same year, at a casual engagement party, glinting in the lamplight in jewels worth some 40 million sesterces – forty times the total property qualification required for membership of the Senate. 'She was enveloped in emeralds and pearls', he remembered, 'alternately interwoven and glittering all over her head, in the locks and the braids of her hair, at her ears, around her neck and on her fingers.'[27]

Caligula was not one to be outdone by his wife. The emperor appeared at his parties arrayed, Suetonius claims, 'not as a Roman, nor as a citizen; not even as a man and, finally, not as a mortal'. One night he would don a woman's silk gown with stacks of bracelets and dainty slippers; the next he would be dressed in the special ceremonial garb of a triumphing general, although he had never been on campaign; the next (as witnessed by the contemporary ambassador Philo) he would assume the guise of a hero or a god – Hercules, Diana, Mercury, Juno, Apollo, Mars, or Mars' lover Venus, Neptune, Dionysus, and finally, Zeus.[28] Caligula was playing dress-up with sacred taboos of gender, politics and religion.

The Caligulan court was built on conspicuous consumption. Suetonius claims that Caligula blew the nearly 3 billion sesterces he had inherited from the parsimonious Tiberius in 'less than the turning of a single year'.*[29] Messalina – rich though she had always been and married to an imperial prince though she now was – would not have been able to keep up with a woman like Lollia Paulina. Claudius had been overlooked in both Augustus and Tiberius' wills: his total bequest from Augustus had been little over 800,000 sesterces, from Tiberius 2 million.[30] These inheritances, even taken together, did not reach a tenth of the value of Lollia's diamond and emerald parure. Although he had inherited at least three properties from his father, and may also have received a portion of his mother's estate upon her death in AD 37, cash flow remained an issue. When Caligula required his uncle to join the priesthood of his own cult – or, more likely, the cult of his *numen* or *genius* – in AD 40, Claudius was forced to borrow the 8 million sesterce entrance fee from the public treasury, putting up, and eventually losing, a portion of his property as collateral.† The pressures of keeping up with Caligula had left Claudius bankrupt.[31]

Messalina was wealthy in her own right. She would have inherited a significant fortune on her father's death and may have been given additional funds from her mother and other members of the family to supplement her dowry. The majority of her property would have remained under her control even after her marriage and would thus have been unaffected by Claudius' bankruptcy, but the financial crisis may nevertheless

---

* Dio gives him two years for the squandering but the end result remains the same.

† The worship of the emperor's *genius* – the divine nature possessed within each person – or his *numen* (name) was a compromise already established under Augustus for a city still not entirely comfortable with the idea of worshipping a living man. Tiberius, for example, appears to have dedicated an altar to Augustus' *numen* while the emperor was living – perhaps on the occasion of his adoption in AD 4 or of his triumph in AD 9.

have caused tension in the household.*³² Messalina may well have resented a situation that required her to support her older husband from the proceeds of her own inheritance; he may have felt uncomfortable with any arrangement that left him financially beholden to his wife; and if limits were imposed upon the family spending habits after the default of AD 40, they would have frustrated Messalina's attempts to make her mark on what was a conspicuously flashy court. Besides, as it would later become clear, Messalina had a growing personal taste for material luxury and beautiful things.

The endless banquets funded nightly by the dwindling imperial treasury provided Caligula with the perfect arena for indulging his penchant for the mixing of pleasure and pain. On one occasion he executed a man's son and invited the father to stay for dinner after the event, showing him all the assiduous attention of a host, telling him jokes and expecting him to laugh. On another particularly dissipated evening, Caligula is said to have begun laughing quite suddenly. When the presiding consuls begged him to let them in on the joke, the emperor replied 'What do you think? Except that with a

---

* Because both her father and paternal grandfather were dead, Messalina was *sui iuris* and could own property in her own right. As was conventional in this period she was probably married to Claudius *sine manu*, meaning that her property did not pass into the ownership or control of her husband. Important decisions regarding the disposal of the property of a woman *sui iuris* were officially subject to a male guardian known as a *tutor muliebrum*, but by the mid-first century their control was increasingly limited: women could turn to the courts to force their *tutor* to act in accordance with their wishes or apply to change *tutor* altogether. In practice, Messalina probably administered her property herself through a hierarchy of slaves and freedmen. Her dowry was legally under the control of Claudius but cultural convention frowned upon men selling property that formed part of their wives' dowries in order to settle personal debts.

single nod from me, both of your throats could be slit within the minute?'[33]

Claudius was the perfect target for the more casual of Caligula's dinner-party put-downs. If he arrived late, Claudius would have to fight for a seat; despite his nominal position of precedence no one in the company would make space, forcing the emperor's uncle to walk a humiliating round of the dining room in search of the last available couch. If, as he often did, Claudius fell into a postprandial nap, fellow diners would pelt him with the pits of dates and olives, the court jesters would whip him awake, or some joker would slide slippers gently onto his hands and wait for him to rouse and rub his eyes with them.[34]

Messalina would have been at many of these dinner parties, watching as they spiralled into excess.* Whether Messalina – fighting for a couch with Claudius and feeling the breeze of the jesters' whips as she reclined next to him – laughed along with her husband's abusers or felt humiliated by association is impossible to say.

Unsurprisingly, talk of Caligula's extravagance and psychological sadism was interlaced with rumours of sexual depravity. He was known to keep unsavoury company; he dined with the charioteers in the stables of his favourite team and socialised with actors, greeting them with kisses in the theatre.† There was

---

* Unlike the Greeks, the Romans had always found that the inclusion of women made for better parties. In the late 30s BC the writer Cornelius Nepos had commented on how bizarre the Greek segregation of the sexes appeared to Roman observers. 'Who among the Romans is ashamed to take his wife to a dinner party? And which lady of the house does not hold court in the reception rooms of her own home or show herself in public?' Nepos, *On the Great Generals of Foreign Nations*, preface, 6–7.

† Both charioteers and actors were regarded as among the lowest of the low in Roman society. Along with prostitutes and convicted adulteresses they were classed as *infames* – a group of citizens whose legal rights and protections were limited on account of their perceived immorality.

talk of homosexual affairs too.[35] These would not necessarily have been perceived as aberrant in themselves, had one of Caligula's rumoured lovers not been his brother-in-law Aemilius Lepidus. Or had another, the young aristocrat Valerius Catullus, not claimed to have taken the penetrative (and thus, in classical thought, masculine) role in the encounter. Or had a third – the handsome Mnester, who would later be executed for his fling with Messalina – not been a dancer. The old rumours of incest reared their ugly heads too, with Caligula now accused of bedding both his surviving sisters, Agrippina the Younger and Julia Livilla.[36]

The pleasure that Caligula evidently derived from observing the humiliation of others does seem to have spilled over into his sex life. When he leant in close to kiss the neck of his latest lover, he liked to use the opportunity to whisper: 'off comes this pretty head the moment I give the order'.[37] Caligula had a whole host of acceptable mistresses at his disposal: actresses, dancers, slaves and prostitutes, women whose sexual honour, even their bodily autonomy, was perceived to be beyond the protection of the law – but Suetonius claims he took particular pleasure in the debauching and debasing of elite Roman wives.

He would generally invite noble-women to dinner with their husbands and, as they passed before his couch, he was accustomed to inspect them, slowly and deliberately, as if buying a slave, even lifting up her face with his hand, if she had lowered it in modesty. Then, as often as he wished, and with whomever had pleased him best called to join him, he left the dining room; returning to his place a little later, marked by all the signs of vigorous passion, he would brazenly praise or disparage his partner, enumerating every aspect, good and bad, of her body and her sexual technique.[38]

The emperor demonstrated little more respect for the women he married. Caligula's first wife had died childless before his accession and so, between AD 38 and 39, he took three more in quick and disastrous succession. His marriage to his second wife, Livia Orestilla, occurred *during* her wedding to another man. Reclining opposite the happy bridegroom at the wedding banquet, he is said to have turned to him and remarked 'don't have sex with my wife', before having the bride removed to his own house. It was not a beginning that boded well for wedded bliss. Within a few months the marriage had soured and Caligula – suspecting Orestilla of maintaining relations with her original husband – had the couple banished.[39]

Caligula's third wife, the famously rich and beautiful Lollia Paulina, was recalled from the eastern provinces where her then husband was commanding Caligula's armies and married to the emperor later that year. Lollia, quickly suspected of being infertile, was divorced in the spring of AD 39.[40]

Caligula took no such chances with his fourth wife; Milonia Caesonia was at least heavily pregnant with, and indeed may have already had, Caligula's child before the emperor married her towards the end of AD 39.[41] The new empress was neither beautiful nor young and yet she exerted a strange power over Caligula. Suetonius accuses Caesonia of using love potions, and the hold she had on him seems to have troubled even Caligula himself: he is said to have repeatedly threatened to have her tortured until she revealed what she had done to mesmerise him so entirely. The pair, it seems, were well matched in their proclivities; Caesonia was a woman, Suetonius claims, of 'ruinous luxury and licentiousness'. Suetonius also describes her riding out alongside Caligula on military inspections, crossing the boundaries of gender by donning a soldier's cloak, helmet and spear, and appearing naked, at the emperor's instruction, before gatherings of his friends.[42]

Stories of imperial sex are always a little suspect; tales of what occurs behind closed doors are difficult to disprove and it is the most salacious rumours (as would be the case with Messalina) that tend to spread the fastest and the furthest. It is impossible to know if Caligula really worked his way through the wives of his courtiers and whether, if he did, Messalina ever felt herself at risk of selection. But Caligula certainly did impregnate Caesonia – a married woman of senatorial rank with three daughters by her first husband – well in advance of their wedding. Within the first year of her marriage, Messalina may have come to believe that a little discreet adultery might be tolerated within the upper echelons of Caligula's court.

As the pregnant Caesonia began to solidify her place in Caligula's affections during the spring of AD 39, Messalina would have joined the rest of the court on sojourns in the Bay of Naples, staying at the villa Claudius owned in the area and enjoying the opportunities for entertainment.

Caligula had had pleasure boats built for amusements on the water. Suetonius describes 'bejewelled sterns, sails of many colours, vast thermal baths, airy porticoes and banqueting halls and even a great variety of vines and fruit-bearing trees'.[43] It is a description that we might take for hyperbole had two such pleasure barges, with inscriptions bearing Caligula's name, not been discovered sunk in a lake known as the 'mirror of Diana' near the emperor's villa outside Rome. Each of these boats was more than two hundred feet in length, with walls and floors decorated with mosaics and inlays of coloured marble. On board one of the ships, a porticoed temple with fluted marble columns was decorated with sculptural friezes. The other was furnished with all the paraphernalia of feasting. Water for a floating bath complex was heated by a hypocaust and flowed out through bronze taps. The roof tiles of the temple, the porticoes and dining rooms were plated in gold.[44]

In Campania, the company, Messalina perhaps often among them, would spend long lazy days on ships like these, cruising down the coast, entertained by dancers and musicians, lying down to dinners early and not leaving them until late in the night.

But Caligula also had a more ambitious project in mind that summer: he had conceived a desire to bridge the bay and ride across its waters in a kind of faux triumph. The pageant that resulted would be one of the most surreal and extravagant in all of Rome's history.[45]

Ships, built or commandeered, were anchored in a double line stretching all the way across the bay from Baiae to Puteoli – a distance of some 2.25 miles. The string of boats was then covered with packed earth and transformed into an imitation of the Appian Way, with lodges and rest stops supplied with fresh running water. When the preparations were complete, Caligula – wearing what he claimed was the breastplate of Alexander the Great and a campaign cloak of gold or purple silk embroidered with Indian gems – rode onto the bridge at Baiae. He sacrificed to Neptune and Envy and, at the head of a large train of soldiers, led a cavalry charge towards Puteoli.

The following day he rode back on a chariot drawn by a team of racehorses followed by a stream of courtiers – Messalina and Claudius almost certainly among them – in flowered robes. Behind them came the Praetorian Guard, followed by the hostages and spoils of a triumph and, finally, by the general public. When he reached the centre of the bridge he mounted a dais and addressed his 'troops'. He handed out cash and praised them for their bravery, for the hardships and perils they had undergone, and for their miraculous success in crossing the sea on foot. The company then feasted on the bridge and on boats anchored all around. Thousands of torches had been lit in the hills around the coast, illuminating the semi-circle of the bay as though it were a theatre. It would have been a remarkable sight for anyone to witness, but it must have made a particular impression on a young woman like Messalina.

In a way, of course, the bay *was* a theatre – and the performance was not over. When the company was well fed and tanked up on what Dio describes as 'good and strong drink', Caligula began throwing some of his fellow diners from the bridge, pushing those who tried to clutch the rudders back down into the water with oars and boat hooks. When he tired of that he used a fast boat with a sharpened ram to sink some of the vessels that had dropped anchor next to the bridge for the feasting.

Explanations of Caligula's actions vary wildly between (and even within) the sources. The Jewish historian Josephus sees the project as a sign both of the emperor's madness and his aspiration to divinity; Seneca of his madness and his aspirations to Eastern-style tyranny.* For Dio, Caligula intended the event as a critical comment on the insufficiency of a traditional Republican-style triumph. Suetonius suggests that he sought to rival the Persian kings Xerxes and Darius who had (in the course of military campaigns) constructed similar bridges across the Hellespont and the Bosphorus; or that he hoped news of his feat would terrify British and Germanic tribes into submission. Suetonius, however, also reports another explanation, relayed to him by his grandfather, who must have been alive at the time of the event: Tiberius, concerned about Caligula's ability to rule, had consulted an astrologer who predicted that the boy had

* Josephus was writing under the Flavian emperors (the dynasty that followed the Julio-Claudians) in the 70s, 80s and 90s AD. A Jew born in Judea, his extraordinary life story saw him take on a major role fighting against the Romans in the Great Jewish Revolt that broke out in AD 66 as military governor of Galilee. Captured and enslaved in AD 67, he became close to his Roman captors, the future emperors Vespasian and Titus. Following the war he was freed and granted Roman citizenship, a house in Rome, land in Judea and an imperial pension – it was at this point that he turned to writing history.

more chance of riding a horse across the Bay of Naples than of becoming emperor. Caligula had been desperate to prove him wrong on both counts.[46]

Whatever Caligula's precise motivations, the bridge – and its violent end – was not the product of an irrational madness. In fact, it fits perfectly logically within the wider programme of his political messaging. Caligula knew that the thing that people feared most about an absolute ruler – in fact, the thing that *defined* an absolute ruler – was not the power to punish violently, but to punish arbitrarily. In public and in private, in bed and at dinner, Caligula liked to remind his subjects that they were just that – entirely *subject* to the merest turn of his whims. His actions on the Bay of Naples in the summer of AD 39 was the ultimate test of this theory: first, Caligula conceived a seemingly irrational ambition, then he made it an extraordinary, surreal reality. He spoiled his guests with a feast for the senses, he lulled them into a sense of security with music and wine. Finally, and quite without warning, he demonstrated his arbitrary and immediate power over their lives and deaths.

The intensity of the environment in which Messalina passed the first few years of her married life – in which she served her apprenticeship in court politics – cannot be overstated. This was a world of constant sensory overload; of luxury, physical pleasure, display, and of competitive conspicuous consumption which Messalina and Claudius could ill afford to keep up with. It was also a world that turned entirely on the arbitrary whims of its leader. A world of sadism, humiliation, sexual harassment, intrigue at the imperial court and rumour in the forum. Perhaps most insidiously of all, it was a world of unrelenting anxiety.

VII

The King is Dead, Long Live the King

'He used to say that the condition of the princeps was a most
miserable one, for whatever conspiracy he might uncover, would
never be believed until he had already been killed'

Suetonius, *Life of Domitian*, 21

September brought an abrupt end to the summer social
season of AD 39. The first days of the new month saw the
sitting consuls deposed on Caligula's orders; their *fasces*, the
symbols of their constitutional authority, were smashed, and
one of them was driven to suicide.[1] Caligula then announced,
quite suddenly, his intention to travel north immediately, across
the Alps, to the Rhine.

A northward push appears to have been planned for some
time: Suetonius talks of the recruitment of new legions and
large numbers of auxiliaries. All previous emperors had proven
themselves, to some extent, in battle and Caligula must have felt
the memory of his father and grandfather's heroism in Germany
weigh heavy on his shoulders.

The timing of his departure, however, was sudden and the
march was undertaken at a remarkable pace. The Praetorians
were forced to lay aside their pride and strap their standards
onto the backs of pack animals in order to keep up. The towns
lining the route were ordered to wet the roads with water to

prevent clouds of dust being kicked up and slowing the pace of the horses and men. Behind Caligula and his soldiers trailed a great train of attendants: gladiators, actors, and a tight inner circle of courtiers including the emperor's sisters Agrippina and Julia Livilla, and the widowed husband of Drusilla, Aemilius Lepidus.[2] Claudius and Messalina – her first pregnancy likely beginning to show – stayed behind in Rome.[*]

The official justification for Caligula's northern expedition was the pacification of the Germanic tribes who, as a result of poor discipline among the border legions stationed too long under the same lenient governor, were making increasingly frequent sallies into Roman territory. Towards the end of October, however, confirmation of quite a different impetus – one that better explained the sudden announcement and unprecedented pace of Caligula's travel – reached the ears of Messalina and Claudius in Rome. The long-time governor of Upper Germany, Gnaeus Cornelius Lentulus Gaetulicus, had been executed, not for the negligent laxity of his discipline, but for conspiracy against the emperor.[3]

By the end of October priesthoods back in Rome were

---

[*] There is some confusion over the year of Messalina's first child Claudia Octavia's birth. Tacitus claims she was twenty upon her death in AD 62 (Tacitus, *Annals*, 14.64) but this would have made her uncommonly young upon her marriage to Nero in AD 53 (Tacitus, *Annals*, 12.58; Cassius Dio, 60.33.11). More persuasively, Suetonius (Suetonius, *Life of Claudius*, 27) presents her as older than her brother Britannicus (born in February of AD 41), and an Alexandrian coin from AD 41 depicts Messalina holding images of *two* children, confirming that Octavia must already have been born by the time her mother became pregnant with her brother. The firmly dated birth of Britannicus means that Octavia could not possibly have been born later than the early months of AD 40, while the likely dating of her parents' marriage in mid-38 AD means she could not have been born before AD 39. The timing of Octavia's marriage to Nero in AD 53 and the confusion over the order of the siblings' births suggests a birthdate towards the latter end of this range, i.e. the winter of AD 39/40.

making sacrifices in thanks to the gods – 'on account of Cornelius Lentulus Gaetulicus' nefarious schemes against Gaius Germanicus [Caligula] having been discovered' – but the affair was far from over.[4] Gaetulicus had shown himself to be a shrewd political operator before; he had survived the fall of his close associate Sejanus by sending Tiberius veiled threats regarding the strength of his support among the legions under his command.[5] It is possible that the ensuing crisis was the result of an unsuccessful last-ditch attempt to save his own neck.

Three further conspirators were accused following Gaetulicus' execution: Caligula's sisters Agrippina and Julia Livilla, and Drusilla's widower Aemilius Lepidus. It was claimed that Aemilius Lepidus had been engaged in affairs with both his dead wife's sisters and that together the group had plotted to murder Caligula and install Aemilius Lepidus on the throne. Proof was soon discovered – or fabricated – in the form of secret letters in handwriting said to match that of the conspirators. All three were convicted of treason before a hastily convened imperial court.

Caligula had three swords – one for each of his betrayers – sent to the Temple of Mars the Avenger in Rome. It was likely through the arrival of these souvenirs of Caligula's northern travels that Messalina first learnt of the drama playing out on the Rhine that winter. Further confirmation soon appeared in the figure of Agrippina herself. Caligula had had Aemilius Lepidus executed and condemned his sisters to exile on the same barren islands that had seen the deaths of their mother and grandmother. But first he sent Agrippina to Rome, requiring that she carry the ashes of her alleged lover every step of the way.[6] Caligula had been devoted to his sisters, his only close blood relatives to survive the persecution of their family – his belief that they had betrayed him must have been unbearable. The penance he imposed on Agrippina was a masterclass in public humiliation and psychological vengeance.

Caligula may have been paranoid, but it is also not impossible that Aemilius Lepidus, Julia Livilla and Agrippina really were involved in a plot in the winter of AD 39. The same season saw Caesonia married and delivered of the emperor's child – a daughter whom Caligula named Julia Drusilla after his dead sister. The emperor doted on the child, his first and the first ever to be born to a reigning emperor. He also made his intentions for her future prominence crystal clear: soon after her birth, Caligula carried Drusilla up to the Capitoline and, laying her in the lap of one of the cult statues, commended her to the gods as a sort of divine foster child.[7]

Before the birth of Drusilla, all three alleged conspirators might have cherished hopes of being or bearing the next emperor. With his wife as proxy, Aemilius Lepidus had been briefly named Caligula's heir in the winter of AD 37, and when Agrippina had borne a son that same December, she had asked Caligula to choose a name – hoping he would alight on his own name 'Gaius' as a sign of future favour. Sensing her intention, he had instead suggested 'Claudius', a snide joke and a suggestion which Agrippina dismissed out of hand.[8] She chose Nero instead. With the birth of a daughter who could carry on Caligula's own bloodline, and the possibility of more children to come, the group must have felt that, in the absence of some quick and decisive intervention, these prospects were slipping away.

The accusations of three-way adultery are more dubious. It had become common under the early empire to find political accusations combined with sexual ones – especially when those accusations were levelled against women. Messalina would use this strategy herself as empress; and it would be used against her in turn. These charges were clearly felt, even by contemporary observers, to be politically motivated fictions. The Augustan reforms to adultery laws had made it illegal for a husband to remain married to a convicted adulteress, or for a woman convicted of adultery to remarry; the return of Julia Livilla to her original husband and the quick remarriage of the widowed Agrippina following their recall from exile in AD 41 prove that the sisters had been acquitted of the charges of adultery, as well as treason.

The sudden public fall of Agrippina and Julia Livilla must have been particularly shocking for Messalina. These were women only a few years older than herself, whom she knew personally, and who had seemed successful players at the game of palace politics. They were, perhaps, women to whom she had once looked for models of how to behave, exert power, and survive as a woman in Caligula's court.

After Agrippina's appearance in Rome, the Senate received a letter from the emperor. It contained the official announcement that a plot had been discovered, the danger averted and its originators punished. The Senate sprang into action, praising Caligula for his foresight, thanking the gods for his deliverance, and voting him a triumphal ovation for his 'victory' over the conspirators. They assembled a delegation to travel to Caligula's winter camp at Lugdunum (the city of Claudius' birth) to announce their resolutions to Caligula in person. Eschewing the regular process of lot drawing, they specifically selected Claudius to be among the delegates.[9] The move would prove to be miscalculated.

It was, perhaps, around the time Claudius left the city to begin the journey north that Messalina felt the first pangs of labour. Her first child, a daughter – named Claudia Octavia (after her father and Octavia, the great-great-grandmother who had furnished both Claudius and Messalina with Augustan blood) – was most likely born into the height of the tumult and confusion of the winter of AD 39/40.

Messalina would have received the very latest medical attention that the empire had to offer. But, as in every pre-modern society, childbirth was a risky business. From the first signs of labour, Messalina would have been attended by a team of at least three highly trained midwives.[10] A male physician would be on call should complications arise. Household slaves would have rushed back and forth fetching olive oil, warm water, bandages, blankets, softened sea sponges, pillows and fresh-smelling restoratives: mint, apple, quince, melon, barley, cucumber, lemon, even freshly dug earth. A room was chosen – cool but not cold, spacious but not so big as to be draughty in the depths of the Roman winter – and readied. A birthing chair was brought in and two beds made up: one firm and low for the delivery, the other soft and piled with cushions and blankets. It was on this second bed that Messalina would rest after the delivery – if she survived.

In his *Sixth Satire*, Juvenal castigates rich Roman women for their unwillingness to risk pregnancy and endure childbirth: 'barely any lie in labour on a gilded couch' he spits with all the confidence of a man who'll never have to.[11] Juvenal presents this as proof of moral decline and the dereliction of feminine duty, but the fear of labour, of its pains, complications, and potential fatality, must have been very real – particularly for a young, first-time mother like Messalina.

The anxieties naturally attendant on the birth of Messalina's first child must have been compounded by the atmosphere at Rome and in Claudius' household that winter. The crisis on the Rhine had precipitated a full-scale reorganisation of the emperor's inner circle, but exactly what form this would take must have been difficult to assess while Caligula remained away from the city. The drip feed of clues back to Rome that autumn – the suddenness of Caligula's departure, the announcement of Gaetulicus' execution, the arrival of the three swords for Mars Ultor, the appearance of Agrippina, and finally the emperor's letter to the Senate – must have fostered a combustible environment of suspense and paranoia.

The full consequences of the failed conspiracy for Messalina and her expanding family would only have become clear upon

Claudius' return to the city from Lugdunum. The emperor, it transpired, had not taken kindly to his uncle's inclusion in the senatorial delegation. His reaction had been so hostile, in fact, that one contemporary story had Caligula throwing Claudius, fully clothed, into the river upon his arrival.[12] This is probably apocryphal, but Caligula's rage at his uncle's presence was clearly intense, and Suetonius judges Claudius to have been in genuine danger of his life that winter in Gaul.

The explanation Suetonius provides for Caligula's reaction is unconvincing: 'Gaius bristled and seethed', he claims, 'chiefly because it was his uncle that had been sent to him, just like to a little boy in need of disciplining.'[13] While the sense he was being patronised might have added fuel to the fire of Caligula's anger, the real issue was probably Claudius' connection to the conspirators. He was uncle to Agrippina and Julia Livilla just as much as he was to Caligula; under other circumstances – had he not been so overlooked within family circles and had he accompanied the emperor on his initial trip north that autumn rather than staying behind in Rome – he could easily have been implicated in the conspiracy itself.

Caligula accompanied his repudiation of Claudius with a directive to the Senate: there were to be no further honours voted to members of his father's family.[14] The changing of the guard was complete. Caligula's birth family, who had played so important a role in his early image-making, had fallen, and the future of the emperor's court now lay with Milonia Caesonia and their daughter.

The news of his reception at Lugdunum can hardly have gone down well when Claudius relayed it to his wife upon his return to the city. Messalina was likely just out of the most dangerous postpartum period, her breasts still uncomfortably bound tight with the bandages soaked in astringents used to stay the flow of milk that was redundant now Octavia had been placed in the care of a wet-nurse called Hilaria.[15] She had her newly established position at court and the future of her new baby to think of. Her husband, she knew, owed his position, his prestige – most likely even his marriage to her – entirely to Caligula's favour. The recent turn of events could spell a disastrous decline for their new family.

It was perhaps the influence of Messalina's network of connections that averted such a crisis. Following Agrippina's exile, the care of her son Nero was entrusted to Domitia Lepida (Messalina's mother and Nero's paternal aunt).[*16] Given that Nero's future prospects had likely been a driving force behind the conspiracy of AD 39, the placement of the boy in the care of Domitia Lepida suggests that Messalina's side of the family, at least, retained Caligula's trust.

Messalina and Claudius were hanging on to their position within the Caligulan establishment by a thread. But it seemed that the establishment itself was crumbling around them.

The emperor remained in the north for the next few months, his absence punctuated only by the stories reaching the city of his bizarre conduct on the front.[17] Rather than fighting the enemy, it was said that Caligula sent members of his own German bodyguard to hide in the forests across the Rhine before hunting them after lunch with a cavalry of friends and Praetorians. Other reports claimed he was having the richest Gauls picked off and murdered to recoup his losses at cards; that he was cutting down trees and arraying them like triumphal trophies; that he wanted to obliterate, or failing that to decimate, two entire legions. Perhaps the most peculiar tale of all involved Caligula marching his troops to the coast of the English Channel, drawing them up in battle lines and ordering them to collect sea-shells – these were the spoils, he claimed, that the ocean owed to Rome.

---

* Nero's father Gnaeus Domitius Ahenobarbus had died not long after his mother's exile.

The veracity and the source of these tales have been the subject of much scholarly debate; some have seen them as mangled reports of genuine attempts to stabilise the border, or of a mutiny by troops unwilling to cross the sea to Britain. The real story behind Caligula's actions on the front makes little difference to Messalina's experience in Rome that winter. Arriving so soon after the turmoil of the plot, rumours of the emperor's erratic behaviour must have added to the atmosphere of angst and uncertainty that pervaded the city at the beginning of AD 40.

When the news arrived that spring that Caligula had left Gaul and was travelling south, it would have been met with a mixture of relief and trepidation. Perhaps to gauge the emperor's mood, or to flatter him, or perhaps in response to increasing instability in the city, the Senate sent a large delegation to meet Caligula en route and beg that he hurry his journey back to Rome. His response was unequivocal. 'I will come,' he shouted, slapping the hilt of his sword. 'I will come, and *this* will come with me'.[18] An official proclamation followed: the emperor was returning, but only to those who truly desired his return – the equestrians and the people; to the *Senate* he would be neither princeps nor fellow-citizen from this day forward.

By May Caligula had reached the environs of Rome, taking part in a sacrifice arranged by the priesthood of the Arval brethren at their sacred grove outside the city walls and meeting a delegation of Jews, concerned about recent pogroms in Alexandria, at his palace near the Tiber.[19] Caligula did not, however, actually enter the city. Perhaps to avoid the urban heat, or perhaps in anticipation of an official triumphal entry after his 'victories' in the north, he carefully avoided crossing the sacred boundary of Rome. Instead he continued down the coast to Campania.[20]

As Caligula continued to avoid city and Senate, moving from one of his luxury villas to the next, the rumours kept coming, thicker and faster than before. It was said that he was considering moving the capital from Rome to Antium, or to Alexandria; that he was planning a wholesale massacre of the Senate; that he kept two little books, one labelled 'sword', the other 'dagger', in which he made long lists of the names and appearances of those he intended to execute.[21] The end of AD 39, it seemed, had dealt a fatal blow to Caligula's already shaky relations with the aristocracy – their anxiety is palpable in the character of these rumours.

For all that Caligula claimed the equestrians and the plebs longed for his return to the city, the emperor's relationship with the general populace was also becoming increasingly strained. In AD 40, he raised new taxes on the bare necessities of life: food, taverns, brothels and legal proceedings.[22] Public protests were dealt with using a combination of police brutality and characteristically Caligulan psychological signalling: on particularly hot days, it was said, he would have the awnings shading the amphitheatre drawn back, before blocking the exits and letting the people burn.[23]

After an absence of nearly a year, Caligula finally re-entered the city on 31 August AD 40 – his twenty-eighth birthday.[24] He immediately set about remodelling the character of his imperial power. Up until now, the old senatorial aristocracy had played a crucial, if paradoxical, role in the definition of Julio-Claudian authority. The emperor had presented himself as the ultimate senator – literally the *princeps senatus*, or the 'first of the Senate' – and it was from senatorial votes that all his powers and honours officially derived. This set-up (so cleverly conceived by Augustus) had bound together the fates of the Senate and the emperor. It forced the emperor to continually reinforce the honour of the senatorial order so as to maintain the dignity of his own position, and the Senate to remain loyal to the emperor in order to retain their position in a social hierarchy which he enforced.

Now Caligula demonstrated his disregard for this understanding, quite literally, upon the public stage. Augustus had instituted complex regulations to govern who could use which tiers of seating in the theatre and amphitheatre, transforming the stepped banks of benches into a visualisation of the hierarchy of Roman society. Caligula abolished these rules, allowing any member of the great unwashed to fight for the front benches previously reserved for the Senate.[25] The scramble that resulted was a manifestation of the promise that the emperor had made on his journey back from the north – he would no longer protect the status and the honour of the Senate.

In his repeated public humiliations of the Senate, Caligula broke the most delicate of ententes and left himself in a difficult position. He could no longer play the *princeps senatus*, but nor, given the increasing breakdown of his relations with the people, could he straightforwardly play the demagogue. Having exhausted the traditional Roman models of supremacy – so carefully reworked by Augustus, and so conscientiously, if clumsily, preserved by Tiberius – Caligula looked eastwards and upwards to the models of monarchs and gods.

Caligula increasingly eschewed the toga – the universal mark of the male citizen and Republican magistrate – in favour of his more unconventional outfits. Just over a hundred years before, in 70 BC, the great orator Cicero had felt that an extortion defendant's appearance at a private party in a tunic and Greek-style cloak rather than in a toga was so indicative of corrupt and abandoned character that he included the detail in his prosecution speech. Now Caligula appeared in the silks and jewels of Eastern monarchs and wore (as he had on the bridge at Baiae) what he claimed was the breastplate of Alexander, the ultimate Hellenistic ruler-god.

Others were expected to alter their behaviour accordingly. At the beginning of his reign, Caligula had banned the deferential ceremonial greetings with which senators had previously hailed the emperor in public. Now Caligula encouraged senators to prostrate themselves before him as subjects did before Eastern kings. These Hellenistic monarchs presented themselves as living gods – leaders whose authority theoretically flowed not from the support of their aristocracies, but from the sanctity of their blood.

Some sources go further still, claiming that Caligula *truly* believed himself to be divine.[26] The emperor, Dio says, saw himself as a sort of Jupiter, and whenever a thunderbolt was heard, or a lightning flash seen, Caligula devised ways to return a flash and a bang as if to prove he was not to be outdone. He apparently also believed that he could commune with the gods directly. Suetonius records that he saw apparitions of Oceanus; Dio that he claimed to speak to the moon goddess Diana. On one occasion Caligula was said to have paused mid conversation with the senator Lucius Vitellius, and asked if he could see Diana too. Vitellius kept his eyes fixed on the floor and chose his words carefully, 'Only you gods, master,' he replied, 'may behold one another.'[27]

Claims that Caligula genuinely *believed* himself to be divine are dubious, to say the least. The accusation is absent from the earliest Roman sources – those written in the decades after his assassination by Caligula's contemporaries, Seneca and Pliny – which otherwise display extreme hostility towards him. Claims that the 'mad Caligula' saw himself as a god and expected to be worshipped as one, with a temple and a full cult in Rome, are found only in the later histories of Suetonius and Dio, and in accounts written by Jewish authors (undoubtedly coloured by contemporary concerns that Caligula planned to desecrate the Temple of Jerusalem as well as by the unbridgeable theological disparity between Jewish and Greco-Roman ideas regarding the separation of the mortal and the divine). There is also a telling lack of archaeological evidence: had the emperor really declared himself a living god we would expect to find a slew of temples, statues and altars dedicated to the worship of his cult.*

In this context, Caligula's flirtations with the aesthetics of the Olympians and the customs of Eastern kingship should not be read as evidence of mental derangement, but as a new humiliation for the Senate. In insisting that the consuls kiss his shoes and requiring men who knew full well that he was no god to enter into sincere discussions about his nightly tête-a-têtes with Diana, Caligula forced his senators to prove their own hypocrisy; to demonstrate that they were not really free and to confirm that their claim to social, if not political, parity with their 'princeps' had long been void.

Dissension among Rome's upper classes may already have been brewing over the long hot months that Caligula was absent from the city in the summer of AD 40 and it seems that matters came to a head not long after his return. That autumn saw the execution of a number of prominent senators. Some of these Caligula had decapitated after dinner by candlelight on the terrace of his gardens beside the Tiber in front of a company of guests – Messalina, quite possibly, among them.[28] The hostile Seneca claims the executions were carried out merely as entertainment, but it seems that a number of the executed senators had actually been implicated in plots on the emperor's life.[29]

These rumblings of conspiracy confirmed all of Caligula's worst fears about the Senate. In a speech he had made to the Senate the year before, Caligula had imagined the cautioning voice of his late uncle Tiberius – 'show no affection for any of them [the Senate] and spare none of them, for they all hate you

---

* Caligula may have encouraged the worship of his *genius* (a person's guiding god or the divine elements within their character) – a practice well established in the private sphere during the reigns of Augustus and Tiberius – on a newly public stage and in increasingly official terms. It was probably the priesthood of this cult which Claudius was required to join, paying a co-option fee which nearly bankrupted him.

and they all pray for your death; and they will murder you if they can. Do not stop to consider then, what acts of yours will please them nor mind it if they talk, but look solely to your own safety and pleasure'.[30] These words, rhetorical constructions though they were, must now have seemed more apposite than ever.

With the Senate's loyalty in doubt, Caligula seems to have attempted to concentrate political power within what remained of his inner circle. The sources express concerns about the growing influence of his wife Caesonia and the imperial freedmen – ex-slaves who made up much of the Palatine administration and constituted a new brand of political player. Anxieties about the power of women and freedmen would only continue to grow after Claudius' accession, reaching what was, perhaps, their apogee with the fall of Messalina. For now, however, these were the only allies whom Caligula found it easy to trust – neither a woman nor an ex-slave could pose a genuine challenge to his supremacy – but their presence at the heart of government added insult to senatorial injury.

The gravity of the Senate's situation was thrown into stark relief one day in the late autumn. When the freedman Protogenes – one of Caligula's closest confidants and, it was said, the man to whom he had entrusted his hit-list of senatorial enemies – entered the Senate House on imperial business, the senators rushed en masse to greet him. Such a response would have been unthinkable for the Roman aristocracy a generation or two before, but now it was merely a prelude to the action. Protogenes returned the senators' greetings until his eyes fell on one man in particular. He stared the man down for a moment and then asked: 'Do you greet me too when you hate the emperor so?' The implication was sufficient: the senators surrounded their colleague and 'tore him', as Dio delicately puts it, 'to pieces'.[31]

Claudius and Messalina occupied a strange position in all this. Messalina's step-father and step-brother were members of the old senatorial aristocracy, unrelated to the imperial family. Less than a year before, Claudius had headed the delegation to the north, representing the views and interests of the Senate. Now, however, as the wedge between the Senate and the emperor grew ever greater, the couple found themselves tied increasingly to the imperial rather than the senatorial circle: Claudius commonly appeared alongside Caligula in public and, along with Caesonia, was co-opted into the hyper-exclusive priesthood of the emperor's *genius*.

Although they were closely associated enough with the emperor to render them increasingly isolated from their senatorial peers, Messalina and Claudius' position in Caligula's inner circle remained precarious. The 'honour' Caligula had done Claudius in his appointment to the priesthood had bankrupted the family, forcing them to borrow money and flog heirlooms on the open market just to keep afloat. Perhaps around this time, Caligula took the unprecedented step of allowing one of Claudius' own slaves (usually banned even from testifying against their masters) to bring a legal case against him.[32] Josephus claims the charge was a capital one initiated by Caligula as a means of ridding himself of his uncle. This version of events is implausible: had Caligula wanted to oust Claudius, he would have had no need of an enslaved proxy. Still, the authorisation of the prosecution sent a clear message that the couple's situation at court was far from secure.

In the winter of AD 40/41, Claudius and Messalina must have felt themselves in an extremely vulnerable situation. Caligula's behaviour was as cruelly unpredictable as ever, but they remained reliant upon his favour. They were inextricably linked, in the eyes of the Senate at least, to his court. The couple might well have feared for their own futures, particularly given that Messalina was pregnant once again.

The mood in the imperial palace as Caligula and his circle celebrated the Saturnalia that winter was evidently still febrile. When a soothsayer warned Caligula to 'beware of Cassius', the emperor, thinking immediately of Julius Caesar's assassin Gaius

Cassius, had his descendant Cassius Longinus recalled from his provincial posting and executed.[33] Caligula, it would transpire, had got the wrong Cassius, but he was right to be worried: the executions of the autumn had not stamped out dissent.

The central players in the new plot that emerged over the winter of AD 40/41 were not senators but members of the imperial administration: two high-ranking officers of the Praetorian Guard, *Cassius* Chaerea and Cornelius Sabinus, were among them, as was the prefect of the guard and Callistus, one of Caligula's most influential freedman-advisors.[34] The precise trigger for this new round of conspiracy is obscure. The ancient sources, ever in search of colour and anecdote, make it personal. Chaerea, they claim, despite being a rugged and experienced soldier who had served on the German front under Caligula's father, had an unusually high voice. It was an insecurity that Caligula could not resist needling: whenever Chaerea was sent to receive a new Praetorian password, the emperor would pick something effeminate and sexualised, 'Venus', for example, or 'Priapus', or 'Love'.[35]

Whatever personal grudges the conspirators might have borne against Caligula, however, the key motivation was almost certainly political. Caligula's leadership style was clearly becoming unsustainable, and Dio and Josephus both claim that the conspiracy found wide support at court and in the Senate.[36] It is plausible that this new operation found its roots in a regrouping of the senatorial dissension that had been revealed earlier that autumn.

Caligula's household saw in the new year of AD 41 with the celebration of the *ludi Palatini*. Established by Livia after Augustus' death to mark their anniversary, the entertainments usually lasted three days, but this year Caligula had doubled its duration.*

---

* The *ludi Palatini* was a private festival intended mainly for the imperial family and the Senate, along with their wives and children, that was most likely held in a temporary theatre constructed in the forecourt of the imperial palace on the Palatine.

There were a number of false starts and hesitations and it was 24 January – the final day of the festival – before the conspirators made their move.

Everyone agreed that Caligula was in uncharacteristic good humour that morning. The emperor found it particularly funny when the toga of one senator was splattered with the blood of a flamingo as he sacrificed to Augustus. Caligula didn't know it then, of course, but this would later be interpreted as an omen.[37]

Given that this was the final day of the festivities, the imperial box was full.[38] Claudius was among Caligula's entourage, although Messalina – then in the dangerous final weeks of her second pregnancy – may not have been with him. For all Caligula's affability, the mood was tense, with the conspirators seated near Caligula finding it hard to hide their restlessness. The morning programme that day was a conspicuously gory one with both the scheduled plays ending in the violent deaths of their protagonists. 'The stage', Suetonius claims, 'overflowed with blood'.

Around noon Caligula became restless – should he stay for the whole afternoon or should he slip away for lunch and a bath and come back, refreshed for the evening's entertainments? Those of his attendants who were in on the plot urged him to bathe, and one of them, a senator, slipped away to alert Chaerea. As the imperial party entered the palace, Caligula left Claudius and the rest of the group. Planning to catch a snippet of some choral rehearsals and bathe before lunch, he turned down a passageway. It was here that the conspirators caught up with him.

There are three separate accounts of exactly how Caligula met his end, each more violent and theatrical than the last. Josephus has Chaerea approach Caligula to ask for the day's Praetorian password, receive a predictably humiliating answer, draw his sword and strike the emperor in the neck. Hurt but not dead, Caligula makes to run, before being caught by Sabinus, forced to the ground and hacked to death by the assembled group. Suetonius provides two versions. In the first, Chaerea approaches the emperor from behind, shouts 'Do the deed!' – a phrase also uttered by priests officiating sacrifices – and lands the inaugural blow. In the second, Sabinus strikes first. He asks the emperor for the password, and when Caligula says 'Jupiter' – the god of thunderbolts and sudden death – Sabinus cries 'So be it!' and drives his sword straight through the emperor's jawbone. The blows continue as Caligula writhes on the floor. Suetonius claims his stab wounds number thirty, significantly more than Julius Caesar's twenty-three, and notes, specifically, that some of the assassins aim for his genitals. Dio remarks only that the assault was so savage, and the conspirators so committed to the task, that some of them were rumoured to have eaten the emperor's flesh. 'Thus', as Dio succinctly puts it, 'Gaius Caligula learned by actual experience that he was not a God.'

The divergence in detail regarding the assassination is testament to the general chaos of the scene. As the assassins fled into the warren of the imperial palace, Caligula's German bodyguards set upon the stragglers, searching the rooms and cutting down conspirators and innocent noblemen indiscriminately. There was a rising tide of panic as reports began to reach those still trapped in the theatre: some said Caligula was dead, some that he was clinging to life in the care of the imperial surgeons, some that he had escaped and was – although wounded and soaked in his own blood – already addressing the mob in the forum.

It was later that evening, while the city remained in a state of anarchy, that the conspirators began to wonder if they had really finished the job: Caligula's wife and daughter, after all, remained alive. Opinion was split.[39] Some argued the two were innocent and that the murder of a woman and a child would devalue the heroism of the tyrannicide. Others placed the blame for the degeneration of Caligula's reign with Caesonia: 'what sent him mad, they said, was a drug she gave him, calculated to enslave his mind and direct his passions to her; so it was she who had been the architect of total disaster for the fortune of the Romans and their world empire'.[40] Fear and the latter stance won the day.

Josephus claims that the soldier sent to do the deed found Caesonia and her child in the passageway with Caligula's body, which still lay where it had fallen. Caesonia – kneeling by her husband, her skin and dress stained with his blood – was crying, 'I warned you, I warned you again and again.' Later, Josephus tells us, people would dispute what these words had meant. Had Caesonia caught wind of the new plot? Or was it possible that she had read the darkening political mood and urged him to moderate his behaviour before it was too late?

The question was already irrelevant. Caesonia guessed the soldier's purpose as he approached: 'Don't wait,' she ordered, offering him her throat. 'Finish the last act of the drama you have written for us.'[41] The soldier obeyed and ran Caesonia through with his sword. Drusilla – just past her first birthday – had her brains dashed out against the wall.[42]

Claudius did not come home on the night of Caligula and Caesonia's murder. Messalina, eight months pregnant, must have been beside herself with fear. The city was in uproar; crowds rushed through the streets towards the forum where the senators were speaking for their lives as they struggled to contain the anger of the mob (with whom Caligula remained relatively popular) and maintain order in the army. The air was febrile with the threat of chaos, riots and looting. The friends or messengers who brought Messalina updates on the developing situation could have told her little with any certainty – the conspirators, it seemed, had not planned much further than Caligula's assassination. They certainly could have given her no reassurances as to the fate of her husband.

The story of how Claudius became emperor – 'by', as Suetonius puts it, 'a miraculous accident' – has an apocryphal flavour.[43] As the commotion of Caligula's death flooded the imperial palace, Claudius was said to have taken refuge behind the curtains of a balcony. A common soldier caught sight of his feet beneath the folds and dragged him out. Horror-struck when he recognised who he was man-handling, he fell to his knees and acclaimed Claudius '*Imperator*'. Claudius – still, we are told, in a state of confusion and terror and begging the soldiers to spare him – was bundled into a litter and conveyed, under armed escort, to the fortified Praetorian Camp near the city walls. The crowds who watched him pass, Suetonius tells us, 'were all pity, thinking him an innocent man being carried off to his execution'.[44]

The Senate, meanwhile, was enjoying a heady flirtation with freedom. When the crowds in the forum demanded to know the name of Caligula's assassin, the consular Valerius Asiaticus responded, 'I wish it had been me'.[45] It was a remark that Messalina would remember and use against him nearly a decade later. The Senate had transferred the contents of the imperial treasury to the easily defensible Capitol, and it was here that they called their meeting that evening. Summoned to join his fellow senators, Claudius sent word that he could not attend: he was being held by force in the Praetorian Camp.[46] On the Capitol, the Senate seemed resolved on the restoration of the Republic. Men who had never experienced a time before Augustus gave rousing speeches denouncing tyranny and, when Chaerea asked the consuls for a new watchword, he was given 'Liberty'. Outside, the urban cohorts – a small group of soldiers loyal to the Senate, who functioned as a quasi-police force – maintained a precarious peace on the streets.

As day turned to night, the hours must have passed slowly for Messalina. News would now have been beginning to circulate of the violent deaths of Caesonia and the baby Drusilla; Messalina would have been acutely aware that the Senate's Republican plan, if it was carried through, could spell disaster for her and her family.

Luckily for Messalina, the Republican ideal of 'Liberty' that meant so much to the Senate meant precious little to anyone else. The plebs – who had enjoyed little more freedom and significantly fewer freebies under aristocratic than under autocratic rule – were still baying for the blood of Caligula's killers. Although Chaerea himself appears to have been a man of genuine anti-imperial – or at least anti-Julio-Claudian – principle, the common interest that had bound the Senate to most of their co-conspirators among the Praetorian cohorts and imperial administration had evaporated at the moment of Caligula's death. Both the Praetorian Guard and the Palatine administration were intrinsically *imperial* institutions that served no role, either practically or ideologically, in a Republic. These men cared little for high Republican principle. They required a new Caesar – just one a little more predictable than Caligula. Claudius seemed the perfect candidate.

Sensing the Praetorians' intentions, the Senate sent a delegation to Claudius to demand that he respect senatorial authority and make no illegal bid for supreme power. For a man who had, allegedly, been cowering behind a curtain just hours before, Claudius' response was remarkably unequivocal. He spoke, in fact, as though his power was *already* confirmed. He said that he understood that the Senate had their concerns about the principate after Caligula's behaviour in the role but promised they had nothing similar to fear from him. He had experienced the fears and trials of the old regime just as they had, and he would do all in his power to ensure they were not repeated – the senators would soon discover *by experience* just how different a ruler he would be. Claudius' words, backed up by Praetorian force, constituted a coup only faintly disguised as a promise. To seal the deal, Claudius addressed an assembly of the Praetorian troops, promising them each a reward of at least fifteen or twenty thousand sesterces in return for their loyalty. Similar promises were sent to the armies stationed outside Rome.

The Senate met again before dawn the next morning. Only a hundred of the six hundred members were brave enough to attend. Outside, the crowds bayed for an emperor and called for Claudius by name; even the troops who had backed the Senate were beginning to demand that a single ruler be chosen in the interests of stability. The Senate toyed with the idea of proposing one of their own number as the new princeps. Marcus Vinicius (husband to Caligula's exiled sister Julia Livilla) was suggested, as was Valerius Asiaticus. No candidate could be agreed on, not least because Claudius had all but taken the principate already. For the Senate to propose an alternative now would have constituted a declaration of all-out civil war – one that they were almost certain to lose.

By the morning of the twenty-fifth, it was clear that the jig was up. Soldiers and subjects were converging in ever greater numbers on the Praetorian Camp, keen to pay their respects and pledge their allegiance to the new emperor. It was now Claudius' prerogative to deign to summon the senators to meet *him* at the imperial palace on the Palatine; and to *allow* them to 'confer' upon him the official titles and powers of the emperor.

VIII

Domina

'The female sex was not merely weak and unequal to real work but, if given free rein, savage, ambitious, and voracious for power'

Tacitus, *The Annals*, 3.33

Although it marked an end to the immediate dangers of the twenty-fourth, Claudius' accession on 25 January AD 41 left Messalina in an ambiguous position.

Claudius' formal acclamation as emperor was accompanied by no correspondent 'coronation' for Messalina. Indeed, the exact nature of Messalina's new position upon her 'accession' that January was far from clear. There existed no official office of 'empress' in the Roman state. The role of the emperor's wife was an undefined and fluid one delineated only by the limits of her personality and the precedents of her predecessors. Before Messalina, only one woman, Augustus' wife Livia, had really held the sort of position in Rome that might merit the term 'empress' – she had proved that it was possible, but she would be a difficult act to follow.

Rome believed itself to have been a city founded almost entirely without women. The story goes that the ultimate ancestor of the Roman people, Aeneas, was born not to a mortal woman but to Venus, and the city's mythological founders, Romulus and

Remus, were suckled not by their own mother but by a she-wolf. The original population of the city too was said to have been entirely male – made up of brigands and escaped slaves – a situation rectified only by the mass abduction of women from the neighbouring Sabine people. Even Lucretia – the noblewoman whose rape at the hands of the prince Tarquinius and subsequent suicide sparked the ousting of the kings and the birth of the Roman Republic – was more influential in death than in life.

The mental gymnastics required to erase the political, social, and even the *biological* role of women so completely from their foundation myths tells us something of Roman attitudes to the public role of the feminine. The story of the Sabine women perhaps encapsulates it best: women were crucial to the *continuation* of the city's population, but Rome as a body politic had already been established in complete and functioning form before their arrival. For the first six hundred or so years of Roman history this separation held strong: all magistrates were male, and so were the Senate and the electorate.

Given that the Republican system was designed in express opposition to the corruption and secret scheming that defined the tales of Rome's early tyrant-kings, it was structured so as to confine political discourse, as far as possible, to the official, transparent and exclusively male public sphere. In doing so, it severely limited opportunities for the exertion of soft power and behind-the-scenes influence – the main conduits for female political power in the ancient world.

The traditional ideal of the Roman woman was defined by her disengagement from public life. One second-century BC epitaph for a woman named Claudia ends with the lines 'She kept the house, she worked wool. I have said all I have to say. You may go.'[1] Another, a hundred years or so later, commemorated 'Amymone, wife of Marcus, the best and most beautiful, worker of wool, pious, modest, frugal, chaste, a *stayer-at-home*.'[2]

By the final, painful years of the late Republic, these boundaries were beginning to blur. Elite women were gaining a degree of economic freedom as their dowries were increasingly held in a sort of trust rather than passing wholesale to the control of their husbands.* Even more significantly, the Republican constitution which had kept them well out of Roman politics was breaking down. In the last century of the Republic's life, a succession of dictators and dynasts, usually with military backing, had bypassed the constitutional checks and balances that had long prevented any one individual becoming pre-eminent in the state. Power was becoming tied ever less to the office and ever more to the man.

The creation of new channels to power that circumvented the traditional magistracies – ones that emphasised personal reputation and relationships – opened up opportunities for elite women to exert some control. So too, strangely enough, did the militarisation of politics. As Rome convulsed itself in spasm after spasm of civil war, women whose husbands were in exile were expected to advocate for them in Rome; others joined their husbands in their camps, at their diplomatic conferences or on the front. Fulvia, the then wife of Mark Antony, was even said to have strapped on a sword and led an army against Octavian.[†] [3]

It was the advent of the principate, however, that would really reshape the parameters of female involvement on the Roman public stage. The solidification of Augustus' sole supremacy in

---

* By the first century BC *cum manu* marriage (in which control of a woman, and her property, passed to her husband) was increasingly replaced by *sine manu* marriage (in which the woman, and her property, remained under her father's *potestas*). This arrangement tended to provide her with greater independence.

† This was the Perusine War, fought between 41 and 40 BC while Mark Antony was in the East. Dio 48.10 records the story that Fulvia girded on a sword and addressed the troops. Though the veracity of such claims is dubious, Fulvia does seem to have played a significant role in events.

28/27 BC, and the growth of his dynastic ambitions over the decade that followed, changed the game when it came to female power. Procreation could no longer be a political afterthought, as Republican storytellers had imagined that it had been in the days of the Sabines: the continuation of the Julio-Claudian dynasty was dependent on women. The definitive reorientation of power away from the Senate towards the figure of the princeps, moreover, made access to the ear of the emperor arguably more valuable a political tool than any of the old magistracies; such access was naturally granted to the women of the imperial family.

Augustus also actively promoted the public profile of the women in his family. In order to defuse some of the anxieties about his novel position in the state and promote social cohesion in the wake of the civil wars, Augustus sought to present himself as the embodiment of 'old-fashioned family values'. The public promotion of the women of his household as paragons of bygone feminine virtue was central to this programme. It was a strategy that (like so much of the Augustan programme) was intrinsically hypocritical. The traditional Roman ideal of the 'good woman' was rooted in domestic virtue; but now Augustus sought to promote these private virtues publicly. It was a conflict that Augustus' wife Livia understood exquisitely, and one that she would be ruthless in exploiting.

To an extent, the novel position of women within Augustus' new order was openly acknowledged. In 35 BC, Augustus arranged for his sister Octavia the Younger and wife Livia to be granted an unprecedented set of honours and prerogatives: they received public statues, protection from verbal insults and the right to administer their own property and estates.[4] When the Senate set up the *ara pacis Augustae* (the Altar of Augustan Peace) in 13 BC, the relief-carved marble walls of the sanctuary became a billboard for the position of women and femininity within the new dynastic ideology. Allusions to fertility are everywhere: foliage twists up the walls, heavy garlands of fruit sag under their own weight, on one panel a goddess nurses twin infants. In among the usual combination of senators, priests and foreign dignitaries depicted on the carved procession that snakes around its outer walls we find, for the first time ever on a Roman public monument, depictions of imperial women and their children.

The design made two statements: firstly that the prosperity of the empire was tied directly to the fertility of the imperial women, and secondly that 'private' members of Augustus' family were now just as crucial to the 'public' world of Roman politics as the senators. By the turn of the millennium, the idea that the *Domus Augusta,* or the 'House of Caesar', existed as a political entity in its own right was coming into focus.[5] The senator who acclaimed Augustus *Pater Patriae* – the 'Father of his Country' – in 2 BC began his speech with the words 'may good fortune and favour be with you *and your house,* Caesar Augustus'.[6] When Augustus died in AD 14, the concept was well established enough to be set, quite literally, in stone: among the honours voted to the deceased emperor was a public statue group depicting '*Divo Augusto domuique Augus[tae]*' – 'the Deified Augustus and the Augustan House'.[7]

While the political significance of the imperial women was an inescapable fact of the new political order, the Senate – and Augustus – stopped short of defining the position of his wife, sister or daughters in official terms. Augustus' position itself constituted an informal (but increasingly standardised) amalgamation of offices and honours, most drawn directly from the old Republican system of magistracies; in developing the role of emperor, Augustus had not technically altered the structure of the Roman state; instead, he had appropriated enough of the Republic's pre-existing offices to make his personal supremacy indisputable. The process was impossible for the women of Augustus' house to replicate: there were precious few pre-existing offices and honours for them to accrue.

The moment at which Livia – Augustus' wife and, in the truest sense of the word, his partner – became Rome's first 'empress' is not entirely clear. In the years immediately following the solidification of her husband's supremacy in 27 BC Livia took a back seat, deferring in large part to Augustus' beloved sister (and direct ancestor to both Messalina and Claudius), Octavia. Octavia had been popular ever since her display of heroic stoicism in the face of her husband Mark Antony's affair with Cleopatra and, for much of the 20s BC, she occupied a more public role than Livia.[8]

During this period, Octavia took advantage of her popularity and reputation for traditional virtue to initiate an unprecedented project for a Roman woman: the commission of a public building in her own name.[9] The Porticus Octaviae – the bastardised façade of which still stands in Rome today as the entrance to a medieval fish market – was a vast colonnaded square, enclosing two temples, Greek and Latin libraries and a public art gallery. It was the death of Octavia's son in 23 BC – an event that triggered Octavia's effective retirement from public life – that brought Livia increasingly to the fore. Over the next fifty years she would originate and shape the role of 'empress' in her own image.

Ten years or so after her death, Livia's great-grandson Caligula would call her 'Ulysses in a *stola*'.[10] As was so often the case with Caligula, the observation hit dangerously close to the mark. The *stola* was the dress that marked out the respectable Roman matron, and in public Livia presented herself assiduously as a woman cut very much from this cloth; the kind of traditional Republican woman, untouched by the insinuations of luxury and vice, whose epitaph might call her a 'worker in wool' and a 'stayer-at-home'. With a slave staff so numerous that it included an in-house pearl setter, Livia can hardly have been called upon to do much in the way of housework.[11] Yet it was put about that the empress wove her husband's togas herself and, as late as the fourth or fifth centuries AD, recipes were in circulation for 'Livia's' home-remedies for sore throats and chills.[12] The working of wool and the nursing of sick family members were symbolic examples of traditional women's work – in laying claim to these practical domestic skills Livia invoked a particular brand of dutiful and comforting womanhood.

In contrast, Ulysses (the Latin name for Odysseus) was famed in the ancient world for his cold intelligence and underhand cunning. Livia undoubtedly possessed a remarkable intelligence and her self-presentation as a domestic goddess was both genius and deeply disingenuous. Roman ideals of uxorial virtue were rooted in a private world, but now Livia began to project them onto the public stage. Around 15 BC she followed Octavia's example and commissioned her own portico.[13] As a 'genre' of civic building, the portico suited Livia's programme of self-presentation perfectly. With its enclosed colonnade, verdant planting, refreshing fountains, and offers of shade or shelter as the weather required, the portico allowed Livia in some sense to play ideal wife to the public at large – providing them with a pleasant space removed from the urban crush and designed for their comfort, health and rejuvenation, just as a wife was expected to do in keeping her husband's *domus*. It was a message that Livia hammered home in her inclusion of a shrine to Concordia – the personification of 'concord' and a goddess who conveniently governed both harmony in marriage and harmony in politics – within the portico or its vicinity. When Livia dedicated her portico in 7 BC she did so with her son Tiberius conspicuously at her side.

Livia also rebuilt the sanctuary of Bona Dea, or the 'Good Goddess', an ancient fertility goddess whose rites were overseen by Vestal Virgins and only celebrated by respectably chaste married women. She may also have been involved in the restoration of two other female-centric cults, those of Feminine Fortune and Chastity. Another philanthropic effort recorded by Dio – the making up of dowries for poorer girls – was once again focused conspicuously on the feminine and familial.[14]

Livia's hinting hit the mark. In his *c.*8 BC *Fasti*, the poet Ovid wrote that Livia 'reconstituted Concordia in her deeds and in her altar/she the one woman deemed worthy of the marriage bed of mighty Jove'.[15] Later, as an exile, Ovid would focus much of his increasingly desperate sycophancy on the same themes: now Livia 'with her virtue shows the former ages of antiquity/Cannot best our own in the glory of their chastity/ Who, possessed of Venus' beauty and of Juno her morality/ Is alone deemed worthy for the marriage bed of a divinity'.[16] Even Tacitus (otherwise notable for the singular negativity of his characterisation of Livia) admits that 'In domestic virtue she followed the mores of a previous age – although her obliging elegance overstepped the boundaries sanctioned by the women of old – and, though a difficult mother, she was an easy wife.'[17]

The reputation Livia created for herself radiated out across the empire; an inscription in Andalusia calls her 'mother of the world'.[18] Perhaps the most conclusive testament to the success of Livia's self-imagining, however, is to be found in silence: almost uniquely among the Julio-Claudian imperial women, no one, no hostile historian or upstart satirist, ever dared accuse her of adultery.

Livia's strategy was suffused with an inherent tension: she was employing the traditional preference for *private* feminine virtues to promote herself on the *public* stage.[19] Tacitus called Livia 'a good match for her husband's artfulness and for her son's dissimulation', and although the passage is undoubtedly meant as an insult, the traits which Tacitus found so distasteful and dangerous in a woman were at the heart of Livia's political success.[20] The empress, just like her husband, possessed a remarkable instinct for the distinction between political image and political reality; like Augustus, Livia understood how wide this gulf might be stretched and how to take advantage of the grey area this created. Augustus had built his position on a precarious web of subtle hypocrisies and Livia did the same in her origination of the role of empress. Livia's promotion of her domestic virtues provided a comforting veneer of traditional continuity or restoration, one that largely protected her as she went about building an unprecedented base of political power.

Clever, well educated and with a remarkable political instinct, Livia had probably acted as a key advisor to her husband from the beginning. Her and Augustus' inability to produce living heirs together (although both had children by other partners) would, in the normal course of things, have led to an amicable divorce – the fact that they remained married indicates that Augustus believed his partnership with Livia was indispensable.

Although much of her influence took place behind closed doors, the sources record a number of specific instances of Livia's intercession on behalf of her sons, friends, petitioners and provincial communities. One example from relatively late in Augustus' reign is related in (imaginative) detail by Seneca. Apprised of a plot on his life led by a man he had previously thought a loyal and complaisant ally, the emperor – torn on how to respond – was experiencing a dark night of the soul. 'Finally his wife Livia interrupted: "will you take the counsel of a woman?" she asked. "Do as doctors are in the habit of doing when the usual remedies don't work; try the opposite. Up to this point you have profited nothing through severity [...] Now try clemency, see what that might grant you: pardon Cinna. He has already been intercepted; he cannot kill you now, but he can be useful to your reputation".'[21]

Perhaps Livia intervened on principle, perhaps she was simply bored of listening to her husband talk about his problems out loud and at length in the middle of the night, but Augustus took her advice; Cinna was spoken to, forgiven, freed and transformed into a genuine supporter of the regime. The episode, as it is related by Seneca, provides a series of insights both into the potential power of the empress and into how Livia was perceived to employ that power. Seneca sets the scene during the night and in the couple's bedchamber: a time and space where the empress, as wife, possessed privileged and uninterrupted access to the emperor. Livia's choice of words – as they were relayed to Seneca or as he imagined them – also reflects the double-faced genius that suffused all her political strategy. She begins with an allusion to her femininity, a claim that she would not usually venture to offer her husband advice unprompted, and the rhetorical suggestion that he need not heed it. She then, however, proceeds to give clear and practical advice in a manner evidently designed to sway Augustus' actions. Although her counsel is mercy, Livia's argument is cynically pragmatic; there is none of what the Romans might have considered 'feminine emotion' here, the construction of her speech is rhetorical and the rationale she offers is political.

Livia acted as a political advisor, but she was also a crucial colleague for her husband when it came to public relations. In the creation of her unimpeachable public image, Livia added credence to Augustus' presentation of himself as a guardian of traditional Roman mores. Even more significantly, Livia's work in associating herself with Concordia provided the link upon which Augustus would base much of his dynastic ideology: the harmony of the state and the empire, she suggested, was directly related to the harmony of the imperial family.

Literary acknowledgement of Livia's power emerges relatively early. The author of the anonymous poem of consolation for the death of Livia's son Drusus writes: 'Fortune set you high and bade you to defend/your place of honour, Livia, your burden bear [...] Could we seek in you a sweeter exemplar of virtue/Than when you bear the work of a Roman prince?'[22] From his exile on the grimly provincial shores of the Black Sea, the poet Ovid begged his wife to plead his case not to Augustus but to Livia.

> Let your lips beseech the wife of Caesar [...]
> Leader of women, our femina princeps [...]
> If she is engrossed in some weighty business of the state,
> Put off your plan, [...]
> You're better to follow on among the crowds of cases[23]

Such poetic entreaties are intended to flatter of course, but flattery would have been pointless had its target possessed no influence. In a world in which much of the princeps' supremacy was based on personal *auctoritas*, Livia's influence was as serious and official a source of political power as any and it is not hard to imagine that Livia's atrium was often filled, as Ovid suspects, by the bearers of public and private petitions.*

The sense that Livia possesses not just wifely influence but political authority in her own right permeates Ovid's poems, especially in their repeated use of the word 'princeps'. An adjective meaning 'first' or 'foremost', or a noun that might be rendered 'leader', 'principal', 'founder', 'chieftain', 'prince' or 'sovereign ruler', it is almost impossible to capture the full tenor of the Roman term in translation – or its context and history. The plural, *principes*, had been used in Cicero's day, and was still sometimes used even under the empire, to refer, in undefined

---

* The Roman concept of *auctoritas* is related, although not directly analogous, to the modern idea of 'authority'. Often contrasted to 'potestas' (power, sometimes backed by force), 'auctoritas' was a powerful kind of legitimate influence derived from status and reputation.

terms, to the foremost men of Rome, while the old title *princeps senatus* had traditionally designated the most senior member of the Senate.[24] This was now a title held always by the emperor and, by the middle of Augustus' reign, the shortened form princeps had begun to be used to summarise and describe the position of the emperor, for which there was no pre-existing Latin term.[*] The association of Livia with this term of legitimate, masculine, political authority is nothing less than revolutionary.

When Augustus died in AD 14, it became clear that Livia's influence and authority was not reliant on her position as wife of the reigning emperor. The death of her husband – a moment which, for most royal consorts, might mark the decline of their power – resulted in a promotion for Livia. In his will, Augustus broke convention and, indeed, the law, in leaving Livia a full one third of his vast estate – a portion valued at around 50 million sesterces. More important, however, was the bequest of his name. In his testament Augustus legally adopted Livia, as his daughter, into the *gens Julia*. This action was designed not to give Augustus some incestuous kick from beyond the grave, but to augment Livia's status.[25] The *gens Julia* was one of the oldest and most noble families in Rome; they even claimed to have traced their lineage back to Rome's mythical progenitor Aeneas, and his mother, the goddess Venus. It was Julius Caesar's posthumous adoption of Augustus into the *gens Julia* that had given the future emperor his political start and he had spent the intervening years using everything – from the artistic iconography of his new forum to the narrative of Virgil's *Aeneid* – to promote the idea that the fates of Rome and the Julian family were indelibly intertwined. His adoption of Livia into the *gens Julia* asserted her continued centrality to the success of the state.

---

[*] The Latin term *imperator* – the source of the English word emperor – was a specific military acclamation, not a title denoting political supremacy.

Livia's husband/adoptive father also took the remarkable step of transferring to her the honorific 'Augustus' – a name which had, by the time of his death, come to be used as a quasi-political title designating the office of emperor. There was no precedent for the transfer of an honorific title from a man to a woman in Roman history; Augustus' action was a clear statement of the power that he intended Livia Augusta should hold after his death.[26]

Augustus' transformation into a god brought about a further expansion in Livia's prestige. The dead emperor's accession to heaven had been handily witnessed by a senator; his good eyesight was rewarded by Livia, who personally paid him a million sesterces for his testimony.[27] Livia was made a priestess of her husband's new cult. The position carried official public duties and Livia was assigned a lictor – an axe-carrying attendant and the ultimate, unsubtle symbol of Roman state authority – to accompany her as she undertook them.

The advent of the Tiberian age saddled Livia with no new rivals to challenge her position. Tiberius never remarried after his second divorce; his ex-wife Julia the Elder still languished in exile in Calabria. Upon his accession Tiberius revoked her few remaining properties and privileges and she died later that same year. Tiberius had no sisters, no mistresses powerful or long-lasting enough to be named in our histories – there existed no woman in any position to compete with Livia. So, Dio claims, Livia Augusta received crowds of senators at her morning salutations, she received petitions, she even co-signed Tiberius' letters.[28]

Perhaps the greatest testament, however, to Livia's influence in this period is to be found in the impotent anxieties of the men who wrote about it. Tacitus in particular sees her machinations everywhere. 'Then there was his mother,' he comments darkly at the outset of Tiberius' reign, 'with her feminine lack of self-control; they were to be slaves to a woman.'[29] For Tacitus, all of Livia's political interventions are motivated by feminine passions – jealousy, hatred, maternal ambition – all take place behind closed doors, all are nefarious, almost all are illegal and the majority are murderous.

Tacitus' vitriol is apparent from the opening scenes of his narrative. 'Tiberius had only just entered the province of Illyricum', he writes,

> when he was summoned back by a hasty letter from his mother; nor has it ever been satisfactorily established whether on reaching the city of Nola he found Augustus still breathing or already dead. For Livia had put the house and surrounding streets under strict guard, with positive reports being put out periodically, until, with provision for the demands of the moment, a single report brought the news that Augustus had died and Tiberius was in control of affairs'.[30]

Tacitus' claims are dubious but the story's literary heritage is illuminating: the episode, as Tacitus relates it, is essentially identical to a story told of the scheming, pre-Republican Roman queen Tanaquil.[31] After her husband's assassination in 578 BC, Tanaquil shut off the palace and appeared at an upper window claiming that her husband lived but that he had entrusted the regency of the state to Servius Tullius (her favourite) until he recovered from the attack. By the time Tanaquil announced the king's death, Servius Tullius' authority was secure – making him the first king of Rome to assume the throne without popular election. In the story of Tanaquil we find underhand feminine intervention bypassing the institutions of male public control – the comparison to Livia is not a subtle one. For Tacitus, the power of Livia and of the other empresses to come – Messalina among them – was a mortal symptom of Rome's descent into monarchy and, as such, that power was invariably sinister.

When Livia died in AD 29 she had, in many ways, achieved a feat comparable to that of her husband: through the combination of traditional roles and novel powers she had gradually created for herself an unprecedented position in the Roman state. On her death, however, the package of honours and prerogatives she had accumulated was not passed on to an heir. That the position of 'empress', as Livia had created it, essentially died with her is testament both to the genius of its amorphousness and the extent to which it had relied on the personal *auctoritas* of its holder.

Between the death of Livia in AD 29 and Messalina's accession in 41, no woman had had a real shot at establishing herself in the role of Rome's 'First Lady'. Caligula's sisters had been exalted, but their pre-eminence had been short-lived: Drusilla had died just over a year after his accession and Agrippina and Julia Livilla had fallen just over a year after that. The first two wives that Caligula took as emperor lasted less than six months each, and even Caesonia – the only one credited with any real influence – survived little over a year in the role, hardly long enough to reassemble anything like the portfolio of power and privileges that had been left to lapse upon the death of Livia Augusta.

Upon her husband's accession in January AD 41 Messalina inherited no established power base. She possessed no title, no specific legal privileges, no official role in the public life of the state. Indeed, the early predominance of Octavia over Livia and – within Messalina's own experience at the imperial court – of Caligula's sisters over his wives Orestilla and Lollia served, quite conclusively, to demonstrate that being married to the emperor was not enough to guarantee pre-eminence. The situation presented Messalina with both a challenge and an opportunity: she would, to some extent, have to mould the role of 'empress' in her own image.

Livia's death, and the relative dearth of female power that had followed it, had demonstrated that the role of empress relied, in large part, on personal reputation. For all Livia's genius in this respect she had bequeathed a blueprint that was of limited use to Messalina. Livia was in her eighties when she died in AD 29; she had been nearing forty and mother to two grown sons when she'd stepped to the fore of Roman public life in the late 20s BC. The public image that she'd created for herself – that of the mature matron, sober, level-headed, gracefully ageing and long-experienced in marriage and motherhood – had been dependent upon her age and *gravitas*. Messalina, a very young mother to a baby daughter, could hardly look to replicate it precisely.

Besides, Messalina knew that times had changed. In the twelve years that had elapsed since Livia's death, much of the old Augustan facade of tradition and Republicanism had been stripped away, first by the paranoia of Tiberius' final years and then by Caligula's performative despotism. Both the forms of politics and the norms of public life had shifted. The Senate could no longer pretend that the locus of power lay in the forum rather than the palace: that question had been resolved by the wholesale move of the Tiberian court to island isolation on Capri. They also knew that a new cast of characters was ascendent: where Augustus and even Tiberius had been assiduous in displaying their respect for the Senate, Caligula had revelled in explicit demonstrations of contempt for the old aristocracy, while making no secret of his reliance on an inner cabal of women, courtiers and ex-slaves. Messalina was well versed in these new norms: she'd been a child when Tiberius had upped sticks for Capri and she'd married into the inner circle of the Caligulan court just as the young emperor was shaking off his last pretences of deference towards the Senate.

The time was ripe for a new, more unabashed, model of what it meant to be a Roman empress, and Messalina – young, beautiful, fertile, modern, noble, and undeniably a child of empire – seemed the perfect woman to create it.

IX

Madonna Messalina

'Fertility and fame'

Tacitus, *Annals*, 2.43

If we buy into the canonical narrative of Claudius' accession, the events of 24/25 January AD 41 saw Messalina's life transformed completely without warning. Eight months pregnant with her second child and barely out of her teens, she had swapped the relatively anonymous life of an imperial princess on the edge of the emperor's entourage for an existence as one of the most famous women in the empire. The position she now occupied carried endless opportunities and risks but offered precious few defined powers and privileges to help her navigate them. Overnight, Messalina's daughter and unborn child had been transformed into the future heirs of empire and her husband had become the most powerful man in the known world.

It is possible, however, that the news of her elevation, when it came, did not strike Messalina so entirely as a surprise. The stories the sources tell of Claudius' accidental accession are highly suspect: in each we find Claudius transformed over the night of the twenty-fourth from a quivering wreck hiding behind a curtain and pleading for his life, to a man intent on holding supreme power, unequivocal in the face of civic unrest and senatorial opposition. The tale of the scared, reluctant emperor fits far too neatly with the overall narrative that would later be constructed for Claudius as ruler; competent, at times, but weak and far too easily influenced. The chaos that followed Caligula's assassination constituted the perfect environment for the proliferation of rumours. As the forum filled with people, the factions of conspirators repaired to their respective camps, leaving behind them a vacuum of uncertainty. A whole host of alternative accounts must have flown back and forth as people tried to get a handle on the situation. The tale of Claudius behind the curtain – so appealing in its equal parts drama and farce, and so useful as a narrative shorthand for Claudius' character – probably emerged from this chaos and stuck.

It seems likely that Claudius was aware of the plot on his nephew's life before it came to fruition. He may have been actively involved or he may simply have indicated to the Praetorian faction that he would be prepared to stand as their candidate for princeps should the assassination be successful. As the storm clouds had gathered in earnest in the autumn of AD 40, and an attack on Caligula began to look less like a likelihood than an inevitability, Claudius may have felt that he had no option but to risk participation. If Caligula fell to a wholly Republican plot, Claudius could have gone the way of Caesonia. Any danger he faced – as the murders of Caligula's wife and daughter would soon demonstrate – might extend to Messalina. Given the advisory role she would later play in his administration, it is not unreasonable to imagine that he might have shared his plans with her as well.

Even if Messalina was forewarned, the days that followed the assassination of Caligula were fraught with risk. Claudius may have been in on the conspiracy, but the conspirators had been far from unified. His candidacy had been opposed in the Senate both by other would-be emperors and by hard-core Republicans. The threat of Praetorian violence had forced these men to accept Claudius' authority in the short term, but they had not been neutralised. For the first time since the establishment of the principate, an emperor – who had little political and no martial experience – had been carried to power by a military coup against the avowed wishes of the Senate. Claudius had a long way to go if he was going to legitimise his power.

Messalina's stake in all this could not have been higher. Even during the bloodiest and bitterest excesses of the civil wars, wives and children had generally survived the proscription of their husband and fathers unharmed. The fate of Sejanus' children and double murder of Caesonia and Drusilla proved that the situation had changed. If Messalina had been aware of the conspirators' plans, she might now have begun to feel that she was getting more than she had bargained for. She would have known Caesonia well, and her own daughter Octavia was around the same age as Drusilla. The daunting reality of her situation – that a failure on Claudius' part to consolidate his power might well constitute a death sentence for herself and her children – was now inescapable.

From the very moment of her accession, Messalina shared in the risks of her husband's supremacy as well as in its rewards. This is key to our understanding of Messalina's actions over the next few years. Like Livia, she would play an active part in shaping and promoting the image of her husband's principate; she would position herself at the centre of the shadowy structures of internal palace politics; and she would systematically, at times brutally, root out potential sources of opposition to his rule as well as to her own position. These were actions that she undertook for herself and her children as much as for Claudius.

Messalina's tenure as empress (if we politely ignore the bloodshed that had marked her accession) could not have begun on a better note. On 12 February, not twenty days into her husband's reign, she delivered her second healthy child – and this time it was a boy.[1] The birth of Tiberius Claudius Caesar – who would later come to be known as Britannicus – marked the first time, after the years of succession crises that had blighted Augustus and his heirs, that a reigning emperor had been blessed with a son.[*]

---

[*] For simplicity, Messalina's son is referred to as Britannicus from here on.

Britannicus' lineage was exemplary. Positive memories of Claudius' parents, Drusus the Elder and Antonia, had survived the reign of their grandson Caligula; and Messalina (unlike Caesonia) brought with her an illustrious descent of her own, boasting the blood of the revered Octavia on both her father's and mother's side. To the people, the birth of such a prince was undoubtedly a cause for celebration.

The timing of the boy's birth, as much as his lineage, stirred excitement. In his quest to transform his dictatorship into a dynasty, Augustus had worked hard to equate the fertility of his house with the prosperity of the empire and, in doing so, he had imbued the wombs of the imperial women with something like the power of prophesy. The birth of an imperial son, just three weeks into Claudius' new regime, must have seemed a good omen for a coming era of peace and prosperity. A new type of coin was minted that year: on one side, Claudius' dignified, laureate profile; on the other, a female personification of 'Spes' or Hope stepping forward and proffering a flower, accompanied by the legend 'SPES AUGUSTA'. The implication was that, with Claudius on the throne and Britannicus as his heir, the Roman people might hope for better days to come.

To the Roman mind, the birth of Britannicus also reflected well on Messalina *personally*. Physical fertility was one of the greatest 'virtues' an ancient woman could possess, and the bearing and rearing of large broods of children was heavily morally loaded. One well-worn anecdote told about Cornelia, an icon of old Republican feminine virtue, illustrates the moralising that surrounded fertility.* Sometime in the middle of the second century BC, Cornelia had found herself hosting a rich Campanian matron as a guest at her home in Rome. The woman was in

---

* Cornelia, the daughter of Publius Cornelius Scipio Africanus, was the mother of the Gracchi brothers, tribunes of the plebs famous for their reforming zeal and subsequent assassinations.

possession of the finest jewellery collection of her day which she flaunted endlessly to her hostess. Cornelia bided her time, keeping the woman talking until her *twelve* children returned from school before announcing, no doubt with insufferable self-satisfaction, '*these* are my jewels'.[2]

We have already seen how, some three centuries after Cornelia's death, Juvenal would castigate the women of his day for avoiding the dangers of pregnancy and labour in his seethingly misogynistic *Sixth Satire*.[3] Childbirth and feminine morality were so intertwined in the Roman mind that a failure to give birth could be shorthand for a failure to be a good woman. After Messalina's death, Juvenal would cite her as another example of feminine depravity. But in AD 41 – after the birth of Britannicus, and before the rumours about her sex life had begun to spread – she seemed to be doing everything right.

The expectation of fertility weighed heavily on all Roman women, but it weighed heavier still on the women of the House of Caesar. Under the dynastic system, childbirth was a duty they owed to the state as well as the family, and their fertility was advertised across the empire. The message was everywhere: in the carved procession of imperial princesses leading their small children by the hand on the Ara Pacis; in the promotion of the cult of Venus Genetrix ('Venus the Ancestress'); in the family statue groups arranged in town squares and public buildings across the provinces; in the fertile abundance of the foliate patterning that defined much of the Augustan aesthetic.* An

---

* Large imperial family portrait groups, including statues of women and children and comprising at least twelve and seventeen statues respectively, have been found, for example, at Veleia in northern Italy and Nerona in Croatia. These displays were not static compositions: statues of new brides or children were added, statues of fallen emperors and empresses removed. The statue of Agrippina at Veleia seems originally to have depicted Messalina: the old empress' head was removed and replaced with a portrait of the new.

imperial woman's fertility could make or break her career and public popularity. Caligula had divorced Lollia Paulina for failing to conceive within six months of their marriage; he had married Caesonia only upon her completion of the job. Tacitus could even argue that the fact that 'Agrippina the Elder, the wife of Germanicus, surpassed Livilla, the wife of Drusus in both fertility and reputation' was a catalyst for court factionalism during the early years of Tiberius' reign.[4]

Indeed, for an imperial woman, fertility was a virtue significant enough to hide a multitude of sins. In Macrobius' *Saturnalia*, a fifth-century AD collection of Roman dinner-party anecdotes mined from old authors and oral history, the discussion turns to Julia the Elder, who had been exiled for adultery in 2 BC, and all agree that it was only her famous fertility (she produced five living children) that had prevented her downfall from coming sooner:

> When Augustus considered his crowd of grandchildren and their evident resemblance to her husband Agrippa, he blushed with shame to think that he had ever doubted his daughter's chastity. Thenceforth Augustus deluded himself that his daughter's high spirits went so far as to give the *appearance* of wantonness but that she was innocent of any real charge.[5]

The equation of 'crowds of children' with 'chastity' might seem an incongruous one to anyone with a basic conception of the fundamentals of human biology, but to the Romans, for whom 'chastity' meant not Christian abstinence but marital fidelity, the two were natural bedfellows. The 'good woman' slept with her husband alone but a lot and bore him countless children, each bearing slight variations of his name – to do so was both a duty and a virtue. To the Roman observer the birth of Britannicus not only boded well for Claudius' regime, it also reflected well on Messalina's character.

The Senate reacted accordingly: soon after the boy's birth they voted that the baby should be honoured with the title 'Augustus' and that Messalina should be 'Augusta'.[6] The proposal was an extraordinary one. The title Augusta was the most exalted available to a Roman woman; Livia had been a widow in her sixties before the honour had been conferred upon her, Messalina was little more than twenty years old and only weeks into her term as empress. For some senators, the offer must have been made through gritted teeth. For those among them who, just three weeks before, had hoped for the re-establishment of the Republic, the concept of the Senate rewarding a *woman*, and particularly a *young* woman, with a public title for doing nothing more than giving birth to a son was a painful admission of the reaffirmed dynastic reality. For those senators who had harboured hopes of gaining the throne for themselves, the birth of a son and heir to Claudius was an unmitigated disaster.

The Senate's offer may reflect the strength of pro-Messalina feeling on the streets of Rome. In the confusion that had followed the death of Caligula, the mob had almost broken down the doors of the Senate's meeting place and had come within a hair's breadth of lynching one of its consuls. The Senate had relationships to repair both with the princeps and the people – honouring Messalina while the crowds were still rejoicing over the birth of Britannicus may have seemed a good place to begin.

Valeria Messalina, however, was not destined to become Messalina Augusta. While Messalina rested from birthing Claudius' child, pre-anaesthetic and pre-antibiotics, her husband took it upon himself to decline the honours on her behalf. For Claudius, this was a way of reassuring the Senate that he was not aiming at some Caligulan aping of Eastern monarchy – it showed, as the historian Dio gushed, 'great moderation'.[7] For Messalina, it was a serious blow. Accession to the title of Augusta had marked the beginning of the most illustrious phase of Livia's career. Claudius' decision made it clear that the prominence women had enjoyed in the court of Caligula was not something that the new emperor necessarily intended to preserve – Messalina was going to have to fight for her position.

Messalina's frustration may have been particularly acute in the face of Claudius' extravagant celebration of past generations of Julio-Claudian women. Despite the contempt she had shown him while she lived, Claudius lavished posthumous honours on his mother Antonia. Circus games were to be held each year in her memory and, unlike Messalina, *she* was to have the title 'Augusta'.[8] The long-dead Livia received new honours too: she was deified in AD 42 on what would have been her wedding anniversary.[9] The only woman worthy of celebration in Claudius' Rome was, it seemed, a dead one.

The old Roman qualms about the public glorification of women that had induced Claudius to turn down the Senate's offer held no sway in the provinces. Messengers setting off down the network of post-roads carried the news of Messalina's successful childbirth to the furthest reaches of the Roman world and the empire rushed to celebrate. On 10 November AD 41, Claudius wrote a letter to the city council of Alexandria in Egypt authorising them to begin setting up statues of himself and his family.[10] Alexandria also minted coins bearing the image of Messalina, draped and veiled, holding the bunch of corn sheaves associated with fertility goddesses. Her other arm is held straight out and the small statue-like figures of her two children balance easily on the palm of her hand. The Greek-language legend inscribed on the coin tells us that this is 'Messalina, Empress and Augusta'. The eastern provinces were more than willing to acknowledge the princeps' wife explicitly and concisely as what she really was – an empress.

Messalina's unilateral provincial promotion to the position of 'Augusta' reflected a deep-seated cultural difference. The Greek East, after more than three centuries of Hellenistic monarchy, had an established conception of the position of 'queen' as an official office carrying a set of inalienable powers assumed automatically by the wife of the ruler. But the coins Alexandria issued in AD 41 also reflect Messalina's personal prestige. The design of coins in the provincial city mints was a matter left to the provincial cities – Alexandria's decision to depict Messalina attests to the new empress' popularity beyond Rome.

To the provinces, the stability of the empire mattered far more than its ideology, and stability was the primary promise of the Claudian regime in its early years: coins minted in AD 41/42, for example, often bear legends that proclaim the emperor's *Constantia* – his steadfastness. While the senatorial conflicts rumbled on at Rome, the provinces (along with the politically disenfranchised urban poor) were simply relieved to see a clear line of succession – one that lessened the risk of destabilising coups, conspiracies and civil wars. It was Messalina who had (quite literally) delivered this stability, and the Alexandrian mint wanted to celebrate her for it.

Of course, Messalina also held another appeal for the die cutters at Alexandria. The eastern provinces did not share Rome's tedious hang-ups about the moral implications of luxury and beauty, and Alexandria was the city of Alexander the Great and Cleopatra – they had an illustrious tradition of royal magnificence to uphold. In comparison with the drooling fifty-year-old Claudius, whose laureate head stamped the obverse of every coin, Messalina brought a much-needed injection of glamour: she was young, noble, and, as the provinces were just beginning to discover, beautiful.

The business of propagating a person's image across the breadth of the empire was a complicated one in AD 41, but one at which the Julio-Claudians, masters of publicity as they were, had become remarkably adept. Messalina would have sat for a sculptor in Rome, probably in the very earliest days of her reign. The portrait that resulted (known from the few copies that survive) is flattering, perhaps, but not idealised beyond recognition as the likeness of a real individual.[11] Messalina wears her hair in the fashionably contrived style of the Caligulan court: parted in the centre, with long screws of curls laid out like vertical furrows over her crown. At the back of the head, the hair is braided and twisted into a low loop. In some versions of the portrait, a few locks are loosed to fall in waves over the shoulders. At the front of the head, a fringe of small, tight, flat curls meets the forehead of a heart-shaped face, with a broad brow, full cheeks and a softly pointed chin. The mouth is small but the lips are full, curving themselves into a cupid's bow and turning up into the slightest smile at the corners. The sculptor has carved a deep, shadowed groove between the lips, giving the impression that the sitter has slightly parted them, in easy relaxation, or as if about to speak. The nose is classically straight, but Messalina's most striking feature is, without a doubt, her eyes. Large and wide-set beneath elegant brows that curve in precise parallel with the upper lids, these eyes lend Messalina's face an open expression that feels at once both innocent and exposing. She looks beautiful, sensual even, but she also looks young.

Once inspected and altered and approved, the prototype portrait would have been copied and disseminated as a model for cities across the empire. These copies would be copied until images of the empress could be seen everywhere. Life-size statues in marble and bronze would have stood in the temples and town squares; busts and statuettes – rendered in precious coloured stones or metals or clay, depending on the budget – would have graced private sitting rooms and household shrines; more transient images, painted on banners or panels of wood, would have hung in public sanctuaries and shop windows.

Most of these images were destroyed in the course of the *damnatio memoriae* that was ordered after Messalina's fall from grace. As news of the circumstances of her execution spread throughout the empire her statues were pulled down from their pedestals: the bronzes were melted down, the marbles smashed to pieces. In some thriftier communities her statues were sent back to the workshop to be recut to resemble Claudius' next wife. Paintings would have been burnt, or Messalina's face quite simply scrubbed away. To retain her picture or her statue even in the privacy of one's home was an act of treason.

A statue head identified as a depiction of Messalina carries the scars of its attempted destruction. Now in Dresden, it bears the characteristic markers of the Messalina portrait type: the complicated hairstyle with its framing rows of ringlets, and the round face with its soft, large features. The Dresden statue imbues the empress with attributes associated with the divine: she wears a laurel wreath and the turreted, city-wall-shaped crown of the goddess Cybele.[12] The image is not intended to be taken literally – Messalina was not worshipped as a living god – but it is a bold statement of power, making the deep cracks that criss-cross the marble all the more striking. The destruction appears to have been deliberate, with the face split into four clean pieces by one heavy blow to the back of the head.[13]

One statue survived this systematic destruction unscathed. Discovered in Rome, spirited into the royal collection at Versailles and confiscated for the Louvre during the revolution, this over-life-size portrait of Messalina and Britannicus is remarkably well preserved.* It likely dates to the earliest years

---

* The statue was discovered in Rome. Although there was some damage that required restoration – the head of Britannicus, for example, was missing – it reflects the natural ravages of two thousand years rather than any deliberate destruction.

of Messalina's reign, when Britannicus could still be depicted as a baby. Perhaps it survived in a workshop where, for some reason, the face was never recut as had been intended; or perhaps it was secreted away in the villa of some private admirer.

This Messalina is not given any explicitly divine attributes. Her dress is conspicuously modest. The patterning of the drapery around her neck suggests that she is wearing the *stola,* the long garment, pinned at each shoulder, that was the mark of the respectable Roman matron. Atop this, she wears the *palla* or mantle, pulled taught around her middle, folded over her left arm and drawn up over her head as a veil. The thumb and forefinger of her right hand pluck at the side of the veil, lifting the fabric from where it would otherwise fall on her shoulder. The gesture is one well known in Roman art and intended to indicate *pudicitia,* or modesty, as the woman moves to draw her veil closer around her face.

This intended iconography of virtue must have been easily recognisable to any contemporary viewer, but the action itself retains a certain ambiguity. There is a coyness, a flirtation even, in Messalina's delicate grasp of the fabric, in the open gesture of the rest of her hand, and in the action itself: she lifts the veil, we are expected to imagine, in order to draw it modestly close around her face – but in the moment captured by the sculptor all she has done is to draw it open and away from the exposed skin of her neck. The Romans were well aware of the potentially transgressive sexiness of the 'modest' woman: speaking of Nero's wife Poppaea Sabina the Younger, Tacitus wryly claims 'she exhibited modesty but enacted debauchery; she rarely went out in public, and then only with her face half-veiled, so that her appearance might never quite satiate her viewers or, perhaps, simply because it so became her.'[14]

The presence of the baby Britannicus cloaks this hint of sexuality in a celebration of fertility and motherhood.

Britannicus sits in the crook of Messalina's left arm, his torso naked but his legs and right shoulder swathed in drapery just like a miniature Zeus. He twists towards his mother, tilting his head upwards to gaze at her face – as she, in turn, tilts her head slightly towards him – and reaching out his arm, with little finger splayed, to touch her chin or, perhaps, to pull at the neckline of her *stola*.

To the Western eye, steeped in two thousand years of Christian iconography, Messalina looks remarkably like a Madonna. The real inspiration for the composition, however, can probably be traced back to a fourth-century BC Greek masterpiece: Kephisodotos' *Eirene and Ploutos*.[15] The original image of the personified goddess Peace (Eirene) holding her reaching infant, Wealth (Ploutos), which had stood in bronze in the Athenian Agora, had been much copied and its form would have been recognised across the Mediterranean world: the borrowing of its iconography for this imperial image would not have been lost on ancient eyes.

This single sculpture encapsulates Messalina's public image during the earliest days of her reign. The birth of her son had allowed her to lay claim to the highest imagery of traditional feminine virtue: her *stola* signalled her marriage, her gesture signalled her fidelity, and her child signalled her fertility. After the endless uncertainty of Caligula's reign, the birth of Britannicus promised a new era of stability and security, of peace and prosperity: in equating her with Eirene, the personification of peace, the composition proclaims Messalina's part in achieving this.

But the statue also reveals another element of the empress' public image. She was young and beautiful; her toying with her veil and the inclusion of her child spoke as much of flirtation as of modesty and as much of sexuality as of fertility. Messalina had weapons in her arsenal that the matriarchal Livia – in her forties before she came to the fore – had never had. Beautiful, young and quite suddenly one of the richest, most famous and most influential women in world, Messalina must have learnt quickly that glamour could be as powerful a weapon as virtue.

X

The Court of Messalina

'Review the many complete dramas and their settings, all
so similar, which you have known in your own experience,
or from bygone history: the whole court-circle of Hadrian,
for example, or the court of Antonius, or the courts of Philip,
Alexander, and Croesus. The performance is always
the same; it is only the actors who change.'

Marcus Aurelius, *Meditations*, 10.27

To tell the story of Messalina's public image during the first
part of her husband's reign is to tell only half, perhaps
less, of the story of her real political prominence. Most of her
work – and most of her power – existed in the space behind the
scenes: moving not through the Senate House and the forum
but through the corridors of the imperial palace that had spread
itself out across the top of the Palatine Hill.

Augustus (then Octavian) had bought his first house on the
Palatine Hill while he was still a private citizen.* Although
situated at the centre of the city's most fashionable district, the
dwelling was a modest one by the standards of the time; relatively
small, with columns carved from pitted grey peperino stone
rather than from marble.[1] It may have been the location that
attracted the future emperor. The house lay on the south-western

---

* The Palatine Hill provides the root of the English word 'palace'.

corner of the hill's summit, just up the slope from the Lupercal
– the cave where Romulus and Remus were supposedly suckled
by the she-wolf – and next to the site thought to have been
occupied by the house of Romulus.*

Suetonius notes that Octavian acquired the house from the
great aristocratic orator Hortensius; he omits to mention that he
probably acquired it in a fire-sale after Hortensius' proscription
during the civil wars of 43 BC.[2] The turmoil of the following
decade was a good time to buy property in Rome – if one had
retained one's head and the ready capital – and while Octavian
traversed the Mediterranean with his armies, his agents acquired
many of the surrounding houses too. Over the years that
followed, walls were knocked through, entrances closed up,
and extensions added to create an interconnected complex of
apartments designed to accommodate Octavian/Augustus' ever-
expanding household of relatives, step-children, foreign princes,
visiting dignitaries and slaves. A second palace, sloping down
the hill from the first (and now lying primarily under the Farnese
Gardens) was built by Tiberius and extended by Caligula until
it reached almost into the forum itself.[3] It was this sprawling
complex of palaces that Messalina would now call home.

The visitor who tried to walk from one end of the palace to
the other would have been struck not only by its size but also
by the range of styles he encountered. In some rooms he was
met by original frescoes in the old Augustan fashions, elegant
and coherent with their grand, illusionistic designs. In one room
a colonnade of carefully fluted trompe l'oeil columns is strung
with heavy garlands of foliage and plump fruit, with Dionysiac
accoutrements, lyres and ivy vines, hanging from thick red
ribbons at their centres. Another is decorated as an art gallery

---

* The remains of Iron Age huts have been actually excavated in this
area of the Palatine, explaining the Roman tradition regarding Romulus'
dwelling place.

complete with faux-framed mythological paintings – copies of the old Greek masters: on one side we find Io, freed from the captivity of Argos only to be raped by Zeus in bull form, and on the other the sea-nymph Galatea, attempting to flee her harasser Polyphemus on a seahorse.[4]

The restrained Augustan schemes gave way to a very different style of decoration as one entered the newer parts of the palace. These had been decorated by Caligula, who – like all the best bloodthirsty autocrats – had a real taste for interior design.[5] Here, rooms were clad in coloured marble or decorated in the new baroque fashion. On these walls, anything went: architecturally unworkable concoctions of columns and stacked arches turned flat walls into stage sets populated by actors, grotesque creatures and gods, with fictive windows opening out onto imagined vistas or dramatic moments from mythology.[6] These rooms immersed the visitor in layers of fantasy.

Despite all its luxury, the imperial palace was something of a mess. In Messalina's day, the Palatine palace consisted of a warren of old Republican houses and shiny new-builds connected by wooden staircases, knocked-through doors, passages and long colonnaded walkways. It must have been a strange experience to pass from the manageable domesticity of the upper sections of the palace into the vast halls of the *Domus Tiberiana*; or to emerge from a narrow staircase or low passage into a high-domed hall. The visitor moved through grand atria, reception halls and banqueting chambers; private baths, courtyards, gardens and fish ponds; accommodation for the family, for hostages and visiting dignitaries; living quarters and workshops for the vast hierarchy of imperial slaves; libraries, offices, record rooms, treasuries, workshops and stores. The structure – which had by now overrun a whole slope of one of Rome's seven hills – was closer to a town than to a home.

In the imperial palace as Messalina found it in AD 41 there was little to delineate public space from private. Careful as ever of the optics, Augustus had designed his home as a conspicuously traditional Republican *domus*. He had developed the public spaces of the city, its temples and forums, into people's palaces of shining marble, but for his own home he avoided anything excessive or palatial. Still, the demands on the space had grown: the home was now the heart of an empire as well as a space for family life and social networking. Meetings here determined imperial policy, and the guests included a steady stream of foreign dignitaries and delegations. The extensions built by Augustus' successors added wider halls for receptions, bigger dining rooms for banquets, and more expansive courtyards in which to wait one's turn to approach the emperor, but there was still no real sense of separation between home and office.

In 28 BC Octavian (as he was still then known) had dedicated a new temple to his patron god Apollo. The ground had been marked out for consecration – the young dynast claimed – by divine intervention when a lightning bolt struck a portion of his own home.[7] It was a remarkably convenient miracle. The doors of his *domus* would now open directly onto the terrace of the temple, creating an architectural conduit between man and god that recalled, implicitly but unavoidably, the palaces of the Hellenistic kings. It was a strategy that Caligula would repeat some seventy years later, extending the palace down the hill until it reached right into the Temple of Castor and Pollux on the forum. 'He made through it', Dio claims, 'an approach to the palace running directly between the two cult statues, in order, as he was wont to say, that he might have the Dioscuri for gate-keepers.'[8] The Julio-Claudians were building themselves and their private lives into the public fabric of the city.

By the time of Augustus' death, both his home and his dynasty had come to be called by one and the same name: the *Domus Augusta*, or the House of the Caesars. As the palace had been altered and extended to serve the changing needs of the imperial family, the physical structure of the building had come to reflect the political structure over which its residents presided. The lack of separation between the public and private areas of the emperor's palace mirrored an increasing blurring of the boundaries of power. As one approached the emperor socially, as his client, as his guest, or as his *wife*, was one necessarily also approaching him politically?

These boundaries, complex at the best of times, were to become particularly porous under Claudius. Mistrustful of the Senate and portions of the army in the wake of the violent circumstances of his accession, Claudius was more reliant than perhaps any emperor before him on his *chosen* associates, the men and women with whom he had surrounded himself on the Palatine and whom rightly or wrongly, he felt he could trust. The power of women and the imperial freedmen had been building behind the scenes for years; now their prominence would explode in a way that had never been seen before.

It is under Claudius that the word 'court' first emerged in Latin as a political term. The word the Romans used – *aula* – does not come from Latin. It is a Latinisation of a Greek word αὐλή or *aule*, a term which had originally meant 'hall' or 'courtyard' but which had long been used to refer to the court circles of the Eastern and Hellenistic kings. The word had first appeared in Latin during the late Republic, but for nearly a century it appears to have been applied strictly and exclusively to foreign lands. Eastern lands, mainly – places that the Romans had always, with a delicious horror, branded tyrannical and luxurious. It is Seneca – a man who (as we shall see) knew the realities of court politics all too intimately – who provides the first known application of the term to Rome sometime around AD 44 or 45.[9] It is telling that this linguistic development occurred bang in the middle of Messalina's supremacy on the Palatine.

The Claudian court has been described as 'a series of concentric circles of diminishing power' beginning with the emperor's bed and bedroom (a venue of intimate meetings as well as sexual intimacy in the Roman world), moving out through his dining rooms, his offices, his baths and his private gardens, to the offices of his freedmen and the great reception halls and petitioning rooms of his palace.[10] The currency of this political landscape was no longer eloquence on the Rostra, or vast amounts of ill-gotten wealth, or even a good old family name – it was proximity to, and influence with, the emperor. This was a world in which Messalina – as the emperor's wife – was better placed than any senator.

The good press Messalina garnered with the birth of Britannicus could not have come at a better time for the imperial couple. Claudius' position at the head of the state remained precarious and he knew it: a full month of his reign would elapse before he felt confident enough even to enter the Senate House.[11] That he finally did so a week after the birth of his son was, perhaps, not entirely a coincidence.

The first months of Claudius' rule were consumed by efforts at conciliation. Chaerea – the man who had struck the first blow against Caligula – was put to death, alongside a number of his fellow Praetorians. For all that Claudius might have appreciated, or even encouraged, Chaerea's actions, emperor-murder was a dangerous act for an emperor to condone. Chaerea's inner circle were also pathologically anti-Julio-Claudian. While the majority of the Praetorians had hailed Claudius emperor, Chaerea had supported the Senate and sought the restoration of the Republic: it was he who, in an attempt to extinguish the dynasty, had ordered the murders of Caesonia and Drusilla and he would no doubt have had Claudius killed too, had he been better at hide and seek. Nonetheless, Chaerea's memory remained popular and the people, Josephus claims, made offerings 'appealing to his ghost to be gracious to them and not to be angry at their ingratitude'.[12]

In general, however, Claudius sought to prove that he was serious about forgiveness. Even Sabinus, one of the primary ringleaders of the plot among the Praetorians, was pardoned and allowed to retain his position as an officer.* There was to be a total amnesty for the Senate: the magistrates were left in office and Claudius intervened personally to prevent the lynching of one of the consuls.[13]

Suetonius records a story which, though likely apocryphal, sums up something of the atmosphere of the early days of Claudius' reign. After Caligula's death, he tells us, 'a huge chest was discovered, filled to the brim with every form of poison. They say that this chest was thrown into the sea by Claudius and that it infected the waters, killing many fish whose corpses the tide cast up along the neighbouring beaches.'[14] The first order of business for both Claudius and Messalina was to suck the poison out of the wound that Caligula's reign had left on the Roman body politic.

Over the months that followed, Claudius treated the Senate with kid gloves, greeting its members with conspicuous respect and consulting it on even the most minor of matters.[15] These demonstrations of deference of course meant little in reality. That Claudius owed his throne to military force rather than to the consent of the Senate was a fact that was impossible to hide. At the same time as Claudius was pointedly petitioning the consuls for the right to hold markets on his private estates, assets were being liquidated to pay the huge bribes he'd promised to his Praetorian supporters. A new coin type was minted that showed Claudius standing outside the gates of the Praetorian Camp shaking hands with an officer.[16] Claudius was walking a lot of fine lines, but his calculated insincerity was beginning to pay off. Within a few months, order had been restored to

---

* Sabinus, however, found it impossible to deal with the guilt of surviving his colleagues and killed himself.

the streets of Rome, the provinces had fallen into line, and the Republican talk of 24 and 25 January was already beginning to look laughably naive.

Claudius courted the public too. A genuine fan of spectacle and keen to prove that he was no dour Tiberius, Claudius filled the calendar with games, plays and chariot races. Although he had declined the honours offered to Messalina by the Senate and insisted that the birth of their son be celebrated only as a private family event, Claudius wasted no opportunity to show off his baby in public. According to Suetonius, 'Even when his son was still a tiny baby, he would carry him in his arms incessantly to show him off before the rallies of soldiers and the people at the games, holding him on his lap or out in front of him and, joined by all the applauding crowds, he would pray for his good fortune.'[17]

The PR programme was effective. Not long after his accession, Claudius was on the road to Ostia when a report was put about in Rome that his convoy had been ambushed and he had been killed. 'The populace fell into a tumult and with ominous curses assailed the soldiers as traitors and the Senate as no better than parricides, not ceasing until first one, then another and finally several men were brought out onto the rostra by the magistrates to confirm that the emperor was safe and approaching the city.'[18]

For all the success of his public policy during these early months, in private Claudius was a mess. The sources speak constantly of his cowardice. 'There was nothing', Suetonius tells us, 'equal to his timidity and mistrust [...] there existed no suspicion, no agent of suspicion, too petty to drive him to be on guard or to seek out vengeance once the slightest anxiety had taken root'.[19] Some of these accusations we can discount as literary hyperbole, but it does appear that Claudius' court began its life in a state of real paranoia. Not only did the emperor shun the Senate, he upped his personal security measures to a draconian degree. He went nowhere without a bodyguard and even his dinners were attended by ranks of heavily armed soldiers.

Petitioners, clients and friends alike were searched, and their possessions were rifled through or even confiscated. Later relaxations of these measures reveal just how severe they had been in the early days of the new reign: 'it was long overdue and then only with some hesitation', Suetonius claims, 'that women and children were spared manhandling and that cases for pens and writing reeds stopped being snatched away from men's scribes and attendants'.[20] As a man carried to power on the back of a clandestine coup, Claudius was ever aware that that which had been given might also be taken away. He was not entirely wrong, of course, but he must have been a nightmare for Messalina to live with.

Behind closed doors the new court sought desperately to settle itself. Two royal weddings and a betrothal were celebrated in quick and quiet succession. Claudius' elder daughter Claudia Antonia was married to Gnaeus Pompeius Magnus; Messalina's infant daughter Claudia Octavia was promised to Lucius Silanus, and his distant relative Appius Silanus was recalled from the governorship of Hispania Tarraconensis and married off to Messalina's mother Domitia Lepida as her third husband.[21] Each of these men had the potential to challenge Claudius' power: Lucius Silanus was a direct descendant of Augustus via his granddaughter Julia the Younger, Appius was one of the most distinguished men in Rome and Pompeius Magnus was heir to the name of Pompey the Great, the illustrious dynast of the civil wars.[*][22] These two marriages and the somewhat premature betrothal of a two-year-old were

---

* Pompeius Magnus was descended from Pompey the Great on his mother's side. On his father's side he was a descendant of Crassus, another Republican dynast who had, along with Pompey and Caesar, formed the First Triumvirate.

evidently attempts to shore up the imperial couple's position; tying these men closer than ever into the imperial family would, it was hoped, align their interests and buy their loyalties. The two weddings were celebrated privately within the imperial palace and neither union was marked with public festivities. The sources do not ascribe either the marriages or the betrothal directly to the machinations of Messalina but, given that one involved her mother, one her step-daughter and one her infant child, it seems likely that the empress had some involvement in the planning of these early dynastic moves.

There was a scramble for positions in Claudius' administration too. The centralisation of power around the figure of the emperor had created a need for new bureaucratic structures designed to put the emperor's will into practice. Republican Rome had never had much call for anything resembling a professional civil service – executive posts were elected and responsibility for delivery was farmed out to private contractors – but the emperor needed to delegate. The office of the emperor had, by Claudius' time, evolved into a vast operation comprising clerks, secretaries, accountants, administrators and advisors.[23] Almost all of these roles would have been filled by members of the euphemistically named 'familia Caesaris': highly educated slaves and ex-slaves of the imperial family who, legally as well as conventionally, owed their masters unflinching loyalty.

Three freedmen in particular emerged as power players during the early days of Claudius' reign: Callistus* took charge of petitions, Pallas headed up the treasury, and Narcissus wangled for himself the position of private secretary to the emperor.[24] These men were immensely powerful; they essentially ran large state departments and, perhaps more importantly still, they enjoyed direct access to the emperor himself.

---

* The same Callistus who was involved in the conspiracy to bring down Caligula.

Indeed, their power was such that the old establishment, however much it might gall them, could not fail to acknowledge it. The tomb of Pallas, which would be erected on one of the main roads out of Rome, commemorated the fact that 'the Senate decreed that he should receive the ornaments of a praetorship and fifteen million sesterces in recognition of his dutiful and loyal service to his patrons'.[25] The aristocratic Pliny the Younger, who came across the monument some forty years after Pallas' death, was horrified; 'this inscription, more than any other,' he wrote bitterly to his friend, 'has reminded me how farcical it is and how absurd an age it is, when such honours might be abandoned to such dirt, such filth; and when that servile scoundrel might dare to refuse to receive them, and all that he might be able to exhibit some great example of moderation'.[26] The money was an honour that Pallas boasted he was too modest to accept, but it is also likely that he had little need of it. A job in the upper echelons of the imperial administration could make a man extremely rich: in his *Natural History* the Elder Pliny recalled seeing thirty large columns of solid onyx decorating Callistus' dining room.[27]

Pliny may not have approved, but it was in the imperial freedmen that Messalina would find her most natural allies. In a society as patriarchal as that of first-century AD Rome, an empress had a lot in common with an ex-slave: both could hold extreme wealth and extreme power, both might command the ear of the emperor, but neither could ever hope to hold power openly and in their own name.

After recovering from the birth of Britannicus, Messalina spent the first few months of her husband's reign developing her connections within this new hierarchy. She would have been given apartments of her own – perhaps situated in Livia's old house or in one of the newer parts of the palace – large enough to accommodate her growing establishment. As empress, Messalina had the freedom to employ a large household of slaves and freed-people, and funerary inscriptions allow us to identify a few by name. A woman called Cleopatra was a needlewoman for the empress, while a man named Amoenus was employed *ab ornamentibus* – to supervise her dress for ceremonial occasions.[28] Hilaria was engaged as a nurse for Octavia, Philocrates as a tutor to one or both of the children.[29] Idaeus was *supra argentum* – in charge of the silver – and men, including one Lucius Valerius, were trained as secretaries and archivists.[30] All were overseen by *dispensatores* or stewards, one of whom we know was called Sabbio.[31] If, as we might imagine, Messalina's household resembled that of Livia, we can add a litany of ladies' maids, hairdressers, doctors, gynaecologists, pharmacists, perfumiers, secretaries, record-keepers, treasurers, footmen, atrium-attendants and cup-bearers.[32]

Messalina's apartments and staff would have afforded her all the space, luxury and comfort she could have desired but, more importantly still, they also afforded her the freedom to entertain independently. The Roman emperor was expected to play the role of host *par excellence* when he was in residence on the Palatine. Vast crowds of petitioners, senators and friends attended his morning receptions; the lucky few were acknowledged, the even luckier invited to dinner.

The empress, it seems, was expected to match her husband's hospitality drink for drink. Livia received political petitioners at her own morning salutations and there is no reason to believe that Messalina did not do the same. It is possible that Claudius expected his wife to take some of the 'women's issues' off his plate, or perhaps to try and convert the wives of some of his senatorial enemies into supporters of the regime: Messalina became close friends, for example, with Arria, the wife of Caecina Paetus, who would fall for his part in Scribonianus' revolt in AD 42.

Although Claudius might have encouraged his wife to develop her connections among the ladies of the aristocracy, the empress' quarters were no segregated harem. The women of the imperial family had always cultivated mixed-sex circles. In the early fifth

century AD, Macrobius – a great collector of old anecdotes –
recorded the following story about the women of the *Domus Augusta*.

> At a gladiatorial game the difference between the
> retinues of Livia and Julia the Elder had caught the
> people's attention, and naturally so – for while Livia was
> surrounded by serious and grave men of substance, Julia
> the Elder was hemmed in on every side by a flock of young
> men unmistakably self-indulgent in their luxury and
> exuberance. Her father cautioned her in writing, observing
> how great the difference between the two First Ladies.
> Julia the Elder, in turn, sent an elegant reply: 'and these
> men will grow old with me too.'[33]

If Livia – with her toga weaving and unsullied reputation
– had been happy to publicly entertain male friends alongside
female, we can be confident that Messalina – whom the sources
never associate either with weaving or with unsullied reputations
– did too.

The circle that Messalina cultivated in her apartments on the
Palatine encompassed a range of characters: aristocratic wives,
politically engaged senators, the privileged and idle, the most
powerful of the freedmen, the richest of the equestrians and
the most fashionable of the wits. Her parties were apparently
unmissable. On one occasion, Dio tells us, a large group of guests
received simultaneous invitations to two parties: one hosted by
Claudius, the other by Messalina and her favourite freedmen.
The empress found her party full; the emperor received a string
of polite but watertight excuses.[34]

Perhaps Messalina's parties simply had better wine and better
music, but the empress' social power was far from frivolous.
However great her influence, as a woman Messalina was still
excluded from the actual processes of administration, justice

and legislation. If she wanted to exert any real power she would have to go through a man, and if she wanted to exert that power *independently* of her husband, she would need to develop a network of other men willing to put her ideas into practice.

We can identify three of the most important members of this network by name. From her accession in AD 41, until just before he arranged for her to be run through with a sword in AD 48, the freedman Narcissus was the empress' most trusted ally at court. As Claudius' wife and private secretary, Messalina and Narcissus had every excuse to be in constant contact. The sources associate the two constantly, particularly during the early years of Claudius' reign, when the empress' position was less independently secure – whenever we find Messalina accused of some conspiracy or some crime during these years, Narcissus is almost always named as her accomplice. Writing after Messalina's fall, Seneca would summarise their relationship thus: they were, he claimed, 'enemies of the state long before they became enemies of one another'.[35]

Together Messalina and Narcissus possessed a dangerous degree of power. The empress' influence over her husband was intense: she had constant access to his presence and his bed and she knew how to use it. The fifty-one-year-old Claudius had always been in thrall to women – he was, Suetonius tells us with a hint of classical surprise, 'unbridled in his passion for the female sex, but totally uninterested in the male' – and to none more so than his pretty young wife.[36] Even in the midst of her fall Messalina was confident that if Claudius could just *see* her all would be forgiven; and her enemies were equally anxious that the execution be completed before Claudius could repair to his bed and all the marital memories it held.

Messalina's influence was on the rise; an alliance with Narcissus might extend it further still. As Claudius' private secretary, Narcissus controlled the emperor's papers and correspondence: dispatches from the provinces, personal appeals, letters of recommendation, minutes of official business, drafts of edicts or speeches, little notes sent over by his senatorial friends. Suetonius paints a dark picture of their *modus operandi*, with Messalina and Narcissus revoking the emperor's grants, rescinding his judgements, and forging, destroying or amending his official memos.[37] But even without resorting to such straightforward corruption, Messalina saw that Narcissus could offer her something priceless: access to *information*. Information about the emperor's personal affairs, the business of the Senate and law courts and the administration of every reach of the empire might now, through Narcissus, come early and directly to the empress.

Messalina had allies in the Senate too; primary among them Lucius Vitellius and Publius Suillius Rufus. These men, eloquent and well connected, acted as agents for Messalina. Defending her interests in the Senate and prosecuting her cases in court, they were her public mouthpieces in those spaces where, because of her gender, she could not speak for herself. When Publius Suillius and Vitellius brought the charges against Valerius Asiaticus (one of the empress' last and most prominent victims) in AD 47, Tacitus wrote that Asiaticus was destroyed by 'feminine fraud and the iniquity of Vitellius' tongue'.[38] In AD 58, a decade after Messalina's death and four years into the reign of Claudius' successor Nero, Publius Suillius found himself hauled up before the courts. He tried to blame everything on Messalina. He had, he said, *just been following orders*. The defence did not fly, but not because anyone doubted that Publius Suillius' actions had been undertaken at Messalina's instigation; instead his prosecutors demanded to know why *he* and not some other man 'had been chosen above all others for the service of that savage whore?'[39] The 'agents of atrocities', it was decided, had to be punished as well as their instigators. The verdict against Publius Suillius and Tacitus' cutting comment on Vitellius encapsulate how the relationship between Messalina and her senatorial allies was perceived – the plans were Messalina's, it was simply responsibility for their execution that fell to her male associates.

These senators needed Messalina as much as she needed them. Their relationships with the empress provided social cachet, information and a channel of communication that connected them directly to the imperial administration and to the emperor himself. So long as she remained ascendant on the Palatine and influential over her husband she could protect them and their families from the vagaries of court politics and senatorial infighting. With so much to offer, Messalina would not have struggled to find senators willing to promote her interests – in fact, they came to her. In his biography of Vitellius' namesake son (emperor for a brief few months in AD 69), Suetonius gives us a taste of the effort the elder Vitellius devoted to courting Messalina. He begged her to allow him to remove her shoes and kept the right one on his person at all time, carried between the folds of his toga, only taking it out, on occasion, to kiss it.⁴⁰ Other senators vied to do her honour too: Dio tells us that a number of the praetors took it upon themselves to arrange public celebrations to mark her birthday, although the day had not been decreed an official holiday.* ⁴¹ That they thought such efforts worth their while attests to the empress' perceived influence on the Palatine, as well, perhaps, as to the popularity she enjoyed on the streets.

The networks of influence and control that she developed among the freedmen and senators were crucial to Messalina's primacy on the Palatine – but also to her survival. Messalina was well aware that her husband's power did not depend upon her in the same way as hers did upon him. Just as there were men at court with the capacity to challenge Claudius' position,

---

* Dio does not specify in which year the empress' birthday was first publicly celebrated, although he discusses it in close proximity to Claudius' refusal to grant Messalina the title Augusta, suggesting it may have occurred relatively early in the reign. From this point on, he says, her birthday was sometimes publicly marked and sometimes not, depending on the preferences of that year's praetors.

there were women who might threaten the new empress. Claudius' second wife Aelia Paetina had almost certainly been divorced to make way for a richer, younger and better-connected replacement; Messalina must have been intensely aware that the same thing might happen to her in her turn. Her husband's refusal to grant her the title of Augusta following the birth of Britannicus – a title which she would have held in perpetuity and in her own right – must have been particularly concerning. It demonstrated not only 'moderation' but also an unwillingness to formalise Messalina's claims to power, to grant her a position independent of her status as 'current wife' and 'mother of the current heir'.* As emperor, Claudius could have any woman he chose and there were undoubtedly women better qualified for the role of empress, more experienced in court politics, richer, better connected, with more Augustan blood coursing through their veins. Messalina recognised that there were only two ways to shore up her position: to render herself utterly indispensable to Claudius, or to eliminate her competition. She appears to have attempted to do both.

One of Claudius' first acts as emperor was to recall a number of political exiles, among them Caligula's sisters Agrippina and Julia Livilla, who had been exiled on the dual charges of adultery and conspiracy in the winter of AD 39/40. Julia Livilla was close in age to Messalina and she was said to be strikingly beautiful. During the early days of Messalina's marriage to Claudius, when Messalina watched Julia Livilla and her sisters seated in the front row of the theatre and beside their brother at banquets, the balance of power between the two had been clear: Julia Livilla was the exalted sister of the emperor, publicly

---

* It is interesting to note that Agrippina, more experienced and more impeccably royal than her predecessor, was granted the title of 'Augusta' soon after her marriage to Claudius following Messalina's fall in AD 48.

honoured and socially powerful; Messalina was the young wife of an impecunious old joke at court. Now the tables had turned. Messalina was ascendant: established on the Palatine, with access to the imperial treasury and the ear of the emperor, she was the natural centre of the social world of the court.

Julia Livilla does not seem to have taken well to her new inferiority. According to Dio, Julia Livilla refused to pay her new empress court, choosing instead to spend as much time as possible alone with Claudius.[42] Dio thinks Messalina was jealous – and well she might have been. Julia Livilla was beautiful and a well-practised player of the social and political game of court life. She had held on to a group of old allies from before her exile and, perhaps most importantly of all, she was a direct descendant of Augustus. Julia Livilla wished to re-establish the position and the prestige that she had lost so abruptly on the Rhine in the winter of AD 39 and it looked like she was planning to do so at Messalina's expense.

The empress' response was swift and brutal. Before the year of her return to Rome was out, Julia Livilla found herself accused of an adulterous affair with Seneca.[43]

The jowly, forty-five-year-old writer, philosopher, and staple of the court social scene, seems, at first glance, an unlikely partner for the twenty-two-year-old imperial beauty. This rules nothing out, of course – some people claim to find intelligence and moral character as attractive as superficial charm and a good jawline – but the tale of adultery was not necessarily founded in fact. Seneca appears to have been a member of Julia Livilla and her sisters' social circle since their time as It-girls under Caligula: the anecdotes of his letters reveal his web of connections among the sisters' friends. In AD 39, Seneca had nearly fallen prey to one of Caligula's attacks of paranoia before an unnamed lady of the court had intervened to secure his safety – this anonymous benefactress likely came from among Julia Livilla's circle; she may even have been Julia Livilla herself.

If Seneca and Julia Livilla had long been close, Messalina would have found it easy to put it about that they had become closer still, especially given that this was not the first time that Julia Livilla's reputation had been called into question. There had been the rumours of incest that had clung to all her siblings and, upon her exile in AD 39, Caligula had accused Julia Livilla and Agrippina not only of treason but also of adultery. It would not have been hard to get rumours of an affair to stick; the groundwork could have been laid before the official charges were brought. The gossip, whether or not it had any foundation in fact, seems to have been widely believed; Seneca continued to be accused of having an affair with Julia Livilla even after Messalina fell and he was recalled from exile.[44]

When Julia Livilla was indicted, the charge of adultery with Seneca was combined with unspecified others – charges of conspiracy, perhaps, or some further sexual deviancy. There was no real trial to speak of – certainly not a fair one – and Julia Livilla was once again banished from Rome. It is likely that she was returned to Pandataria, the island that she had left only a few months before. A narrow rock set far out in the Tyrrhenian Sea, the island was remote and bleak, famously wind-whipped and with space for little more than a villa and its attendant out-buildings. Seneca fell too. To 'corrupt the bedrooms of principes' women' (as a later opponent would put it) was a crime tantamount to treason and Seneca was hauled up before a senatorial jury.[45] His judges promptly sentenced him to death, allowing Claudius the opportunity for a display of clemency in mitigating his punishment to a Corsican exile.[46]

Messalina's part in all this is confirmed both by the fact that Seneca would not be recalled until after her death and by an off-hand remark made by the man himself. In the dedication of Book IV of his *Natural Questions*, Seneca praises his dedicatee Lucilius for remaining loyal to his 'friends' (i.e. to Seneca himself and perhaps to a wider faction of his sympathisers) even in the face of pressure from Messalina and Narcissus.[47] Dio claims that Seneca continued to plead with Messalina from exile, sending her a book filled with praise of her and her freedmen friends so sycophantic that he tried to have it suppressed out of shame upon his return.[48] The direction of his appeals speaks volumes about where Seneca, a consummate insider, felt that influence lay on the Palatine of the early 40s AD.

Seneca would be recalled to court in AD 49, after Messalina's fall and Claudius' remarriage to Julia Livilla's sister Agrippina, but Julia Livilla would not be so lucky. Within a year of her return to the barren island of Pandateria she was dead.

The sources present the whole episode as a catfight – Julia Livilla was popular and hot, and Messalina was jealous – but in reality the conflict was undoubtedly a political one. Claudius' marriage to Agrippina after Messalina's death shows that the new empress was perfectly justified in judging her husband's niece's threats to her own position; Messalina may have seen the removal of Julia Livilla as a necessary act of pre-emptive self-defence.

Messalina was not the only person whom Julia Livilla's renewed prominence threatened. In all our surviving accounts of the intrigue, Claudius is presented as an innocent, if gullible, bystander, played first by Julia Livilla's flirtations and then by Messalina's accusations. Yet the emperor had perhaps just as much reason as his wife to wish himself rid of Julia Livilla.

Julia Livilla's husband Vinicius had been considered as a possible replacement for Caligula during the brief interregnum of the previous year. He was a statesman, it appears, of genuine ability. Tacitus describes his 'gentle temper and well-groomed speech', while Dio praises him for having the political instinct to know when to shut up.[49] He was clearly held in high esteem by his contemporaries too; Velleius Paterculus had dedicated his Roman history to Vinicius in the run-up to his first consulship in AD 30. These personal qualities were admirable, but it was their combination with the illustriousness of his marriage that had made Vinicius a plausible candidate for the principate at the start of AD 41. Vinicius came from an old and dignified country family, but not an imperial one. If, however, his union with Julia Livilla (Augustus' great-granddaughter on her mother's side) produced children they would have the blood of the dynasty's founder in their veins – something that neither Messalina nor even Claudius could claim. The removal of Julia Livilla would go a long way to reducing the risk posed by Vinicius.[50]

Messalina may have been jealous of Julia Livilla; she may have disliked her personally and felt that she threatened her pre-eminence on the Palatine; but she may also, in part, have been acting in the interests of the regime. For all his gentle, slightly bumbling reputation, the new emperor had shown himself remarkably willing to countenance the murder of his peers. In the first seventeen years of the reign of Tiberius there is not one recorded senatorial execution. In Claudius' significantly shorter time on the throne he racked up an impressive 35 senators, and either 300 or – if you'd prefer to give him the benefit of the doubt – 221 equestrians.[*][51] The regime of which Messalina was a part – in which she and her children had what would indeed turn out to be a life-and-death stake – had been born out of intrigue and violence, and relied on intrigue and violence to maintain its stability. Messalina's role in the fall of Julia Livilla and Seneca was not a corruption of Claudian policy, it was a continuation of it. The destruction of Julia Livilla killed, as it were, three birds with one stone: Seneca was well connected, clever and potentially hostile; Julia Livilla's dynastic credentials

---

* Suetonius gives a total of 35 senators and 300 equestrians. The *Apocolocyntosis* (a satire of Claudius' death and deification, historically mis-attributed to Seneca) agrees on the number of senators but when it comes to the number of equestrian victims, the manuscript is damaged. The text appears to read 221 although some scholars reconstruct 321 on the basis, in part, of comparison with the numbers provided by Suetonius.

posed a threat to Britannicus; and Vinicius' combination of talent and imperial connections made him a potential rallying point for senatorial opposition to Claudius' principate.

The removal of Julia Livilla and Seneca went a long way to stabilising Messalina's own position; it protected the regime upon which she and her children were reliant, allowed her to present herself to Claudius as an active and indispensable part of his political programme, and removed Julia Livilla as a potential rival for the position of empress – perhaps before Claudius had even begun to think of her as such.

Although less than a year had elapsed since her husband's accession, the Julia Livilla affair demonstrates that Messalina had already established a court of her own on the Palatine. She had the social connections to sow the rumours of her rival's adultery and the political connections to have official accusations brought before the courts. She had no official position and Claudius had refused her even those honours that the Senate had offered, and yet Messalina had already become powerful enough both to contribute to the survival of the regime and to intervene to ensure her own. The new empress had shown herself to be something of a prodigy at the game of palace politics.

XI

The Triumph of Messalina

'High above the crowd you ride, Caesar, in the chariot of victory,
And as you go, your people applaud you all around
And falling flowers, cast from every side, cover your way'

Ovid, *Tristia*, 4.2.47-50

As part of the precarious tacit agreement that he had reached with the Senate in the months that followed his seizure of power, Claudius had been careful to leave the incumbent consuls in place until the end of their tenures. He waited until 1 January AD 42 (the beginning of the traditional Republican consular term) to assume the office himself. This was his second consulship, his first as emperor.

The new year may have been cause for reflection in the imperial household. Claudius' assumption of the consulship on his own initiative underlined just how far he had come from his situation in AD 14, when he had begged Tiberius for the office and been refused in the most humiliating terms, and even from his position in AD 37, when the longed-for appointment had been granted on the whim of his young nephew Caligula. The contrast may have struck Messalina too: when she had married Claudius fresh out of his first consulship she could hardly have imagined that she would ever see him hold the office again, far less that he would hold it as emperor.

The approach of the anniversary of Caligula's, Caesonia's and Drusilla's executions may also have weighed on Messalina's mind. She and Claudius had maintained their power for a full year. Just how remarkable a feat this was for an emperor brought to power by military coup would be demonstrated some three decades later by the violent succession of four emperors in the single year that followed the coup that ousted Nero. With the birth of Britannicus, her popularity in Rome and in the provinces, and her manoeuvres behind the scenes, Messalina could rightly feel that she had contributed no insignificant amount to the hard-won stability of her husband's position. The dawn of 24 January AD 42 – which brought with it the ghosts of Caesonia and Drusilla – was a timely reminder of the necessity of her work.

That reminder may have seemed less welcome as the year progressed. Sometime in AD 42 a letter reached the imperial palace from the province of Dalmatia, on the eastern shore of the Adriatic. Its author, the governor Camillus Scribonianus, pulled no punches.* Clearly a proponent of the 'if you don't ask you don't get' school of thought, Scribonianus 'not doubting that Claudius could be frightened into submission without the need for war, ordered him, in an abusive, menacing and insolent letter, to cede supreme power and enter upon a private life of leisure'.[1] It was a gamble, if we believe the sources, that almost paid off. A number of prominent senators and equestrians were found to have pledged their support to Scribonianus, and Dio and Suetonius both paint a scene of panic in the palace: Claudius, they report, genuinely considered abdication. The idea was a preposterous one – whatever promises Scribonianus might make, there was no such thing as an ex-emperor; abdication would

---

* Furius was his birthname and the name used by Suetonius but he was officially, by this point, known by the name L. Aruntius Camillus Scribonianus after his adoption by the powerful consul of AD 6.

have meant death for Claudius, and perhaps for Messalina and her children too.

The rebellion was short-lived. Before the end of the revolt's fifth day, Scribonianus' men had deserted him. Dio claims they had no interest in his rhetorical promises of a restored Republic. Suetonius blames 'piety': the troops, he claimed, found their standards ominously difficult to raise and interpreted this as divine disapproval of their betrayal of their oath of loyalty to the emperor. In reality the legions, who can have had no inherent ideological interest in an aristocratic civil war, had probably weighed Scribonianus' chances of winning and rewarding them – and had found them wanting.

Scribonianus fled to the tiny Adriatic island of Issa (now Vis in Croatia) and either fell on his own sword or was assassinated.* The legions that had turned on their commander were rewarded for their (albeit slightly delayed) loyalty to the emperor with the hopeful title 'Claudius' own legions, loyal and trustworthy'. A number of prominent senators and equestrians were identified as supporters of the revolt and executed in Rome – this urban aftermath was messy, and Messalina's alleged part in it will be explored more in the next chapter. Although the immediate danger was stamped out within the week, Scribonianus' actions had revealed the fissures in Claudius' authority: he enjoyed the support of the troops, but he could not count on the respect of their leaders. This realisation may have been a factor in the decision that Claudius made towards the end of the year: he was going to invade the mysterious land to the north of Gaul that the Romans called Britannia.

As an addition to the empire, Britain's value was negligible, but as a weapon of propaganda it was unparalleled. It was Julius

---

* Cassius Dio, 60.15 cites suicide; Tacitus, *Annals*, 12.52 implies that Scribonianus died later, either of illness or by poison.

Caesar who had first set his eyes across the Channel to Britain. He had landed, received the submission of some chieftains, and made notes on local druidic cultures – but he had never *conquered* it. Claudius' fulfilment of these old ambitions would, he hoped, serve to align his own image with that of the great and respected general.

In AD 43, Rome was an empire of seas, the Mediterranean and the Black, bordered by well-charted lands, but they knew that the water between Gaul and Britain was part of something different – an ocean. They didn't know how far the water stretched, or whether the land that they could see was an island or a continent. Somewhere beyond Britain, it was thought, lay a place called 'Thule' – the northernmost land in the world – but it was almost impossible to reach; the sea, it was said, became thick and un-rowable as one approached. All these unknowns only added to the glamour of the project. It had been a long time since the Romans had last really felt themselves explorers. Britain, with its wildness, its 'savagery', its strange priests and unknowable dangers, was perfectly placed to reawaken the old Roman pioneer spirit.

The imperial excuse for invasion, as ever, was that there had been a minor attack on some client king whom Rome had sworn (entirely altruistically) to protect.[2] Preparations were made throughout the winter and spring of AD 42/43, with some 40,000 troops marched out of their provinces and amassed on the northern coast of Gaul. The first crossing was made without Claudius, who may have remained at Rome with Messalina. Only once a firm passage and landing had been established did Claudius himself set out by boat from Ostia to Massilia (modern Marseilles), before travelling by road and river to Bononia (Boulogne), and crossing the Channel with reinforcements sometime in July AD 43.

The emperor arrived – as planned – a little late to the party. His generals had already fought their way up from the south coast to the Thames, flushing out British resistance and bringing the Catuvellauni – the powerful tribe who had become threateningly dominant in the region – into line. Claudius' progress to the Thames was a journey through conquered territory. When he reached the banks of the river, he assumed command of the troops and readied them for the taking of Camulodunum (Colchester) – a stronghold of the Catuvellauni. Dio, reliant on official reports from the front, describes a battle against a massed barbarian force, but it is unclear how much active resistance really remained by the time Claudius approached Camulodunum.

Claudius used his triumphal entry into the captured city as an opportunity to make a display of Roman military might. British chieftains were summoned to look upon the captives and watch parades of tightly ranked soldiers, men from unfamiliar places in unfamiliar armour, led by a contingent of African war elephants. One can only imagine the logistical nightmares involved in shipping these elephants across the English Channel – Claudius was clearly keen to leave an impression. It worked: in all, Claudius received the submission – enforced or 'encouraged' – of eleven kings and queens during what was likely little over two weeks spent on British soil. He then handed the clean-up operation over to his generals and returned to the continent in search of a proper bath and a distinguishable summer.

Messalina's movements in this period are difficult to establish. It is not impossible that she accompanied Claudius along at least part of the route to the edge of the empire. It was not uncommon for imperial women to travel with their husbands on diplomatic or military campaigns: Claudius himself had to contend with continual jibes about his Gallic origins because his mother had given birth to him at his father's winter camp of Lugdunum. We generally trace the travels of these imperial women using the over-excited inscriptions often set up by the provincial towns they passed through – in Messalina's case any such evidence would have been destroyed in the process of *damnatio memoriae* that followed her death.

It seems more likely, however, that Messalina remained behind in Rome, at least until Claudius' victory was assured. The journey north was not a diplomatic tour, where an empress' presence might be useful as a weapon of soft power; this was a mission intended to project an image of military masculinity. Messalina, who does not appear to have been the kind of woman to take pleasure in discomfort, is unlikely to have felt she was missing out. Long-distance travel was arduous and Britain would come to be acknowledged as one of the empire's more notable provincial shitholes. During the reign of Hadrian, after a hundred years of concerted efforts at 'civilisation', the poet Florus could still write: 'I don't want to be a Caesar, no!/To roam among the Britons and to suffer Scythian snows.'[3]

It may also have seemed politically safer for Messalina to remain at home in the capital. Claudius was taking a serious risk leaving the capital so soon after Scribonianus' revolt – and he knew it. As a series of Republican dynasts had discovered to their detriment, the man who held Rome almost invariably held the empire; if unrest blew up while Claudius was away at the front it could deal a fatal blow to his rule. The list of aides that accompanied him on his British campaign reads like a roll-call of the most illustrious senators in the Roman state: Claudius was evidently anxious to keep them out of Rome while he was away. He may also have thought to use the invasion, and the military honours it promised, to put these potential rivals distinctly in his debt. In this context, Messalina's residence at Rome reads as a responsibility as well as a reprieve.

Since the birth of Britannicus, Claudius had been careful to avoid singling out any one man as his second in command. Strangely for what was essentially a monarchy, imperial Rome was not a society particularly wedded to the idea of biological descent. Adoption, nomination, bequests and patronage all had their roles to play alongside blood relationship in the selection of heirs, and a lieutenant given too much power might easily begin to think himself well placed to challenge Britannicus' succession. Still, someone needed to hold the fort while Claudius was away. The two most obvious candidates for the role were Claudius' present and future sons-in-law – Pompeius Magnus, recently married to Claudia Antonia (Claudius' daughter by Aelia Paetina), and Lucius Silanus, still betrothed to Messalina's infant daughter Octavia. Claudius, hyper-vigilant as always, had been careful to keep both men at his side throughout the journey and campaign. When they were eventually dispatched back to Rome it was as the first messengers of Claudius' success, ensuring that their arrival in the city could engender only celebration in the emperor's name.[4]

Instead, Dio claims, Claudius entrusted 'affairs at home' to Messalina's close ally Vitellius, the emperor's colleague in the consulship of AD 43.[5] While Vitellius kept control over the Senate House and the Praetorian Camp, the administration of the imperial court may well have fallen to Messalina. She was popular with the public; she was *au fait* with all the workings of court politics; and her interests were, for the moment at least, perfectly aligned with Claudius'.

However much she might have been enjoying his absence, the news of her husband's success – when it arrived in Rome with Pompeius Magnus and Lucius Silanus – would have been a source of relief for Messalina. Even though she knew her husband would see little active service, the journey alone involved real dangers. A number of imperial princes had died of wounds sustained while riding or on military exercises and here there was a sea crossing to contend with, over ocean waters that were poorly charted and into ports that were unfamiliar; it would be just Claudius' luck to die at the age of fifty-three in some undignified accident on his first ever military campaign.

Were he careless enough to do so, Messalina's situation would be dangerous in the extreme. The line of succession lay wide open: her son was far too young to inherit and yet his existence posed an existential threat to any man who managed to wrest power in the meantime. The tone of Scribonianus' letter, moreover, had made the delicate state of Claudius' credibility painfully clear; a military disaster, or even an anti-climax of the sort Caligula had seen in Germany, might well induce another pretender to throw his hat into the ring.

The announcement of victory in Britain took much of this immediate pressure off the regime. Messalina may have felt secure enough to leave the city and travel northwards to meet her husband at some point on his route back to Italy. Imbued with a new confidence, the imperial party was in no rush and there were festivities at every stop. In Lugdunum, the city of Claudius' birth, the imperial party were likely present for the dedication of monuments to Jupiter and Victory in honour of Claudius' success and safety; at the mouth of the Po they sailed the Adriatic on a boat that Pliny the Elder would later call 'more a palace than a ship'.[6] These galas and amusements were nothing, however, compared to the celebration being prepared for them in Rome.

Whether she had met him en route from the north or at the gates of the city, when Claudius officially re-entered Rome – after an absence of at least six months, of which no more than sixteen days had likely been spent in Britain – Messalina was certainly at his side. Confronted with the news of the success of his campaign in Britain, the Senate had voted Claudius a series of fawning honours.[7] He was granted the honorific name Britannicus – a name that would be used primarily by Messalina's son – and triumphal arches were planned in Rome and at his point of embarkation in Gaul. When these arches were finally completed in AD 51, they would be decorated with statues of the emperor's new wife, Agrippina, but when the projects were announced Messalina would have expected to see them adorned with her own likeness.

The Senate voted honours to Messalina too, and this time they were not refused. She was granted two of Livia's old privileges – the right to sit in a place of honour with the Vestal Virgins in the front row at the theatre, and the right to travel through the city (usually pedestrianised during daylight hours) in a special form of covered carriage called a *carpentum*.[8] Messalina might still be unable to lay claim to the title Augusta, but these honours marked a shift in her position; both were designed to render her more visible, more conspicuous in the eyes of the public, and in allowing her to accept them Claudius signalled a change in policy. Now that his rule was more established, it seemed he was finally willing to begin to acknowledge the power and importance of Messalina's position.

Finally, the Senate voted Claudius a triumph.[9] An ancient form of victory celebration that dated back, the Romans believed, to the triumph of King Romulus himself, this was one of Rome's most storied – and most loaded – traditions. As the Republic had grown older, richer and more cut-throat, the ceremony had swollen exponentially to become a statement *par excellence* of the personal status of the victorious military commander.[10] It was a process of development (or degeneration) that Augustus had all but ended with his celebration of a magnificent triple triumph in 29 BC. From then on (with just one exception), triumphs were to be reserved for the emperor and his heirs – and even these celebrations were to be few and far between.*

---

* The reasons for Augustus' soft repression of the triumph were probably twofold: firstly, he conceived the empire as having reached its fullest reasonable extent and explicitly warned his successors off further wars of expansion; secondly, he was well aware that the triumph was an intrinsically Republican institution and one that had become tightly bound up in the frenzied competition that had characterised the era of the civil wars.

188

Claudius' triumph in AD 44 was the first in twenty-seven years.[11] Many among the (overwhelmingly young) urban population would not have been old enough to remember the last time the rite had been celebrated, by Claudius' own brother Germanicus in AD 17, and the excitement in the city as it waited in anticipation of Claudius' return must have been palpable. Messalina may have been involved in the frenzy of preparation: streets had to be cleared, sacrificial animals chosen, feasts prepared, outfits embroidered, decorations made and hung. The satirist Persius described the role played by Caesonia in preparing for a Caligulan triumph that never came to fruition: 'a laureate letter has been sent by Caesar describing his remarkable defeat of the men of Germany. The cold ashes are swept from the altars and even now Caesonia is arranging arms to decorate the doorposts, now those kingly cloaks, now the "Celtic" war-chariots and blonde wigs for the "captives" and now towering images of the river Rhine'.[12] We might imagine a similar role for Messalina as her husband tarried in Gaul and on the Rhine at the end of AD 43.

Early in the morning on the day of the triumph a vast crowd would have gathered on the Campus Martius, the old military exercise grounds which lay just beyond the sacred boundary of the city known as the pomerium. Claudius was present, with his generals and his soldiers, as was Messalina, with Britannicus and Octavia in tow. Heaped on carts, arranged on floats, or chained in lines were the prisoners and spoils of war. Britain was not generous to her conquerors in this regard – she offered none of the monumental art of Greece or Egypt, and less gold and fewer jewels than might be plundered from the Eastern potentates – but its fair-haired prisoners of war were highly prized and someone, Messalina perhaps, would have arranged for the creation of images of the country's most suitably strange-sounding places. These may have been paintings, or sculptures, or costumed personifications. There might have been depictions of Oceanus too, that great and unknowable god, over whom Claudius could also claim, in some ways, to have triumphed.

The first ceremonial role of the day fell to Messalina. When Livia was young and it was still expected that she would have children with Augustus, a story had been put about that an eagle had dropped a laurel sprig into her lap. The empress had planted this branch in the garden of her villa outside the city, and it was said to have given growth to a whole grove sacred to the imperial family and untouchable to all but its members.[13] It seems to have been the job of the most senior imperial woman – in this case Messalina – to cut branches from this laurel grove to decorate the triumphator's moon-shaped chariot.[14] The triumph over, a portion of those garlands would be carried back to the grove and replanted – the whole cycle handily integrating the tradition of the triumph and the expansionary glory of the imperial project with the fertility of the Julio-Claudian family.

Once Messalina had finished decorating the chariot, and its four horses had been reined, the triumphal procession began its progress across the pomerium and along the sacred way towards the temple of Jupiter Optimus Maximus on the Capitol. Claudius came first, riding the chariot, wearing a laurel wreath and dressed in the traditional *toga pikta* of the triumphator – heavily embroidered with designs of palm fronds, symbolising victory. The emperor was probably joined in the triumphal chariot by his two young children – the four- or five-year-old Octavia and the two- or three-year-old Britannicus.

Directly behind Claudius, in the place of honour usually reserved for the triumphator's heir, rode Messalina. The inclusion of a wife in a triumphal procession was entirely without precedent at Rome. Women had been totally excluded from participation in the old Republican ritual and even under the empire the roles played by imperial wives had thus far been limited to the garlanding of their husband's chariots and the sponsoring of segregated celebratory banquets for women and children.

Now here was Messalina, in pride of place, *before* the generals and the senators and the foreign dignitaries, directly following her husband and her children as they made their way past the cheering crowds, through the streets of their city and up the slopes of the Capitol. She rode in the *carpentum* – the covered carriage she had only just won the right to use – ornately carved and highly decorated for the occasion. Like her husband's chariot, this was a ceremonial vehicle specially granted by senatorial vote on the occasion of a victory: the *carpentum* was, in a sense, Messalina's own *currus triumphalis*, and Claudius' triumph was, in a sense, equally a triumph of her own.

Messalina was now approaching the height of her public prominence. New coins were issued across the empire; one from Anatolia shows a bust of Messalina on one side, her children and step-daughter on the other.[*] It is perhaps to the period following her husband's triumph that we should date the portraits that show Messalina in semi-divine guise: wearing a laurel wreath (also donned by triumphing generals) and the turreted crown associated with the goddesses Cybele or Fortuna-Tyche. These depictions were not intended to be taken literally – Messalina was not being worshipped as a living goddess – but they were intensely flattering.[†] In public,

---

[*] This is a silver didrachm minted between AD 43 and 48 in Caesarea Mazaca, an example of which is now in the British Museum: BM 1893,0804.3.

[†] We cannot date these statues precisely but the addition of divine attributes might suggest that they were commissioned in the years that followed the granting of the empress her first official public honours in AD 43. For a discussion of the iconography and an attribution of the portraits as depictions of Messalina, see Wood, 'Messalina, wife of Claudius: propaganda successes and failures of his reign'.

the empress' popularity appeared ascendent and assured – it all seemed, in fact, to have come easily to her. Behind the doors of the Palatine palace, the reality had been, and would continue to be, much more complex.

XII

Intrigues and Anxieties

'All other men rule their wives; we rule all other men,
and our wives rule us.'

Plutarch, *Life of Marcus Cato*, 8

In his description of her bigamous wedding to Gaius Silius, Tacitus stresses that Messalina was terrified most of all that she would lose her '*potentia*'.[1] The historian picked his words carefully; '*potentia*' carried connotations that were darker and more complex than its English descendant, 'power'. Often contrasted with '*auctoritas*' or 'authority', '*potentia*' meant something closer to the power of force. This was power that went beyond its proper bounds, power that might challenge the state itself. In the account he wrote of his own life, Augustus claimed: 'I stood before all in authority [*auctoritas*], but I had no more power [*potestas*] than the others who were my colleagues in the magistracies.'[2] If *potentia* was a dangerous thing even in the hands of a magistrate, it was certainly not something to be touched by a woman.

Anxieties about Messalina's power pervade the historical narrative of her husband's reign. 'Surrendered to the freedmen and to his wives', Suetonius claims, Claudius 'behaved not as a princeps but as a servant; he bestowed accolades and armies, pardons and punishments, according to *their* interests – no, actually according to their fancies and their lusts. All this he did blindly and for the most part utterly in the dark.'³ Dio agrees – Claudius, more than any emperor before or after, was 'ruled by slaves and women'.⁴ It is this sinister influence that Dio identifies as the cause of every weakness in Claudius' rulership and every cruelty of his reign.

Our sources present Claudius as a man endlessly susceptible to the domination of women. After his father's death he had been raised in a largely female household. His mother had controlled his activities and bullied him for the same physical disabilities that barred him from taking part in boys' games and men's military training. He was addicted to women physically too; to love and sex and wine-drenched sensualities that clouded his mind and tied his tongue until he could not refuse his partner's insinuations or demands. The sources also claim that the emperor was prone to fear and that his paranoia made him pliant; the merest insinuation of danger was enough to render him incapable of rational thought and vulnerable to feminine suggestion.

Messalina, if we believe the sources, exploited every inch of her husband's weakness. She toyed with his love and stoked his fears and – freed by his seemingly endless obliviousness – she planned her political manoeuvres as *she* saw fit. For a woman to hold such unfettered power was a dangerous thing in and of itself; but perhaps more sinisterly still, it was a symptom of a dangerous and unmanly weakness on the part of the emperor.

These anxieties are deep-rooted and they cloud almost every sentence that we read about Messalina's political activities. In our ancient narratives, the empress' every exertion of her power – unchecked and murky in its extra-constitutionality; passionate and irrational in its femininity – is presented as an abuse, and almost every Claudian abuse of power is laid squarely at Messalina's door. Rooted in misogyny and in the narrative demands of ancient history writing, these descriptions require interrogation.

Before Claudius had sailed to Britain, and before she had ridden in his triumph, Messalina was said to have opened AD

42 – her first full year as empress – with an unprecedentedly audacious intrigue. The removal of Julia Livilla and Seneca had been successful, but the Julio-Claudians had been around long enough that accusing an imperial woman of adultery was beginning to look a little trite. Messalina's next project – if we believe the sources – was to be more theatrical.

Her adversary in this instance was Appius Junius Silanus.[5] A distinguished man in his mid-fifties – of old family, long public service, and honoured position at court – Silanus had been married off, just the year before, to Messalina's mother Domitia Lepida as part of Messalina and Claudius' programme of stabilisation. It had not taken long for the step-daughter/ step-father relationship to sour quite spectacularly. Dio claims, dubiously, that Messalina developed a sexual infatuation with her step-father, and when he repulsed her advances the empress naturally began to plot his total destruction.

Silanus was a trickier target than Julia Livilla had been: a woman might be taken down with the merest implication of adultery, but Silanus was well respected and, remarkably, there seem to have hovered around him no pre-existing rumours of misconduct which Messalina might exploit. The empress, aided by Narcissus, would have to think outside the box.

The scripts were written and the parts divvied up: it was Narcissus who was to begin the charade. Before dawn had broken on the appointed day he rushed, headlong and visibly panicked, into the emperor's bedroom. When Claudius – still in bed and trying to shake himself from the hazy edges of sleep – asked him what the matter was, Narcissus, now visibly trembling, told the emperor that he had been racked that night with the most terrible dreams. He claimed to have seen a vision of Silanus stalking the corridors of the palace in the early morning light, approaching Claudius and unleashing a brutal attack on his emperor.

It was now that Messalina – appearing from the corridor to her own apartments or emerging bed-headed from beneath her husband's sheets – cut in. She also looked sincerely shaken. She had seen it too, she said – the same horrible vision had been visited upon her night after night for days now. She had assumed it was just a nightmare and had felt it would be foolish to say anything, but now she heard Narcissus describe her dream word for word she was beginning to feel that it had a new significance, that it might have been less a dream than a *premonition.*

Suddenly there was a noise heard outside the bedroom door, the guards parted, and in walked Silanus. Silanus' 'fortuitous' appearance was, of course, carefully choreographed. Messalina and Narcissus had sent him word the night before, notifying him that the emperor required his presence *first thing* the next morning. To Claudius, however, Silanus' early-morning appearance was proof positive that the visions of the previous night were coming to fruition. Silanus was seized by the guards and put to death immediately, without even the semblance of a trial. 'Thus,' Dio concludes grimly, 'Silanus perished because of a mere vision.'[6]

The emperor appeared before the Senate the following day and recounted the events to a shocked house. He explained that the dreams had constituted premonitions of a real conspiracy, and that Silanus had been arrested in the act of forcing his way into his apartments. Finally, he heaped praise on Narcissus – here was a man who watched for his emperor's safety even in sleep.

This whole episode, as the sources tell it, has a suspect stench of the theatre to it. The first half of the affair, with its erotic motivation and complex deception, verges on the farcical. Our cast of stock characters appears to have walked straight off the stage of a Roman comedy: Claudius, the foolish old man; Narcissus, the cunning slave; Messalina, appearing in the role of the jealous and duplicitous courtesan. The second act plunges unavoidably into tragedy. In the report that Claudius makes to the Senate we even seem to find an echo of the chorus' final chant, sung directly to the audience, in which the events of the play were summarised and moral warnings drawn out.

This is not to say that the story that we find in Suetonius and Dio is entirely fabricated. If, as Suetonius tells us, 'Claudius did not hesitate to lay the whole affair as it happened out openly before a meeting of the Senate the following day', the emperor's account must have been recorded in the senatorial minutes for our sources to read and reference.[7] The essentials of the intrigue are, therefore, probably accurate – Narcissus and Messalina probably did claim to have dreamt of Claudius' destruction, and Silanus definitely was killed – but the construction of the story and the attributions of blame are warped by the anxieties of the age.

The fall of Silanus appears in the sources as the sinister court intrigue *par excellence*. The story begins 'before dawn', under cover of darkness and the action occurs in the privacy of the emperor's bedroom; everything about the setting is designed to emphasise secrecy and conspiracy. The motivation for the affair has its roots in a woman's irrational, uncontrolled passions, her lust and her jealousy. The key players, a woman and an ex-slave, have no right to political power – they have co-opted control from the senators, who are informed of events only after they have occurred. The use of a concocted dream, with all its connotations of the mystic and unexplained, is as far from the logic and transparency of senatorial debate, fair trials, and public oratory as one can get. In the tale of Silanus we find a confluence of every Roman fear about the dark possibilities of court politics.

An awareness of these undercurrents forces us to re-evaluate what we are told of Messalina's motives. Dio's claim that 'Silanus had offended Messalina, the most abandoned and lustful of women, in refusing to lie with her' serves two purposes: it feeds the growing image of Messalina as nymphomaniac and it adds to the image of the whole affair as something intimate and corrupt.[8] The empress may have made a sexual approach to Silanus – we will never know – but his fall was the result of politics rather than passion.

Appius Silanus had been recognised as a threat from the start of Claudius' reign. Silanus came from a dangerously distinguished family and had thus far successfully navigated the pitfalls of a political career: he had been consul in AD 28 and had survived an accusation of *maiestas* connected with the fall of Sejanus in AD 32.[9] Upon his accession, Claudius had wasted no time in removing Silanus from the governorship of Hispania Tarraconensis, which, as the largest of Rome's silver-rich Spanish provinces, looked concerningly like a potential power base. When he arrived back in Rome, Claudius and Messalina had arranged for Silanus to be married to Messalina's mother Domitia Lepida.* At first glance, this was both a compliment and an opportunity; the marriage afforded Silanus a position of honour at court and all-important access to the emperor's inner circle.

In reality, the swiftly arranged wedding was an attempt to neutralise any potential risk Silanus might pose to the new regime. In marrying him to Domitia Lepida, Claudius brought Silanus into the imperial fold but relegated him to the generation above his own. Domitia Lepida – now in her late thirties or early forties – was unlikely to start a new family with Silanus. His position as the emperor's father-in-law also made Silanus look like the illustrious past, rather than the potential future of the principate.

---

* Domitia Lepida's previous husband, Faustus Cornelius Sulla, has not been heard of in the decade since his fraught consulship in AD 31; it is possible that he died, but it is not inconceivable that his step-daughter and her husband arranged for him and Domitia Lepida to divorce in AD 41 in order to clear the way for their plans.

As the year progressed, however, it evidently began to be felt that Silanus' prestige remained dangerous. The dream charade was likely designed as a cover to justify what was essentially a summary execution – allowing it to take place without senatorial oversight and without direct blame attaching to the emperor himself. Whether this charade was planned independently by Messalina and Narcissus in an effort to protect Claudius – and their own positions – or whether the emperor was involved from the very start is unclear. What *is* clear is that this was not an unhinged intrigue based on uncontrolled feminine passion.

The sources were twisting the tale of Silanus in the same way that they had twisted the Messalina vs. Julia Livilla saga of the year before. Clear-sighted – if brutal – political strikes are transformed into personal crimes of desire and jealousy. The sources seem to insist that the power of a woman like Messalina must be sinister, irrational and threatening to the stability of the state. The story of Silanus encapsulates the confluence of a range of deeply rooted imperial anxieties: about the concentration of power on the Palatine, the opacity of court politics, the eclipse of the old senatorial aristocracy and the rise of previously disenfranchised groups, and even about the *nature* of women. It was these anxieties – perhaps more than any single one of her actions – that shaped how Messalina's reign went down in history.

Fears about the empress' power continued to fester as the year wore on. It was not long after the execution of Silanus that Scribonianus mounted his short-lived rebellion. Although the revolt itself was suppressed within the week, its reverberations were felt for some time. A number of prominent men were discovered to have pledged their support for Scribonianus' plot: this was evidence of sedition in the highest ranks and it would have to be rooted out.

Dio claims that Messalina saw the chaos of this crisis as an opportunity to remove her own enemies at court.[10] He describes the empress, Narcissus, and a crack-team of freedmen setting to work immediately, collecting or fabricating evidence to bring accusations of *maiestas*. They employed a network of informers, paid the slaves and freedmen of the accused for information and pressured wives into betraying their husbands. The empress initiated a more drastic 'data collection' campaign too: wealthy equestrians, well-connected plebeians, suspicious-looking foreigners, young aristocrats and old senators alike were rounded up without distinction and questioned under torture.

Once the information had been collected, the cases prepared and the charges brought, the real negotiations began. Those who could afford to – 'some of the most guilty', if we believe Dio – began to collect the capital necessary to make the sort of bribe that might satisfy the empress. For these men, Messalina interceded with the emperor, encouraging him to drop the charges or to mitigate an execution to an exile. Those who were not so lucky or so rich were tried in the Senate, not only before the senators and the emperor but also, extraordinarily, before the Praetorian Prefects and the freedmen.

'Justice' in AD 42 was decidedly bloody. A number of the accused, recognising that the conclusion of the trials was foregone, killed themselves upon receiving the summons. Among them was Vinicianus (a relative of Julia Livilla's husband Vinicius) who had been one of the key movers in the assassination of Caligula. Of those who endured their trials and were convicted, some were granted the opportunity to make their own arrangements for immediate death; others were murdered in prison or executed in public, their bodies thrown down the Gemonian Steps or their severed heads put out on display.

A number of women fell too – led up to the executioner's scaffold, Dio claims, like chained captives. One did not have to be directly implicated in the conspiracy to find oneself at risk: a woman called Cloatilla was hauled up before the court and charged with having arranged for the burial and the last rites of her husband, despite his conviction as a traitor. She escaped only narrowly, with an imperial pardon.

Dio does admit that one of the deaths of AD 42 might have grieved even Messalina.[11] Arria, one of Messalina's most intimate friends, was devoted to her husband Caecina Paetus. He had joined Scribonianus' troops in the Adriatic and when everything had fallen apart he had been arrested and forced on to a ship bound for Rome. Arria had begged to join him, even offering to act as the customary servant allowed to consular prisoners – to serve his meals, arrange his clothes, tie his shoes. When this was refused she had hired a local fishing boat so she could follow in the ship's wake. Back in Rome she attacked those wives who, afraid for their own lives, revealed information to Claudius' inquisition. As her husband's trial wore on, her mood became suicidal. Her friends, growing more worried by the day, tried first to reason with her and then to enforce a strict suicide watch. When Arria realised that they had hidden anything with which she might harm herself she declared, 'there is nothing you can do, for you can make me die painfully but you cannot prevent me from dying', and smashed her head against the wall.[12] When she came to she was satisfied that she had made her point: 'I told you I would find myself a difficult way to die, if you kept me from an easy one.' In the midst of all this drama, her husband Paetus was found guilty by the Senate and offered the opportunity of killing himself. The deal was a good one – it allowed him to avoid the indignity, discomfort and dishonour of an execution – but when the crucial moment came Paetus found himself frozen. Arria pulled the sword from his hand, plunged it into her own breast and said: 'Look Paetus, it doesn't hurt.'[13] Arria went down in the history books as an exemplum of female fortitude and marital fidelity – and it is interesting to find such a paragon of virtue among the empress' inner associates – but for Messalina the drawn-out anguish and eventual suicide of her friend cannot have seemed so edifying.

The fall of one of the empress' close friends in a spate of prosecutions that had allegedly been directed by Messalina herself might give us pause for thought. It is possible that Arria was simply collateral damage, but Dio's account of Messalina's part in the purges of AD 42 is, in general, highly suspect. Although the rebellion never gathered sufficient momentum to pose a serious military threat, Claudius knew that he had got lucky. Scribonianus had managed to attract a number of serious men to his cause, both abroad and in Rome, and the rebellion had confirmed what the imperial couple already knew: that the circumstances of Claudius' accession had left a deep-rooted residue of resentment among their senatorial peers. The executions of AD 42 cannot be dismissed as the result of the empress' personal grudges; they constitute a systematic removal of the most prominent and vociferous enemies of the regime, many of whom may have been genuinely involved in Scribonianus' conspiracy.

Although Messalina – whose fate was, as ever, intimately entwined with that of her husband – may have supported this political purge, its impetus must have come from Claudius. The password that the emperor chose for the Praetorian Guard at the height of the crisis provides an insight into his state of mind. It was a quotation drawn from Homer's *Iliad*: 'revenge on those who struck first'.[14] Nor would Claudius have had need of Messalina's help in the execution of his plans. These were not adultery charges, rooted in court gossip; men like Caecina Paetus had *physically* joined Scribonianus with the clear intention of marching on Rome – they could be prosecuted openly, immediately and confidently. If Messalina was involved at all in the prosecutions of AD 42 it was likely only as an advisor to her husband, or in the use of her social network to collect information. Implausible though it is, it is a remarkable testament to the perceived reach of Messalina's political power that we find such a major regime-level enterprise attributed to her personally.

The following year, AD 43, finds Messalina accused of two far more plausible crimes: the elimination of the Praetorian Prefect Catonius Justus and of the imperial princess Julia Livia (referred to from here on as Julia).

Catonius was a career soldier with years of illustrious service behind him. He had been present in Pannonia when the troops had mutinied against Tiberius in the wake of Augustus' death. A 'first rate centurion', Catonius had remained loyal to his commander and was dispatched as part of a deputation to consult with the emperor in Rome.[15] His loyalty to the imperial family had not wavered over the decades that followed and had finally been rewarded with the command of the Praetorians. His promotion must have been a relatively recent one – he was certainly not in the job at the time of Caligula's assassination.

Dio lays the blame for Catonius' execution in AD 43 squarely at Messalina's feet.[16] The historian claims the prefect discovered evidence of the empress' wild behaviour – her debaucheries, her partying and her infidelities – and was preparing to reveal everything he knew to the emperor; the empress 'put him out of the way' (Dio does not record how) before he could do so.[17] The tale of the honest soldier done away with by the scheming empress, before he can expose her for what she really is, is a tempting one, but ultimately difficult to credit. In AD 43 Messalina was well protected against allegations of adultery; given that a report of infidelity so soon after the birth of Britannicus would have cast doubt on the legitimacy of his heir, Claudius would have been disposed to believe his wife and any accuser could well have found himself in more danger than the accused.

Catonius' fall was probably the result of more routine political tension. The assassination of Caligula had demonstrated just how dangerous to an emperor – and how opportune to his enemies – a hostile Praetorian Camp could be. If Catonius' loyalty was in doubt he would need to be removed; Messalina may have used her contacts to seed the requisite rumours or bring official charges against him. The regime was clearly concerned about the allegiance of the Praetorian leadership in this period: Catonius' colleague in the prefecture, Pollio, would be executed by Claudius the same year or early the next.[18] Both men seem to have been appointed in the immediate aftermath of Caligula's assassination, when the weakness of Claudius' position may have forced him to settle on candidates he knew would be acceptable to the Senate and Praetorian conspirators.[19] By AD 43 the imperial couple may have felt the time had come to bring to the forefront men who were unquestionably 'their own'.

Messalina's personal involvement in the removal of Catonius, and perhaps Pollio too, is also reflected in the identity and behaviour of their successors. The men who replaced them – Lusius Geta and Rufrius Crispinus – were both suspiciously staunch supporters of Messalina's cause. It would be Rufrius Crispinus who was sent to arrest Valerius Asiaticus on Messalina's instigation in AD 47 – and he was rewarded with a massive cash bonus for his loyalty. When Messalina fell a year later, Narcissus felt it necessary to temporarily relieve Lusius Geta of his control of the guard to prevent him intervening. Both men would be removed from their positions within two years of Agrippina's accession; too loyal, it was feared, to the memory of the old empress and the interests of her son.

The same year saw the fall of another imperial princess – in circumstances eerily similar to the Julia Livilla affair of AD 41.[20] Julia, the princess in question, was (like Julia Livilla) Claudius' niece, and although she did not carry Augustan *blood*, she was his great-granddaughter by adoption, courtesy of her paternal grandfather Tiberius.

Fifteen years or so Messalina's senior, Julia had spent more than two decades trying to avoid falling foul of court politics. Her first husband had been her first cousin, Caligula's elder brother Nero Caesar. They had married, while both still young teenagers, to an outpouring of public excitement in AD 20; the marriage appears to have been childless, and when Nero finally fell at the end of the decade, Julia survived.*[21] When her mother, Livilla, was accused of adultery with Sejanus and complicity in the murder of her husband (Julia's father, Drusus) and starved to death the following year, Julia survived that too.

In AD 33 Tiberius arranged for Julia to be remarried. The appropriately named Rubellius Blandus was in his mid-fifties and distinguished in a sensible, modest and entirely unthreatening way.[22] The grandson of an oratory teacher from Tibur (modern Tivoli) – essentially the Roman equivalent of a home county – Rubellius had been the first man in his family to hold the consulship. This was all very impressive and aspirational, but it hardly made the man a match for an imperial princess. The people apparently agreed: Tacitus places the marriage first on his list of the 'dismal events which grieved the citizenry' in a year that also saw the deaths of many illustrious men. The couple were married nonetheless, and Julia may have been shipped off the following year to accompany her new husband during his governorship of Africa.[23]

If Tiberius' intention had been to keep Julia out of the dangers of high politics, then her marriage served its purpose for a decade; she does not reappear in the history books until

---

* Nero Caesar was accused of various crimes in a letter Tiberius wrote to the Senate in AD 29 and exiled. He died in AD 30 or 31 either as the result of starvation or forced suicide.

AD 43. By this time her son Plautus (whose blood was as much imperial as it was uppity gentry) was nearing his tenth birthday. It is also possible that her husband had recently died, leaving her once again on the marriage market.*

Messalina is said to have grown jealous of Julia. It was the same charge that was levelled against her in the case of Julia Livilla and here it probably reflects much the same reality. Julia, like Julia Livilla, was a seasoned player of court politics and Messalina may have been concerned that, if she took a new, more illustrious, husband, Julia might become a source of competition on the Palatine. Like Julia Livilla, Julia boasted an imperial lineage stronger than Messalina's – and this made her son a potential future rival for Britannicus. In AD 43 Plautus was still too young to fend for himself – the removal of his mother now would deprive him of his most powerful proponent on the Palatine before he had the opportunity to embark on a public career. This was, once again, a carefully calculated political murder, committed to protect Messalina's own position and the dynastic future of Britannicus.†

---

* Rubellius Blandus is not mentioned in the discussions of his wife's downfall and indeed has not been heard of since his appointment to a board investigating fire damage in AD 36 (Tacitus, *Annals*, 6.45), although the couple's four probable children suggest that he survived at least a few more years.

† It has been argued that the deaths of Julia and Catonius (who had once served with Julia's father in Germany) were connected and that both may have been involved in a nascent conspiracy against the regime. Although it is always dangerous to form arguments based on *omissions* in the ancient sources, in this case it seems unlikely that, had such a connection been suspected at all, it would not have appeared in our accounts of the events. Julia's mother Livilla had fallen as the result of an alleged alliance with a Praetorian Prefect; if there had been even the slightest whiff of suspicion that the daughter had repeated her mother's mistake the story would surely have been too tempting for ancient commentators to ignore.

We are not told exactly what crime Messalina chose to charge Julia with – only that the charge, when it came, was 'unsupported' – but we can make a well-informed guess that she may have turned once again to that old (ironically) faithful option: adultery.* As a crime that occurred – unless the participants were feeling particularly adventurous – behind closed doors, adultery was notoriously difficult to prove or disprove. Julia appears to have had no pre-existing reputation for Messalina to prey on, and the empress may have been forced to falsify evidence. This was no serious obstacle. The empress had endless powers of patronage at her disposal: she could offer money or position to anyone willing to testify that they had witnessed secret glances, meetings or embraces, or to admit that they delivered love letters on Julia's behalf – perhaps incriminating letters were even produced, in a hand that seemed to match Julia's own. Some of these witnesses may have come from within Julia's own household: a legal loophole instituted by Augustus allowed slaves to testify against their masters and mistresses in cases of adultery.[24]

Julia's alleged paramour was irrelevant. Unlike married men, who might sleep with prostitutes or slaves with impunity, for a married woman, sex with anyone other than her husband constituted adultery. Perhaps Messalina linked Julia to some court wit or rich equestrian; perhaps she added insult to injury by suggesting she'd slept with some low-class plebeian or slave.

Messalina passed the dossier of 'evidence' to her most feared prosecutor – the shamelessly self-serving Publius Suillius – and once the charges had been admitted by a presiding magistrate (perhaps, in this case, one of the consuls, or Claudius himself) Julia received a summons to appear before the Senate for trial.[25] Although the sources agree that Julia was innocent, the

---

* The legal intricacies of the adultery laws will be discussed in the next chapter.

outcome of her trial was forgone and Julia was killed or, more probably, was forced to kill herself.*

Her attack on Julia – a dignified and popular princess, mother to three or four children and now approaching the early years of her middle age – did not win Messalina universal approbation at court. Pomponia Graecina – a woman of distinction who held significant standing at court as the wife of Plautius, Claudius' most trusted general and the man with whom the emperor was just now beginning to plan his invasion of Britain – donned mourning clothes in protest and refused to give them up until her death some forty years later.[26] It was a blatant condemnation of the empress' actions. Tacitus tells us that Pomponia received no punishment, suggesting that she enjoyed enough support among the aristocracy for neither Claudius nor Messalina to think it worth the risk of stirring up a hornet's nest.

The pace of Messalina's political activity appears to have slowed significantly after AD 43. Perhaps the response to Julia's death threw her. That Pomponia Graecina – a well-respected woman but certainly not one who should have been in any position to challenge the empress – had been able to voice so openly her belief that the death of Julia had been a miscarriage of justice was a concerning development, and perhaps a timely reminder that her power as empress was not an impermeable shield against criticism and backlash. Messalina had worked hard to build networks of influence on the Palatine and position herself as an indispensable asset to the Claudian regime; she could not

---

* The sources all agree that the affair ended with Julia dead, but there is some disagreement about the method. Only Tacitus notes specifically that Julia killed herself (Tacitus, *Annals*, 13.43); Cassius Dio, 60.18.4 and Suetonius, *Life of Claudius*, 29.1 tell us she was killed but do not state how. On balance, suicide seems the more likely option. The official punishment for adultery was exile; an execution would likely have been mentioned specifically.

risk losing her status as a leader of court opinion – or, worse still, begin to look like a political liability to her husband.

However, it is also possible that by the time Julia's ashes were being cleared from the pyre, Messalina felt that much of her work was complete. The loyalty of the Praetorian Guard was assured; Silanus, her husband's most immediately viable competitor, was dead; the regime had weathered a rebellion and kept its troops on side; and she had rid herself of the two princesses perhaps best placed to threaten her present supremacy and the future of her son. In playing the strategist, informer, advisor and enforcer, Messalina had not only protected her own interests, she had also rendered herself indispensable to the regime and transformed herself into a political partner that her husband could not, it seemed, afford to lose.

There would be new risks to deal with in the future. There was the couple's son-in-law, Claudia Antonia's husband Pompeius Magnus, who might as he grew older become a credible contender for supremacy. Another 'unresolved problem' might have played on Messalina's mind in the months that followed Julia's death. Just one of Claudius' nieces remained alive: Agrippina the Younger, a direct descendant of Augustus, a sister of Caligula and the mother of a son – then called Lucius Domitius Ahenobarbus, but better known to history as Nero.

It seems inconceivable that Messalina had not identified this last imperial princess as a threat. Any attack on Agrippina may well have been deferred in the wake of the response to the death of Julia, but Messalina might also have felt that she had time to waste. Nero was still only five or six years old and after her recall in AD 41 Agrippina had been safely married off to Passienus Crispus, a caustic wit but a genuine favourite of Claudius and a loyal adherent to the regime.[27] Perhaps most crucially of all, Agrippina may not have physically been *in* Rome for much of the early, volatile period of the new reign. In AD 42 Passienus was appointed proconsul of Asia, one of

Rome's richest and most prestigious provinces (covering an area now in western Turkey), a post from which he would only have returned shortly before the end of AD 43. Agrippina may well have accompanied him – it was, by now, common for the wives of high-ranking officials to accompany their husbands to their provincial postings and there were far worse places to play governor's wife than in the luxurious urbanity of Asia. An inscribed statue base from a temple in Cos honouring her as Passenius' wife may be testament to her travels eastward.[28] Agrippina may, therefore, have missed the diciest years, bookended by the murders of Julia Livilla and Julia, altogether. By the time she returned to Rome with her husband at the end of AD 43, Messalina was comfortably in control of the court; any threat posed by Agrippina no longer seemed so immediate or existential.

Between AD 43 and 47 – when we next find Messalina accused of politically motivated murder – the empress, and the regime, were both in strong positions. There were few people left at court with the resources to challenge the emperor or empress; Claudius' expansionist campaign in Britain had proved his mettle, winning him swathes of support among the populace and soldiery; and, following his triumph, Messalina had finally won public recognition to go with her private power. Although the title of Augusta that had slipped so narrowly through her grasp after the birth of Britannicus still eluded her, senatorial votes had deemed her worthy of symbolic visible honours. During the middle years of the 40s AD, Messalina's position as empress was secure – and she knew it.

The slowing of Messalina's intrigues in the years that followed the fall of Julia blows a serious hole in the picture painted by the ancient sources. If the empress' actions were really driven by her irrepressible and irrational passions – jealousy, lust, greed, pride and desire – it seems unlikely that they could have been brought under such control during the middle years of her reign.

The fluctuation of Messalina's intrigues implies, instead, a cool-headed and sensitively reactive strategy. During those early, febrile years of her husband's reign she worked to remove the most serious threats to herself and to the regime systematically, ruthlessly and, largely, dispassionately. And after the death of Julia, with her most immediate rivals dead and a backlash brewing that looked set to threaten her influence – at the point, in other words, that her activities no longer seemed rational and politically expedient – *she stopped*. The image of Messalina as a slave to her passions is not rooted in the evidence; it is a projection, born of men's fear of female power and fuelled by the rumours that would soon start to swirl about her sex life.

XIII

Political Perversions

'A sin which is pleasurable deserves graver censure
than one which is painful...'

Marcus Aurelius, *Meditations,* 2.10[1]

In the middle of the 40s AD, Messalina's position was more
exalted and more secure than it had ever been. Her two children
were healthy heirs for the principate; she had ridden in her
husband's triumph; her image was blazoned across the empire;
her major rivals (bar, perhaps, Agrippina – but she would have to
wait her turn) were dead or banished; her network of associates
was ascendent on the Palatine. The title of Augusta must have
seemed closer than ever.

And yet by the end of AD 48 Messalina was dead. The reason,
our male historians tell us, was a sort of madness. Adultery, they
say, was a fever that stole over the empress gradually and then
all at once, stripping her of her capacity for rational action and
precipitating an all-consuming cycle of self-destruction, one
that ended in a bigamous marriage and an unparalleled tally of
executions.

When Messalina fell, a string of prominent men fell with her.
Gaius Silius, Titius Proculus, Vettius Valens, Pompeius Urbicus,
Saufeius Trogus, Decrius Calpurnianus, Sulpicius Rufus, Juncus
Vergilianus, Mnester, and Traulus Montanus are named among

those executed.[2] A Helvius, a Cotta and a Fabius may also have been killed in the same efficient batch.* Plautius Lateranus and Suillius Caesoninus were spared.[3] Some of these men were accused of committing adultery with the empress themselves, others may have been accused of aiding her infidelities. Claudius' freedman Polybius, who is also said to have conducted an affair with the empress, was lucky to already be dead.

The list of Messalina's paramours is remarkable in its length – even the notorious Julia the Elder was only ever credited with five named lovers (only one of whom was executed) – but also in its breadth. Vettius Valens was a renowned physician; Sulpicius Rufus ran a training school for gladiators; Juncus Virgilianus was a senator; Decius Calpurnianus headed up the cohorts of night watchmen; Mnester was a pantomime dancer and Gaius Silius was the consul-elect.

The Romans believed that lusts bred new lusts, and the sources would later claim that Messalina had begun to crave not only new lovers but new sexual experiences. Rumours spread that she wanted to flaunt her adulteries openly; then to watch her friends watch their wives sleeping with other men; then to engage in competitions of sexual stamina; then to play at being a prostitute. Finally, it was said, the old thrill of adultery became so mundane to her that *marriage* (albeit a bigamous marriage to her lover Silius) began to look like the last remaining taboo.

In the years that followed Messalina's death, tales of her sexual exploits would metastasise until she had become an abstracted exemplification of feminine desire, and all the fears and fantasies that attended it. In the tenth book of his *Natural History*, Pliny the Elder takes a sharp detour from his systematic categorisation of species of birds: 'There is a fixed time of the year', he observes, 'for the mating of all other animals, but humans – men will

---

* The *Apocolocyntosis* (13) includes Helvius, Cotta and Fabius in a list of victims, the rest of whom fell with Messalina.

take any and every hour of the day and of the night. All other animals can sate themselves on sex; man can almost never get enough.'4 Pliny produces only one piece of evidence to support his hypothesis: Messalina. The empress, he claims with a gleeful horror, sought out the most notorious prostitute in the city and challenged her to a duel. Each had a full day and a full night to sleep with as many men as she could – Messalina won with twenty-five. Pliny comments archly that she considered this a victory well worthy of an empress. Less than three decades after the empress' death, her sex life was already notorious enough to be presented as incontrovertible scientific proof.

Sex lives are hard to study at the best of times. We know so little about what our friends – even sometimes our own lovers – *really* do or desire. These things are harder to study at a distance of over two millennia. They are harder to study still when they have been gossiped about and mythologised, and few sex lives have been as mythologised as Messalina's.

The most outlandish tales told about Messalina's love life – including Pliny's sex competition – should be dismissed out of hand, but the situation is more complex when it comes to claims of more mundane adultery. For all that the accusations of adultery that took down Messalina in AD 48 may (as I will argue) have been politically motivated, it is hard to believe that they were entirely unfounded. The sheer weight of rumour militates against it and besides, there is something in the character of the detail that makes it doubtful. Occasionally Tacitus takes a break from the flow of names of the executed to tell us something about the man or the affair; there is little in these tales of desire, flirtation, rejection and caprice that smells of politics. In fact, the closer we look at the list of Messalina's adulterers, the less feasible it seems that this is simply a poorly camouflaged political proscription list. The young and beautiful Traulus, the nameless equestrians, the dancer Mnester and Sulpicius Rufus, who ran some gladiatorial school, all seem like strange candidates for involvement in a serious Palatine plot. If the set of accusations levelled against Messalina was not constructed purely to destroy the empress and her faction, we have to consider that we may be looking, at least in part, at the remnants of real affairs.

Until 18 BC, adultery had not been considered a criminal offence under Roman law. For more than seven hundred years of Roman history, the conduct of extramarital affairs had been viewed as an issue of private morality, something to be dealt with within the family. These private punishments could be very harsh: the murder of a wife actually caught *in* the act appears, under certain circumstances, to have been deemed an admissible, if frowned upon, response. It was not until the reign of Augustus, however, that Rome began to see the punishment of adultery as the business of the state.

The Romans viewed history as essentially a process of cyclical decline. Their mythology told them that the world had begun in an Age of Gold, which had tarnished into the Ages of Silver, Bronze, and the Heroes, before finally deteriorating into the hard-edged Age of Iron. Men living in the middle of the first century BC believed that they had witnessed a similar cycle of decline in their own lifetimes, and they attributed it to the same driving cause: the decline of the Republic, like the decline of the mythological ages, was blamed on human vice.

When Augustus came to power he promised the people a new Golden Age; a fresh start free from the debaucheries, derelictions of duty, deviancies and dissipations that were believed to have destroyed the Republic. The stability of the Augustan settlement relied in large part on its leader's promise to return Rome to its traditional roots, to the upstanding virtues of the *mos maiorum* or 'the ways of the ancestors'. A programme of sexual reform was central to this value-signalling and, in 18 BC, Augustus passed the *Lex Iulia de Adulteriis Coercendis* ('The Julian law for the restraining of adultery) which promised to enforce old morals with new threats.[5]

The law defined the crime of *adulterium* entirely by reference to the status of the woman involved: in Augustus' Rome 'adultery' meant sex with a respectable married woman.* A husband's playing away was of no consequence at all, provided he picked his partners prudently: a married man might fuck a prostitute, a madam, a convicted adulteress or a slave-girl with total impunity, but an unmarried man who slept with another man's wife was an adulterer. For a married woman, the status of her partner was irrelevant – she was an adulteress either way.

Augustus established a permanent sitting court to hear what he correctly predicted would be a steady stream of cases. Penalties were carefully prescribed for those convicted: the woman was to lose a third of her property and half her dowry; the man half his total property; both were to be sent away for some time to separate islands far from the city; and both were to be subjected to some form of *infamia*.[6] A Roman legal term meaning, in a literal sense, the state of being entirely without a reputation, *infamia* stripped an individual of many of the privileges, markers and duties of citizenship. *Infamia* signalled that its bearer was unworthy of full inclusion in state and society; the stigma, in many cases, must have been unbearable.

Your situation was (of course) worse if you were a woman. In addition to the punishments suffered by her male counterpart, the convicted adulteress could never remarry.†[7] Nor would she be allowed to forget her shame. The adulteress may have been expected (at least in theory – there is little evidence that the

---

* The separate charge of *strupum* that covered sex with an unmarried but respectable woman was designed to punish the debauching of virgins and the seduction of widows.

† At least not legally and to a Roman citizen unless pardoned – as Julia Livilla and Agrippina must have been following their recall from exile in AD 41.

custom was rigorously enforced) to give up the dress and mantle of the matron and don the toga.[8] This radical change in dress made a woman's conviction impossible to hide – her new status as an adulteress and an *infamis* trailed, quite literally, behind her. But it also said something more specific about the nature of her crime. The toga was the quintessential symbol of Roman masculinity – this was the defining dress of the citizen, donned by boys as they came of age, worn by the advocates in court, the senators in the *curia* and the magistrates on the Rostra. On the adulteress the toga was transformed from a symbol of masculine pride to one of feminine shame. The Roman conception of feminine virtue was rooted in the private sphere, but in straying beyond the settled domestic bounds of her marriage the adulteress had rendered herself in some way *public*. She'd lost her role as wife and mother, she'd lost the protection of her home and her family, she'd lost her place in respectable society and, in doing so, she'd also lost something of her femininity.

Augustus was determined to force men to take the crackdown on women's morality seriously, whether they wanted to or not. To this end, he included an extraordinary clause in his law: any man who failed to divorce an adulterous wife was liable to be prosecuted as a pimp.[9] The message was clear. Adultery was no longer a private issue, a crime against one's partner and a thing to be thrashed out between the couple themselves. A married woman's affair was now a crime against the state of Rome itself.

Telling women that their sex was a sin against the political establishment seems to have done little to cool desires or alter behaviour, even within the imperial family. In the last few years of the first century BC rumours began to circulate about Augustus' only daughter Julia the Elder, then unhappily married to the absent Tiberius. At thirty-seven, she was a leader of fashion and a famous wit, displaying a self-confidence that bordered on arrogance as she held court at the centre of a fast set of Roman aristos. She was seen everywhere and was talked about endlessly. Initially Augustus dismissed the rumours as idle gossip but, in 2 BC, it seems that the emperor was presented with incontrovertible proof of his daughter's misbehaviour. His response was swift and brutal. Julia the Elder was banished to the island of Pandateria just off the coast of Italy in the Tyrrhenian Sea. Here her every movement was to be watched and restrained: no wine, no luxuries, and certainly no men.[10]

Augustus – too ashamed to appear in person – sent a long letter of explanation to the Senate laying bare all the tawdry details of her affair.[11] Rumours about her were still being related, with barely disguised relish, more than half a century later. In one of his moral essays (penned after he was recalled from his Messalina-inflicted exile) the philosopher Seneca would claim that Julia the Elder had slept with 'herds of adulterers', led debauched nightly revels through the city that culminated in drinking parties in the Forum Romanum and taken part in orgies with strangers on the very Rostra from which her father had propagated his laws on adulteries.[12] In AD 8, her pregnant daughter – Augustus' granddaughter Julia the Younger – was also accused of adultery and followed her mother into exile.[13]

The Augustan adultery laws brought new risks for imperial women, but they provided new opportunities too. Augustus had transformed affairs, adulteries and accusations from the stuff of gossip into cold, hard political ammunition. As Messalina's early intrigues have shown, adultery *alone* was now enough to end a political career – to ensure the exile of a court lady or a consular.

Accusations of adultery became the weapon of choice for imperial women looking to get rid of their rivals. Two birds – or more if you were feeling adventurous – could be killed with one stone. An adulteress required an adulterer, or two, or three, and, provided the prosecution was successful, all would be exiled. Here, if you played your cards right, was a way to take down a whole faction. Besides, evidence of adultery was so much easier to fabricate than evidence of treason or corruption. Slaves of the accused were allowed to give evidence in adultery trials and could easily be forced to give the correct sort of statements about the messages they carried and the assignations they caught glimpses of. The seeds of an adultery accusation could be sown *by* women – ensconced as they were in the social life and talk of court – against whomever they chose; unlike in most sedition or treason cases, a person need not be a magistrate or in control of an army to be credibly accused of adultery. Augustus, wittingly or not, had created a political tool perfectly suited to the new politics, a politics obsessed with the personal and centred on the dynastic court. From the very start of her reign, Messalina had mastered the art of weaponising the laws surrounding *adulterium*. She used adultery accusations in AD 41 against Julia Livilla and Seneca, and in AD 43 against Julia; and she would return to the same strategy in her campaign against Poppaea Sabina the Elder in AD 47.

Anti-adultery laws could be employed to break the political power of one's rivals, but the consummation of an adulterous affair could also be used to *create* political power for oneself. Sex, for all its dangerous unpredictability, was a powerful tool of alliance, and despite the sources' cries of '*Madness!*' Messalina's first forays into infidelity might well have been pragmatic.

By the mid-forties AD, the strength of Messalina's position was such that she may have reckoned that, if rumours of an affair were to get out, it would, for once, be the male partner who came off worse. Everyone knew that Claudius was desperately in love. The emperor only had to see Messalina at dinner or spend the night in her bed for any quarrel between them to be settled. The ancient writers swear that the emperor knew nothing of his wife's affairs, and they may have been right. Love tends to breed blindness and few at court would have been brave enough to risk their necks relaying rumours of Messalina's infidelities to her husband. There were more pragmatic factors in play, too. Messalina's two children – Claudius' heirs – were still young; the emperor would not be keen to countenance rumours about his wife's fidelity that might encourage people to whisper that his heirs were not his at all.

Confident in her own safety, Messalina may have begun to consider adultery in a new light – not as a potential risk to her position, but as a means of getting what she wanted politically. Illicit affairs offered obvious opportunities for persuasion: Messalina was young and beautiful and men have always done stupid things for sex. Even more importantly, an affair might act as an assurance of loyalty. Once a man had slept with the empress, his fate was tied to hers. Adultery with the emperor's wife was the most serious of crimes; an ex-lover could not launch an attack on Messalina without destroying himself in the process. Her lovers were tied to Messalina by their bonds of sexual intimacy, but also by the secrets that they shared.

Perhaps we see this impetus at work in Messalina's alleged relationship with Polybius. One of Claudius' most powerful freedmen, a sort of literary advisor to the emperor, Polybius was highly learned, incredibly widely read, and a well-received author in his own right.[14] Although his role was not strictly political, the ex-slave's influence at court was immense and notorious: he often appeared walking between the consuls, and once, when an actor spoke the line 'a prosperous whipstock can scarce be endured', the entire crowd of theatre-goers turned to look pointedly at Polybius.[15] He shouted back another quote from the same playwright: 'who once were goatherds now have royal power'. It was an extremely risky response, and the fact that Polybius could make it without consequence demonstrates the extent of the favour he enjoyed with the emperor.

Unfortunately for Messalina, Polybius, with all his power, appears to have proved difficult to win over. He had, in all likelihood, served Claudius for some years, perhaps since they were both young men and his master had looked destined for a life of literature, drinking, history and gambling. Since then, the lives and fortunes of the two men had been inextricably intertwined. Claudius had granted Polybius his freedom; Polybius had watched, perhaps even advised on, Claudius' accession. Polybius may have been well acquainted with Claudius' previous wife – the Aelia Paetina whom he had set aside for Messalina; he may have seen and celebrated the birth of their daughter Claudia Antonia around AD 27; and he may not have taken immediately to his old mistress' younger replacement.*

Claudius evidently valued Polybius' judgement sufficiently highly to allow him a degree of freedom in thought and speech. When Seneca decided to begin canvassing for a return from exile around the years AD 43–44, he turned to Polybius, sending him a sycophantic, self-pitying and decidedly unstoic letter of 'consolation' upon the death of his brother that quickly dissolved into a transparent plea for Polybius to intercede with the emperor on his behalf.[16] It was at Messalina's instigation that Seneca had been exiled in the first place; his decision to appeal to Polybius suggests that he thought him the weakest link in Messalina's control of the Palatine court – the man most likely and most able to stand up to the empress' will.

Perhaps Polybius' independence seemed attractive to Messalina – there were few left on the Palatine willing to question her – and he was certainly a clever and witty conversationalist. But their affair, if Dio's assertion that it occurred is to be believed at all, may have been rooted more in policy than in chemistry.[17] Messalina wanted to bring Polybius on side, and sex may have seemed an expeditious way to do it. It would all end predictably

---

* Polybius had certainly been freed by Claudius himself – Seneca emphasises his total debt to the emperor in the letter of consolation he wrote to the freedman following his brother's death – implying that they had worked closely together for some time before his accession.

badly for Polybius, but the coming rift was some years down the line and for now everything was suffused with the illicit promise of a new affair – Seneca was not recalled and Messalina had a staunch new ally in her husband's inner circle.

Other entries on the list of Messalina's adulterers and accomplices could also have been chosen, at least in part, with political motivations in mind. Gaius Silius was consul-elect when he became Messalina's 'second husband' and he appears alongside a healthy sprinkling of other senatorial names. Decrius Calpurnianus was prefect of the *vigilles*, the paramilitary night-watch; Plautius Lateranus was the nephew of the Plautius whose British victories had won a triumph for Claudius and an unimpeachable position at court for himself and his family; Suillius Caesoninus was the son of the feared Publius Suillius who did so much of Messalina's dirty work in the courts and the Senate.

These men were useful allies, and by drawing them into affairs, or into a dangerously complicit knowledge of them, Messalina could have gained guarantees of loyalty that might just as well have been signed in their blood. In all this – as wrong as it might have been and as illegal as it most certainly was – Messalina displayed none of the sex-crazed madness with which she would come to be so associated.

Still, no one can be rational all the time.

XIV

Adulteresses Have More Fun

'So give me a thousand kisses, then a hundred,
Then a thousand more...'

Catullus V

Just a few years after Augustus passed his anti-adultery
legislation, the poet Ovid published his *Amores*. An original
five books of collected elegies (later edited down to three) were
copied out and bound and sent to friends and read aloud at
salons and dinner parties. He might have called them his *Loves*
– but if they are love letters to anything, Ovid's *Amores* are love
letters to the *game* of adultery.

Come before, before your husband – though I see
There's naught that your arriving first can do.
Yet still I say, come first. And when that he
Presses his place upon the couch and you –
Now with that face of sweetened modesty –
Come in to lie companion at his side,
Reach to touch my foot with yours in secrecy.
Watch me and there is much I will confide
In my nods and in the language of mine eyes;
Catch my concealments and return them bound
Written o'er with your own signals on this wise:

My brows shall speak you words without their sounds,
And you will read the words my fingers write in wine.[1]

This account of the illicit thrill of an affair appears near the start of the first book of the *Amores*. For all that the poet professes to wish his rival dead – 'Your husband will be present with us at the party/I pray this supper be your husband's last' – the husband is the lynchpin in Ovid's games of love. There's no need, after all, to trace your words in wine if your lover is single.

Later, the poet is more up front about what really turns him on.

If you fool feel no jealous urge to guard her
Still stand guard for me that I might want her
What is licit always starts to cloy for me
The banned alone inflames so bitterly.[2]

Ovid, with his versified indiscretions and his charming faithlessness, came at the end of a brief, golden-age flourish of Latin love poetry. Writers such as Propertius, Tibullus, Catullus, and the female poet Sulpicia had built a language of love that relied on secret letters, stolen glances, and the delayed gratification of the locked door. They were young, rich, and bored, beautiful and well versed in the Greek literary canon, with its elegant love ballads, tragedies of ill-fated attraction, and epic tales of the base appetites of the gods. The political world around them was falling apart and reforming itself, but money and luxuries hadn't stopped flowing into the city: the old Roman aristocracy had never been richer or more useless. The reckless sense that one might die tomorrow, which had pervaded the civil war years, was giving way to the ennui of Augustan safety: either, if one squinted hard enough, might look like justification for an affair. These men and women had time and money to spend on sensual pleasures and they were used to excess and to variety. Marriage among the upper classes was largely a socio-economic affair – the loves, lusts and pleasures that they craved were necessarily the stuff of adultery.

Messalina had been married off to Claudius when she was in her late teens and he was around forty-eight. He stuttered and drooled and took Caligula's humiliating jokes with a passive resignation. He can hardly have been her dream man. But whatever she felt about her husband on a personal level, marriage had drawn Messalina right into the whirl of the Caligulan court. This was a world defined by sensuality, by banquets and pleasure barges, emeralds and pearls and foreign perfumes. Caligula was an emperor obsessed with the breaking of boundaries as he tested the limits of his own power: in his bridge over the bay of Naples he blurred the line between fantasy and reality; in his dress he blurred the line between male and female; in his behaviour he blurred the line between man and god. He delighted in the crossing of sexual barriers too, displaying his nude wife to his friends and openly cuckolding his courtiers. To have observed all this so young must have been an overwhelming and formative experience for Messalina.

Things calmed a little after Claudius' accession, but it was a question of scale rather than radical reformation. This was still a court that concerned itself *seriously* with pleasure. Claudius knew, given the unusual circumstances of his accession, that he would have to work harder than most to curry favour with the people, and he embarked upon an unprecedented programme of public shows.[3] There were all the usual crowd pleasers – gladiatorial fights, wild beast hunts, mock battles – alongside more novel offerings; some newly devised, some that Claudius claimed to have found and revived from the archives of the ancients. He gave chariot races in a Circus Maximus which he had adorned with marble railings and gilded turning posts, he imported panthers from northern Africa to be hunted down by mounted squadrons of Praetorian Guards, he brought over horsemen from the northern Greek plains of Thessaly to wrestle wild bulls by the horns. One single spectacle saw the killing of three hundred bears and three hundred Libyan lions. After the British triumph, Claudius built reconstructions of British towns and laid successful siege to them for the urban populace to watch. Messalina, straight off the back of her own starring role in the triumphal procession, would have been there in the front row, visible and glowing.[4]

Some fifty years before, Ovid's *Ars Amatoria* – a satirical poetic guide to the 'Art of Love' (how to find it, how to keep it and, quite literally, how to make it) – had taught its readers to focus their efforts on events like these.[5] The party spirit, the crush of the crowds, music, refreshments, the well-staged performances of the great love stories or the adrenaline of watching men live and die, all of these contributed to the sort of heightened atmosphere that greased the wheels of seduction. Obviously, no man could have approached Messalina as Ovid did his unprotected targets, but the sensual intensity that aided the poet's seductive pursuits would have suffused the imperial seats too – and it may have lingered on the empress' person as she returned with the rest of the court to the Palatine.

These public spectacles would have been followed by private parties. Held in the newer, grander halls of the imperial palace, their guest lists often numbered over six hundred.[6] On these evenings – which in fact occurred almost *every* evening – guests in newly starched togas or diaphanous Chian silks reclined on feather-bedded couches with gilded or inlaid legs. They were served dish after dish in moulded golden bowls, as experts mixed the best wines with the perfect quantities of water, before sending slave boys off to ensure that glasses never ran dry.

A fresco from the Pompeian House of the Golden Bracelet reflects the Roman obsession with landscaped gardens' mixture of nature, art and artificiality.

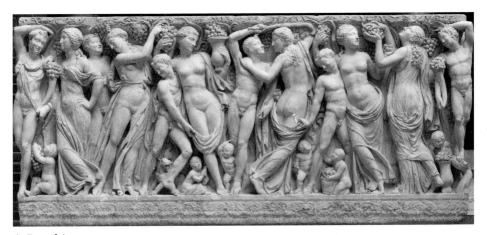

A Bacchic company celebrates the grape harvest on the Farnese sarcophagus. As in Messalina's story, the theme links wine, sex, pleasure and death.

A maenad, hair loose and grasping a leopard's leg, dances ecstatically inside this early fifth-century BC Athenian drinking-cup – suggesting both liberty and danger.

Poppaea shows Nero the severed head of his executed ex-wife Octavia in a fantastically tacky 1876 imagining of imperial cruelty and splendour.

The dank hallway of the Pompeian Lupanar. Juvenal imagines the empress slipping from the palace nightly to work in just this kind of brothel.

Toulouse-Lautrec returned night after night to draw during performances of the opera *Messalina*. In the resulting paintings, the empress is unmistakable in red.

Messalina remains well-dressed and composed while
burning in hell alongside the emperors Tiberius
and Caligula in a c.1415 illuminated manuscript of
Boccaccio.

Part of a series of paintings commissioned to celebrate the marriage of a Venetian nobleman, Francesco Solimena's Messalina becomes a tragic warning against adultery.

The Danish royal painter Nicolai Abildgaard presents a remarkably sympathetic 1798 vision of Messalina: safely dead and mourned by her mother Domitia Lepida.

The Dutch painter Nikolaus Knüpfer re-imagines the raucous wedding party of Messalina and Silius within what looks like a contemporary seventeenth-century brothel.

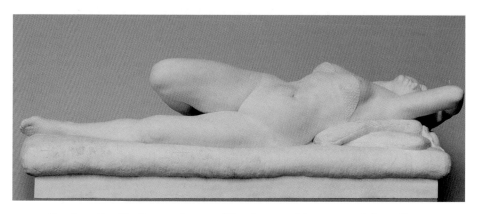

Eugène Cyrille Brunet's over-life-size marble statue, *Messaline*, introduced the empress – who is depicted alone but clearly aroused – to the Paris Salon of 1884.

The marketing team of *The Affairs of Messalina* (1951) had a field day with their tag-lines.

A rococo Messalina, both wig and bodice proving ineffective cover, heads for the brothel in one of Aubrey Beardsley's illustrations of Juvenal's *Satires*.

The French symbolist painter Gustave Moreau presents
a beautiful, statuesque and ultimately unsatisfiable
Messalina – the ultimate fin de siècle femme fatale.

Flames flickered on the golden candelabra, clouds of perfume sat low in the air, and processions of dancers and musicians wended their way between the tables. There could be no better environment for the discreet exchange of looks and the writing of words in wine.

If these were games which Messalina wished to play, she possessed one distinct advantage – her husband's well-known love of the bottle. Claudius had found solace in drink ever since he'd been young and overlooked, and his days had stretched out long and free from any hope of a career. He'd drunk in taverns then, like a pleb, or at home with groups of insalubrious associates, or at banquets in the palace, to dull the humiliation of the continual jokes made at his expense.[7] These were not habits that were easily broken and even after his accession Claudius regularly ended his nights throwing up the contents of his stomach or being carried, unconscious, from his own banqueting hall.[8] Even on his more lucid nights, other distractions lay in wait for the emperor. Claudius' weakness for women was notorious and Messalina was said to keep him supplied with a constant stream of pretty serving girls to temporarily take her place in the marital bed.[9] With hundreds of men to pick from and her husband passed out cold – or fucking someone else – the empress had the means as well as the motive to pursue affairs of her own.

Messalina's flirtations and adulteries – such as they were – probably only began in earnest in the middle of the 40s. Even once it had become expedient under Nero, no one ever succeeded in casting serious aspersions on the paternity of Messalina's children. By this point, the empress had given her husband – middle-aged, physically unappealing and often intoxicated beyond the point of all use – two healthy children as heirs for his dynasty. She had plotted, killed even, to support the stability of the regime and worked to establish her position on the Palatine and in the public consciousness.

After all this effort and stress and success, Messalina was still a woman in her twenties, still young and beautiful. She had hairdressers, ladies' maids, and endless funds to buy the kinds of silks that skimmed her body and precious stones in all the colours that suited her best. Her body was softened by daily steam baths and shaved and massaged with perfumed oils. She possessed her own beauty and she had access to all the sensuality that comes with luxury. Messalina, with her duties and her old husband, may have begun to feel that her own passions had been overlooked for too long.

The Romans believed that the desires felt by women were more powerful than those experienced by men. 'Our gentler passions aren't so full of fury', Ovid warned, 'man's flaming knows a lawful boundary.' One had only to look to the myths – magnifications of every human strength and weakness – with their tales of incest, adultery, bestiality and crimes of passion. 'All these horrors were stirred up by women's lust', the poet would conclude, 'sharper than ours, it bears more of madness.'[10]

These sharp cravings crept up upon the women of Rome just as much as on their mythological sisters. At the very start of his first book of poetry, Catullus sets a scene loaded with double entendre:

Sparrow, my girl's delight, with whom she toys
And holds upon her lap and feeds her finger-tips
And urges ever on to harder bites
Whenever sleek lust for me lingers on her lips.
My love, I cannot know if this kind of play
Is pleasing, but I believe the tender irritation,
Abates the harder heat of love and gives
My girl some short relief from her frustration.[11]

These unsatisfactory distractions could not hold forever and before long the object of Catullus' desires – the married and aristocratic Clodia – was stepping over the threshold of a house that the poet's friend had lent him for their secret meetings.[12] Another poet, Tibullus, imagines his mistress taking even more drastic initiative; tricking her guards and unlocking her husband's door, stealing out of her marital bed and avoiding those floorboards that had tendencies to creak, sending her lover secret signals and fabricating palatable lies, mixing herbal ointments to lighten love bites.[13]

This is female passion imagined by hopeful men but, very occasionally, we hear a Roman woman express her cravings in her own words. The poems of the first-century BC noblewoman Sulpicia, collected among the corpus of Tibullus, are an exceptional survival. Within her lines, we find every inch of the passion expressed by her male counterparts.

> *I burn more than every other, I flame first*
> *But I joy, Cerinthus, in this burning*
> *If within you too there thrives and glows a flame*
> *Kindled off my own flame-fire glaring,*
> *May there be a shared and equal love I pray –*
> *I pray by all our stolen pleasures,*
> *By your eyes and by your soul.*[14]

Sulpicia is careful to specify that her love (at least as she constructs it poetically) is neither chaste nor marital. After all her burning, she writes a new poem in which she thanks Venus for bringing her Cerinthus to her, for placing him *physically* in her arms. She rails against the pressures of convention too. 'My sin pleases', she proclaims, 'and I am sick of wearing masks for reputation: I will declare that we were one, him fitting me as I fit him.'[15]

Sulpicia writes her verses and makes her libations to the goddess and waits for Venus to deliver her beloved to her.

Messalina, accustomed to employing earthier methods to get what she wanted, was not willing to entrust her affairs to divine intervention.

Traulus Montanus was a young man from a good, but not a seriously distinguished, family.[16] His comfortably wealthy equestrian parents might have expected to be able to enjoy Julio-Claudian prosperity without getting themselves entangled in the dangers of its high politics. They had been careful to bring up their son well, with proper manners and old-fashioned values, and their efforts had been successful; Traulus had turned out modest in his behaviour and moderate in his tastes. He had also turned out exceptionally, unluckily, good-looking.

As night fell one evening, Tacitus tells us, Traulus received a sudden summons to meet Messalina at the palace. He went, of course and found himself conveyed directly to her bedroom. They spent the night together and he was dumped before the sun had risen the next morning. Messalina's summary dismissal of his person and performance cannot have been good for Traulus' ego, but that would prove to be the least of his worries: despite his youth and passivity Traulus would be executed with the rest of the empress' lovers. It was a heavy price to pay for a one-night stand.

Messalina's brief affair with Traulus, as Tacitus describes it, is driven unapologetically by lust rather than love. It speaks of an attitude to adultery that was not always so serious as the one reflected either in the fiery passion of Sulpicia or in the puritanism of the Augustan laws. However much the old moralists might have railed against it, there seems to have been a sense in some circles that to be judgemental about a little adultery was terribly *bourgeois*. In his *Amores*, Ovid (obviously *entirely* without agenda) pokes fun at those provincial stick-in-the-muds who valued marital fidelity:

It's just those rustic men who care about a wife's adultery
The boors who never studied how we do it in the city
Of Romulus and Remus, twin founders formed by Mars'
crime
You'd have no precious Rome if Ilia never crossed the
line.[17]

Ovid, it would transpire, had not read the mood entirely right. This was the age of Augustus now, not of Catullus, and the rules of propriety had shifted. He was exiled in AD 8 for, in his own words, 'a poem and a mistake'.[18] The poem was the *Ars Amatoria*; the 'mistake' was most likely adultery, perhaps even with Augustus' granddaughter, Julia the Younger, who was banished in the same year. If Ovid was exiled, in part, on account of the *Ars Amatoria*, the emperor had used the opportunity to display a little humour of his own. In book three, Ovid had breathed a sigh of relief that he lived not in the brutal Caucasus mountains or in unrefined Mysia on the north-western coast of what is now Turkey but in Rome, where the girls knew to keep their armpits smelling fresh and their legs shaved.[19] Now he found himself confined to Tomis, a provincial backwater on the western coast of the Black Sea; Mysia lay tauntingly to the south and the Caucasus rose to his east across the water. Ovid may have overstepped the boundaries, but his crime lay less in his attitudes or actions than it did in his playful, brazen openness.

It was less acceptable now to glamourise infidelity as openly as Ovid had, but that did not mean adultery itself had gone out of fashion. Far from it: fears about the frequency of feminine infidelity were on the rise. Around the turn of the second century AD, Juvenal's stinging satire on the morality of the women of the Roman upper classes, included Messalina – 'the Whore Empress' – as one of its key examples, but there was a litany of others. Eppia, who fled her senatorial husband to follow her gladiatorial lover to Egypt; the rich Caesennia, who flaunted her love letters before her husband's very eyes; Tucia, Apula, Thymele, all lovers of the pantomime dancer Bathyllus.[20]

Besides, the new world of the imperial court was governed by a code of rules that overlapped only partially with the law. Here, where secret intrigues and dynastic planning were the order of the day, sex could never simply be an issue of old-fashioned morality. The absolute power of the emperor had also rendered personal scruples an irrelevance – if the emperor decided he wanted you, there was very little that you could do about it. This was particularly true of Caligula. Some degree of sexual licence was a key aspect of the court culture – sensual, young, unbeholden to the 'ways of the ancestors' – that the young tyrant was trying to create, and for a certain minority of the courtiers who had, like Messalina, come of age under his auspices, adultery may have seemed simply one aspect of an upper-class, cosmopolitan social life.

This certainly appears to have been the attitude of the group that coalesced around the young empress. Cassius Dio accuses Messalina of *forcing* her female friends to prove their promiscuity by sleeping with other men as their husbands watched. It was the men who didn't care at all, Dio claims, whose company she enjoyed.[21] These visions of orgiastic social hazings are far-fetched, but Dio's story perhaps reflects some flicker of the prevailing atmosphere in Messalina's milieu. As this group of young nobles – men and women who'd known each other forever and who had all been paired off in their teens or early twenties to fulfil familial ambition or expectation – fell from one party to another, spent their money, and tried to avoid exile or execution, extramarital flirtations (even if they stopped short of consummation) may have become the order of the day.

Traulus had been a short-lived, light-hearted fancy, but on other occasions it seems Messalina's experience of love involved all the pain and joy of the poets.

Mnester had first emerged as a star of the Roman stage during the reign of Caligula. He was a dancer in the pantomimes, a Greek art form in which a single male dancer danced every role, male or female, transforming physically from character to character, in time to music and a sometimes sung, sometimes spoken narrative. The movement was expressive and balletic, the subject matter was tragedy and myth. There were certainly no shouts of 'he's behind you'.

The pantomime had exploded in popularity under Augustus and its stars developed huge and fevered followings. In AD 15 Tiberius had been forced to intercede after a fight between two groups of fans had ended in the deaths of a number of civilians, soldiers and a centurion.[22] Among his new measures, the emperor banned senators from the homes of pantomime performers and stipulated that equestrians should no longer flock around them when they appeared upon the streets. These laws speak of an anxiety provoked by something other than the rowdiness of the crowds: Tiberius clearly feared that proximity to pantomime dancers might corrupt his aristocracy.

Like the convicted adulteress, the pimp and the prostitute, the professional stage performer was an *infamis*: at best a sort of half-citizen, deemed too unreliable to give testimony in the courts and barred from marriage with the better sort. Roman law held these men in such disdain that one could beat a dancer up, perhaps even kill him, with total impunity if you could prove you had just cause. *Infamia* was a life sentence – no matter how far a performer rose, no matter how much his dress, his house or the invitations that his slaves brought each morning resembled those of his senatorial acquaintances, these were restrictions that would bind him forever.

Yet the stars of the pantomimes still possessed a dangerous, ambiguous glamour. Brought over, generally enslaved (as Mnester had once been), from the Greek East and given romantic stage names, these dancers were transformed into sex symbols. Strong but lithe, they appeared on stage in clinging silks and seemed to be able to move every sinew of their bodies separately; transforming from hero to villain, man to god, even masculine to feminine, all on the turn of a note. They had academic educations and were expected to be familiar with the whole canon of Greek myth and Homeric epic, as well as the historical stories and Latin poetry that inspired the newer librettos; but when they performed they seemed to be the very incarnation of raw emotion. Their movements were smooth, sensual and rhythmic, often suggestively so, but their subjects were exalted: the pantomime dancer transformed something carnal into the stuff of tragedy and myth.[23]

There was something dangerous and romantic in all this ambiguity. In the second century AD, the famed physician Galen was called in by a worried husband to attend to his wife – she couldn't sleep, she'd hardly speak, her pulse was wild and irregular. Galen's diagnosis was clear-cut: the woman was love-sick for Pylades the pantomime dancer.[24] The second century AD writer Lucian of Samosata judged these men to be worse than sirens – sirens only sang, but the pantomime dancer drew his audience into 'a captivity of ear and eye, of body and soul'.[25]

Whatever special quality a pantomime dancer required to captivate his audience, Mnester had it in spades. Caligula had been obsessed with him: the two had allegedly been lovers and the emperor had kissed the dancer openly in the theatre. Anyone caught talking during one of his favourite's performances was dragged from their seat and beaten on the spot.[26] Messalina apparently fell equally hard. Dio specifies cattily that it was Mnester's looks that entranced the empress, but given the intensity and apparent longevity of the affair there must have been something else too.[27] Perhaps it was the quick wit he would later display at Messalina's expense or the easy way he filled his conversation with references to poetry and myth. Perhaps it was the fact that she knew everyone wanted him, that she could see other noblewomen (and men) seething with jealousy over dinner. Perhaps it was the thrilling forbiddenness of it all, she an empress and he an *infamis*. Perhaps it was the way he moved, so easily and so elegantly – and *so unlike* Claudius.

If we believe the sources, to say that Messalina did not play hard to get would be the understatement of the first century AD.[28] At first (Mnester claimed) he resisted her. Attractive though Messalina may have been, cuckolding the ruler of the known world was something of a risk to take for a shag – particularly for an ex-slave who was just trying to get on with his acting career after the assassination of his last imperial lover Caligula. Besides, it wasn't as though Mnester didn't have other options. He had begun an affair with Poppaea Sabina the Elder. She was rich, widely acknowledged as the greatest beauty of her day and castigated for her promiscuity.[29] There seemed little more a man could want – Mnester had no need to entangle himself in the risks and complications of an affair with Messalina.

Still, the empress would not take no for an answer. She tried promises, she tried threats, and eventually she tried the most generally ill-advised of seduction strategies: she turned to her husband.[30] Messalina allegedly complained to Claudius that Mnester was failing to follow her orders, conveniently omitting to specify exactly what those orders had been. Claudius, ever keen to please his wife and doubtless a little confused about why he was being drawn into such a trivial issue, called in Mnester and ordered him to obey his empress' instructions without further question. Mnester, with no option but to obey the emperor, obliged. The story, brilliant though it is, is implausibly farcical; but it does contain a grain of truth – if Messalina wanted Mnester, he had little power to turn her down. Later, when he fell, Mnester would show the scars from the beatings he had received while enslaved and argue that, unlike Messalina's senatorial lovers, he had had little choice in the relationship.[31] It was an argument that almost swayed

Claudius, and Mnester might have survived had Narcissus not intervened.

Her conquest apparently did nothing to dull Messalina's obsession – and this affair at least appears to have lasted some time.* She lavished gifts on her new lover; people accused her of having siphoned off all the Caligulan bronze coins that Claudius had ordered to be re-minted to rid them of the image of the old emperor, and of having them melted down to cast statues of Mnester.[32] In return the empress made ever more voracious demands on the dancer's time. She wanted to be with him every minute and Mnester's attendance at the palace grew increasingly notorious, just as his absence from the stage grew increasingly conspicuous.[33] On one particularly humiliating occasion, Claudius was allegedly forced to publicly state that Mnester was *not* at the palace when he failed to appear at the theatre. On another, Mnester was said to have told crowds that he could not perform because he was detained 'in bed with Orestes'.[34] The allusion was to the mythological son of Clytemnestra and Agamemnon, a member of the doomed house of Atreus, driven mad by the relentless furies after he killed his mother to avenge the murder of his father. Mnester was – in the most highbrow possible way – calling his girlfriend a psycho.

The affair with Mnester appears to have been different from those that had come before it. It had none of the careful secrecy of Messalina's political entanglements, nor any of the easy flippancy of her affair with Traulus. The empress, it seemed, was in love, and therein lay the root of the problem. In her infatuation with Mnester we see the seeds of all those actions

---

* Discussions of Messalina's affair with Mnester appear at two different points in Dio's narrative – 60.22 and 60.28. The events of a number of years are described in between the two passages, suggesting that Messalina and Mnester's affair may have been, or may have been rumoured to be, ongoing for some time.

that would prove so ruinous when it came to her final affair, the one that made the others pale in comparison – her liaison with Silanus. Messalina was not mad, but she may have been too up front about her wishes, too aggressive in her pursuit, too antagonistic to her rivals. She was too overwhelming in her affection, too needy for their attention; she had, quite clearly, not learnt to shrink and repackage her passions in ways that made them more palatable to men. Worst of all, she was too public about her attachments – and that was a contravention not only of the law but also of the *rules*.

It was humiliating for Claudius, who appeared to be the last to know, and it undermined the dignified, almost inhuman, inaccessibility required of an empress who aspired to the title of 'Augusta'. But while the Mnester debacle was embarrassing, Messalina's attachment to an actor and an *infamis* posed no real threat to the stability of the regime, so the rumours simply continued to brew. These were rumours that would, after the empress' death, mutate into talk of 'madness', nymphomania, and twenty-four-hour sex-tournaments; but they would carry no serious consequences for the empress until AD 48, when her affair with Silius would force them to a head.

XV

A Garden to Kill For

'Whole dynasties have been destroyed by the yielding
Of the gods to the wishes of their members'

Juvenal, *Satires*, 10.7–8

In the spring of AD 47 Claudius assumed the censorship. Once the most eminent of the old Republican magistracies, the office had fallen into abeyance with the emergence of the principate. Now Claudius, ever the antiquarian, revived it after a hiatus of some sixty-eight years.[1]

The censor's task was the maintenance of public morality.[*] He held jurisdiction over the lists of citizens, equestrians and senators with the power to place a black mark by the name of any man whose conduct – public *or private* – he felt to be improper. Citizens could be stripped of the right to vote; equestrians and senators could be demoted from their respective orders. At the end of their term, the censors led the whole community in a ritual of purification known as the *lustrum*. This was a celebration of rebirth for the body politic – the dead wood had been cut away, the venom of corruption sucked out of the city.

---

[*] A number of the censor's other original tasks – for example the letting of contracts for public works and the constitution of army ranks – had been rendered entirely obsolete by the powers of the emperor.

For Claudius to take on this role *now*, as Messalina's affair with Mnester raged on, gossiped about from the Palatine to the theatre, was horribly ironic. The emperor did try not to veer too laughably far into the hypocritical. When a man notorious for corruption and adultery appeared before the censor's tribunal, Claudius admonished him only to reduce the number of his indulgences, or at least to be more subtle in his pursuit of them. 'For why should I know,' the emperor shrugged, 'what mistress you have?'[2]

As spring ripened into summer and Claudius continued to work his way down the citizenry rolls, Messalina's passion for Mnester showed no signs of abating. Nor could she quite shake off the anxious jealousies she harboured towards his ex-lover Poppaea Sabina. But she had other concerns on her mind. Earlier that year, or in the year before, Messalina had broken her dry spell when it came to murder. Perhaps she felt that sufficient time had passed since the backlash that followed her attack on Julia; she had re-fortified her networks of support and could now afford to return to the programme of pre-emptively and systematically removing rivals which she had pursued with such efficiency during the early years of her husband's reign. Or perhaps a lack of forward momentum was beginning to play on her mind. A few years had passed since the British triumph and the honours that had accompanied it, and Messalina knew that if you weren't moving forward in the ultra-competitive world of the Palatine court, you could only be falling behind. Claudius' assumption of the censorship was a statement of confidence and intent; it was also the perfect opportunity for the conferring of new honours on an empress – Messalina may have felt that this was a good moment to consolidate her own position.

One individual who had for some time been maturing into a serious concern was Pompeius Magnus. Heir to the name of Pompey the Great, the Republican dynast who had been Caesar's last real rival, Caligula had seen enough threat in the honorific

'Magnus' to ban Pompeius from using it entirely. Claudius, as we have seen, took a different approach, reinstating Pompeius as 'the Great' and marrying him off to Claudia Antonia, the daughter of his previous marriage to Aelia Paetina. This might have made Pompeius loyal to Claudius, but to Messalina it only increased the threat he posed to her own children, both to Britannicus and to the future family of her daughter Octavia, who had been betrothed to Lucius Silanus in the same year that Claudia Antonia had been married to Pompeius. With his old name and his independent connection to the emperor, Pompeius owed Messalina no loyalty at all – he was the weakest link left in the empress' network of dynastic control and he would have to be replaced.

Pompeius Magnus did not prove particularly hard to take down – in this instance there would be no need for the fabrication of dreams. The emperor's son-in-law was stabbed to death while in bed with his male lover.[3] This summary execution was justified on the basis of spurious charges of conspiracy – though whether these were concocted before or after the deed was done is altogether less certain.[4] For his family, Pompeius' death meant ruin – his father (stupid enough, the writer of the *Apocolocyntosis* comments, that he could have been emperor) and his mother were killed or forced to commit suicide – but for Messalina it provided an opportunity to strengthen the ties between her family and the dynasty.[5] Her step-daughter, Claudia Antonia, was remarried immediately to Faustus Sulla Felix, Messalina's half-brother, bringing her, and any children she might have, firmly into the empress' sphere of influence.

Now Messalina turned her mind to another target – one that was altogether more serious, both in risk and reward. Decimus Valerius Asiaticus had been born at Vienne, a wealthy Gallic city near Lyon. It had once been the fortified capital of the tribe of the Allobroges, but now it called itself the *Colonia Iulia Augusta Florentia Vienna* and boasted a temple dedicated to Livia and

Augustus. Asiaticus' family had likely once been Allobrogian kings or chieftains but they had shrewdly elected to work with the Romans so Asiaticus was born a citizen, and a rich one at that. As a young man he'd been sent to Rome to build a public career and transform a prominent provincial name into one known across the empire. It was a task in which he could hardly have been more successful. To his vast landholdings in southern France, he added estates in Italy and Egypt.[6] Popular, proud, bold, clever and athletic, Asiaticus rose to the rank of senator and then, in AD 35, to the consulship – becoming the first man from Gaul to hold the highest office of the state.[7]

By the time of Caligula's accession, Asiaticus was prominent enough both to be counted among the emperor's closest associates and to be in serious danger. Although the emperor did not immediately enter Asiaticus' name on any of his proscription lists, he did begin to make attacks upon his dignity. On one occasion, in the course of a large drinking party, Caligula turned to Asiaticus before the assembled company and loudly criticised his wife's performance in bed.[8] Asiaticus said nothing – after all, what was there to say? – but it was not an affront that he would forget.

Asiaticus had been seated near Caligula in the theatre's imperial box on the day of his assassination and when the news spread it did not take long for fingers to begin to point at the Gallic consul. Asiaticus rose to meet the accusations in the Senate: he hadn't done it, he said, but he wished that he had. It was a bold comment, but that was what the moment required – the world outside the *curia* was in turmoil, it needed a leader. Asiaticus, it seemed, was preparing to throw his hat into the ring.

Once his power had been secured, Claudius made no moves to punish Asiaticus for his comments about Caligula or for the ambitions that they seemed to imply. Instead, he followed his usual policy and drew Asiaticus more closely than ever into the imperial orbit. When the emperor went to Britain, Asiaticus was at his side, and in AD 46 Claudius put him forward to be consul for a second time.[9] It was an extraordinary honour – to reach the consulship once was the apogee of a senatorial career, to hold it twice was exceptionally rare.

During the first half of AD 47, Asiaticus might have felt very blessed indeed. He was fresh off a successful second consulship, with all the privileges and prestige that that entailed. He had just purchased the vast pleasure gardens of Lucullus and begun to subject them to an extravagant programme of restoration. It was even said that he was sleeping with Poppaea Sabina, Mnester's ex-flame and the most renowned beauty in the city.[10] Asiaticus, it seemed, was a very lucky man.

The reasons why Messalina chose to move against Asiaticus now, at the very height of his power, are not entirely clear, but in the summer of AD 47 Asiaticus was arrested on charges of sexual impropriety and treason, convicted before an imperial tribunal and forced to suicide. Tacitus identifies Messalina as the driving force behind the affair and ascribes her two motives, neither one of which is entirely convincing.[11] First, he tells us that the empress attacked Asiaticus because of his connection with Poppaea Sabina. Messalina had long been jealous of Poppaea on account of her beauty and her past with Mnester; now the new rumours that she was committing adultery with Asiaticus offered the perfect opportunity to get rid of her without implicating Mnester in anything. Second, he claims that Messalina was desperate to get her hands on the gardens of Lucullus. The word he uses, *inhians*, or 'gaping', has an inescapably sexual quality.*

The gardens recently purchased by Asiaticus had first been laid out during the 60s and 50s BC by Lucullus, a man famed just as much for his love of luxury and the extravagance of his

---

* The phrase 'gagging for it' perhaps carries a similar sense in modern English.

dinner parties as for his military conquests. The middle of the first century BC had seen an aristocratic craze for the planting of vast private pleasure grounds, ironically known as *horti* or 'vegetable gardens'. In these spaces – vast, green gaps in the urban landscape – nature was blended with artifice. Imported plants were grown in mechanically irrigated ground; whole areas were landscaped to create stepped terraces punctuated by 'wild' crags and caves; caverns and channels were dug out and filled with water to create artificial lakes and streams. Moralists – or those who could not afford to compete – complained that these gardens were dangerous and un-Roman. They co-opted public space in an already overcrowded city, walling off vast plots for no other purpose than private pleasure. They also seemed concerningly Eastern, far too like the verdant 'paradises' planted for the Persian satraps. They were violations of nature, with their hanging terraces and hot-house flowers and man-made caves and rivers – these were corruptions of the perfection of the Italian landscape, alterations that interfered with the *equilibrium* of things.

Lucullus, conscious that he had a reputation to maintain, ensured his gardens were among the most luxurious (and most criticised) in Rome. Sloping down from the summit of the Pincian Hill, they looked out right across the city and down the Tiber towards Ostia.[12] The top of the hill was crowned with a semi-circular court, its walls dotted with statue-filled niches. From here monumental stone staircases descended from terrace to terrace until they reached a man-made lake, generally serene but wide enough for the staging of mock sea battles as after-dinner entertainments.[13] His terraces were planted with trees and topiary, lawns and wildernesses, orchards and banks of flowers chosen so that their blossoming was staggered and the gardens seemed to live all year round.[14] Some plants were selected for their beauty, some, like verbena or saffron, for their smell.[15] Some were native to Italian soil, others were exotic imports – Lucullus had discovered the sour cherry tree during his campaigns in the East and he had been the first to introduce the plant to Italy.[16] Seeds and cuttings were not the only things Lucullus had collected in the course of his victories: the gardens were filled with masterpieces of Greek sculpture in marble and bronze, carefully placed to enhance the landscape around them or to interact with one another in erudite recollections of mythological tales. People who saw the gardens joked that Lucullus was the Persian king Xerxes in a toga.

Asiaticus set to work embellishing these renowned gardens even further – doing so, Tacitus tells us, with *insigni magnificentia*, a 'conspicuous magnificence'.[17] Perhaps he constructed new follies and porticoes and fountains, laid out new walks, added newly collected statues, planted new varieties of trees and new patterns of banked flowers, herbs and hedges, superimposing a new layer of imperial excess over the old Republican one. Writing some fifty years later Plutarch observed, 'even now, when luxury has increased so much, the Gardens of Lucullus are counted among the most costly of the imperial gardens'.[18]

If Asiaticus could be convicted of high treason, he would be executed and his whole property – gardens included – could be confiscated by the state. According to Tacitus, it was a desperate, almost lustful desire to acquire the Gardens of Lucullus – the same gardens where she would meet her violent end – that drove Messalina to make her accusations. Dio agrees: those gardens, he claims, 'more than anything else were the cause of her ruin'.[19]

Jealousy of Poppaea or desire for a garden – neither of these are sufficient explanation for Messalina's actions in AD 47. If Messalina simply wanted Poppaea gone she had no reason to accuse Asiaticus of treason as well as adultery. Besides, even if the rumours of his affair with Poppaea were true, Asiaticus' popularity and position made him a risky co-defendant. Messalina clearly had few scruples when it came to the fabrication of legal evidence and she would likely have found it easier to level her accusations against a 'lover' who was insignificant and innocent than one who was powerful and guilty. Equally, if the empress had simply wanted to possess his gardens, there were easier, more legal, ways to go about it. The financial instability that had blighted the first years of her and Claudius' marriage was long past; in AD 47 Messalina was at the height of her influence and had the weight of the imperial treasury behind her. Asiaticus could surely have been convinced or coerced into abandoning his renovation project and selling up. Although the gardens certainly passed into the empress' possession upon Asiaticus' downfall, they can hardly have been the primary motivation for her attack.

The claim that Messalina killed for a pleasure garden bolstered the narrative that the male writers were building around her. Gardens had always excited something sexual in the Roman imagination. The luxury of a pleasure garden had a taboo indulgence to it; its irrigated verdancy spoke of wet fertility; the smells of its plants, the sights of its walks, the sounds of its fountains and birds carried a heavy sensuality. These were spaces where leisure could easily transform into desire. Tacitus' description of Messalina 'gaping' for a garden fits far too neatly with the image of the empress as an insatiable nymphomaniac, driven purely by the immediate demands of appetite, to be taken at face value.

Messalina herself – when the moment came to move against Asiaticus publicly – would naturally give quite a different justification for her actions.[20] She claimed that Asiaticus was plotting against the throne. Rich enough to bribe the troops, popular in the Senate, and renowned across the empire for his meteoric rise; on paper, Asiaticus had the resources to make a bid for power. Now Messalina alleged that he was planning a visit to the armies of the north. He felt confident, she claimed, that he could convince these legions to support him, particularly as his family owned vast tracts of land around Vienne where the people still remembered the loyalty they owed to their old chieftains. The other tribes of Gaul would support him too: they shared age-old bonds and allegiances with his family and knew, on a more practical level, that there would be advantages to having one of their countrymen on the imperial throne. With the forces of Gaul on his side, Asiaticus would put his case to the armies in Germany. Once they'd been won over by a combination of charisma, threat and promise, he would march on Rome. Asiaticus had openly said he wished he'd killed the emperor Caligula; now it looked like he was hoping to fulfil this old ambition with Claudius.

The real reason for Messalina's attack on Asiaticus probably lay somewhere between these two extremes – on one hand the genuine fear of conspiracy that Messalina claimed herself, and on the other the petty jealousies claimed for her by the sources.

It is unlikely that Asiaticus was really preparing to make a play for power on his own account. For all his success, he remained a New Man from Vienne. He was the first senator in his family, he had no long line of consular ancestors to point to, and he most certainly was not related to Augustus. The empire was not yet used to the regular chopping and changing of dynasties – it had never had an emperor who was not a Julio-Claudian. Besides, if Asiaticus had really been preparing to usurp control of the northern legions, he would have begun by ensuring that he had a network of powerful associates whom he could rely on to support his bid for supremacy back in Rome. But when Asiaticus fell, only two equestrians fell with him; had there actually been a conspiracy under way, it could never have been unravelled with so few casualties.

Although the circumstances of Asiaticus' birth probably precluded him from seeking the principate himself, they did not stop him being a threat. With his wealth, his connections in the north and the senatorial relationships he'd just spent his second year as consul consolidating, Asiaticus held considerable influence, even if he could never have held power. He'd be a powerful ally for any pretender to the principate and, as a man who had publicly avowed his support for the last tyrannicide, would be an obvious port of call during the early sounding-out stages of any nascent conspiracy. If Asiaticus' support for Claudius, Messalina and their children was not rock-solid, then he was a danger.

As AD 47 wore on Messalina may have become increasingly anxious about the possibility of a resurgence of rival camps at court. Sometime between AD 45 and early 47, Agrippina's second husband Passienus Crispus had died.* Crispus had been rich but loyal and now his death had left his widow dangerously wealthy and dangerously unattached. The timing of his demise was so convenient for Agrippina that rumours began to spread that she had had him poisoned. Agrippina, who had been conspicuously absent from the court intrigues of the 40s, now returns to the fray.

The Secular Games were meant to be held once every *saeculum* – a period of either 100 or 110 years, reckoned to be the maximum span of a human life. As a symbol of post-civil war regeneration, Augustus had held them in 17 BC but Claudius, with an academic precision, was resolved to celebrate them again in AD 47; it was only sixty-four years since they had last been held, but it was exactly eight hundred years since the date traditionally held to mark the original foundation of the city. These games were laden with symbolism of fertility, renewal and prosperity, and, interestingly, they had historically been associated with Messalina's family, the *gens Valeria*.[21] The festivities spanned three days and one of the events was a performance known as the Game of Troy – a horseback display performed by young, noble boys. The six-year-old Britannicus took part and so did Agrippina's nine-year-old son Nero. The

---

* Crispus was consul in AD 43 and if his death had occurred in the latter part of AD 47 (where book 11 of Tacitus resumes) or later it would doubtless have been mentioned.

crowd cheered for both boys, but some people thought they heard them cheer just a little louder for Nero.[22] Messalina was rattled – a rumour, albeit propagated most likely by Agrippina, spread that the empress had sent assassins to strangle Nero as he slept. The assassins had fled, the story went, after being spooked by what looked like a snake slithering out from under the child's pillow – when a shed snakeskin was later found in the room, Agrippina had it encased in a gold serpent-shaped bracelet for Nero to wear on his right arm as an amulet of protection.[23]

If Messalina was concerned that a faction might form around Agrippina and Nero or that senatorial conspiracy might flare up again as it had in AD 42, then an Asiaticus whose loyalty was wavering – who might be convinced to throw his considerable weight behind an alternative claimant – was a dangerous man. It was probably these fears that Asiaticus might act as a lightning rod for sedition that finally pushed the empress to show her hand.

As the spring of AD 47 turned to summer and an unhealthy smog of humidity rolled down the seven hills into the forum, anyone who could afford it got well out of Rome. The richest and most fashionable went to Baiae, where villas with terraced gardens and private beaches lined the cliffs around the Bay of Naples. Asiaticus was among them, and Messalina seized the opportunity of his absence to make her move.[24]

The faithful and reliably amoral Publius Suillius was recruited to act as prosecutor, but first Britannicus' tutor Sosibus was sent to sow the seeds of doubt in Claudius' mind. His warning was worded with a friendly concern. Claudius would do well, he said, to 'beware power and wealth hostile to the principate'.[25] The Latin word Tacitus has him use for 'power' – *vis* – is heavy with the threat of physical violence. Next Sosibus enumerated the many advantages Asiaticus enjoyed – his fame in the city and the provinces, his leverage in Gaul, his vast network of connections – and reminded Claudius of the willingness Asiaticus had shown to countenance the murder of another Caesar, Claudius' own nephew Caligula. Finally, he laid before the emperor Asiaticus' 'plan' as Messalina had constructed it: his intention to rally support in Gaul, seize control of the armies of the north and finally march upon Rome itself.

Perhaps Claudius believed the accusations laid before him in full, or perhaps he too felt that Asiaticus' influence was risky and his removal would be expedient – either way the thing had been set in motion. Without waiting for harder evidence, Claudius summoned Crispinus, prefect of the Praetorian Guard, and tasked him with the pursuit and arrest of Asiaticus. The prefect set out from the city at the head of his troops as if there were a rebellion to quell. When he found Asiaticus, in the middle of his summer holiday on the Bay of Naples, he shackled him like a common criminal and dragged him back to Rome.

Asiaticus was not granted the opportunity to account for himself before his peers in the Senate. The trial was held in the emperor's bedroom, before Claudius, his advisors, and Messalina. The hearing began and the charges were brought: treason, incitement to mutiny, adultery with Poppaea Sabina. A final, bonus accusation was added – that Asiaticus took the passive role (an illegal enjoyment for a respectable male citizen) in his sexual affairs with men. Although it was the least serious, the last charge wounded Asiaticus' pride: 'question your sons, Suillius', he shot back, 'they will acknowledge my manhood'.[26] This was a puerile insult to Publius Suillius (whose sons do appear to have had something of a reputation), but it was also an attack on Messalina: one of Publius Suillius' sons was a close friend of the empress who would be indicted among her associates in AD 48.[*]

---

[*] Publius Suillius' son was granted an imperial pardon. Tacitus claims he was actually saved by his 'vices' before hinting once again that his preference was to take the passive part in homosexual affairs. Tacitus, *Annals*, 11.36.

The hearing soon devolved into further farce. Asiaticus claimed not to know any of the witnesses supplied by the prosecution and so one of the soldiers who'd been brought in to testify against Asiaticus was asked to identify the defendant with whom he'd allegedly conspired. He pointed to a random bald man standing nearby – baldness being the only feature of Asiaticus' appearance of which he had been pre-informed. The court erupted into laughter.[27]

Once order had been restored to the courtroom, Asiaticus embarked upon his defence proper. He claimed to have no knowledge or association with the men testifying against him. He spoke exceptionally well – so well that Claudius appeared to be beginning to soften and tears seemed to be coming even to Messalina's eyes. Perhaps the empress was genuinely overcome with emotion, with some guilty mixture of pity and resolve. Perhaps she was scared; if Asiaticus carried the day she would have a now mortal enemy in a more unassailable position than ever before. Either way, Messalina knew that now was not a time for a show of weakness. When the empress left the chamber for a moment, seemingly to wipe away her tears, she drew her old ally Vitellius aside and ordered him to do everything in his power to secure a conviction.

As the hearing adjourned for deliberation, Messalina turned her attention to her second target. Messalina had supplemented the main treason charge against Asiaticus with a charge of adultery with Poppaea. If Asiaticus and Poppaea *were* actually sleeping together, the addition of a real charge would add credence to the fake ones. It also offered the empress an unmissable opportunity to rid herself of an old rival.[28]

A beauty who'd shone at the centre of a particular Roman social scene, Poppaea knew the rules on adultery. She was perfectly aware of how bad things might be about to get. When Messalina sent her men to describe the horrors that awaited her in a prison in the city and then a prison island off the coast, it didn't take long for them to convince Poppaea that her best available option was suicide.

Claudius, it seems, was unaware of this part of the plan. At a palace dinner a few days later he asked Poppaea's husband Scipio why he attended without his wife – Scipio responded simply that she had lived out her fate. Later, when Scipio was required to comment on the affair before the Senate, he replied: 'Since I believe the same as all of you about Poppaea's admission, imagine me to say the same as you do.'[29] Scipio's position was impossible and Tacitus judges his response an 'elegant middle road between marital love and senatorial necessity'.

With Poppaea dead and her memory roundly condemned in the highest arenas of state, the focus turned back from adultery to treason. The speech Asiaticus had made in his own defence hung uncomfortably in the air as the emperor and his advisors met to discuss their verdict. For a moment it looked as though Claudius was being swayed towards an acquittal. Finally Vitellius – Messalina's order still ringing in his ears – spoke up. He had been close to Asiaticus for years – they had both been favourites of Claudius' mother Antonia and, despite everything, Asiaticus' son would one day marry Vitellius' granddaughter. But Vitellius, already up to his neck in Messalina's intrigues and with a known associate on trial for high treason, was in no place to contravene the empress' orders. He cried as he spoke – crocodile tears, or perhaps he regretted every word. He recounted his own friendship with Asiaticus and the man's long history of good service to the state and then, as though it was the best that could possibly be asked for even by the accused's friends, he begged that, rather than suffer the indignity and shame of execution, Asiaticus be allowed to take his own life. Claudius mercifully acquiesced.

Asiaticus' other friends had not deserted him, but now, faced with the desperation of his situation, they urged him to consider self-starvation as his quietest and most painless option. Asiaticus thanked them for their advice but refused – he had no desire for a drawn-out death. Instead, he exercised as usual, bathed, and dined in good spirits, commenting only that he would rather die by some Tiberian plot or Caligulan madness than by the betrayal of Vitellius and the fraud of a woman. When dinner was finished, he inspected the funeral pyre that he'd had built and ordered it moved a little so as not to risk burning some nearby trees. Then he slit his veins and bled to death.

Messalina had got what she wanted – both Poppaea and Asiaticus were dead – but the full cost of her victory was yet to become clear. The popularity, respect and connections that had given Asiaticus influence in life gave him influence in death too. A number of Asiaticus' closest companions had remained by his side to the last. This was a miscarriage of justice that they felt personally.

The reverberations of Asiaticus' fall were felt beyond his close circle of grieving friends. Before AD 47, Messalina had generally restricted herself to attacks on members of the imperial family (Appius Silanus, Julia Livilla, Julia) or men outside the inner circles of the senatorial elite (a relatively early-career Seneca and the equestrian Praetorian Prefect Catonius Justus). But Asiaticus was something different: he had never married into the imperial family – with all the well-known risks that that entailed – and he seemed to have played his senatorial role to perfection – he had been consul for the second time only the year before. Messalina's pre-emptive attack on Asiaticus overstepped all the careful lines she had drawn for herself during those challenging early years of her reign. If it could happen to Asiaticus, every senator now knew that it could happen to him too.

Paranoia grows quickly, it feeds off itself, and it appears the Senate now began to fear the empress. It is perhaps to this period that we should date the development of a rumour that Messalina had had Vinicius poisoned.[30] The irreproachable widower of Julia Livilla had survived his wife's downfall in AD 41 and when he had died of seemingly natural causes five years later he had been granted a state funeral. People now began to whisper that his death had not been natural at all, but that the empress had poisoned him in retaliation for his rejection of her sexual advances or because he suspected her (most likely correctly, but hardly controversially) of having arranged his wife's death in exile. The story is almost certainly unfounded – the motives are unconvincingly recycled and the *modus operandi* is not typical of Messalina – but the development of the rumours reveals an increasing nervousness in senatorial circles. They believed that the empress' actions were growing unpredictable, her methods criminal – what had once been ascribed to the natural work of time was now the nefarious work of Messalina.

More dangerously still, the Asiaticus affair had sown discord within Messalina's own inner circle. It divided her senatorial allies deeply. Publius Suillius clearly had no compunction about his part in the affair, but the tearful Vitellius may have violently resented the role that he had been forced to play in the death of his old friend.[31] When it was Messalina's time to face the music in AD 48, Vitellius would be carefully non-committal in his speech, but he would certainly not leap to defend his long-time ally.

The affair may also have weakened the empress' position with her strongest powerbase of all – the imperial freedmen. Curiously, we find no mention of the otherwise ubiquitous Narcissus in Tacitus' dramatic account of the trial; this seems to be one plot of the empress' in which Narcissus was uninvolved. Perhaps he had felt that the risk was too great. Asiaticus was a powerful man and a persuasive one, too; when his defence had almost carried the day, Messalina had been staring down the barrel of a real crisis. Even now he was dead the whole mess was still causing controversy. And for what? The removal of a man who could never have held enough power to challenge the throne? If Narcissus felt that Messalina's judgement of risk was slipping – that she was losing sight of the boundaries of what she could get away with – then he must have felt himself in danger. He was up to his neck in the empress' schemes; he could not countenance her turning into a loose cannon.

XVI

Re-Reading an Ending

'I am not unaware that it will seem like fiction...'

Tacitus, *Annals*, 11.27

The Asiaticus affair had bothered the Senate. So much so in fact that they decided, for the first time in some time, that something really must be done. The senators were in no position to attack the empress directly, but they could attack her agents among their own order.

There was an old law, the *lex cincia*, that prohibited advocates from accepting payment in fees or gifts in return for pleading their cases.[1] The stipulation harked back to a time when the aristocracy had been expected to advocate on behalf of their friends and clients purely in pursuit of honour and out of a sense of communal duty: the law, which had been passed in 204 BC, had been long in abeyance.

Still, the *lex cincia* remained on the statute books and the actions of Publius Suillius, the most prominent of Messalina's pet-prosecutors, were certainly in contravention of it. Only recently a leading equestrian by the name of Samius had stabbed himself to death in Publius Suillius' atrium. He had paid a ruinous 400,000 sesterce fee for Publius Suillius' service as an advocate before discovering that he was colluding with the prosecution.[2] Now Gaius Silius – a glamorous young aristocrat, an avowed

255

enemy of Publius Suillius, and an ambitious rising star on the political scene – proposed that the *lex cincia* be enforced.

Publius Suillius and his associates tried to shout the proposal down but Silius stood firm.[3] He reminded them of the exempla set by those famous Republican orators who had asked for only honour and lasting fame in return for their labour. What had once been the best and most beautiful of the liberal arts was, he said, being soiled by the sleaze of its representatives. He had more practical arguments too: if there was no profit to be had, prosecutions would be fewer. As things stood, 'enmities, accusations, hatreds, and old injuries were fostered that the foul putrefaction of the forum might bring profit to the advocates, in just the same way that the spread and violence of disease brought profit to physicians'.[4]

Opinion was on Silius' side and the house began to prepare a motion to bring the most corrupt advocates to trial under the laws governing extortion. Publius Suillius and those senators who had pursued similar strategies began to panic. Their guilt was so obvious and well-evidenced, Tacitus tells us, that they felt that it was not their trial, but rather their *punishment* that was being arranged. Desperate, they appealed directly to the emperor.

The arguments they chose were pragmatic. During the earlier years of the Republic it had been easy to maintain the life of a senator on the proceeds of an estate; as the empire grew and the civil wars raged, there had been vast fortunes to be made on the battlefield. The situation was different now and senators needed to make a living. The practice of advocacy took time, time that might otherwise be consumed with attention to more profitable affairs. If every potential reward of the profession were removed, the profession itself would wither; good advocates would be hard to come by and men would be left to defend themselves against miscarriages of justice and the whims of the powerful. No mention was made, of course, of the fact that Publius Suillius and others like him more often gained from giving voice to those whims than from protecting people against them. The emperor, Tacitus tells us, found these arguments less noble than those advanced by Silius, but not without their truth. Perhaps he also had an eye to the services that Publius Suillius, in particular, had rendered to him and Messalina. Claudius alighted on a compromise: advocates could accept fees up to the value of 10,000 sesterces; anything more and they would be liable to charges of extortion.

Perhaps it was Silius' open attack on her closest senatorial ally that first brought the young man to the serious attention of the empress. Regardless of the circumstances, she evidently liked what she found. Silius was clever, with a fluent eloquence that he was unafraid to turn against those more powerful than himself – even against agents of the empress. He had an innate aristocratic self-assurance; the kind that the oft-bullied Claudius, despite his high birth and his highest of positions, would never truly possess. It helped that he was wildly good-looking – more handsome, Tacitus claims, than any other young man in Rome.[5]

By the end of the summer, Messalina's affair with Mnester appears to have been cooling off. Perhaps Messalina's murder of Mnester's ex, Poppaea, had created a tension in the relationship; or perhaps, ironically, the empress found herself bored in the absence of a worthy love-rival. Maybe Mnester was simply eclipsed as Silius began to occupy Messalina's thoughts. Whatever the reason, there was a space in the empress' bed, and she was determined it would be filled by Silius.

Messalina's decision to embark upon an affair with Silius may, at its outset, have been a partially pragmatic one. With his impeccable pedigree, natural leadership and talent for speaking, Silius was a rising political star; one of the consulships of AD 48 had already been set aside for him to assume once he reached the requisite age. He'd shown himself willing to attack Publius Suillius – the most powerful and dangerous of all Messalina's allies – and he'd almost succeeded: left to his own devices he might mature into a dangerous enemy. If Messalina's relationship with Silius began as part of a plan to keep her enemies close – to bind him to her interests through an adultery that functioned as political collateral – it would not be long before it mutated into something far less sober. Something more akin to an obsession.

Using a phrase that evokes every simmering Roman anxiety about female sexuality, Tacitus tells us that Messalina now 'burnt' with a passion that was 'new and verging on madness'.[6] The empress had been indiscreet with Mnester, but she was worse by far with Silius. Messalina was always at his house, and she never arrived alone and in secret – instead, she trailed a perpetual retinue of friends and companions in her wake. She clung to Silius constantly in public too, whenever and wherever he went out. The word Tacitus uses – *adhaerescere* – means, quite literally, to be stuck fast.[7] She lavished wealth, honours and political resources on Silius; she had done the same with Mnester and his statues, but there was more that one could bestow upon a consul-to-be than on an actor. When she was done, Tacitus tells us, 'the slaves, and the freedmen and even the furnishings of the emperor were on show in the house of the adulterer'.[8] It was as if 'the fortunes of the emperor had already been transferred to another'.[9]

Much had been added to Silius' house, now all that was left was for one thing to be removed: Messalina saw to it that her lover divorced his wife, Junia Silana, a noblewoman of impeccable lineage and a very close friend of Agrippina.[10] Silana was swiftly 'evicted from her marriage bed', as Tacitus puts it, so that the empress might have Silius wholly and perfectly to herself.[11] Messalina had now broken all the rules of polite adultery – not only had she humiliated her husband but she had destroyed another aristocratic marriage in the process.

Of course, Silius' part in his divorce from Junia Silana may have been more proactive than Tacitus is willing to admit. Tacitus tells us that Silius was well aware of the peril of his position and the extent of the outrage he was committing against the emperor; but to refuse Messalina would have marked him out as a potential threat and to accept her might reap him rewards of the most serious political kind. Besides, there were more immediate perks to a relationship with Messalina, of the sort that required savouring – Silius, Tacitus tells us, 'consoled himself by shutting out thoughts of the future and enjoying the pleasures of the present'.[12]

Messalina's passion for Silius left her very exposed – in theory at least. The brazenness with which she revelled in the joy of this new love affair perhaps reflects less 'feminine madness' than a certain degree of 'masculine arrogance'. What Messalina was doing was a crime and her victim was the most powerful man in the world: in conducting the affair so openly she was potentially handing her enemies a weapon with which to bring about her destruction. The only thing standing between her and that destruction was the bold bet that to bring an accusation against her – even one that was irrefutable – was simply too great a risk for anyone to take. Messalina was relying on the unassailability of her own position – her position in Claudius' affections and her position at the head of a network of powerful allies.

It was a risk that the empress – in love and confident of her own power after nearly seven years on the throne – clearly felt was worth taking. Her allies among her husband's freedmen, Narcissus and Polybius in particular, may have felt differently. The reckless intensity of Messalina's affair was romantic, but it brought no benefits to the freedmen; indeed, for Polybius, who had allegedly once occupied the empress' bed himself, the whole thing may have been trying to watch. Nevertheless, the *downside* of the empress' affair was potentially just as great for the freedmen as it was for Messalina. Accusing the empress of adultery, particularly in the light of Claudius' continued infatuation with her, would be a dangerous undertaking: if someone – a senatorial friend of Asiaticus' perhaps – *did* decide to do so, they would be unlikely to accuse her of adultery alone. Any potential prosecutor would almost certainly also bring other charges too; charges like conspiracy or corruption, designed to scare Claudius into taking rumours of his wife's infidelities seriously. These were charges in which Messalina's long-time allies among the freedmen might easily be implicated. If Messalina's destruction was instigated by her enemies in the Senate or the imperial family, there was little chance that her favourite freedmen – Narcissus primary among them – would survive unscathed.

The risk only seemed to be worsening as the ranks of allies, upon whose protection Messalina relied, began to thin. Her attack on Asiaticus had alienated much of the Senate – including, perhaps, her old favourite Vitellius. Now relations with the prosecutor Publius Suillius, her other great senatorial ally, may also have been souring. He had had no compunction about aiding the empress in her destruction of Asiaticus, but Messalina's new affair was a different matter entirely. Her new lover Silius was his sworn enemy; the younger man had attacked him openly in the Senate, even tried to have him hauled up before a court on humiliating and ruinous charges of corruption. Indeed, Tacitus hints that the two men may also have had some personal enmity, one that had existed long before Silius gave it a political face in the Senate. As the affair between Messalina and Silius grew increasingly serious, Publius Suillius may have begun to feel not only betrayed, but also nervous. His greatest enemy had, in the space of a few short months, become the most important man in the life of the woman who had previously been his greatest ally. The ties of loyalty that bound Messalina and Publius Suillius, like those that had bound her and Vitellius, were loosening.

Before the end of AD 47, or perhaps in the early months of 48, Messalina would make one more major mistake. She killed Polybius.[13] Dio gives us precious few details of how she brought this about, telling us only that she did it her usual way – with a false accusation. We don't know what she had Polybius, allegedly her one-time lover, charged with; nor do we know what precipitated the rupture in their relationship. In the context of the messy winter of AD 47/48 it is possible that he raised questions about her judgement – about Asiaticus perhaps, or the affair with Silius. The empress may have sensed a dangerous shiver of personal jealousy.

Whatever her reasons, the empress' murder of Polybius was a serious error. The imperial freedmen had always been Messalina's most natural allies – they'd helped her root her most dangerous enemies out of the Palatine court and in many ways they'd tied their success, their survival even, to hers. But this was an attack on one of their own. If Messalina's destruction of Asiaticus had shown the senators that none of their number was safe, the attack on Polybius sent the same message to the freedmen.

By the spring of AD 48, it must have been becoming increasingly clear to Narcissus that things could not go on as they were. His relationship with Messalina now imperilled him on two fronts: if she was attacked from the outside, he might well fall with her, but if she retained her power, he was forced, for the first time, to face the reality that she might one day turn that power against him.

If we believe Tacitus, it was the empress who moved first. Silius, perhaps sensing that Messalina's power was less stable than before, became restless. Now, for seemingly the first time in the course of their relationship, he had plans of his own. He urged her to make the boldest move of all: breaking what was left of their cover and making a play for the imperial throne *together*.[14] Tacitus reconstructs his arguments thus:

> They had not come so far just to sit and wait for the emperor to grow old. Harmless plans were for the innocent,

manifest wickedness could profit only by audacity. They would have ready accomplices in all those who feared for themselves and he, for his part, was single, childless and ready both to marry Messalina and adopt Britannicus. Messalina's power would continue uninfringed and she would have added security going forward too if only she moved before Claudius, who was just as blind to well-laid plots as he was quick to anger.[15]

Tacitus considers two possible reasons why Silius might have proposed such a scheme. Either he was blinded to the risks by his growing obsession with Messalina – a 'fatal madness', Tacitus calls it – or he had finally realised the magnitude of the danger that his position had placed him in.[16] The situation had gone so far, he thought, that there was no going back now: the couple had already shown their hand. Playing it out was risky, but doing nothing was an automatic death sentence.

At first, Tacitus tells us, Messalina was unconvinced. It was not because she loved her husband that she hesitated, far from it, and nor was it because she had made an assessment of the political situation and found the scheme wanting (this is the silly, slutty, almost apolitical Messalina of Tacitus, after all). In fact, she had few qualms at all about the coup itself; it was what would happen *afterwards* that played on her mind. If she trusted Silius, married him, installed him on the throne, was she truly confident that she could trust him in return? Most of all, Tacitus claims, she was scared that once Silius had attained all that he desired, he would drop her like a stone. The adultery that had seemed so tempting and harmless while she was *someone else's* wife would suddenly seem repugnant: 'he would spurn an adulteress', Tacitus imagines Messalina thinking, 'because he would soon estimate the true price of that wickedness which he had endorsed in the uncertain heat of danger'.[17]

But Silius could be convincing and in the end, according to Tacitus, the empress' own perverted obsession with taboo-breaking got the better of her. Just as Ovid had found that 'the licit always starts to cloy', Messalina had 'come to disdain the ease of her adulteries' and now she was 'drifting into untried lusts'. Most of all 'she craved wedlock – the *name* of marriage – in pursuit of that magnitude of infamy that is the last pleasure of the prodigal'.[18] It is a motivation that suits perfectly the character that Tacitus was creating for Messalina, and her place in his tale of tyrannical debauchery and moral decline. The idea that the empress played the blushing bride to fulfil a sort of kink, and that she was willing to set aside everything else to do so, encapsulates all her immorality and all the dangers she posed to the traditional order. This is a woman who cares only about the immediate and sensory, a woman *so bad* that her understanding of right and wrong has flipped totally. Messalina makes marriage, the reassuring glue that held society stable and made sex respectably procreative, into something dirty, illicit, sexy – and soon enough a wedding would nearly destabilise the entire regime.

Once Messalina has decided to risk it all, Tacitus' version of the story unfolds much as it did in the first chapter of this book.[19] The couple waited until Claudius was called away on business to Ostia and set about preparations for the wedding that would inaugurate their coup. They picked a day, an auspicious one; Messalina had the palace decorated and the marriage couch garlanded; she consulted on a menu for the banquet and drew up a guest list of those friends whom she could trust to support her bid for power and be lively in conversation. It was autumn, so the harvests were fresh and the wine was good. She bathed and had oils rubbed into her skin and sat patiently as her hair was separated, scented, braided and piled high on her head. Perhaps she gossiped as she waited, or touched up her makeup – a little red ochre on the cheeks, a little kohl around the eyes – in the polished silver of a hand mirror. When it was done, she donned the yellow-red veil of a bride, the kind she had not worn since her marriage to Claudius a decade before, and set out.

Tacitus claims that Messalina and Silius followed the conventions of the marriage ceremony to the letter. Nothing (excepting the fact of its bigamy) was to be contrary to tradition. The witnesses pressed their seals into wax on the marriage contract; Messalina listened to the speeches and well-wishings of their chosen friends and offered the customary sacrifices to the gods. Now the more enjoyable business of the evening could begin. Messalina took her place among her guests, reclining next to her new 'husband'; they kissed, publicly tangled up together, and enjoyed every inch of their 'conjugal licence'.[20] New vats of wine were tapped, and Messalina and Silius danced together, 'throwing back their heads', to the lewd songs being played by the bands installed on each of the garden terraces. It was now that Vettius Valens climbed the tree and saw the storm brewing over Ostia.

It is only at this point, in Tacitus' narrative, once Messalina's actions have already 'shaken the house of the princeps', that Narcissus and the other freedmen realise they have no choice but to intervene.[21] They were concerned not with Messalina's immorality, nor even her bigamy, but with the outcome of the political coup they knew it portended. Silius had all the makings of a princeps – an aristocrat, the consul-elect, blessed with noble good looks and a razor-sharp intellect – and the celebration of a wedding went well beyond indiscretion. This was a point from which there would be no coming back; it constituted both a dissolution of Messalina's marriage to Claudius and a declaration of insurrection. These men owed their positions, their prosperity, their freedom even to the emperor – they had a great deal to fear from the prospect of a revolution. Still, Messalina was a powerful woman, and in the end it was only

Narcissus who was willing to tell the emperor the truth: it was his revelation of the empress' conspiracy that set the events of her fall in motion.

This narrative satisfies from a storytelling point of view – and Tacitus is a consummate storyteller – but it cannot satisfy from a historical one. By the final months of AD 48 Messalina had been married for ten years and empress for almost eight. In that time, she had created a position for herself right at the centre of a political world that had been dominated by men for the best part of a millennium. She had maintained this position – destroying her most dangerous political enemies in controlled, carefully planned bursts – for the best part of a decade. She had made serious errors of judgement in the past year, but Messalina had otherwise shown a capacity for foresight and a single-minded instinct for the preservation of herself and her children. The idea that she would have risked everything she had worked so hard for – risked her own life and those of her children – in pursuit of some passing fancy, is difficult to credit. It is perhaps even harder to believe that a woman who had witnessed the chaotic aftermath of the long-planned coup against Caligula would have made a move so irrevocable as the public celebration of a marriage – a move that had to signal insurrection – with no apparent plan for what was to come next.

Tacitus knows that his narrative tests the boundaries of credibility. 'I am not unaware that it will seem like fiction,' he admits, 'but nothing here has been fabricated to cause wonder, truly I impart only that which was said or written by my elders.'[22] Tacitus' proposed solution feels like an attempt to fit the tales that he had heard, tales which suited his characterisation of Messalina and her age, into a frame they simply do not fit. Suetonius records an even more outlandish rumour: Messalina had tricked Claudius into backing the marriage, even getting the emperor to sign her dowry contracts himself, by claiming that omens had prophesied the death of the emperor and that the only way to avoid disaster was to temporarily install another man (Silius) on the imperial throne. Even Suetonius – not usually a man to let credibility stand in the way of a good anecdote – acknowledges that the story 'surpasses all belief'.[23]

So what are we to make of it? Some historians have argued that Messalina *did* marry Silius in AD 48 as part of a plot to overthrow her husband. Contrary to Tacitus, however, they contend that the plan was initiated by Messalina and motivated by political necessity rather than the madness of love. The prominence of Agrippina and her son Nero, they argue, had been growing ever since the Secular Games and now Messalina was terrified that Agrippina was plotting to take her place in Claudius' bed and on the imperial throne. The empress was growing frantic, she feared for her own power and for Britannicus' future, and she began to feel that her only option was to forestall Agrippina's seduction of Claudius by installing Silius on the throne in her husband's place.

The theory is problematic on a number of levels. There is no evidence to suggest that Agrippina was angling to supplant the empress prior to Messalina's fall – had it existed, it would doubtless have been exploited to the full by ancient historians keen to present Agrippina as an endlessly ambitious schemer. Even if Agrippina *was* making plans, Messalina's actions remain inexplicably rash. Agrippina could hardly have been more powerfully positioned in AD 48 than the emperor himself; if Messalina was worried about her own safety in the face of Agrippina's growing influence she would have attacked her swiftly and directly – as she had Julia Livilla in AD 41, or Julia in AD 43 – rather than attempting to bring down Claudius.

The only real way to make sense of the events of AD 48 is to flip the roles around. There *was* a coup, but Messalina was not its instigator – she was its victim. Narcissus had been conscious for some time that the empress was becoming more of a danger to him than an asset: the Asiaticus affair had shown her to be a liability, and the murder of Polybius had made her seem a threat in much more direct terms. At first Narcissus and the other freedmen considered whether some judicious threats might convince Messalina to change course and end her affair with Silius; but by the early months of the new year, it was becoming clear – to Narcissus at least – that she would have to go.

The removal of an empress, even one who had recently been busy accruing enemies, was a treacherous undertaking. Messalina had built a remarkable public profile for herself and the influence she exerted over Claudius seemed disquietingly intense. It was decided that there could be no last-ditch attempt to reason with Messalina – it seemed inevitable that it would fail, and it would only serve to put the empress on guard against the coming attack, perhaps even spur her to try and strike first. Narcissus had to pick his moment carefully and, when that moment came, manage events to perfection.

The months between the murder of Polybius and the autumn fall of Messalina must have been fraught ones on the Palatine. Narcissus and his associates were scoping out support. Callistus and Pallas, the two most powerful of Narcissus' surviving freedman colleagues, appear to have agreed that Messalina's removal was to be desired – Tacitus describes their frenzied discussions with Narcissus (although he dates these to after Messalina's 'marriage') and both men certainly showed themselves ready, once she was dead, to turn immediately to the task of finding her replacement – but they were unwilling to commit themselves to action. After all, they were not so closely associated with Messalina as Narcissus was or Polybius had been, and they had less to fear either from her destruction or her survival.

Narcissus may have received similar murmurs of qualified assent from other quarters too. He recruited two of Claudius' mistresses, Cleopatra and Calpurnia, to first break the news – these were expendable women who could be used to sweeten the blow and test the temperature of the water. Turranius, the long-time prefect of the all-important corn supply, indicated that he might be willing to back Narcissus' story. So too did Lusius Geta, one of the Praetorian Prefects and a man who most likely owed his job to Messalina's machinations. It was clearly felt, however, that this was as far as his support could be trusted: fearing that his loyalties might swing back towards the empress once the affair was under way, Narcissus would have Geta temporarily relieved of his control of the troops until his old patroness was safely dead. Her old senatorial ally Vitellius – still resentful, perhaps, of the role that Messalina had made him play in the destruction of his friend Asiaticus – may also have hinted that he would not stand in the way of an attack on the empress. In the tension of the carriage ride back from Ostia to Rome, Narcissus would press Vitellius again and again to follow through and condemn Messalina outright before the emperor – Vitellius demurred, preferring to keep his position defensibly ambiguous, but he certainly did nothing to defend the woman whose shoe he had once begged to be allowed to kiss.

Narcissus knew that whatever support he could canvass would mean nothing if he could not prise Claudius away from Messalina. Messalina could be persuasive, manipulative even, and Claudius was in love. On a more pragmatic level, the emperor may have been aware of how much he owed his empress. The couple had, in many ways, built their dynastic power together. Messalina had bolstered Claudius' image with her fertility, her youth and her glamour; she had taken on the risk involved in the removal of enemies who threatened not only her position but her husband's too; she had given him a son, a PR coup and the promise of a legacy – a princely bloodline of Claudius' own. These were not minor matters, especially not when combined with the empress' physical allure, and Narcissus seems to have been desperate to prevent Messalina from making her case in person.

It was likely this concern that drove the timing of events. In the autumn Claudius had to be in the port city of Ostia to inspect the grain supply and make sacrifices for its safety. He would be away for some days, perhaps even weeks, while Messalina remained behind in the city. The distance offered Narcissus the perfect opportunity to act – it was the ideal breeding ground for mistrust and, when the moment came, it would prevent the empress from doing anything to influence her husband.

But the question remained – what exactly should Messalina be charged *with*? Narcissus may have guessed that accusations of adultery alone, however true and well-evidenced they were, would not be enough to sink the empress, and he seems to have been right. The sources agree that it was fear of a coup and humiliation at seeing his possessions laid out in Silius' house that would finally turn the emperor against his wife – not the immorality of her alleged infidelities. Claudius might have been complacent about flirtatious indiscretions but he had always been terrified of attempts on his life. His fears were understandable, given the mode of his accession, and deep-seated. So, if Narcissus could convince the emperor that Messalina was a threat to his rule and his very survival, he had a shot at taking her down.

The autumn in Rome was always a good time for a party. The aristocrats who'd spent their summers on the coast had returned to the city, the evenings were mild, the vine harvests had come in in September, and ancient festivals celebrating the shortening of the days and the safety of the crops provided traditional excuses for feasting. With Claudius in Ostia, Messalina had little to do but make the most of it.

The party Messalina held in the autumn of AD 48 – with its feasting and music and dancing – might not have been a wedding at all. Instead, the celebration may actually have been a festival held in honour of Bacchus, the god of wine.[24] Tacitus tells us that the empress transformed the imperial palace into a pageant of wine-making. Grapes were pressed before the eyes of the guests and the great vats set up throughout the house of the Caesars brimmed with wine of the finest vintage. The guests were dressed for a bacchanalia; Messalina not least, with her hair worn loose and clutching a *thyrsus* – the distinctive vine-woven, pine-cone-topped staff carried by Bacchus and his band of followers. Bacchus was a god of dual character: he entertained, brought warming pleasures, loosened limbs, but he also drew his followers right up to, and sometimes over, the edge of a violent, barbaric madness. Even the *thyrsus* Messalina carried was *double-edged*: usually, in Bacchic legend, it was a dancing staff, thrown between maenads and used to beat rhythm – but sometimes it became a deadly weapon.

Events had conspired to offer Narcissus the perfect opportunity to strike. Messalina and Silius' behaviour had been raising eyebrows for some time but this latest display was something new for Narcissus to exploit. The mysterious festivities of Bacchus appeared to have borne some similarity to the rituals of a Roman wedding, and *this* might be the root of the implausible tale of Messalina's bigamous marriage; if Narcissus could claim that what had been celebrated in Rome was not a party got out of hand but a *wedding*, he could accuse the empress not only of adultery but of conspiracy too. Claudius' isolation in Ostia made him reliant on Narcissus and his other advisors for the relay of such information – 'information' which Narcissus now resolved to provide.

After breaking the news to Claudius through his mistresses Calpurnia and Cleopatra, Narcissus presented his case. He began by apologising that he had concealed the empress' infidelities for so long. It was a well-calculated admission – he had been so close to the empress that it was impossible for him to claim he knew nothing at all, and owning a minor, contained complicity early on gave him an appearance of repentant integrity. Those were minor scandals, but this was something entirely different:

an issue not of adultery, he stressed, but of insurrection. 'Are you aware of your divorce?' he asked, 'because the people, and the Senate, and the soldiers – *they* all saw the marriage of Silius and if you don't act fast, your wife's new husband holds the city.'[25]

The speech was designed perfectly to push Claudius' buttons. He had always had a tendency to paranoia and now – isolated in Ostia, betrayed by his wife, far from the city, which he knew well could turn in a night, reliant on Narcissus and unsure of whom else he could trust – his thoughts turned immediately to the worst. Was Silius still his subject? The emperor asked again and again. Was he still in control of the empire? Additional witnesses were brought in, the Praetorian Lusius Geta and the corn-prefect Turranius among them, and a council of the emperor's advisors was convened. They validated the emperor's fears, as planned, advising him to go straight to the Praetorian Camp and secure the city.

Narcissus remained in control as the imperial convoy set out for Rome. He demanded that he be given a place in the emperor's carriage and hijacked the direction of the conversation. He pressured Vitellius to denounce Messalina explicitly – as, perhaps, he had indicated he might in the months that had followed the death of Asiaticus – but the senator sensibly refused to commit himself. Frustrated, he turned his attention to the problem of the Praetorians. Lusius Geta had been convinced to speak against Messalina in Ostia but Narcissus was concerned that his co-operation, and that of his colleague Rufrius Crispinus, could not be relied upon back in Rome. To ensure against disaster, Narcissus persuaded Claudius to hand over temporary command of the Praetorian forces to him. Before Claudius' carriage reached Rome, Narcissus had secured command over both the ear of the emperor and the forces that controlled the city.

Messalina must have retained some friends among her husband's circle because messengers arrived at the Palatine palace well before her husband and his convoy. They warned the empress that 'everything was known to Claudius and that the emperor would soon be on his way, ready for revenge.' What exactly Claudius thought he knew may not, at this point, have been entirely clear.[26]

It is what Messalina and Silius did next, more than anything else, that makes it clear that this was not a conspiracy on their part. They made no attempts to rally support, to sway the Senate, to bribe the Praetorians, or to secure the city. Instead they split up: Messalina fled to the garden of Lucullus, her haven on the Pincian, while Silius repaired to the forum and continued with the usual business of a consul-elect. They clearly still felt confident that the scandal could be quieted, Claudius could be placated, and that their lives could return to normal.

In the space and calm of her garden, Messalina recalibrated and planned her next move. Even now there is no evidence that she thought of conspiracy – instead, her deliberations centred on how her husband might be mollified. She prepared a defence that focused not on politics but on optics and emotion.

She enlisted the support of Vibidia. As the most senior of the Vestal Virgins, Vibidia could demand an audience with the princeps whenever she chose, but her position also rendered her the ultimate arbiter of feminine chastity. Support from her would be a good look. Messalina also decided to send her children to Claudius – the seven-year-old Britannicus and the eight- or nine-year-old Octavia, reminders of the family unit they had created and the dynastic service she had done him.

Finally, the empress resolved that she would go and face her husband herself. She was certain, Tacitus tells us, that if she could just *see* him, he could be won over: it was a strategy that had always worked before. The journey across the city from the Pincian Hill to the Via Ostiensis was a humiliating one. It took Messalina down through the forum and past her home on the Palatine. By this point she had only three companions and she was travelling on foot – the *carpentum*, the special carriage which she had been given as a special honour after her husband's triumph, was nowhere to be seen.

When she reached the gate that marked the beginning of the road out to Ostia, she found a cart that was willing to carry her. Tacitus' claim that it was a cart of garden waste seems too neatly symbolic to be true. Equally dubious is his assertion that 'the vileness of her scandals were so well established that she was pitied by not a soul'. Messalina had spent years building up a public image for herself – she had appeared alongside her husband at the triumph, the circus and the games; she had sponsored banquets and led the women in processions at the festivals; she had made benefactions and sacrifices; she had given the populace a pair of royal babies; she had sat for portraits that made her look glamorous but maternal, chaste but fertile. The empress had made missteps that had earned her enemies, but those enemies were in the Senate and on the Palatine; there is no reason to believe that she did not remain popular on the streets of Rome.

As his carriage moved towards the city, Claudius was vacillating. Sometimes he berated his wife and her betrayals, at other times he was swayed by memories of their marriage and young family. In part no doubt he thought of love, but he may also have thought of politics – of the work she had done to stabilise their regime, and of the dynastic future that their children represented.

It was now that Messalina appeared and, as soon as she was in earshot, began to plead her case – begging that her husband hear out the mother of his children.

This was the eventuality that Narcissus had feared, the reason he had waited until Claudius was isolated in Ostia before making a move. He knew that, at this point, failure to retain control over the narrative he had created could prove fatal and so he began, quite literally, to shout the empress down;

'roaring', as Tacitus puts it, about her marriage to Silius and the conspiracy it revealed.[27] He made sure he had Claudius' visual attention too, handing him sheet after sheet of evidence to distract him from the sight of the woman standing before him on the road.

From this point on Narcissus kept a stranglehold on access to Claudius, on whom he saw and on what information he received. When Octavia and Britannicus tried to approach their father's carriage, Narcissus ordered their immediate removal; when Vibidia appeared to demand that the emperor give his wife a fair hearing, Narcissus simply lied – Messalina would have a chance to defend herself, he promised. In the meantime, he continued darkly, Vibidia would do well to attend to her proper duties as a Vestal.

Narcissus directed the emperor's coach to continue straight to Silius' house, where he showed him the gifts his wife had given her lover – things taken from the imperial palace, heirlooms of the dynasty even, which could only have come from Messalina. He was careful, too, to point out the statue Silius kept of his father – an illegal image given that Silius the Elder had been condemned in AD 24 on charges of corruption and insurrection. The implication was clear: like father, like son.

From here it was straight to the Praetorian Camp, where Narcissus had arranged for an assembly of the forces temporarily under his command. Briefed and prompted by his freedman, the emperor made a short address and then the throng of defendants – already arrested and brought to the camp on Narcissus' orders – were called up one by one, starting with Silius, and executed. When the emperor hesitated over Mnester, who argued that he had been in no position to refuse the empress' advances, Narcissus was firm: after the execution of so many senators, an actor who had cuckolded the emperor could hardly be allowed to live. The optics were just too bad. Just two of the accused were pardoned: Plautius Lateranus and Suillius Caesoninus.

The first probably through his military uncle's intervention with the emperor, but the second, perhaps, because his father, the empress' feared prosecutor Publius Suillius, had agreed not to support his old ally against Narcissus. The executions complete, Narcissus took the emperor home for dinner.

After Narcissus' intervention on the Via Ostiensis, Messalina had returned to the Gardens of Lucullus. At this time of year, in the middle of the autumn, they must have been beautiful with colour and the sleepy heaviness that had begun to weigh on the flowers and the leaves. The empress was panicking, veering between hope and indignant anger, composing and rewording appeals to her husband. Her mother Domitia Lepida was there; the two had been estranged – perhaps she had objected to Messalina's murder of her husband Appius Silanus in AD 42 – but she was here for her daughter in this final crisis.

Domitia Lepida was advocating suicide: the game was up, she argued, and the only thing left was to die with the sort of dignified fortitude that looked good in the history books. Messalina disagreed: despite everything, she was sure that if she could only see her husband, *speak* to him, then the situation might still be rescued. Had Narcissus not intervened at the final moment, it is not impossible that she would have been proven right. As dinner continued back on the Palatine, Claudius began to grow warmer and softer with each glass of wine. Finally, he called over an attendant and ordered that a message be sent to "the poor woman" – she should come tomorrow and tell him her side of the story.[28]

This was a risk that Narcissus could not afford to take. His success so far had rested on his control of access and information to the emperor, and on the precision of his stage-management. Everything had been choreographed so as to leave no gaps for vacillation, nor for the advancement of any alternative version of events. Messalina was persuasive, and if she had the opportunity to make her case to her husband – particularly, of course, if her 'marriage' to Silius, with all its implications of conspiracy, had been a fabrication on Narcissus' part – she might just come out on top. Narcissus knew that if Messalina survived, 'ruin', in Tacitus' words, 'would turn on the accuser'.[29]

Narcissus slipped out of the dining hall and spoke to the soldiers who had been stationed by the door. They were to go ahead with Messalina's execution immediately, he said – emperor's orders. He sent a colleague of his, the freedman Evodus, to ensure the job was finished.

Messalina was crying, Tacitus claims, when they found her in the garden. It was only when she saw the soldiers, and heard the way that Evodus, an ex-slave, was speaking to her – she who had been the most powerful woman in the world for the best part of a decade – that the irremediable nature of her situation finally dawned on her. Now she tried suicide, raising a sword to her throat, and then to her chest – but she couldn't do it. In the end it was a tribune who dealt the blow that killed her. It was a death that Tacitus considered cowardly, ignoble and unstoic, evidence of 'a soul so corrupted by lust as to retain nothing of honour'.[30]

It is difficult to perceive it that way now.

XVII

The Whore Empress

'And what of her who bound our arms, not long ago, with shame,
...The Whore-Queen of the dissolute Nile'

Propertius, *Elegies*, 3.11.39

Claudius was still at dinner when he was told the news of his wife's death. No one said whether Messalina had killed herself or been killed and he did not ask. Instead, if we believe our sources, he lay back and called for another glass of wine. The emperor remained an emotional blank in the days that followed. Nothing seemed to rouse him – not the celebration of the freedmen, not the grief of his children – he showed no human feeling at all. Tacitus calls it an 'oblivion'.[1]

If it felt good for Claudius to forget, then the Senate were willing to help him. They decreed that Messalina's 'name and images were to be removed from all places, public or private'.[2] It was only the second time in Roman history that such an order, known as *damnatio memoriae*, had been made officially.[3] Across the empire, statues set up over the past eight years were removed from their pedestals.*[4] Some had their heads smashed in, others were carted

---

* The north African city of Lepcis Magna, for example, removed Messalina's statue from the imperial portrait group that stood in the city's Temple of Roma and Augustus, and erased her name from the honorific inscription that had adorned the pedestal.

back to the workshop. Their features would be re-carved until they looked like portraits of Agrippina or Octavia and you couldn't tell that they'd ever been Messalinas at all.[*5] Inscriptions were altered too, great public ones in the forum at Rome and provincial city centres. In private, in a Roman necropolis, 'Valeria' was chiselled off the tomb of one of Messalina's freedmen.[†6] The Senate's decree even reached into people's pockets: in the city of Tralles (on the western coast of Turkey) the empress' name was erased from individual coins.[7]

But even after her statues had been smashed and her name had been erased, people still talked about Messalina. The downfalls of great and powerful women have always made good fodder for scandal, particularly when they involve sex, and the sheer number of men who fell with the empress, combined with the accusations of bigamy, made this a scandal without parallel. Claudius might have ensured the city's corn supply, but Messalina had fed it gossip enough to make it through the winter.

The story changed as it was told – they always do – and this one was told often enough to mutate almost beyond recognition. This section of our book is no longer the history of Messalina: it is the history of her reputation.

*

It was around the turn of the second century AD that the poet Juvenal composed his *Sixth Satire* – perhaps the most unpleasant and most famous of his works. For nearly seven hundred lines

---

* The statue of Agrippina in the imperial portrait group that stood in the basilica of the northern Italian city of Velleia had originally depicted Messalina. Here the head was removed and replaced but another portrait from Naples was simply recut until the features looked sufficiently different.
† This was the tomb of a barber named Antiochus. 'Valeria' has been carefully scraped off, but interestingly, the empress' second name 'Messalinae' has been left untouched.

the poem's rampantly misogynistic speaker advises his friend never to marry via a wholesale denunciation of every form of womanhood and woman that he can imagine. If your wife is beautiful, she'll be vain; if she is ugly, she's worthless; if she is rich, she'll lord it over you; if you love her, she'll torture you; if she can play the lyre, she's too good with her hands; if she speaks Greek, she's too emotional; if she is sporty, she's too masculine; if she is religious, she'll turn to witchcraft; and if she is clever, of course, she'll prove to be an utterly unbearable nightmare. Even the perfect woman – beautiful, fertile, rich, aristocratic and virginal – finds a way to anger Juvenal. Her very perfection, he warns, will make her proud, and who can stand *that* in a wife?

You might be forgiven for assuming that this constitutes an exhaustive list of Juvenal's criticisms of womankind, but in fact it excludes his most significant concern: woman's capacity for infidelity. There was not a single chaste woman in the Rome of his day, Juvenal claimed – the city was simply too steeped in sin and sensuality to allow for it – and Messalina was the worst of them all. As proof of his argument, Juvenal tells an astounding story about the empress, one that goes far beyond the boundaries of run-of-the-mill adultery.[8]

> *You want to worry over Eppia's crimes –*
> *Those of a private home and a private wife?*
> *Look on the rivals of the gods and hear*
> *What Claudius bore in his married life.*
> *When she felt her husband safely slumber,*
> *His wife would nightly slip herself away,*
> *With one serving-girl alone as escort,*
> *She would dare – as she preferred – to lay*
> *Upon a rough mat on the floor instead*
> *Of in her own palatine marriage bed.*
> *The Whore-Empress dared to don her night-time hood*

And to hide the black curls of her own head
Under the cover of a blonde-weaved wig.
She slipped into the brothel's heavy heat
And on into an empty cell – her own –
Hung with the ancient stench of soiled sheets.
Then there she stood, naked but for gilded
Nipples and for sale, right beneath a sign
That lied, and that called this girl 'Lycisca'
And here she showed the belly that was thine
Upon a time, well-bred Britannicus.
With sweet allurements she receives the men
Who enter, and demands they pay in coin.
And then unceasing now and now again
Lies back devouring every stroke they make.
And when the pimp dismisses all his girls
She goes away unwilling and she takes
Each last minute that she can to shut-up shop;
And even then she's still aflame and feels
Her clit still stiff with lust – and so worn-out
By men, but still not sated, back she reels,
Her filthy cheeks obscured by oil-lamp soot,
That foul thing bears her brothel odour
Back to the bed of the god-emperor.

The tale that Juvenal weaves is a remarkable one. It takes us from the imperial palace to a slum brothel and back again, destroying, as it goes, the comforting boundaries upon which Roman society was built: there is no separation here between empress and slave, wife and whore. The passage also gives Messalina the epithet that would, perhaps, have the single greatest impact on her enduring image in Western culture: *meretrix augusta* – the Whore Empress. The whole passage is striking, but to understand just how shocking it would have been to a Roman reader we will have to take a detour to Pompeii.

*

The year is sometime before AD 79 and you are approaching Pompeii from the coast, past the suburban baths and under the barrel vault of the Porta Marina that cuts through the city walls which have stood here some seven hundred years. They're obsolete now, but the double fortifications, peppered with slingshot holes, are testament to a time before stable Roman rule spread its wings across the whole peninsula, when Italy was less peaceful and prosperous than it is today. Nowadays the emphasis in these wealthy coastal resort cities around the Bay of Naples is not on war, but on trade, entertainment and conspicuous consumption.

Immediately to your right as you enter the city is a temple dedicated to Venus, the goddess of love and sex, and Pompeii's patron deity, surrounded by landscaped gardens set on artificial terraces looking out over the valley below. You continue on your way, passing the sanctuary of Apollo and the covered basilica where court cases are heard, as the Via Marina widens, drawing you towards the centre of the city and out into the open space of the forum.

You pass over the flagstones of polished Travertine marble and on down the Via dell'Abondanzza, turning left at the Stabian baths into Pompeii's less salubrious side streets. The roads here are narrower and so the balconies that hang out from the second storeys block out much of the light. On the corner of two of these passageways – the Vicolo del Balcone Pensile and the Vicolo del Lupanare – there is an awkward, narrow, wedge-shaped building, two storeys high and with a terrace wrapping, prow-like, around its facade.

Depending on what time of day or night you have arrived, the fork in the road around this building might be very busy indeed. Men spill in and out of the building's two entrances, women lean against the doorways or over the balcony, calling out to passers-by. You have arrived at a brothel or, as it is known to your fellow Latin-speaking travellers, a *lupanar*. In English, the term translates as 'Wolf-Den'.

You slip inside, through the entrance on the Vicolo del Lupanare, and find yourself in a wide corridor.[9] Simple frescoes – red patterns, ornamented with little griffins and swans – decorate the walls. These wall paintings, designed to mimic more luxurious fabric hangings, meet a floor of beaten earth. Five narrow rooms open up off the central passage: some are windowless, some have small windows set high up into their walls, each has a sparse masonry platform abutting the back wall decorated with painted red 'ribbons' and stone 'pillows'. The floor around the doorways inside the brothel is surprisingly smooth; there are no grooves, no post holes, nothing to indicate the presence of doors. It is possible that some privacy was afforded by curtains but it is also possible that no privacy was felt to be necessary.

The space above each of the doorways is decorated with erotic panel paintings depicting pairs of men and women. The scenes are not particularly ground-breaking, the positions not particularly varied. This is not, as is sometimes suggested, a 'menu' of the sexual options on offer to the customer. None of the pictures show, for example, oral or homosexual sex – although both these services are referred to in the graffiti that covers the brothel's walls. These pictures evoke an abstracted, sanitised, intimate, erotic ideal where beautiful, close-looking couples make love on ornamented beds piled high with thick mattresses, pillows and richly coloured sheets. If you dropped your gaze to look through the doorways beneath these paintings, you would quickly have understood that they did not refer to the reality of the brothel at all.

The sections of the walls that are not frescoed are covered with graffiti; names, sketches, sexual boasts. One scribble perverts Caesar's famous claim to have come and saw and conquered:

'I came here, I fucked and then I returned home'. The layers of graffiti – with its desperate statements of identity, its shouts of 'so-and-so was here' – remind us that the now empty space was once in constant and energetic use.

In the wide hallway between the rooms, naked prostitutes display their wares, clients peruse their offerings and the madam ensures payment is made in full. In the loo at the far end, girls wash off the last man, shave their legs and put on makeup. Inside the rooms, hastily discarded clothes are strewn across the floors; a glass of wine sits by the 'bed'; if it's getting late an oil lamp burns steady streaks of soot marks up the walls; and, on the masonry ledge at the back of the room, the prostitute and her client engage in their financial transaction.

We could do worse than to look to the brothel in Pompeii for a model of the type of establishment Juvenal imagined for Messalina. The *lupanar* has the same small individual rooms described by Juvenal; we might imagine a rush-mat like Messalina's rolled out to cover the cold stone of the Pompeian bed-platforms, and the layers of soot that settle on Messalina's face must have come from an oil lamp like ones found in the *lupanar*. In Juvenal's imagining, the empress' hideaway is defined by its seedy, uncomfortable poverty, and the contrast it offers to the material luxury of the imperial palace of her daytimes. The satirist emphasises the stench and the stuffy heat of the place of Messalina's brothel, and with five poorly ventilated rooms in use in a space measuring less than 35 by 35 feet, the same atmosphere must have pervaded the *lupanar* in Pompeii.

Imagining Messalina in *this* brothel, visualising her standing in the corridor and fucking on the masonry platform that stood in for a bed, we can finally grasp the true shock-factor of Juvenal's satire. It doesn't get further from the palace, or from the dignity and the majesty of imperial rule, than this.

Messalina's physical appearance changes with her surroundings. Juvenal imagines her disguising herself by covering her black hair with a blonde wig. Blonde hair was a prized and attractive feature in ancient Rome, but rare among the native population. Blondness was associated much more with the northern European captives brought down from Germania, or even Britannia: these girls were enslaved, sold and often they were forced into prostitution. Later in his *Sixth Satire* Juvenal would talk of a '*flava lupa*' – a 'blonde whore' – who worked out in the open among the ruined tombs on the roadside.[10] Her new blondeness made Messalina *look* like a prostitute, but as the wife of Claudius it might have implied another humiliation. It seems almost a reversal of the couple's British triumph: Juvenal's Messalina has transformed herself from the woman who had headed the procession in her garlanded *carpentum* into one of the fair British captives who had followed, shackled, behind. Messalina's physical transformation continues throughout the night: by morning her cheeks are fully 'obscured' by the dirty residue of smoke from the cheap oil lamps she uses to light her work. It is a 'foul thing', dirty and almost unrecognisable, that slips her way back between the sheets of the imperial bed.

A Roman woman's name carried with it her family history and, in a final erasure of her daytime identity, Juvenal's Messalina changes hers. 'Lycisca' is the feminine, diminutive form of the Greek word λύκος; it means something close to 'Little She-Wolf'. A single name of foreign origin, this was clearly designed to be read as a slave name. We know from Pompeian graffiti that prostitutes tended to work under single names like this. Veneria, Fortunata, Successa, Iucunda.[11] Many of these had sexual undertones, and Lycisca is no different.

The Roman world had a lot of sex for sale and the Latin language had a lot of words for the men and women who sold it.[12] The most neutral – *meretrix* – might be translated simply as 'prostitute'. It meant, in a literal sense, a 'woman who earns'. If you felt inclined to be a little more offensive, you could use the casually pejorative *scortum*. This harsher-sounding word was used for both male and female sex-workers and carried more moral baggage. In its connotations, it is roughly comparable to the English word 'whore' but, translated literally, it means 'leather or hide'. The possible origins of the terms are obscure and universally unsavoury. It may have evoked the relationship between the 'hide' of an animal and the 'skin' of a person, objectifying the prostitute as little more than a sack of flesh. Alternatively, the term might reflect a perceived connection between the act of leather working, the repetitive hammering, banging, rolling and handling of the hides, and the act of sexual intercourse, immortalising a violent and mechanical version of love-making.

The very lowest end of the Roman sex-work spectrum was occupied by the *lupa*. Literally meaning 'she-wolf', this was the term used to describe the most socially degraded, most morally debauched, most easily accessible prostitutes of all; streetwalkers, seedy brothel girls, and women who sold themselves in the sprawling necropolises that skirted the roads leading into and out of town. It was a term in such common use that it spawned the Latin word for the brothel – the *lupanar*. The well-educated Roman spoke Greek as well as Latin and it is impossible that he could have seen Messalina's pseudonym 'Lycisca' without thinking of the meaning of its Greek source word. In his rechristening of the empress as 'Little She-Wolf', Juvenal presents Messalina as the archetypal whore and the personification of an uncontrolled, *bestial* sexuality.

The Roman prostitute routinely risked objectification, coercion, violence, theft and death, and Juvenal provides no explanation as to why the empress would risk everything – her power, her wealth, her respect – to take on one of the most degrading roles in Roman society. In his silence, and his emphasis on the sensual qualities of the stuffy, seedy brothel, Juvenal seems to suggest that it is the material and sexual debasement of the brothel that holds a fetishistic appeal for Messalina.

Juvenal's story is not credible. It is difficult to believe that the wife of the emperor, however powerful she was in her own right, would have been able to slip, nightly, out of a palace complex, heavily guarded by men who answered directly to her husband. And if by some miracle Messalina had made it past the palace walls, across the city and into a brothel, the blonde wig Juvenal gives her would hardly have been enough to protect her anonymity. In the 40s AD Messalina was the most recognisable woman in the world. As empress, her image would have been everywhere; captured in the oversized marble statues that stood in sanctuaries and basilicas, the paintings of the imperial family that hung in shops and atria, even on the coins that jingled in people's pockets and paid for the necessities of their lives. Everyone knew her face; there is simply no way she could have got away with it.

Satire feeds on recognition, and as implausible as Juvenal's tale is, it reflects a pervasive and persistent tradition associating the empress with prostitution. By the time that Cassius Dio was writing at the dawn of the third century AD, these rumours had taken on the appearance of historical fact. He reports that the empress established her own brothel *within* the walls of the Palatine palace, working there herself and forcing other women of the court to do the same.[*][13] The rumour is repeated in the *Epitome of the Lives of the Caesars*, a collection of short imperial biographies written in the late fourth or early fifth century, with the anonymous author adding the detail that Messalina employed both the wives and the virginal daughters of the nobility and punished noblemen who refused to pay the clients.[14] Pliny the Elder's tale of the empress' contest with a

---

* Interestingly, a similar accusation had been levelled against Caligula.

courtesan is another variation on the same theme. The survival of three mutations of the same rumour suggests Chinese whispers-style repetition.

Messalina was not the first powerful woman to be called a prostitute. Less than a century before Messalina's ascendancy on the Palatine, the poet Propertius had dubbed Cleopatra '*meretrix regina canopi*' – the Whore Queen of the Dissolute Nile – and Juvenal's echo of this famous phrasing was almost certainly deliberate.[15] Although this tendency to associate female rulers with prostitutes trades on its shock value, it is less surprising than it first appears. To the ancient mind, both the prostitute and the female politician had transgressed the boundary that divided the feminine sphere of private domesticity from the masculine world of civic life. The prostitute had rendered her body communally accessible, the political woman had interfered in state affairs, but both had shed their domestic feminine identities and embarked upon a new public life; in a way, one was an obvious allegory for the other.

The stories of the empress playing prostitute are just one aspect of the process of mythologisation that Messalina's history was subjected to after her fall in AD 48. During her lifetime Messalina had shown herself a political force to be reckoned with. She had built a public profile for herself, developed new channels for the working of court politics, and systematically removed a number of opponents, big players in the Senate and imperial family, who had looked to threaten her own position or her husband's regime. In the years that followed her death, all this was stripped away. She was transformed from a woman with sexual desires, ones that co-existed alongside the ambitions she harboured for herself and her family, into an undiluted embodiment of what the Romans feared about female sexuality. Everything – Messalina's plans, her failures, her achievements, her innovations – was subsumed into the growing narrative of 'the Whore Empress'.

*

So how did it happen, and why did it happen to Messalina? She was far from the first imperial woman to fall on charges of sexual immorality, so why was it her name alone that became so synonymous with sexual excess? The empress was clearly less chaste than the absolutist ideal of Roman womanhood required – she may have racked up more sexual partners than was usual even among those of her high-society friends who were perhaps a little more *au fait* with adultery, and she certainly flirted with less discretion. But the real key to the mythologisation of Messalina lies not in her life, but in the years that followed her death: in the actions and perception of her successor Agrippina, and in the judgements that came to be passed upon the reign of her husband.

After he watched the execution of Messalina's lovers and associates that autumn in the Praetorian Camp, Claudius turned to the assembled cohorts and ordered them to kill him if he ever tried to marry again.[16] By winter, his feelings had changed, and on New Year's Day AD 49 he married his fourth wife and second empress, his niece Agrippina. When she became empress, Agrippina assumed an established position in the Claudian court – a position with a set of privileges and a degree of influence that Messalina had spent nearly a decade building. Within the year she had been granted the title 'Augusta'.[17]

At the start of AD 49, the Claudian court, still reeling from the fall of Messalina, was riven with competing factions. Agrippina had not been the only candidate for Claudius' hand in marriage; her claims had been advanced successfully by the freedman Pallas, but two other women – Claudius' ex-wife Aelia Paetina and Caligula's third wife Lollia Paulina – had been proposed by Narcissus and Callistus respectively.[18]

Messalina's children Octavia and Britannicus also remained at court and in apparent favour with their father. The loyalties of any surviving adherents of the old empress would transfer naturally to them and even some of her past enemies – Narcissus included – would later show themselves willing to support the claims of her children. There would also probably have been some beyond the Palatine who remained attached to Messalina's memory; many in Rome may have felt aggrieved to see her statues recut in Agrippina's image. Even Claudius himself still seemed conflicted; although he had publicly supported the damnation of Messalina's memory, he had rewarded Narcissus more meanly for the 'service' of her removal than the freedman had hoped.[19]

The insecurity of Agrippina's position during the early years of her reign is reflected in a flurry of activity intended to strengthen her own faction on the Palatine. She arranged for Seneca – an old ally of her and her sisters and no fan of the last empress – to be recalled from the exile Messalina had contrived for him in AD 41 and installed as tutor to her own son Nero. She saw to it that Lollia Paulina, the more threatening of her two rivals for Claudius' hand, was convicted on charges of sorcery (allegedly having consulted astronomers regarding marriage to the emperor), exiled from Rome, and forced to take her own life.[20] She accused Lucius Silanus, who had been betrothed to Octavia since AD 41, of committing incest with his beautiful sister Junia Calvina – he committed suicide on the same day as Agrippina's wedding to the emperor.[21] These events left Octavia free to be betrothed to Nero, strengthening Agrippina's dynastic ties to Claudius.

Given the febrility of the situation, it was crucial to prevent any idealisation of the last empress that might reflect poorly upon the new. Managed carefully, however, the comparison might be a useful tool. If Messalina's flaws, real or perceived – her alleged promiscuity, violence and irrationality – could be played up, Agrippina might bolster her own position with Claudius, the court and the public. Rumours that had begun to take hold in the wake of the suddenness and scandal of Messalina's fall might now have been promoted by her replacement. Members of Agrippina's circle may also have found that adding new exaggerations to old gossip won them favour on the Palatine. Some of these stories would have spread by word of mouth, and repeated until they had solidified into 'fact'. Others may have been written down. We know from citations in Tacitus and Pliny the Elder that Agrippina wrote a set of *commentarii* – a memoir-style 'commentary' on 'the story of her life and the misfortunes of her family'.[22] If, as seems likely, the account was composed sometime in the late 50s AD, Agrippina must have covered the vicissitudes of life in the last empress' court and the details of Messalina's fall.

It is probably to Agrippina's autobiography or to the talk of her circle that we should ascribe the dubious tale of Messalina's attempted murder of the young Nero in AD 48. It is all far too convenient; presenting Messalina as an unhinged maniac and Agrippina as a protective mother while associating Nero with those mythological heroes (Hercules, Oedipus, Romulus etc.) attacked in infancy by enemies who hoped to forestall their fated greatness. The circle may have propagated other stories too: in addition to being good fodder for dinner-party gossip, tales of uncontrolled promiscuity provided a neat contrast to the image of herself that Agrippina would attempt to cultivate after Claudius' death as a single-mindedly devoted mother and a chaste widow. It also suited Agrippina to repeat Narcissus' accusations that Messalina and Silius had been involved in an outright conspiracy. The narrative overshadowed any memories of the fact that Agrippina had herself been convicted (though later pardoned) of treason against Caligula in AD 39 and served to justify the murder which had made Agrippina empress.

Messalina's alleged exploits moonlighting as the prostitute 'Lycisca'
provide the perfect classical cover for eighteenth-century French
eroticism in Pierre Didot's take on Aretino's 'Positions'.

The House of the Caesars, envisioned in marble procession on the *Ara Pacis* or Altar of Augustan Peace.

A young couple make love on the wall of Caecilius Iucundus' peristyle in Pompeii – such explicit scenes were common in fashionable first-century interiors.

Messalina, with her distinctive mid-first-century hairstyle, youthful beauty and famous eyes, as she appears in the official portrait type commissioned early in her reign.

Claudius – a dignified-looking man, Suetonius claims, so long as he remained stock-still – is portrayed as emperor wearing the oak-leaf *corona civica*.

The chaotic moment of Claudius' 'accidental' accession, as imagined by the Anglo-Dutch painter Lawrence Alma-Tadema in 1871.

A wall-painting from the Palatine palace, still in place in Messalina's day. The trompe l'oeil illusionism and abundant foliage encapsulates the Augustan-era second style.

An ironically
Madonna-esque
image of Messalina
and Britannicus. The
composition is based
on a famous statue of
the goddess Peace and
her son, Wealth.

Messalina is given the attributes
of the mother-goddess Cybele.
Later, the statue was smashed
with a heavy blow to the back
of the head.

A coin from Alexandria depicts
Messalina holding the comically
small figures of Britannicus and
Octavia. The obverse shows a
bust of Claudius.

Andrea Mantegna's assiduously researched late fifteenth-century
Triumphs of Caesar includes men carrying images of captured towns
and key battles – as they would in AD 44.

Hans Makart's portrait of Charlotte Wolter as Messalina in the German
play *Arria und Messalina* imagines the empress during her ascendency:
imperious, confident and sensual.

The story of Arria and Paetus provided everything the neo-classical painter could desire: a classical setting, moralising message and high-Victorian melodrama.

Couples banquet on the walls of the triclinium of the Pompeian House of the Chaste Lovers – the perfect setting for Ovidian games of infidelity.

A couple get close over a kithara in this Pompeiian wall-painting. Music and poetry were both viewed with suspicion as potential gateways to adultery.

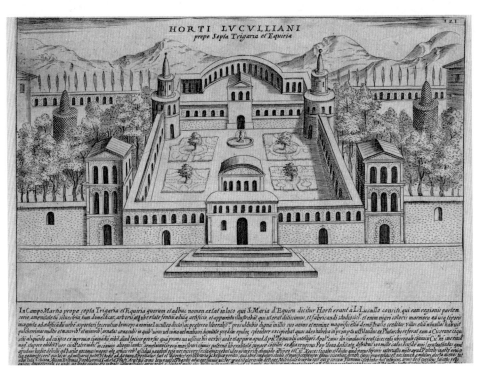

The Gardens of Lucullus – splendid enough to be thought a motivation for murder – re-imagined in an early seventeenth-century print by Giacomo Lauro.

The new empress and her circle might have spread salacious rumours about Messalina but, ironically, it was Agrippina's own fall that did perhaps the most lasting damage to her predecessor's reputation. Agrippina was murdered in AD 59 at the hands of her son, almost exactly a decade after the death of Messalina, and an uprising against Nero brought the end of the Julio-Claudian dynasty in AD 69. In the years that followed, hostile historians went to town on their characterisations of Agrippina. She had certainly given them a lot to work with: she had engineered the accession of her son Nero (an emperor deeply unpopular with senatorial writers), allegedly via the double-murder of Claudius and Britannicus; and worse, by their calculation, she had gone on to place herself at the centre of political life more openly than Messalina or any other Roman woman had dared to do before. While Messalina had kept her exercise of power mainly behind closed doors on the Palatine, Agrippina was not so reticent: the first Praetorian password of the new reign was 'the best of mothers'; coins were issued which showed her profile nose-to-nose with Nero's; she appeared in a golden, military-style man's cloak and even attempted to receive foreign ambassadors in an official capacity.[23] It is this that the historians zero in on: their Agrippina is defined entirely by her ruthlessly single-minded political ambition.

The Ancients viewed the writing of history as an exercise in the creation of literature as well as in the dispassionate recording of historical fact. Arguments might be drawn just as legitimately with setting, structure and character as with analysis – and in the contrast between Claudius' two empresses, Roman historians found an ideal opportunity for an exercise in literary construction. The more ambitious, clever, rational, scheming and sexless they made Agrippina, the more directionless, stupid, irrational, passionate and carnal they made Messalina. The contrast brought both figures into cinematic definition, creating extremes that provided readers with drama and variation, but it also made a point about politics.

For all that Augustus had preached traditional domesticity, his creation of a hereditary dynasty had given the women of the *Domus Augusta* a potential for power that was without precedent in Rome, and the development of structures of court politics in the years that followed had given them new opportunities to exercise it. It was a change that had only really become evident under Claudius: Livia had cloaked her power under a careful veil of old-fashioned modesty, Tiberius had ruled as a confirmed bachelor, and Caligula had chopped and changed his wives too frequently for any of them to make a real impact. The power of the women who emerged under Claudius – first Messalina and then Agrippina – appeared a sinister development to those senatorial observers who wrote the history of the first dynasty: it was a symptom of the new quasi-monarchical political structure and it seemed to portend a dangerous corruption of the natural way of things.

In the contrast they drew between Messalina and Agrippina, these writers (Tacitus in particular) presented two visions of female power: opposite in character but equally horrifying in effect. Messalina, hyper-feminine in her sensuality and passion, *feminises* the political, making affairs of state revolve irrationally around lusts, secret intrigues, jealousies, dreams and love affairs; Agrippina, by contrast, is rendered unnaturally, monstrously masculine by her obsession with the acquisition of outright political power. As he introduces the new era of Agrippina, Tacitus makes this comparison explicit: 'the commonwealth was turned upon its head and the whole state submitted to a woman who, unlike Messalina, did not toy with the affairs of Rome out of wantonness. This was a controlled and quasi-masculine enslavement: in public there was severity and often arrogance; at home there was no immodesty, unless it paved a path to domination.'24 Between the two extremes,

Tacitus makes his argument that female power – and by extension Julio-Claudian-style dynasty – must invariably be a scourge on the state.

Just as Messalina's image was shaped in relation to Agrippina's, it was shaped in relation to Claudius' too. The characteristic flaw ascribed to Claudius by the historians who weighed up his legacy as a ruler was weakness. This was a man who could be clever and shrewd, who could, and indeed *did*, do good for the state, but he was weak: susceptible both to the undue influence of those who had no right to power, his freedmen and his wives in particular, and to the failings of his own self-restraint, especially where women and wine were concerned. Messalina and her misbehaviour are key to the creation of this image.

Control was, perhaps, *the* defining feature of ideal Roman masculinity. The male citizen was expected to exert control on three levels. Over himself, through the exercise of rational moderation. Over his family, through his role as the *pater familias*, or head of the household. And over the state, through his political participation in voting or office holding. Female adultery interfered with the foundations of this second pillar of control. In straying beyond the boundaries of her marriage, the adulteress laid bare her husband's failure to keep his wife in line – in other words, she made a mockery of his masculinity.

These expectations of ideal masculinity rebounded doubly on the princeps. For him, the boundaries between person, household and state were blurred – his person and his household *were* political entities and, on a symbolic level, he was expected to act as a father to the empire. A failure of control in any arena on the part of the emperor was more than just a personal failing – it was a crisis of state.

The most outlandish stories about Messalina, the extremes of her adultery and ventures into prostitution, all play on this obsession with masculine control and fears about Claudius' ability to maintain it. If adultery was humiliating for the deceived husband, for a wife to eagerly engage in sex-work took this humiliation to an undreamt-of extreme. Where adultery contravened the bonds of marriage, prostitution circumvented them entirely; the prostitute was one of the few women in Roman society who was acknowledged to function independently outside the structure of the family, beyond the control of a father or a husband. In accusing Messalina of prostitution, the sources transform Claudius into a sort of über-cuckold, entirely unable to keep his wife or his home under proper masculine control. It's a point they drive home in the detail: in Juvenal's narrative the empress literally transgresses the boundaries of the palace, escaping out into the nocturnal city, before bringing the dirt back home with her to physically corrupt her marital bed; in Dio's account she destroys the sanctity of the domestic space by establishing a brothel within the walls of the imperial *domus* itself. The stories raise a bigger question too – how can Claudius possibly run the state if he cannot keep his own house in order?

Rumours of the empress' prostitution also played on another anxiety about Claudius' leadership. The Roman prostitute was a dangerous symbol of social mobility: she was a woman who made her own money, whose position in society was not defined by the status of a father or husband, she was an *infamis* of likely slave background but she might consort on the most intimate and unguarded terms with the most elite of men. By transforming Messalina into a woman of this kind, the gossip-mongers, satirists and, later, the historians add a new dimension of risk to Claudius' failure of control. It not only set a poor example, they suggest, but also introduced a destabilising element directly into the heart of the state.

The period covered by Messalina and Claudius' reign was suffused with an uneasy sense that things were shifting. The Roman establishment had spent a long time, nearly three-quarters of a century, trying to pretend that all was as it had ever been; that the Augustan revolution had not been a revolution at all, but rather a restoration or, perhaps, a reformation, and that the emperor was really just first among senatorial equals. As the dynasty took root, however, this fiction became less crucial for the emperors to maintain and more difficult for the senators to make themselves believe. The façade had been falling away by the end of the Tiberian period, and by the time of Caligula's accession it had become something to be mocked. Conscious of the fate of his predecessor, Claudius was more careful to pay lip-service to the distinction of the senatorial order, but it went no deeper than that and nowhere was this hypocrisy clearer than in the evident power of Messalina and the freedmen.

The accounts of Messalina's prostitution place a constant, unerring emphasis on transgressive shifts in status. It's a theme that spreads through every line of the Juvenal passage: it's there in the constant references to the seedy environment of Messalina's chosen brothel, in her new name, in her new look, and in the dirt she carries back to the palace in the morning. The sense that Messalina is undermining proper social hierarchies is there in Dio too, in the specification that the other women Messalina recruited to work in her Palatine brothel were nobles too, and in Pliny the Elder's acerbic quip that Messalina considered victory over a prostitute 'a triumphal palm worthy of an empress'.[25]

The accusations of prostitution that were levelled against Messalina after her death did not need to be true to cement their place in the popular memory of the empress – they needed only to tap into anxieties that were widespread, unspoken, and in need of an outlet. And they did just that: they nourished fears about adultery and the endless uncontrollability of female sexuality; they bolstered characterisations of Claudius' weakness as a man and a leader; and they gave fleshy form to contemporary anxieties about shifts in who held power, from senators to freedmen, from men to empresses.

It is an error of history that those aspects of Messalina's image that were shaped least by the realities of her reign were the ones that most enduringly shaped her legacy. The rash, silly girl fashioned in contrast to Agrippina's clever, scheming woman; and the insatiable 'Whore Empress' created as a critical judgement on the politics of her and Claudius' reign – these are the characterisations of Messalina that would haunt her down the centuries.

XVIII

The Tragedy of Octavia
and Britannicus

'I am left over, in the shadow of a great name...'

Pseudo-Seneca, *Octavia*, 71

One evening during the January or early February of AD 55, just over six years since the death of their mother, Octavia and Britannicus dined, as usual, on the Palatine. Britannicus was coming up to his fourteenth birthday; this was the year that would, if everything went to plan, see him assume the *toga virilis* and embark upon the public career to which he had been born.

Their father had died just a few months before, in the middle of the previous October.[1] At sixty-three Claudius had had a good run for a man who had never enjoyed robust health, but nonetheless people whispered foul play. Suspicion had fallen predictably on Octavia and Britannicus' step-mother Agrippina. It was rumoured that she had poisoned her husband – twice over for good measure. The first dose had been infused into a plate of mushrooms, Claudius' favourite dish, but the poison had been slow-working and the emperor had simply seemed drunker than usual. To avoid any possibility of error, a second dose had been smeared onto one of the long feathers that the emperor's physicians used to help him throw up on those common occasions when he overindulged; this time, the effects were immediate.

Whether or not Agrippina had really contrived the emperor's death, she certainly controlled the events that followed. Her son Nero had been adopted by Claudius upon their marriage in early AD 49, and in the intervening years the emperor had showered his step-son with all the honours that had traditionally marked out possible successors. Now aged almost seventeen he, unlike the thirteen-year-old Britannicus, was a young man, arguably old enough to hold the principate.

Agrippina managed her son's succession to perfection. Concealing Claudius' death until all was in order, she had sent Nero first to the Praetorians and thence to the Senate, while she comforted Britannicus and Octavia on the Palatine. Nero was acclaimed emperor both in the camp and the *curia* on 13 October AD 54 – gaining, in one go, every power and honour of the principate. Claudius' will was never read: its contents, particularly as regarded the question of whether he had designated Nero and Britannicus co-heirs to his estate, were already irrelevant.

The couches at dinner that evening in early AD 55 were filled with the inner circle of the imperial court: the new emperor Nero, Agrippina, Octavia and Britannicus were all there.[2] As he was yet to assume the *toga virilis* and with it his full place in adult society, Britannicus reclined at a table of boys around his own age (among them his closest friend, the future emperor Titus) slightly more sparsely furnished than the rest; it was traditional and, given his position, the family had to be particularly careful not to be seen to be spoiling him. It was also on account of his position that Britannicus retained a 'taster', a slave whose job it was to sample each dish as it was brought before him to look for signs of poison. This evening, a glass of wine was served to the prince in the usual Roman way, with hot water added to the vintage. The wine was tasted and passed as safe but it was too hot, far hotter than usual, and was sent back for a dash of cold water. It was not tested again on its return.

Once the glass had been drained, Britannicus had some kind of seizure, losing the power of speech and struggling to breathe. The company panicked; some rushed for help but the quicker thinking among them looked to Nero. The young emperor was unperturbed – he said Britannicus had had these sort of epileptic fits on and off ever since infancy and assured the company that he'd soon regain control of his senses. Britannicus was carried from the room and the dinner resumed.

Despite all Nero's assurances, Britannicus – the one-time 'Hope of the Caesars' – was dead before the night was out. No time was wasted in preparation for the funeral, which was held at first light the next morning on the *Campus Martius*. During the funeral a storm of such violence broke out, Tacitus notes, that people said it must speak of some judgement from heaven.[3] But the bad weather was more than just portentous. Dio claims that as Britannicus' body was carried through the forum on its bier, the heavy rainfall washed away a coat of whitening gypsum that had been applied to his skin revealing an unsightly, livid discolouration. This was believed to be a symptom of poison and everyone thought that it was Nero who had administered it.

It is perfectly possible that Messalina and Claudius' son really did die of natural causes, just as Nero claimed. Britannicus could have been killed by an epileptic fit or, perhaps, by a tetanus infection which might have caused both the seizures and skin discolouration.[4] The true cause of his death ultimately matters little to the history. Britannicus' status as Claudius' son had always rendered him a risk to Nero's hegemony, and his imminent assumption of the *toga virilis*, with all the expectation of new public prominence it entailed, meant that that risk could only increase.

From the moment of Claudius' remarriage to Agrippina and his adoption of Nero, it had been clear that one of the boys would have to die. From the point of view of the reigning emperor, the provision of two heirs carried real advantages.

Rome offered young men so many ways to die (as Augustus' endless succession struggles had shown); if one nominated a single heir and he were to die, the appearance of a power vacuum behind the emperor might create an incentive to factionalism or even regicide. The empire could not be shared, however – the degeneration of triumvirate after triumvirate into civil war during the late Republic had shown that much – and so the second candidate, as useful as he may have been while the last emperor lived, had to go upon the succession of his competitor. It was a situation that had played out quickly and clearly in the winter of AD 37/38 when Caligula had brought about the death of Tiberius Gemellus (named as his co-heir in the emperor Tiberius' will) on charges of conspiracy; if Britannicus had not died, either by poison or illness, in those first months of AD 55, similar charges would likely have been filed against him before the year was out.

Britannicus' only hope, from the moment of Claudius' marriage to Agrippina in AD 49, would have been to have beaten Nero to the top job and destroyed him in the process. The timing of Claudius' death before Britannicus' coming of age made such an outcome unlikely. The convenience of the timing for Nero added fuel to the rumours that Agrippina had arranged for her husband's murder in order to preclude the plans he was formulating for the imminent promotion of Messalina's son. In Agrippina, Nero enjoyed the unwavering support of the most powerful woman on the Palatine; since the death of his own mother, Britannicus had had, and could have had, no such ally.

The fate of Britannicus, whether he was poisoned or not, had been pre-sealed by twin tragedies: the fact of his mother's death and the timing of his father's.

Octavia's situation was less clear cut. As a girl she posed no direct competition to Nero, and Agrippina knew that if she played her cards correctly, Messalina's daughter might be key to her son's success.

At the time of her mother's death, Octavia, then around eight years old, had been engaged to Lucius Silanus for some seven years. Lucius Silanus was a young man of ancient noble stock and a great-great-grandson of Augustus; his betrothal to the infant Octavia had been one of the stabilising arrangements made by Messalina and Claudius during those first, febrile months of their shared reign. It had been the only one to survive the length of Messalina's rule. During that time, Lucius Silanus had been steadily, if quietly, advanced: he had been with Claudius in Britain, and had been chosen as imperial envoy to inform the Senate of Rome's victory; he had ridden in Claudius' triumph and been awarded honorary triumphal insignia of his own; before Messalina's death in AD 48 he had held the praetorship and been granted the rights and funds to stage the sort of lavish gladiatorial show that ingratiated men with the populace.[5]

To Agrippina, this betrothal was an impediment, and she wasted no time in getting rid of it.[6] Lucius Silanus was accused of incest with his sister Junia Calvina – beautiful, party-ish and 'forward', her reputation added a delicious dash of possibility to the charges.[7] Junia was exiled, and Lucius Silanus pointedly committed suicide on the morning of Agrippina and Claudius' wedding.

The way was now clear for the betrothal of Octavia and Nero. The move was crucial to the development of Nero's status as a possible successor to the principate – he was now the emperor's heir twice over, his step-son *and* his son-in-law. The couple were married in AD 53 when the bride was around thirteen, and the wedding was marked with public celebrations, lavish gladiatorial games and wild beast hunts in the Circus Maximus.[8]

A year and a half later, when Octavia sat down to the dinner that saw her brother's death, she sat in a place that had once been occupied by her mother: that of the emperor's wife. If she suspected her husband of her brother's murder that evening, Octavia did not show it. 'Though inexperienced in years', Tacitus claims, 'she had already learnt to hide her grief, her love, in fact her every emotion.'[9]

Octavia may have learnt to mask her feelings, but there is no doubt that her marriage to Nero was a desperately unhappy one. Despite her own reputation, Messalina had brought her daughter up to be a model of old-fashioned virtue, 'noble and proven in her upright honesty'.[10] She was loved by the people, her mother-in-law, Agrippina, and the court – but she was not Nero's type. 'Whether by chance,' Tacitus observes, 'or because the lure of the illicit always wins in the end, he came to abhor her.' [11]

In the years that followed his marriage, Nero embarked upon a series of passionate affairs; first with the freedwoman Claudia Acte and then with the famously beautiful, elegant and manipulative Poppaea Sabina the Younger – daughter of the equally attractive Poppaea Sabina the Elder who had been forced to suicide by Messalina over her alleged affairs with Mnester and Valerius Asiaticus.[12] These were the kind of women Nero wanted: less 'upright' and more fun; less constrained by their morals and the expectations of their birth; less weighed down, perhaps, by childhood trauma and constant marital rejection. Octavia's discontent was evident to all those around her. On one occasion, Nero's friends tried to intervene on her behalf, urging the emperor to treat his wife a little better. She was the wife of the emperor, Nero retorted, shouldn't that be enough for her?[13]

For all the past animosity between herself and Messalina, Agrippina seems to have had a real affection for Octavia. She stood by her daughter-in-law in the early days of Nero's affair with Acte, comforting her and putting her own position on the line to openly censure her son's behaviour.[14] Perhaps unsurprisingly, knowledge of his mother's disapproval did little to cool the teenage emperor's obsession with his lover or to redirect his attentions back towards his lawfully wedded wife; but it did provide Octavia with a degree of protection.

When Agrippina died in AD 59 at the hands of the son she had worked so hard to make emperor, Octavia was left more vulnerable than ever.[15] Nero felt trapped, and the more blamelessly Octavia performed her role of good wife and good empress, the more he resented her. Octavia was unassuming and modest, she betrayed no desire to meddle, as her mother had done, in affairs of state, but still her husband felt 'oppressed', Tacitus says, by her personal popularity with the people and by her father's name – he was aware and resentful of how indebted he remained to her for the power he possessed.[16]

Suetonius claims Nero made a series of unsuccessful attempts to strangle Octavia to death.[17] By the early 60s, and encouraged by his ambitious new mistress Poppaea Sabina the Younger, Nero appears to have resolved to be rid of her by more conventional and reliable means.[18]

Given the frequency of divorce in Rome, and Nero's quasi-totalitarian authority, it is a remarkable testament to Octavia's personal renown that her ousting provoked such a crisis. Octavia was divorced in AD 62, initially on grounds of infertility, and Nero was swiftly remarried to Poppaea Sabina. The move played so badly with the public, however, that new charges of adultery were quickly contrived to remove Octavia from the city for good.

Strikingly, the first prosecution failed outright. Octavia was accused of having an affair with an enslaved Alexandrian–Egyptian flute-player by the name of Eucaerus, but even under torture Octavia's attendants refused to play ball. One of her slave-girls lashed out at Tigellinus, the Praetorian Prefect who was interrogating her: her mistress' vagina, she spat, was purer than his mouth. Unable to gather enough witnesses to carry a court case, the emperor gave up and forced Octavia instead into a 'voluntary' retirement on a set of well-guarded estates in Campania.

The public outcry was immediate and intense and, when a rumour spread that Nero had bowed to public pressure and restored Octavia to her position as wife and empress, the celebrations were equally effusive. The people flooded the forum and the Capitol, giving thanks to the gods for Octavia's safe return. They pulled down statues of Poppaea Sabina and brought out the old images of Octavia, wreathing them in garlands of flowers, carrying them in procession, and setting them up in the forum and the temples.

The strength of the support-base Octavia enjoyed may suggest the public retained some positive memories of her mother. Octavia was only twenty-two and in her seven years as empress she seems to have consciously avoided promoting her own power and image. If the people of Rome had really hated Messalina, really abhorred her as the 'Whore Empress', and really believed her fall had been deserved, it seems unlikely that they would have felt disposed to be so protective of her daughter.

The celebrations of Octavia's supposed return culminated in riotous rounds of applause for Nero and hailings of his restored empress. They were premature. When some of the exultant crowd tried to rush into the imperial palace they were cut down by the guards. It soon became clear that Octavia had not been recalled, and that Poppaea Sabina remained empress.

As the imperial guards struggled to subdue the mob, it dawned on Nero that as long as Octavia was alive she would remain a threat to the regime. This time he decided not to bother with witnesses. Instead, he sent for Anicetus, commander of the imperial fleet near Naples and a man who had played a pivotal part in the murder of Agrippina. Now Nero held his former service over him; the emperor demanded that Anicetus swear, on oath, that he had seduced Octavia into an adulterous affair, threatening to have him executed for murder if he failed to comply. Anicetus, unsurprisingly, agreed to the terms and made his 'confession' before a counsel of witnesses. Nero issued an edict detailing his wife's alleged infidelities and added the accusation that her affair had ended in a pregnancy and an abortion.

Anicetus was 'banished' to a luxurious exile in Sardinia; Octavia was shipped off to the island of Pandateria in the Tyrrhenian Sea. Despite all Nero's accusations, the people, Tacitus says, stood by her.

> No other exile had ever before struck the eyes of the onlookers with a greater sense of misery. At that time some still remembered Agrippina, exiled by Tiberius, and more recent memory had seen Julia sent off by Claudius: but these women had had the strength of age; they had seen something of happiness and their present bitterness was lightened by the remembrance of sweeter fortunes past. For Octavia, her wedding day had been her funeral – brought into a house which could offer nothing but sorrow, where she'd seen first her father and then, so quickly, her brother too, ripped away from her by poison; then a slave-girl made her husband's mistress, and Poppaea Sabina married to ensure her ruin; and, at the last, she'd been the subject of a false accusation more painful than any death.[19]

The people who watched her go feared that they would not see Octavia return from Pandateria – the notoriously barren prison island which had seen the deaths of many other imperial women – and they were right. Only a few days of exile passed before Octavia received a letter from Nero ordering her to commit suicide. As her mother had done before her, Octavia refused. She argued her descent, her services, her silence, even her relationship with Agrippina; she had been miserable in her marriage, she admitted, but she was not ready to die.

It was pointless – the order from the emperor had been clear enough. The soldiers bound her tightly with cords and cut the veins on her arms and, for good measure, those on her legs too. The blood, Tacitus says, still flowed too slowly – it was 'congealed' he says 'by fear' – and so a bath was run, hot enough that the steam might speed the process.[20] Once she was dead, people said, her head was cut off and conveyed to Poppaea Sabina in Rome. Octavia, Messalina's first child and the last of her direct descendants, was dead at the age of twenty-two.

The fates of the other main players in Messalina's story were more mixed than those of her children.

Narcissus received less than he had hoped in reward for all the risks that he had taken to destroy Messalina. Claudius awarded him the ornaments of the quaestorship (one of the lower senatorial offices) in a public show of unity following the empress' fall, but he appears to have thanked him little in private; the affair had damaged the emperor's political credibility and torn apart his family. Agrippina did not trust Narcissus either: he argued against her marriage to Claudius, counselling the emperor instead to return to his unthreatening ex-wife Aelia Paetina.

Narcissus' favour with the emperor and his fortunes, particularly in comparison to Agrippina's favourite freedman Pallas, now entered a slow but unmistakable decline; in AD 52 Pallas was awarded the insignia of the praetorship, two steps above Narcissus' quaestorship in the *cursus honorum*.[21] Narcissus had other problems on his hands. He had been put in charge of one of Claudius' major engineering projects: the draining of the Fucine Lake. When some of the drainage system collapsed, people blamed Narcissus, claiming that the freedman had siphoned off funds and then sought to destroy the evidence.[22]

By the time of Claudius' death, the tensions between Narcissus and Agrippina were such that he was said to be considering supporting Britannicus as the emperor's heir against Nero, despite all his enmity with the boy's mother and the risk that Britannicus might seek to revenge himself on Narcissus should he attain power.[23] If the freedman was planning another bold move, however, he misjudged his timing. In the autumn of AD 54, Narcissus was out of Rome; ostensibly he was seeking a cure for his gout but the trip may actually have been arranged on some pretext by Agrippina. By the time he returned, Claudius was dead and Nero was in power. Narcissus' decision to return at all was ill-judged: he was placed under arrest and, before the year was out, had been executed or forced to commit suicide. Narcissus' last act before he died, it was said, was to burn all the imperial correspondence which had come into his possession as Claudius' secretary.[24]

Messalina's mother, Domitia Lepida, had fallen earlier in the same year. Her relationship with Messalina cannot have endeared her to Agrippina, but the issues between the two women may have dated back to the time of Agrippina's apparently unhappy first marriage to Domitia Lepida's brother Domitius Ahenobarbus. Worst of all, it had been Domitia Lepida who had fostered the infant Nero during the period of Agrippina's exile under Caligula and she had retained an influence over her nephew, whom she apparently doted upon and spoiled, which Agrippina both resented and feared.[25]

The empress had Domitia Lepida charged with a double crime: she was arraigned firstly for employing witchcraft against Agrippina, and secondly on the less sinister but more provable charge of having allowed the huge gangs of slaves who worked her estates in Calabria to run dangerously out of control. Domitia Lepida was sentenced to death and died in AD 54, either by execution or suicide.

Messalina's old associates in the Senate fared somewhat better. Vitellius, the man who had kissed her shoe but later refused to support her on the road from Ostia, died of natural causes in AD 51. Three times consul and one time censor, he had enjoyed a remarkably illustrious career and he was honoured with a state funeral. The Senate raised a statue on the Rostra in the forum with an inscription that declared him 'Unalterably Loyal to the Emperor Claudius'.[26] Later, after the fall of Nero, Vitellius' namesake son would briefly rule the empire.

The notorious prosecutor Publius Suillius lasted longer. He survived for a decade after Messalina's death in all the splendour and consequence he had enjoyed during her life. But in AD 58 his mode of life eventually caught up with him.[27] It was the Cincian law – the same one that Messalina's lover Silius had tried to use against him in AD 47 – that was invoked once again, but this time his accuser, the philosopher Seneca, combined it with accusations of extortion. Publius Suillius did not take the charges lying down – it was not in his nature. He was a man, Tacitus says, 'who would rather seem wicked than weak'.[28] Publius Suillius went on the offensive: he restated the accusations Messalina had made about Seneca's adultery with Julia Livilla, accused him of corruption, and mocked his taste as remarkably expensive for a philosopher.

When the evidence of his career as a prosecutor was laid before him, however, Publius Suillius changed tack: he had, he said, just been following imperial orders. Nero cut him off, stating that Claudius' papers proved he had given no such instruction. No, Publius Suillius clarified, the orders had not been Claudius' – they had been Messalina's. At this point, Tacitus says, 'the defence began to falter'. 'Why', the prosecution asked, 'was it Suillius' voice that had been chosen above all others for the service of *that savage whore*?'.[29] Finally, Publius Suillius capitulated to the foregone conclusion of his conviction; half his property was confiscated and he was exiled to the Balearic Islands, where, it was said, Messalina's last ally lived out the remainder of his life in a state of ease and plenty.

As Publius Suillius gathered enough of his vast estate to support him amply in this legally enforced retirement and left Rome for the final time, the prosecution's designation of Messalina as a 'savage whore' was being noted down in the senatorial minutes.

XIX

Epilogue: The Messalinas

'Death has been able to put an end to her debaucheries, but
it cannot wipe them from memory.'

Francesco Pona, *La Messalina*

The crowd crossing the Place du Casino to the Opéra de
Monte Carlo on the evening of 21 March 1899 would
have been a mixed one. European aristocrats and nouveaux
Americans, society virgins and the courtesans who slept with
their fiancés, men who had won big at the tables and men
who had little left to lose. On the bill that night was the world
premiere of a new opera by the English composer Isidore de
Lara, entitled *Messaline*.

As the orchestra started up, the curtains rose on Victorian-
imagined Rome. A monumental stone staircase was flanked by
Ionic columns and arches were decorated with gilded torches,
heavy garlands and undraped statues. Everything was excess.
Even the chorus of slave girls wore colourfully embroidered
tunics, three-stranded necklaces and golden armbands. When
Messalina finally appeared, played by the renowned Belgian
soprano Meyrianne Héglon, she did not disappoint: her richly
embellished silk gown was tied beneath her breasts with a thick
jewelled band and her heavy velvet veil was held in place by a
crown of golden leaves.

The year was meant to be AD 45 – at the very height of Messalina's power – but the librettists Silvestre and Morand had played fast and loose with history. Their plot centres on a fictional love triangle between the empress and an invented pair of brothers, the poet Hares and the gladiator Hélion. Both embark on affairs with Messalina, before Hélion kills his brother and then himself in a tragic case of jealousy and mistaken identity. The empress survives unscathed. If any of the audience in the Salle Garnier that evening remembered enough of their classical educations to notice *Messaline*'s wild historical inaccuracy, it did nothing to dampen their enjoyment. Perhaps some remembered her better from copies of Didot's 1798 book, with its pornographic engravings of Messalina as Lycisca, that they had found in their great-grandparents' libraries. Either way, the opera provided everything they wanted: Roman decadence, sexual depravity and multiple deaths.

Fresh from the rave reviews it had received in Monte Carlo, *Messaline* cut a swathe across Europe. Henri de Toulouse-Lautrec saw it at the Grand Theatre in Bordeaux the following winter, returning night after night to draw. The six paintings based on *Messaline* that Toulouse-Lautrec produced all inhabit the same strange, somewhat dreamlike and vaguely threatening atmosphere. The characters, in their half-Roman, half-Belle Époque fashions, are bathed in the greenish light of the gas-lamps that illuminated the stage. In each scene Messalina stands out, self-assured and haughty in shocking red.

Messaline played at the Royal Opera House in London too, and in 1901 it became the first opera by an English composer to be staged at La Scala in Milan. By January of 1902, *Messaline*'s success had carried her across the Atlantic to the Metropolitan Opera in New York.

What had flown in *fin de siècle* Europe did not, however, fly in New York. The review that ran in the *New York Times* on the morning of 23 January 1902 was unequivocal.[1]

> The production of a new opera at the Metropolitan Opera House may fairly be described as an 'event' [...] The libretto of Messaline is calmly audacious, frankly unclean. It is based wholly upon the noise-some passion of a foul mouthed, utterly carnal, and debased woman [...] [The librettists] have failed miserably in their attempt to shroud the thoughts of this Messaline in 'poetry'. Their verses do not conceal their own meaning and that meaning is not nice [...] the polite audience who sat through it last night could not plead the operagoer's usual ignorance of the plot and dialogue. There was no mistaking the meaning of this scene.

The reviewer reserves some contorted praise for the performance of the leading soprano. 'It is hardly necessary at this stage of operatic history in New York', he writes,

> to tell any reader of the newspapers that Mme. Calve has a fatal talent for the simulation of seductive fascinations. Those who have seen her Carmen – and who has not? – know that she understands to the letter the nature of that class of women which prays upon the weakness and folly of men, which raises self-gratification to the first position, and which sends its discarded victims to ruin or death without compunction [...] But if we must see the dead Messaline resurrected and in the flesh, let us confess at once that she lived last night and shed her baleful influence across the footlights of the Metropolitan.

Clearly not entirely satiated in his outrage, the same reviewer would return to see a second performance of *Messaline* not three weeks later.

*

Some eight hundred years before *Messaline* roused the indignation (and the interest) of the opera critic of the *New York Times*, the twelfth-century theologian Honorius of Autun had concerns of quite a different nature: nuns, he thought, had begun to behave badly. Honorius claimed that the devil had infiltrated the convent dormitories and encouraged the girls to take part in every kind of debauchery. These women, he said, no longer looked to the Virgin Mary as their model – they looked to the Greek courtesan Phryne, and to Messalina.[2] A millennium after her death, Messalina was being turned into a sort of anti-Christ of female sexuality.

Another millennium later, in 2013, the Danish director Lars von Trier would once again mysticise Messalina's sexual misbehaviour. At the start of the second volume of his controversial two-part film *Nymphomaniac*, in a perverted twist on the tale of the transfiguration of Jesus on the Mount, a twelve-year-old Joe (the titular nymphomaniac) experiences a vision of Messalina and the Whore of Babylon as she has her first orgasm. Messalina appears as she does in the Louvre statue, veiled and holding the baby Britannicus. Recounting her story decades later, in the home of the middle-aged bachelor Seligman, Joe mentions that the woman looked like the Virgin Mary. 'Well, it wasn't the Virgin Mary, I can tell you that', replies the widely read Seligman. 'From your description it must have been Valeria Messalina, the wife of Emperor Claudius, the most notorious nymphomaniac in history.'

As different as Lars von Trier's and Honorius' intentions may have been, both men use Messalina in the same way, transforming her from a woman into an allegory of sexual excess. As Messalina is made first into a demonic false idol and then into a pseudo-saintly vision she is stripped of her historical

reality, and of any non-sexual aspect of her identity. Both the
medieval theologian and the twenty-first-century film director
reduce the complex history of the empress until she functions
only as a symbol of uncontrolled female desire.

In their use of Messalina as an archetype, Honorius and
von Trier are party to a long tradition. Messalina's story was
used as a subject in art and literature, and her name itself
became a noun, an adjective, a warning, a joke, an insult, a
compliment and a benchmark. The figure of 'the Messalina' or
'the Messaline' is not related particularly closely to specific tales
told about Valeria Messalina in the ancient sources; instead, her
name becomes a shorthand for the sexual woman – and for the
bad woman more generally.

Authors, well versed in the ancient tales of the empress' sexual
adventures, return to Messalina again and again as a model of the
overtly sexual woman. Women are likened to Messalina when
they desire sex, when they have a lot of it, when they're good at
it, or when they enjoy it. One 1830 French novel describes 'the
furious desire for pleasure that torments these Messalinas'.[3] The
exhausted madam who supplies the secret society of aristocrats
in Andréa de Nerciat's 1793 *Les Aphrodites* wonders of one of
her clients: 'have I not supplied this certain Messalina with up
to three Swiss Guards in a day? She never gives up!'[4] Another
eighteenth-century French novelist, Restif de la Bretonne, extols
the way that one woman 'moved her hips like Cleopatra and
Messalina', and in the Marquis de Sade's *Juliette*, one lover
promises the eponymous heroine that he will ensure she 'comes
like a Messalina'.[5]

The idea of 'the Messalina' as an embodiment of unrestrained
female sexual desire flourished in Britain too. As early as the
1670s, Messalina's position as the whore-ish archetype *par
excellence* was well established enough to be inverted by the
famous libertine, John Wilmot, Earl of Rochester. In a satirical
address to Hortense Mancini, French mistress of King Charles II,

he writes: 'Lewd Messaline was but a *Type of thee*/Thou highest, last degree of Letchery'.[6]

Sometimes 'the Messalina' was a prostitute or a demi-mondaine, but more often she was a wayward member of respectable society.[7] In the 1770s the prolifically adulterous Caroline Stanhope, Countess of Harrington, was labelled 'the stable-yard Messalina', in reference to the nickname of her house in St James's.[8] A decade later, her daughter-in-law's sister, Seymour Fleming, Lady Worsley – whose famous trial for 'criminal conversation' had named twenty-seven alleged lovers – would be dubbed 'the Messalina of the age'.*[9] As late as the mid-twentieth century, the Duke of Argyll was said to have called his scandalously adulterous wife Margaret 'a Messalina in the family'.

Confirmation of the association between the upper-class adulteress and the cultural memory of Messalina comes with the publication of a letter purporting to be written by an anonymous 'Lady of the Ton' to the *London Courant* in October 1781, slamming the concept of monogamous marriage and praising adultery in the most exalted terms. 'Is it to be supposed', the writer asks,

> that any woman of taste and mettle, deeply tinctured with the gallantries of the age, can reconcile herself to the thought of prostituting all her precious moments upon a battered old fribble of a husband, whose animated pulse no longer beats with any warm, amorous throbbings,

---

* References to Seymour Fleming as a Messalina appear in a number of the popular satirical verses composed around the trial. One, posing as a letter from Seymour to her ex-husband, included the lines:, 'What though for thee I'm styl'd in ev'ry page/The Messalina of the present age;/Be it my praise, my chief delight, to own,/Of all mankind I love not thee alone'. Another, posing as his reply, retorted: 'O thou, whom our young nobles hail divine/Unrivall'd priestess at Priapus' shrine,/Immortal W—Y, or if yet more dear/The name of Messalina greet thine ear'.

whose dying sparks serve only to irritate desire [...] ? [...]
Can these be compared to the sweets of vagrant amours,
and the raptures inseparable from an unlimited range in
the velvet path of levity and dissipation?

The writer's choice of pseudonym is telling: the letter is signed
'Messalina'.[10]

Just two years before 'Messalina' wrote to the *London
Courant*, a correspondent of another London newspaper – the
Morning Post – had also invoked the empress in his pen-name.
A man calling himself the 'Anti-Messalina' wrote to the paper
twice in July 1779, complaining about the general existence and
behaviour of women. His first letter mentions adultery but focuses
mainly on women's luxury and extravagance, which he blames
for a spate of bankruptcies, robberies, murders, and suicides.
His second accuses French prostitutes posing as governesses
of teaching English daughters 'levity of manners and an empty
fantastical behaviour' and leaving them with 'the masculine
air of an Amazon, the wanton leer of a Lais, and nonsensical
bagatelle which would disgrace a chambermaid'.[11] Given his
pen-name, it might seem remarkable how little of the 'Anti-
Messalina's' invective concerns adultery, but by this stage the
epithet 'Messalina' had come to stand not only for an adulteress
but for a bad wife and a bad woman more generally. As the
Victorian age became increasingly obsessed with the ideal of the
good wife, the 'angel in the home', the 'Messalina' morphed ever
more into her opposite. Explaining the unbearable predicament
of his first marriage, Jane Eyre's Mr Rochester ascribes a litany of
faults and vices to his half-Jamaican wife, Bertha. He concludes
by christening her 'my Indian Messalina'.[12]

The transformation of Messalina into a shorthand for
unrestrained female desire, aristocratic adultery and dangerously
undomestic femininity plays on her reputation but does little to
explore the actual narrative of her life. From the first century

AD onwards, however, playwrights, poets, novelists, composers, painters and sculptors recognised the dramatic and symbolic potential of Messalina's story.[13] Their more in-depth interaction with the details of her life did not necessarily render these artists' representations of the empress much more nuanced than those which had used her name as a noun synonymous with promiscuity and harlotry. Instead, these artists employ the rise and fall of Messalina to explore eternal female 'types': the victim, the witch, the political villain, the sex object, the nymphomaniac and the *femme fatale*.

Messalina's story had made its stage debut some 1,800 years before the opening of de Lara's opera in Monte Carlo. The tragedy *Octavia*, composed around the time of the fall of the Julio-Claudian dynasty and the rise of their Flavian successors, tells the story of Messalina's daughter's unhappy marriage to Nero, culminating in her exile and murder.* Messalina is dead before the story begins but her presence looms large from the very first page:

> *Ever must I mourn my mother*
> *First-seeded cause of all of my bad luck [...]*
> *I, crying, watched your wounds and saw your face*
> *Freckled with the filthy gore of its own blood.*[14]

In the *Octavia* Messalina is an agent of tragedy. Her actions and her fall (opening the way, as it did, for the rise of Agrippina and Nero) have placed a transgenerational curse, of the type so

---

* The authorship is unknown. It is sometimes attributed to Seneca but, although the author borrows a number of Senecan phrasings and attitudes, this is now deemed unlikely on both stylistic and contextual grounds. The play is our only surviving example of a *fabula praetexta*, a genre of Latin tragedy based in Roman history rather than Greek myth.

common in Greek tragedies, on the house of Claudius: it has killed Britannicus and Claudius already, and Octavia will be lost to it before the end of the play.

But Messalina is also presented as a victim of tragedy herself. Octavia's description of her 'unlucky' mother's mutilated corpse demands our sympathy, and later in the play the Chorus lists Messalina among a number of innocent female victims of the Julio-Claudian tyrannies. The answer to the question – who exactly was Messalina a victim *of*? – is less clear. Octavia blames the machinations of Agrippina, the Chorus blames Narcissus, but the most interesting and enduring suggestion comes from the character of Octavia's nurse: 'Let your laments alone now, dry your pious tears/and don't disturb the spirit of your mother', she counsels, 'she paid a great price for her madness'.[15] Messalina is both blamed and absolved: her downfall is the result of her actions, but those actions are the result of a 'madness' intrinsic to her nature. Messalina's sexuality becomes a preordained 'fatal flaw', rendering her death inescapable and proper, but tragic too.

It is an idea that is picked up 1,200 years later by the great fourteenth-century Italian humanist Boccaccio in his book *On the Fates of Famous Men*. One day while sitting in his study, Boccaccio imagines himself visited by a series of visions of great men and women from history who recount their lives and attempt to explain or excuse their conduct. Book Seven sees Boccaccio surrounded by a crowd of ancient Romans. His attention is drawn to an argument between Tiberius, Caligula and Messalina.[16] The two emperors castigate Messalina for her adulteries. She fights back, presenting her story as a tragedy and pointing out the hypocrisy of her sexually debauched accusers. She is ashamed of her adulteries, she admits, but they were driven by desires beyond her control. When her father sought the opinion of an astrologer upon her birth, she explains, he stated that all the signs of the child's heavens converged in the sphere of Venus. 'So, I was born,' she says, 'under this urging sky, and as abominable as my deeds might have been, still they were in my nature. Anyone would want and *truly* want to be able to conquer such a nature by strength of will, but even Hercules will excuse a young girl for falling short [...] for he was conquered by the power of love, just as I was.' A French manuscript of Boccaccio's work, illuminated by the Boucicaut Master around 1415 and now in the Getty Museum in Los Angeles, shows Messalina – beautiful, blonde and richly dressed in the fashion of a medieval queen – flanked by an angry Tiberius and an already cowed Caligula.[17] Messalina appears remarkably calm, considering that the flames of hell reach up past her knees. In another illumination produced around 1400, Messalina is being consumed alive by a satanic beast who, it appears, has no taste for Caligula or Tiberius.[18]

Boccaccio invites us to sympathise with Messalina but in doing so he, like the writer of the *Octavia*, strips her of much of her agency. These men encourage us to forgive Messalina because it was beyond her natural capacity to do better. Her actions, they argue, were driven not by choice, but by fate and the weakness of her femininity. These tragic constructions of Messalina rely entirely on her downfall. It is only because we know that Messalina has been properly punished for her sexuality – by her horrible death and, in illuminated interpretations of Boccaccio, by her eternal damnation – that we can feel confident enough to forgive her.

Messalina also appears as a tragic victim in visual art. At the very beginning of the eighteenth century Gerolamo Canale, Venetian aristocrat and second in command to the Doge, commissioned the famed Neapolitan artist Francesco Solimena to paint a series of scenes from mythology and ancient history – among them, the *Death of Messalina*.* This monumental

---

* Interestingly, the series was probably commissioned to celebrate a marriage. Messalina was included, presumably, as an example of what *not* to do. The painting is now in the J. Paul Getty museum in Los Angeles (72.PA.24).

painting, over six feet high and nearly nine feet across, depicts the dramatic climax of Tacitus' narrative: Messalina has been found in the Gardens of Lucullus and a centurion is preparing to strike the fatal blow.

Solimena has used every weapon in his arsenal to heighten the drama of the scene. The soldier, turned away from us, lunges diagonally forward as he draws back his right, sword-carrying arm. His other hand grasps Messalina's wrist, the fingers visibly pressing into her flesh, to hold her still. The sense of movement and the tension visible in his every muscle alerts us to the force of the blow to come.

On the ground beneath him and facing out towards the viewer, Messalina – in a golden diadem and richly coloured silks – puts up a futile fight. Her left hand tries to push him away while her right reaches out, fingers splayed, open, vulnerable and pleading towards the centurion, but also towards the viewer.

Messalina looks young, with round cheeks and a softened chin, and terrified. Her skin appears almost blue-white, especially where it touches the pink skin of the centurion, as though the life-blood has already drained out of her. Her mouth is open, her brows furrowed, her eyes raised towards her executioner and widened in fear. Above Messalina leans Domitia Lepida, her hand grasping the hair of the centurion, trying to push him away from her daughter. Her presence provides the viewer with a model of what pity for Messalina in this moment might look like.

This pity, however, is not encouraged without caveat. Behind the main group in the foreground stands a fourth figure – probably the freedman Evodus commissioned by Narcissus to see the assassination through. Standing tall, straight and still in contrast to the swirling dynamism of the central trio, he wears military dress and leans his right hand with an arrogant dignity on a short staff. His expression is impassive as he quite literally looks down on the fallen empress. This figure, with his calm certainty, seems to reassure us that as tragic and as pitiable as Messalina's end might appear, it can be the only proper end for such a woman.

Another, quite different, vision of Messalina as victim was produced in 1797 by the Danish royal painter Nicolai Abildgaard.[19] Abildgaard shows not the climax of the Tacitean drama, but its aftermath: Messalina is dead, her killers have gone, and only her mother remains to mourn. Messalina's body splays itself out across the entire length of the bottom of the painting. Her head is thrown back, her dark hair is dishevelled and her crown has fallen off. Though her open eyes point directly out at the viewer, they do not *look* – her face has become a death mask. Above Messalina kneels Domitia Lepida, pressing the back of her hand to her daughter's chest as though feeling for a heartbeat. Old and modestly dressed, she does really look at the viewer, presenting us with an expression of resigned despair. There is no violent movement, nor any gore besides a small patch of blood on the floor, and the empress' soft, pale body itself appears untouched.

Abildgaard renders his Messalina morally and sexually ambiguous. There is something Madonna-like about Messalina's simple white dress and blue mantle, and yet there are undertones of the erotic too, in the throwing back of Messalina's arm, the exposure of her breast, her almost ecstatic expression with the taut tilt of the neck and the open mouth. If Messalina had looked pitiable at the point of death, now she is dead she has acquired an aura of tragic romance.

Attempts to present Messalina as a victim reach their apogee in the play *Valéria* by Auguste Maquet and Jules Lacroix, first staged by the Comédie Française at the end of February 1851. In order to render Messalina palatable to their audience, Maquet and Lacroix split the character, quite literally, in two. We have the empress 'Valeria', clever, principled, passionate and devoted to her children; and her promiscuous long-lost identical sister, the courtesan 'Lycisca'. Valeria is adulterous only with Silius; their tragic love affair is presented as faithful, romantic and noble. All of Messalina's wilder sexual exploits are attributed to the conveniently unscrupulous Lycisca. Both characters were played by the same actress, the famed Mademoiselle Rachel, who reigned as the leading tragedienne of the Comédie Française and whose real-life lovers included a count, a prince and an emperor. The real villain of the piece is the scheming Agrippina, and when Valéria dies (by her own hand) it is in an attempt to protect her honour and the future of her son. Maquet and Lacroix's revisionism was highly controversial and rumours spread through Paris that the Assembly was considering cancelling the Comédie's treasury subsidies in the wake of Mlle Rachel's outrageous performance as Lycisca.[20]

Few representations of Messalina were so forgiving. In England, in the mid-1630s, the Company of his Majesty's Revels staged a new play by Nathanael Richards. In *The Tragedy of Messallina, the Roman Empresse* we encounter a Messalina who is as straightforwardly villainous as they come. This Messalina is *the* 'top gallant strumpet, that Strumpet, witch, hell-Cat; most insatiate whore that ever cleav'd to the loynes of Letchers'.[21] She is violent too: torturing her prospective lovers, killing respectable citizens for sport, demanding that Silius murder his wife and plotting the assassination of Claudius. At one point (in case the message wasn't clear enough) Messalina appears on stage brandishing a suspiciously seventeenth-century pistol.

The play is saturated with anachronistic Christian ideology and suffused with endless references to sin and holiness, heaven and hell, angels and devils. Within this framework, Richards transforms Messalina into a sort of Satan, not only revelling in her own corruption but dragging others into sin with her. In her selection of lovers Messalina targets the virtuous; corrupting them with promises, threats, seductions, trickery and even, as we shall see, the supernatural. In touching Messalina, these men sign a sort of Faustian pact, promoted at court and provided with sensual pleasures but put on a path to fornication, murder and ultimately death. The empress does not content herself with the seduction of men; we also find her seeking to debauch paragons of feminine chastity. Three virtuous Roman matrons choose to be killed rather than to be taken to court to be dressed in finery and 'tost on the downy beds of dalliance'.[22] Messalina even plans to end her and Silius' wedding celebration with the rape and murder of one hundred Vestal Virgins.[*23]

Perhaps Nathanael Richards' most striking innovation, however, is his transformation of Messalina into a witch. 'I have not the Court art to kill my lovers,' complains the prostitute that Messalina has just bested in the twenty-four-hour sex contest, 'Nor draw them on with witchcraft, *Circean* charmes'.[24] As the play progresses, we find that these are not idle accusations. The empress slips Silius a drink somewhere between a love and a sleep potion that will ensure that 'when he wakes he may admire and burne/be mad in love to pleasure free in us'.[25] Later on, seeking to reach new heights of seduction and murder, Messalina calls on the aid of the 'great Arck-Ruler of the lowe Abysse' (Hades transformed into Satan) and summons three furies (who, in Richards' version, are transformed into spirits straight from hell). 'Here, here', Messalina incants, 'let Circe and the Syrens charmes,/Poure their inchantments.'[26]

The effect Messalina has on men does, indeed, seem threatening and supernatural. 'O I am all Flame', Silius cries, 'A scorcht inchanted flame and I shall burne/To Cinders with delight'.[27] His interactions with the empress drive Silius

---

* An interesting choice, given that there were only ever six Vestals at one time.

inexorably towards self-destruction: 'O that delicious melting kisse prevailes', he laments a moment later, 'Poysons my blood and braine, and makes me apt/To doe an outrage I should loathe to name.'[28]

Dangerous to men, lustful, in league with the devil, summoning spirits, Richards' Messalina is a seventeenth-century witch – the ultimate symbol of feminine threat in the years that followed the Protestant Reformation.

Richards' audience would have known that his characterisation of Messalina was not only an interpretation of ancient history, it was also intended as a comment on current politics. In her improper religion and her suspect control over the king, it seems that Messalina was meant to be read as an alter-ego of the contemporary Catholic queen Henrietta Maria, wife of King Charles I, who would be overthrown in the civil war that would start in 1642, just two years after the publication of Richards' play.

Messalina is an interesting choice for an attack on Henrietta Maria, who was renowned for her loving, and apparently faithful, relationship with her husband. This incongruity reflects an abiding impulse to accuse the politically problematic woman of being a whore. The association was a natural one – men found it hard to believe that women could build spheres of political influence without recourse to sexual favours. Both the female politician and the courtesan/adulteress broke the boundaries of a woman's proper place within the private sphere: one by swapping domestic concerns for public affairs, the other by rendering her body 'publicly' accessible to men other than her husband. Messalina, as the 'Whore-Empress', was the perfect shorthand for this sort of transgressive behaviour.

In his opening argument before the revolutionary tribunal in 1793, Marie Antoinette's prosecutor Antoine-Quentin Fouquier leant into the dramatics. 'In the manner of the

Messalinas-Brunhildas, Fredegunds and Medicis,' he railed, 'that one called in other times Queens of France, whose names forever hateful will not be erased from the annals of history, Marie Antoinette has been since her time in France the plague and the bloodsucker of the French.'[29] Later in the same case Marie Antoinette and her sister-in-law Elizabeth are called 'Messalinas' again, this time in the context of the bizarre allegation that they had committed incest with the young Dauphin.

The pairing of Marie Antoinette and Messalina in the legal invective comes straight from a vicious culture of pamphleteering which had flourished in the febrile years leading up to the revolution.[*][30] Run off the press in hot print shops in Paris, London, Germany or Amsterdam, and distributed quicker than the royal agents could buy up and burn them, pamphlets attacking the queen alternated long tracts of revolutionary theory with long passages of pornography. In these pamphlets, sex is used as a means to express the chaos, corruption and unnaturalness of the *ancien regime*. The queen's body becomes an ideological battleground. Marie Antoinette is portrayed as a nymphomaniac, driven by unnatural and insatiable desires to every form of debauchery: adultery, lesbianism, voyeurism, exhibitionism, sadism and group sex. These 'secret histories' of the queen's sex life are haunted by the model of Messalina: she is 'a new Messalina', 'the modern Messalina', 'the Royal Messalina', 'that Messalina without shame'. When Marie Antoinette was finally executed in 1793, pamphleteers made

---

* Other powerful women of the age were subjected to similar attacks. Marie Antoinette's sister, Maria Carolina of Naples, was accused of having 'united all the lustfulness of a Messalina with the variegated tastes of a Sappho'. Even the never-married but politically influential Adélaïde d'Orleans was pseudonymised as 'Madame Messalina' by her opponents in the press during the July Monarchy. Empress Josephine is associated with Messalina in an 1805 James Gilray print.

sure not to miss the opportunity to rhyme 'Messaline' with 'guillotine'.

The lengthy (and often illustrated) pornographic scenes that accompanied the naming of Marie Antoinette as a Messalina did have an ideological import – they portrayed Marie Antoinette as corrupting, the aristocracy as debauched, King Louis XVI as too weak to rule – but their sensuously descriptive detail can hardly be attributed to politics alone. The men who wrote about Marie Antoinette had discovered what Juvenal had known at the beginning of the second century AD: that there was a particular type of titillation to be had in the whore-ification of a Great Lady, in the stripping away of the barriers that protected her to render her accessible to the imagination of the common man. Juvenal's treatment of Messalina in his *Sixth Satire* – with its emphasis on *filth*, both physical and sexual – had been a masterclass in the writing of such a fantasy and had opened Messalina up to a future of literary and artistic undressing.

In the middle of the seventeenth century, the Dutch genre painter Nikolaus Knüpfer produced a painting now thought to depict the wedding banquet of Messalina and Silius.[31] At first glance, we might have entered one of the more expensive brothels near Knüpfer's studio in Utrecht late on a Friday night sometime around 1650. A four-poster bed hung in gold silk stands against one wall of a seventeenth-century interior; a variety of glasses and a polished pewter bowl of fruit sit atop a rich damask tablecloth. Playing cards and a pipe have fallen off the table onto the floor. The company is very drunk and very high-spirited. A woman plays the lute, a man falls across the bench in the foreground, two more have climbed the table to look at something outside the window. Three figures cavort on the bed in the background, one of the women dangling the man's feathered hat from her raised foot.

It is only on closer inspection that we discover that this is not a contemporary scene: the man on the bed wears a version of Roman military uniform, while the man in the foreground appears in a seventeenth-century imagining of an ancient tunic. This seems to be a reimagining of Tacitus' description of the wedding feast of Messalina and Silius.* The guests at the window catch the first signs of the approaching 'storm' from Ostia, the man sprawling on the bench in the foreground draws his sword in futile preparation to see off the Claudian forces, and the vine branch and the bottles in the great gold pot to the left of the composition reference the celebration of the new vintage. Silius is the drunken soldier in red and gold sprawling against the pillows of the bed, raising a toast to his new bride. Messalina sits next to him, pretty, rosy-cheeked and blonde, leaning forward and laughing at whatever lewd joke Silius is making. The artist has emphasised the intimacy between the newlyweds – they hold hands and Silius' arm is tangled in Messalina's skirts – and Messalina's sexual availability; her golden hair falls undone around her face, her dress is unlaced and pulled down to fully expose her breasts and a ripe-red apple has rolled across the table to rest suggestively in front of her crotch. Knüpfer has transformed the empress – powerful, demanding and potentially dangerous – into a common, jolly, and easily accessible harlot.

Knüpfer's rendering of Messalina made her seem sexually accessible to the viewer and his imagination, but it was nothing compared to the undressing of the empress that was unveiled at the Paris Salon of 1884. Eugène Cyrille Brunet's *Messaline*, an over-life-size marble statue, is stretched out across a finely decorated mattress.[32] She is totally nude apart from a narrow

---

* Knüpfer's vision was possibly filtered through the lens of a contemporary tragedy written about Messalina by the great Dutch playwright Joost van den Vondel but cancelled before its premiere – out of concern for potential political controversy – and now lost to posterity.

bandeau bra that has slipped down beneath her nipples – emphasising more than it conceals. The statue is carved in the round to ensure there is no angle from which the circling viewer does not have visual access to the empress. One leg is stretched out, the other bent up behind her and raised to give us a view that reaches almost to the top of her slightly parted thighs. Messalina's torso arches back and over the pillows on which she rests, one arm is bent behind her head, her hand tangled in her hair, the other reaches back to grip at the side of the mattress. Her head is flung back, her hair loose, her neck exposed. She seems to be in the throes of an orgasm.

Nearly forty years before, another work in marble had been exhibited at the Paris Salon of 1847. Auguste Clésinger's *Woman Bitten by a Serpent* depicted a female nude similarly stretched out and tensed in ecstasy.[33] The model was Apollonie Sabatier, the young mistress of the Belgian industrialist who had commissioned the work and the hostess of a famous artistic Parisian salon. The sculptor had worked from casts taken from life and reproduced the details of Apollonie's body right down to the folds of flesh at her waist and the pucker of her cellulite. A small snake, curled around the statue's wrist, was hastily added before exhibition as an excuse for what was undoubtedly a depiction of the female orgasm. The statue caused an uproar: 'It's alarming', the composer Chopin wrote home to his family, 'how this statue squirms'.[34] Clésinger's sculpture proved extremely influential, and it is clearly the model for Brunet's *Messalina*. That the body of an empress could be treated in the same way as that of a demi-mondaine – and be met with significantly *less* controversy – is testament in part to the transformations of the Second Empire, but it is also testament to the extent that Messalina was considered fair game for artistic explorations and exploitations of female sexuality.

Messalina was not only exposed in galleries. She had been, and continued to be, undressed between the pages of books too. In Venice in 1633, the polymath Francesco Pona wrote a historical novella which would go on to become one of the most popular – and most banned – books of the century. Pona claimed *La Messalina* was a work of moral instruction, a cautionary tale intended to warn women of the dangers of promiscuity. In reality, it is a work of blatant eroticism, clearly tailored to the literary gaze of the male reader.

The identity of the true intended audience can be sensed in Pona's descriptions of the teenage empress' physical appeal: 'Messalina gave a golden colour to her hair* that she dressed in the supplest wave, beautifully correcting their lascivious disorder [...] On its own, her face was admirably beautiful, but beyond its beauty, there was something dazzling that penetrated when one looked at her, sparkling eyes of a celestial water'.[35] We are led in our desire by Claudius himself: he had 'admired her like a flower', Pona tells us, and now he wished to 'taste her like a fruit'.[36]

If Pona's descriptions of the empress' external appearance are perfectly calculated to arouse desire, her internal life is equally defined by sex. Naturally sexual, the child of immoral parents, and introduced by her husband to galleries of pornography in the imperial palace, Pona's Messalina is both born and trained to be driven entirely by her desires. These desires consume her thoughts in the day and fill her dreams at night: 'Messalina, tossing in the turbulence of her thoughts, did not sleep at night', Pona writes, in a passage that could have been written to caption Brunet's statue, 'and if she did sleep, Morpheus slept at her side, prompting stirrings in her, robing and disrobing a thousand images that her sexual fantasies during the day had suggested. The more filthy and loathsome they were, the more attentive she was.'[37]

Messalina's sexuality does not remain in the realm of fantasy. Pona describes a litany of debaucheries, some of which

---

* Dyed blonde hair was a trademark of the seventeenth-century Venetian courtesan.

are canonical, some newly created. Messalina takes lover after lover; prostitutes herself to forty men in one night; watches the defloration of virgins and hosts extravagant orgies on her country estates. Pona's descriptions of these scenes are detailed in their focus on setting, dress and sensation, inviting the reader to envisage the empress, fantasise about her, and imagine himself with her. As Messalina slips from the palace to the brothel, for example, Pona describes her thus: 'She wore only a chemise of a very fine linen that was perfect for her pleasure – taking care to perfume herself with an essence of amber of great refinement [...] She left visible under her cloak the circle of her little breasts, held up by a cloth of gold'.[38] Pona's Messalina seems to be a creature designed for male fantasy: a beautiful woman who thinks only of sex, and who acts tirelessly on those thoughts.

Unsurprisingly, it was *this* version of Messalina that would make it in Hollywood some three centuries later. Sometimes references to the empress function as a shorthand on camera just as they do on the page. In Fellini's semi-autobiographical *Roma*, the promiscuous wife of a contemporary chemist is reimagined as Messalina, dancing seductively in a transparent red tunic, surrounded by togaed lovers, on the back of a convertible. In other productions we find Messalina's character explored more fully, although not necessarily more accurately. A spate of films excused the empress' presence by constructing fictional stories of redeeming love affairs between Christian slave-girls and their hunky convert lovers in which Messalina could play the antagonist.* The contrast between the innocent chastity of the Christian love interest and the pagan sexuality of the empress allowed the directors free rein to make outright

---

* For example, Guazzoni's 1923 *Messalina* or *The Fall of an Empress*; Gallone's 1951 *Messalina or The Affairs of an Empress*; and 20th Century Fox's 1954 *Demetrius and the Gladiators*.

temptresses of their Messalinas. The slave-girls are pretty, but it is always Messalina who is played by the real star and given top billing.

One film, produced by Penthouse in 1977, *Messalina, Messalina!*, avoids the Christian-romance cliché. The tagline tells us that we are about to witness 'The varied amorous adventures of the most insatiable devourer of men'; the film includes real sex and no plot at all. Messalina became a subject of pulp fiction too. One cover proclaims her 'The wickedest woman in Rome', another makes her 'daughter of the devil, goddess of all delight, empress of all Rome', a third tells us 'She was beautiful, sadistic, tantalising and deadly...from the top of her golden head to the tip of her silver whip'.

These books and films invite us to fantasise about Messalina, but again and again we find these fantasies tinged with a sense of danger. 'A young woman frantic with her desires', writes Pona, 'understands no obstacle. The world can perish; they must be satisfied. The bulimic ardour of her desperation would absorb chasms that would engulf entire cities'.[39] Some of Pona's protestations of horror are disingenuous covers for eroticism, but others seem to betray a genuine conflict between desire and fear. This tension is half the key to Pona's desire; Messalina embodies a particular brand of fantasy – the fantasy of the *femme fatale*.

It is a role that the empress is perfectly placed to play. She is sexually alluring and scheming, and she destroys almost every man with whom she interacts: Appius Silanus and Asiaticus die at her political instigation, Silius and Mnester are executed with her, Claudius' credibility is trashed by her adulteries. Perhaps most significantly of all, the gaps in Messalina's story give her that sense of mysterious unknowability that is so crucial to the construction of the *femme fatale*.

Nathanael Richards prefaced the 1640 print edition of his *Tragedy of Messalina* with a quote from Juvenal's *Tenth Satire*:

Optimus hic et formosissimus idem / gentis patriciae rapitur miser extinguendus / Messalinae oculis. 'This Silius, the best and most beautiful of his patrician race, is being dragged off towards a wretched ending by the eyes of Messalina'. In these lines, Juvenal suggests that Messalina possesses within herself, within her *body*, something which is intrinsically dangerous to men, to the best of men, and thus to all men – she is, in other words, a natural *femme fatale*. It is a view of Messalina that is influential from the Renaissance onwards (indeed, we have already encountered it in Richards' characterisation of Messalina-as-witch), but it really comes into its own in the nineteenth century, building to a spectacular apogee during the decadence of the *fin de siècle*.

In April 1872, a French man by the name of Arthur Dubourg murdered his adulterous wife.[40] The convent-educated Denise Dubourg was hardly a Messalina. She had been in love with a young clerk who worked at the Prefecture of the Seine prior to her family-arranged marriage to the wealthy Dubourg. The marriage was not a happy one: Dubourg was unfaithful, Denise attempted suicide, spent time in an asylum and, upon her return, resumed her relationship with the clerk. Dubourg followed her to her lover's apartment, found them together, and murdered Denise on the spot. Crimes of passion were not afforded special treatment by the French legal codes, but they were by nineteenth-century French legal culture. It was expected that Dubourg would be acquitted, and his sentencing to five years in prison raised an outpouring of public debate.

One of the contributors to this debate was Alexandre Dumas *fils*. Dumas had famously romanticised and rehabilitated the figure of the courtesan in his 1848 novel *La Dame aux Camélias* (the basis of Verdi's opera *La Traviata*), but he would prove himself far less forgiving of the adulterous wife. His pamphlet on the Dubourg affair, *L'Homme-Femme*, or *The Man-Woman*, would run through thirty-five editions and sell

50,000 copies in the six months that followed its publication.[41] 'Since the Dubourg affair', Dumas begins, 'my pen has itched to write'.[42] What follows is a tract (running to over a hundred pages) on the nature of man, woman, marriage, society, and religion in which Dumas presents Messalina as the apex of the evils of unsaved pagan society – the ultimate granddaughter of Eve's original sin. The pamphlet ends with Dumas as a modern Moses, laying down the law for an imagined son on an imagined mountain: try to control your wife, he advises, and if you cannot – if she is born so bad that 'nothing can prevent her from prostituting your name with her body' – then you can, you should, 'kill her!'[43]

The Dubourg affair, Dumas stated at the start of *L'Homme-Femme*, had thrown into relief issues that he had been considering for some time – issues that will, he tells us in an opportunistic flash of shameless self-promotion, be explored in his upcoming play, *La Femme de Claude*. This play, Dumas promises, was to be a modern reimagining of the relationship between Messalina and Claudius.[44] Some things would be changed: 'I need not say', Dumas says, 'that my Claudius will be a modern Claudius, conscientious, Christian; and not the historic and imbecile Claudius who allows his wife to be killed by Narcissus'. Others would stay the same: 'As to the woman, it is the eternal Messalina, after as before Christ'.

La Femme de Claude appeared on the Paris stage, as promised, the following year. The setting is the large provincial home of Claude, an honest, patriotic, virtuous man who has recently invented a powerful new type of cannon which is set to bring him fortune and honours. The play opens at dawn with the surreptitious return of the mistress of the house – she has been gone some three months, indulging in adulteries, unnamed crimes, and perhaps prostitution in Paris. The morning return of Claude's wife is a clear reference to Juvenal's depiction of Messalina, covered in brothel filth, slipping back into the emperor's bed. Claude's wife's name connects her to the empress too: she is Césarine – a female Caesar.

As Dumas had promised in *L'Homme-Femme*, Césarine accords entirely with the image of the utterly corrupt and corrupting Messalina that was well established by the nineteenth century. The child of an adulterous (and German) mother, Césarine has 'that strange irritating beauty which a man finds it difficult to resist', but she is also 'rebellious, frivolous, ferocious and venal'.[45] She 'could not see a man without wishing to make him love [her]', she is afflicted with 'the mania of love'.[46] She is capricious, unpredictable, volatile, irrational and uncontrolled: 'I am extreme in everything', she warns her husband, 'I must love or I must hate'.[47] She is a 'charming monster' and a 'creature of hell'.[48]

Césarine is fatal to the men around her. Lacking conscience and entirely self-interested, she plays on their emotions, she lies, manipulates, entraps and corrupts. 'She dishonours or she kills', her husband says, 'between two smiles'.[49] Within a day of her return to the family home, Césarine has destroyed its safety and stability, seducing her husband's beloved protégé and plotting to steal the secrets of his invention on behalf of a shady foreign conglomerate who plan to use it against France. Through her uncontrolled sexuality Césarine – like Messalina – endangers both essential patriarchal structures: the family and the nation state. The play ends as it must: with the murder of Césarine by Claude.

By transposing the Roman empress to haute bourgeoise France, Dumas demonstrated the enduring power of her myth. The 'eternal Messalina' functions just as well in a nineteenth-century drawing room as in a first-century palace because she exposes fears of ungovernable, destructive feminine desire that are shared by every patriarchal society.

The nineteenth century loved to systematise, and by the 1870s doctors had started to try to classify human sexuality. These men distinguished between 'normal' sexual desire, which could exist

in only one form (heterosexual, monogamous and essentially procreative) and 'abnormal' sexual desire, which could take any number of imaginative forms, all of which required identification, definition and treatment. Each of these new classes of sexual pathology needed illustrative examples and, for a number of feminine perversions, Messalina proved the perfect candidate.

In his seminal 1886 work, *Psychopathia Sexualis*, the German psychiatrist Richard von Krafft-Ebing coined the term sado-masochism. Sadism, he argued, was a generally male pathology – arising, as he thought, when the naturally masculine role of sexual aggressor was intensified to an immoderate extreme. He noted that there were, however, some rare examples of sadism in women. He provides two modern case studies and then turns to the example of two historical women with 'sadistic instincts'. 'These nymphomaniacs', he says, 'are particularly characterised by their thirst for power, lust and cruelty'.[50] One example he cites is Catherine de'Medici, the other 'Valeria Messalina herself'. In this passage, Krafft-Ebing enshrines the vision of Messalina as *femme fatale* in science.

In late nineteenth-century Italy, another new discipline was emerging. Criminal anthropology posited that crime resulted from the biology of the individual and that the degenerate dispositions of 'born criminals' might therefore be identified via a study of the facial features. In 1893, two of the leading lights of this new 'science' published a book entitled *La donna delinquente, la prostituta e la donna normale*, or, *The Delinquent Woman, The Prostitute, and The Normal Woman*. The frontispiece was a drawing of a Roman bust from the Uffizi, captioned 'Messalina'. The bust reappeared later in the work – alongside photos of contemporary female murderers, poisoners, prostitutes and arsonists – as an example of the 'anatomy, pathology, and anthropometry of the female criminal and the prostitute'. The portrait of the young empress might appear attractive, the authors explain, but it betrays tell-tale signs of inborn delinquency: a low forehead and a heavy jaw, thick and wavy hair. It was unfortunate that, upon further research, the bust in question was re-identified as a portrait of Agrippina.[51]

The medicalised Messalina was not only a danger to men and to society; she was also a danger to *herself*. 'Excessive' female sexual desire has been defined as an illness ever since Ancient Greece, but by the nineteenth century the old diagnosis of *furor uterinus* (uterine frenzy) – a disease thought to arise either from the rising of vapours from the uterus to the brain or from demonic possession – was increasingly being replaced by the new and more psychologically focused diagnosis of 'nymphomania'. Messalina was, from the very start, cast as an ambassadress for this new medical trend. Doctors regularly referred to their nymphomaniac patients as 'Messalinas' and on occasion we find the disease itself referred to as the 'Messalina-Complex'.

The association of Messalina with nymphomania was based not so much on her reputation for sexual desire as on her reputation for sexual *insatiability*. 'Lassata viris necdum satiata', 'tired out by men but still not sated' – this is how Juvenal has Messalina leave the brothel as it closes in the morning, and this is the concept that defined the nineteenth-century nymphomaniac. A woman who suffered from 'acute nymphomania', doctors believed, would suddenly be afflicted with an 'unlimited desire for sexual gratification, obscene delirium' which, within just a few days, would result in 'death from exhaustion'. This patient becomes an extreme version of Juvenal's Messalina – unsatisfiable, she tires herself to death. Doctors had, in a sense, gone a step further than Dumas: Messalina no longer needed to be killed, because her own desire was poisoning her from the inside out.

Sed Non Satiata. This slight variation on the wording of Juvenal's description of Messalina entitles one of the poems in Baudelaire's 1857 collection *Les Fleurs du Mal*. Written about the Parisian poet's Haitian mistress Jeanne Duval, '*Sed Non*

Satiata' presents its subject as exotic, mystical, unknowable and, most concerningly of all, unsatisfiable. The poet finds that, 'in the hell of your bed', he cannot 'break the spirit' of his mistress or 'bring [her] to bay'.[52] We sense that here is a woman who might never be satisfied with what a man can offer her – in terms of sex, of wealth, of power – and that the feeding of her desires might consume him before it could ever sate her. It is this Messalinaic quality that both obsesses and terrifies Baudelaire.

Baudelaire was the godfather of the artistic movement – both disparaged and celebrated as 'Decadent' – that defined the *fin de siècle*; a movement for which Messalina would become an emblem and an obsession. The obsession was so intense, in fact, that by 1902 it had driven the literary critic Ernest-Charles to something of a journalistic breakdown: 'There are too many of these novels,' he wrote. 'Far *too many!* [...] For years now it is Messalina... Whose turn is it now? Who *hasn't* written about Messalina?'.[53] The subject may have lost its charm for Ernest-Charles, but it is easy to see Messalina's appeal as a theme for the writers and artists of this period. These men believed (and perhaps they were right) that they were living through the long death of a civilisation that had become too sweet and too heavy for its own good.

In contrast to the Romantic movement which had preceded it, the Decadent movement contended that human nature was not naturally good. Instead, they believed that man, naturally sinful, was intrinsically attracted to (although simultaneously repulsed by) corruption, vice and death. The successes of empire and industrialisation had brought new extremes of prosperity to European society; in the modern urban centres of Paris, London, Vienna and Berlin, any luxury or intoxicant or sexual service was immediately available to those willing to pay. This accessibility, it was thought, bred a boredom or ennui that drove people – by their nature attracted to corruption – to seek out new luxuries and new vices. This cycle of corruption and decay, the Decadent movement believed, could be concluded only by death: the death of the individual and, eventually, of the civilisation itself. The moral and social decline that came as society elaborated itself into new extremes of modernity demanded new forms of artistic expression, ones that privileged ornamentation, form and symbolism. There was beauty to be found, the Decadent movement proposed, both in the macabre process of decay itself, and in the artifice that sought to conceal or transcend it.

Ancient Rome was cited as the classic example of 'decadence', and the story of Messalina held an especially emblematic appeal for the artists of the Decadent Movement.[*] Juvenal's empress 'lassata [...] necdum satiata' was a perfect alter-ego for the Decadent society afflicted with the ennui of excess: tired but unsatisfied. Messalina's status as an archetypal *femme fatale* also contributed to her appeal. The figure of the deadly but alluring woman was a prominent one in Decadent art: she personified the connections the movement drew between death and sex, beauty and decay, attraction and revulsion. The details of the stories told about Messalina encapsulate key themes of the Decadent movement. There is the empress' penchant for adornment and artifice; her capacity for deceit, her disguise, the false identity of Lycisca, and her obsession with the fake nature offered by the Gardens of Lucullus. And there is the combination of luxury and filth that follows her from palace to brothel, and from wedding feast to rubbish cart. Juvenal's description of an insatiable,

---

[*] Eighteenth-century historians such as Montesquieu and Gibbon had linked moral, artistic, political and imperial decline in their analyses of the fall of the Roman empire. Augustan self-discipline gave way to the depravities and luxuries of the later emperors, the restrained golden age of Latin oratory and verse had been ruined by increasingly ornamental styles, and ideals of social and military duty were undermined, until, they argued, the empire had collapsed under its own weight. The artists of the 'Decadent movement' sought to reclaim this process of 'decline' as a source of artistic beauty.

murderous empress working in a low-class brothel under a fake name and wearing a blonde wig, her nipples covered in gold but her cheeks smeared with dirt is, perhaps, the Decadent scene *par excellence*.

The great British illustrator of aestheticism and decadence, Aubrey Beardsley, produced two images of Messalina for special editions of Juvenal's *Satires* commissioned by the controversial publisher Lionel Smithers. The first – probably created around 1895 – depicts the empress leaving the palace en route to the brothel. It is night and she is making her way through a formal garden; a small cluster of drooping flowers and a tiered hexagonal fountain are silhouetted against the pitch black of the background. Her small companion, hunched over and skull-like, stares out at us, but Messalina does not notice the viewer – as she strides forward her gaze is fixed in the direction of her destination and her mouth is set with determination. Beardsley depicts his empress ludicrously over-adorned. Her rococo-style bodice has been pulled down to reveal her breasts and the hood of her black cloak is decorated with feathers. She wears the famous yellow wig but Beardsley has pushed it back so thick black curls escape around the empress' face, revealing the artificial nature of her blondeness.

A few years later, Beardsley would produce a second illustration on the same theme. This time, Messalina is alone and returning to the palace. All her adornment is gone: she wears only a fine shift, ripped down to her waist, and her dark hair is uncovered and dishevelled. She has clearly had a busy night, but her expression remains unmodified. There are bags under her eyes but her eyes remain set, her mouth downturned, her fist is clenched at her side – this is a woman frustrated, vengeful even, in her failure to reach satisfaction.

Around the time that Beardsley produced this second drawing, the Belgian poet Iwan Gilkin addressed 'untamed Messalina' in his ironically entitled 1897 poem 'Prayer'.

You, the eternal love, You, the eternal woman,
Absurd Devouring, ignoble and solemn,
Who sucks out life and empties our brains,
[...]
And with your lily teeth, drunk with cruelty,
[...]
And with your insane nails, flushed red with roses,
Lacerate, knowingly, with exquisite pauses,
[...]
My muscles and my fibres, forever unsatisfied,
Until that day, Madonna, when your too smiling lips
Will press, in vain, the lips of my wounds.[54]

Gilkin's Messalina is the ultimate *fin de siècle femme fatale.*
Insatiable, sadistic and vampiric, she threatens to destroy
the artist – perhaps to destroy man more generally. In doing
so, however, she also allows the poet to play out his own
pretentiously Decadent fantasy; he can borrow the Baudelairian
image of the wound with lips, elide sex and death, and admit
his masochistic attraction to the destructive and macabre.* This
Messalina is both muse and murderess, but she remains in the
service of the artist.

On one of the streets on the hill leading up to Montmartre
in Paris is a townhouse set back a little from the street. The
rooms on the first floor are domestically bourgeois, small and
busily decorated in the style of the late nineteenth century, but
climb to the second floor and you emerge into a vast, two-storey
artist's studio. This was the studio, and is now the museum, of
the symbolist painter Gustave Moreau. Every inch of wall is
covered with his paintings of biblical and mythical subjects and,
among them, hang two depictions of Messalina.

---

* Baudelaire uses the image of the lips of a wound in 'À celle qui est trop
gaie'.

The first, much more finished than the second, depicts Messalina in the brothel. To the right of the composition stands a canopied bed, its white sheets rumpled, its red coverlet slipping to the ground. To the left, beneath a strange bat-like creature, sleep two crumpled figures – another couple perhaps, or two of Messalina's exhausted lovers. Above them, a window looks out over an imperial Rome of monumental buildings and equestrian statues. A column topped with a sculpture of Romulus and Remus being suckled by the she-wolf is illuminated by the light of a full moon. Inside, an elderly woman with her breasts exposed but her head bowed and veiled holds a smoking torch. She lights the room inside the brothel, but her placement also makes her seem to be setting fire to the vista of the city outside. With a pair of scissors hanging from her waist, she might be Messalina's ladies' maid, but she might equally be one of the fates – weaving Messalina's life-thread and preparing to cut at the necessary moment.

In the foreground we find the empress and one of her lovers. Messalina stands, one foot on a stair to the bed, the other knee bent to rest on the mattress. She is naked bar a thin strip of white fabric which clings improbably conveniently between her legs. Her lover, tanned, muscular and naked to the waist, stands below her on the floor. He has flung his arm around her waist and tipped his head back to gaze up at her. Although the empress rests one hand on his shoulder, she does not appear to notice him. Instead, Messalina's head, adorned with an elaborate hairstyle and a diadem, is turned away from him, her hand raised to her chin as though in thought as she stares into the recesses of the bed. Moreau has made his empress appear statue-like: her face is in perfect, classical profile, her skin has the flat whiteness of marble. 'I imagine this daughter of the emperors', Moreau wrote in a note to his mother about his latest work in progress, 'who personifies the unsatisfied desire of women in general, but also of feminine perversity, constantly seeking

341

out her idea of sensuality.' Her lover is clearly alive and feeling, flushed and desperate in his passion, but Moreau's Messalina is impenetrable, unsatisfiable and unreachable – indeed, she seems already to be dead.

*

In 1937 the Anglo-Indian Hollywood film star Merle Oberon smashed through the windscreen of a car. Oberon had been in London shooting the role of Messalina in an epic film production of Robert Graves' I, Claudius, a project that was already in a degree of trouble. Oberon narrowly survived the accident but it was clear that it would be months before she was able to work again. The production, and the role of Messalina especially, seemed cursed; the project was halted and never completed.

Instead, in the autumn of 1976, after a nearly forty-year silence, Graves' novel was adapted into a BBC mini-series. The series caused a furore. My own great-grandfather would, apparently, switch the TV off censoriously every time the opening credits began to roll, but he was undoubtedly in the minority. I, Claudius would become one of the most watched BBC productions of all time, introducing a whole generation to its (not entirely inaccurate) vision of the Julio-Claudians as a sex-obsessed royal mafia. 'I, Claudius getting better and better', ran a short notice published in the TV section of the Sunday Telegraph on 14 November 1976; 'switch on early if you don't want to miss the orgy'. Apparently, the orgy did not disappoint: the morning after, the Telegraph's reviewer judged it 'the first decent orgy we've had since the season started'. It is during these same scenes that we are first introduced to Graves' Messalina. Up until now we have encountered Messalina primarily as a symbol or a type. She has been a victim of the weakness of femininity, and an emblem of its destructive power, but she has rarely been very human. This changed, to an extent, with the publication of

Robert Graves' 1934 novels: *I, Claudius* and *Claudius the God and His Wife Messalina*. Presented as an autobiography written by the emperor himself, Graves makes us feel that nothing really significant separates us from the people who walked the forums. They shared, he imagines, our weaknesses, our prejudices, our desires and our emotions.

We first meet Messalina in *I, Claudius* as a fifteen-year-old victim of sexual abuse. Caligula has removed her from her father's house and brought her to the palace, where he forces her to appear nude before his guests as part of a theatrical pageant. Once the show is over, Caligula comments on the girl's beauty and her virginity. He had been considering raping her himself, he admits, but since he met Caesonia he has lost his taste for underage girls – instead, he suggests that Claudius divorce his wife and marry Messalina.

Claudius acknowledges that much of his young wife's initial affection for him derives from her relief at having escaped Caligula. Within two months of their marriage, she is pregnant. 'When a not very clever, not very attractive man of fifty', Claudius observes with the benefit of hindsight towards the end of the first book, 'falls in love with a very attractive and very clever girl of fifteen it is usually a poor look-out for him.'[55]

It is a prediction we watch play out over the course of the sequel, *Claudius the God and His Wife Messalina*. Claudius grants us privileged access to the imperial bedroom, and we watch in real time as Messalina gains his trust and employs it for her own purposes. Graves has Messalina make herself an indispensable imperial aid but still play up her feminine vulnerability when it suits her. He imagines the conversations that result in the political murders and exiles related by Tacitus, Suetonius and Dio: we watch as the empress mixes advice with jokes and flirtation, as she makes her insinuations casually or dramatically, whatever the situation calls for. This Messalina gains control over Claudius not via some mysterious seductive magic but by intelligence, good instinct and opportunism. His weakness, Claudius admits, is as much to blame as her opportunism.

Graves' Messalina is undoubtedly a villain – or at least, she appears so to our narrator Claudius. She lies, manipulates and murders. She is a bad wife, and little better as a mother. She humiliates and disappoints Claudius, although she does not completely destroy him.

And yet despite her role as an antagonist, and despite the one-sided nature of Claudius' account, we still get a sense that Graves' Messalina is *human*. She is complicated: at once clever, rational, funny and Machiavellian, and also beautiful, sensual and capricious. She comes across less as darkly all-consuming than painfully bored and desperate for entertainment; less insatiable than simply unsatisfied. Graves allows Messalina to be a woman driven both by politics and by sex, who exists both in her mind and in her body.

That Graves' characterisation of the empress as bad but human stands out as peculiarly sensitive says a lot about the treatments of Messalina that preceded it. For two millennia, Messalina has stood as an emblem for everything concerning about femininity. Even the most sympathetic renderings, the ones that invite us to pity her at the moment of her downfall, base their compassion on the belief that Messalina's fault lay in her uncontrolled *womanliness*, with all the sensuality and irrationality that implied, and on their confidence in her punishment. More often, the response to Messalina was one of fear, rage, titillation – or all three together. This was a woman who seemed to make a mockery of men with her imperial power and her sexual unsatisfiable-ness; in return she was made a witch, a weapon of political invective, an unspeaking sex object, a *femme fatale*, a medical case and even a vision of death itself.

Conclusion

In many ways, Messalina's story is the story of the Julio-Claudian dynasty. She was thrust into a position of power by birth and marriage and retained that position via a ruthless exploitation of the Julio-Claudian court's nuanced hypocrisies and tolerance for violence. She was concerned with the creation and survival of her own line, and well aware that failure would mean death, for herself and her children. The changes she made to the political landscape were not open and constitutional, they lay in the gradual pushing of boundaries, clearing of paths and creation of precedent. Her life was lived in a kind of luxury that would have been unimaginable even a hundred years before, in a social world deeply concerned with image and pageant, with the *theatre* of politics. Across the empire, she projected an image of ideal femininity and traditional morality, but people whispered rumours of her adulteries and secret, corrupting, perversions; of things that went on behind closed doors on the Palatine that spoke to dangerous cracks in the foundations of the state. These impulses, anxieties and conditions defined Messalina's life, but they also defined the culture and the politics of the age: little, either in Messalina's story or in her world, was as it seemed.

A story like Messalina's forces us to interact with the processes of mythologisation that shape all of ancient history. We know that the empress cannot really have worked as a low-class prostitute or have expected to bigamously marry Gaius Silius and get away with it – and so we ask where these stories come from, and why they develop, and what they signify. The unpicking of these tales helps us uncover Messalina's real history, but it also reveals something of the essence of an epoch in which the gulf between ideological façade and political reality bred increasingly outlandish tales of intrigues, murders and sexual depravities.

That these rumours centred especially on women is not surprising. The new power of imperial women was a symbol of the new dynastic system and the new court politics – the very existence of an 'empress' triggered all the anxieties that drove the processes of rumour creation. The women of the Julio-Claudian family also lived their lives and made their political moves more in private than their male counterparts; less was known or provable. There was more space for gossip – and no platform for women like Messalina to refute it.

Messalina and her mythologisation is a perfect case study both of the perils of Roman womanhood, and of the peculiar, sensuous, and paranoid world of Rome's first dynasty. But that does not mean that she should be approached merely as a symbol. Her association with sex means that this has occurred far too often and for far too long.

Western society has always been possessed by an impulse to categorise women. To make them neater, more easily consumable as objects or cultural symbols. To sort them into types which can be described succinctly, ascribed a value and pitted against one another. These categorisations have often, as in Messalina's case, centred on sexuality.

A Roman girl became a woman not through the passage of time but with her first marriage and the loss of her virginity. She was either a *virgo* or a *matrona*, and this status defined her rights, the rhythm of her life, her dress, her daily activities, and the way she was treated by others. Should she transgress some sexual boundary, she strayed into new categories still. Now she was an adulteress, or perhaps a prostitute. Her legal rights and protections had changed; society treated her differently and felt justified in doing so.

The drive to classify women on the basis of their sexuality has hardly let up in the years since the fall of Rome. With the advent of Catholicism, a woman became either a 'Madonna' or a 'Whore'. With the advent of cinema, she became 'the sex symbol' or 'the girl next door', or 'the mother', or 'the bimbo', or 'the naked murder victim', or 'the *femme fatale*'. A woman's sexual attractiveness, her choice of sexual partners, the circumstances in which she has sex, the fact of her having had sex at all; these have all been used historically to define a woman's identity and limit the boundaries of her existence – the same has never been true for men.

Messalina's association with sex – with seductiveness and desire as well as promiscuity – has clouded every aspect of her presentation. The career of Messalina's successor Agrippina was not so different from Messalina's own. She pursued similar policies and (although she survived a little longer) was politically ascendant for almost exactly the same length of time. Yet Agrippina has gone down in history as remarkably ambitious, rational, forward-thinking and politically astute. The ancient sources may vilify her, but in emphasising her unnatural, immoral masculinity they betray a grudging respect for her intelligence and success. Messalina's treatment is different. Though equally vilified, she receives none of the respect afforded to Agrippina. Even modern historians have tended to shrug aside questions of Messalina's motivations, to overlook her impact on the era, and to dismiss her as unworthy of serious study. The gap between the two women's careers is not sufficient to justify the gulf in their presentation. The real source of this disparity is not difficult to discern: the major difference between Messalina and Agrippina's characterisation comes down to sex.

For Messalina, a reputation for sexuality has spilled into every aspect of her history, eclipsed every accomplishment, obscured every other personality trait. The Messalina of our sources is mad and uncontrolled in her passions. Capricious, incapable of strategic thinking, and beholden to her immediate, momentary impulses. Her actions are inexplicable to rational men. She is driven only by her sensual, tangible desires for beauty, money, luxury and sex. Messalina's sexual reputation has cast her in renaissance morality tales, Victorian melodramas, and 1970s pornos; it has also affected ancient *and modern* historians' analyses of her motivations, her personal capabilities and her worth as a subject of study.

Worst of all, these narratives have transformed Messalina into a cipher of sexuality, obscuring a story that is more complex and more interesting. For seven years in the 40s AD, Messalina was the most powerful woman in the world. No other woman had lasted so long in a position of such power since Livia. She shaped the political landscape of her day and pioneered new methods of court politics – new templates for the exercise and projection of feminine power – that would last long after she had been killed. Messalina transformed the Roman concept of what it meant to be empress, but she was not infallible: her fall, when it came, was not the result of some sexual 'madness', but it did arise from a series of political and personal miscalculations.

We cannot call Messalina 'good': too much cheating, too much murder. Nor can we cast her as some sort of feminist role model: she worked within patriarchal structures and employed them against her female enemies just as much as she struggled against them herself. But we can say that she was powerful, interesting, audacious, innovative, and intelligent, and that for the best part of a decade she was successful. None of these qualities conflict with the existence of her attractiveness and her sexuality – or with the possibility that she made decisions that were not always sensible and possessed desires that were not always rational.

I do not ask the reader to believe that Messalina was impressively self-controlled, or self-denyingly moral, or blameless in her relationships, or intellectually infallible, or entirely strategically consistent. I only ask that they acknowledge that her achievements and her worth as a historical subject can sit alongside her errors and her failings and her immoralities – just as we allow the sins of Great Men to sit alongside their glories.

Acknowledgements

In my first term at Oxford, I tried to drop out at least twice. Having never studied ancient history before, I felt woefully behind my classmates, and I desperately missed my life in London. My tutor, the incomparable Professor Christina Kuhn, told me to stick it out until Christmas and that Michaelmas term she taught me a module entitled 'Tacitus and Tiberius'. I was hooked. It is to her and her teaching that I owe my involvement in ancient history and my obsession with the Julio-Claudians and their historiography.

It was whilst studying for a masters that I really began to consider Messalina in earnest and I'm so grateful to my supervisor, Professor Katherine Clarke, for taking my proposed thesis topic seriously and for encouraging me to approach the empress from new angles. Her teaching, questions, and insights had a huge impact on the development of the ideas that would form the basis of this book.

There are so many other teachers and tutors to whom I owe a great deal, among them Dr. Thomas Mannack, Dr. Claudia Wagner, Dr. Anna Clark, and Professor Nicholas Purcell. To Juliane Kerkhecker, who taught me not to be scared of Latin. To Irene Brooke, my supervisor at the Courtauld, I owe the ability to look at art and an appreciation of the visual which has transformed my understanding of history. I am also endlessly grateful to my doctoral supervisor, the brilliant Professor Jo Crawley Quinn, for the support, encouragement and crucially the patience she has shown me during the final months of producing this book.

I am forever indebted to Dan Jones and Antony and Nicolas Cheetham at Head of Zeus for taking a chance on Messalina and to the judgment and expertise of my editor, Richard Milbank. His edits and insights not only transformed this book into something fit to be seen by the general public but also taught me a great deal about how to write. Thank you too to Miranda Ward who had the Sisyphean task of copy-editing a dyslexic who never really learnt to use commas. And, of course, to my friend Edward Stanley, who once spotted a typo over my shoulder and who has never let me forget it.

Thanks are due to the whole team at Head of Zeus whose hard work and skill have made this book a reality – especially Aphra Le Levier-Bennett, Ellie Jardine, Clémence Jacquinet and Dan Groenewald. To my publicist Kathryn Colwell for her enthusiasm and energy. To Isambard Thomas for his work on producing the beautiful maps of Rome and the Empire and to Jessie Price for designing the stunning cover.

Thank you also to Clare Wallace, my agent, who has supported and encouraged this project from its very inception as well as to Mary Derby, Georgia Fuller, Salma Zarugh, and Chloe Davis at Darley Anderson Agency.

I have been lucky enough to receive support from a number of incredible historians at every stage of this process. The powerhouses that are Dan Jones and Sara Cockerill have been there to offer support and indispensable guidance from the very beginning – this project would never have happened without them. The legendary Antonia Fraser, long an inspiration, gave me a generous grant for the completion of my research and was equally generous with her advice and encouragement. Thanks are also due to the great Robin Lane Fox who was kind enough to take the time to cast his expert eye over my manuscript and suggest a number of pertinent corrections.

Thank you finally to my family for their unconditional support and to the friends who offered me both endless encouragement and endless distraction.

Bibliography

A Note on Translations

All translations from Latin, unless otherwise stated, are the author's own. All translations from Greek, unless otherwise stated, are taken from the Loeb Classical Library editions.

Primary Sources

Apollodorus, *Against Neaera*.
Aristotle, *Politics*.
Atheneaus, *Deipnosophistae*.
Augustus, *Res Gestae*.
Pseudo-Aurelius Victor, *Epitome of the Lives of the Caesars*.
Cassius Dio, *Roman History*.
Catullus, *Poems*.
Cicero, *On the Republic*.
Cicero, *On the Laws*.
Cicero, *The Verrine Orations*.
Cicero, *For Caelius*.
Cornelius Nepos, *On the Great Generals of Foreign Nations*.
Dionysius of Halicarnassus, *Roman Antiquities*.
Euripides, *Medea*.
Florus, *Poems*.
Galen, *Method of Medicine*.
Horace, *Odes and Epodes*.
Horace, *Satires*.
Josephus, *Jewish Antiquities*.
Julian, *Digest*.

BIBLIOGRAPHY

Juvenal, *Satires.*
Livy, *History of Rome.*
Livy, *The Periochae.*
Lucan, *The Civil War (Pharsalia).*
Lucian, *On Dance.*
Macrobius, *Saturnalia.*
Marcellus Empiricus, *On Medicines.*
Marcus Aurelius, *Meditations.*
Martial, *Epigrams.*
Ovid, *Amores.*
Ovid, *Fasti.*
Ovid, *The Art of Love.*
Ovid, *Tristia.*
Ovid, *Ex Ponto.*
Pseudo-Ovid, *Consolation to Livia.*
Paulus, *Opinions.*
Persius, *Satires.*
Petronius, *Satyricon.*
Philo, *On the Embassy to Gaius.*
Pliny the Elder, *Natural History*
Pliny the Younger, *Letters.*
Plutarch, *Lives.*
Plutarch, *On Talkativeness.*
Propertius, *Elegies.*
Sallust, *The War with Catiline.*
Seneca, *Consolation to Polybius.*
Seneca, *Consolation to Helvia.*
Seneca, *Natural Questions.*
Seneca, *On the Brevity of Life.*
Pseudo-Seneca, *Apocolocyntosis.*
Pseudo-Seneca, *Octavia.*
Soranus, *Gynaecology.*
Suetonius, *Lives of the Caesars.*
Sulpicia, *Poems.*
Tacitus, *Histories.*
Tacitus, *Annals.*
Tibullus, *Poems.*
Ulpian, *Digest.*
Valerius Maximus, *Memorable Doings and Sayings.*
Velleius Paterculus, *History of Rome.*
Virgil, *Georgics.*

Vitruvius, *On Architecture.*
Historia Augusta
The Suda

*

Anon., *Vingt Ans de la vie d'un jeune homme* (falsely dated 1789, c. 1830). Paris, Éditions Séguier (1996).

Baudelaire, C., *Les Fleurs du Mal* (1857). Translation Howard, R.: New York, Everyman's Library, Random House (1993).

Boccaccio, G., *On the Falls of Famous Men* (late 1350s).

Brontë, C., *Jane Eyre* (1847). London, Penguin Classics (2006).

Cossa, P., *Messalina* (1876). London, Forgotten Books (2018).

Croze-Magnan, S-C., *L'Aretin d'Augustin Carrache, ou Recueil de postures érotiques, d'après les gravures à l'eau-forte par vet artiste célèbre, avec le texte explicative des sujets.* Paris, Pierre Didot (1798).

Dumas, A. fils, *L'Homme-Femme: réponse à M. Henri d'Ildeville* (1872). Translation Vanderhoff, G.: Philadelphia, New York and Boston (1873).

Dumas, A. fils, *La Femme de Claude* (1873). Translation, Byrne, C. A. New York, F. Rullman (1905).

Gallois, L. (ed), *Réimpression de l'Ancien Moniteur Vol. 18.* Paris, Au Bureau Centrale (1841).

Gilkin, I., *Prayer* (1897). Translation Friedman, D. F.: *An Anthology of Belgian Symbolist Poets.* Bern, Peter Lang Publishing (2003).

Gorani, J., *Mémoires secrets et critiques vol. 1.* Paris, Chez Buisson (1793).

Graves, R., *I, Claudius* and *Claudius the God* (1934). Penguin Modern Classics, London, Penguin Random House (2006).

Isidore de Lara (libretto Sylvestre & Morand E.). *Messaline* (1899).

Jarry, A., *Messalina* (1900). London, Atlas Press (1985).

Maquet, A. and Lacroix, J., *Valeria.* Paris (1851).

Nerciat, A., *Les Aphrodites; ou Fragments thali-priapiques pour server à l'histoire du plaisir* (1793).

Pona, F., *Messalina.* Venice (1627).

Richards, N., *Tragedy of Messalina, Empress of Rome* (1640).

de Sade, D. A. F., *Histoire de Juliette* (1800). New York, Grove Press (1994).

Von-Krafft-Ebing, R., *Psychopathia Sexualis* (1886). New York, Arcade Publishing (2011).

Wilbrandt, A., *Arria und Messalina* (1877). Norderstedt, Hansebooks (2016).

Wilmot, J., *Rochester's Farewell* (1680).

Secondary Sources

Aali, H. *French Royal Women during the Restoration and July Monarchy: Redefining Women and Power.* Hampshire, Palgrave Macmillan (2021).

Adams, J. 'Words for Prostitute in Latin', *Rheinisches Museum für Philologie vol. 126, no. 3* (1983), pp. 321–358.

D'Ambra, E., *Roman Women.* Cambridge, Cambridge University Press (2007).

Baldwin, B., 'Executions under Claudius: Seneca's "Ludus de Morte Claudii"'. *Phoenix, vol. 18, no. 1* (1964), pp. 39–48.

Baldwin, B. 'The "Epitome de Caesaribus," from Augustus to Domitian', *Quaderni Urbinati di Cultura Classica, new series, vol. 43, no. 1,* (1993), pp. 81–101.

Barnes, T. D. 'Review: Epitome de Ceasaribus', *The Classical Review, vol. 52, no. 1* (2002), pp. 25–27.

Barrett, A., *Caligula: The Corruption of Power.* London, Batsford Ltd. (1989).

Barrett, A., *Agrippina: Sex, Power and Politics in the Early Empire.* New Haven and London, Yale University Press (1996).

Barrett, A. 'Tacitus, Livia and the Evil Stepmother', *Rheinisches Museum für Philologie vol. 144, no. 2* (2001), pp. 171–175.

Bauman, R. A., *Women and Politics in Ancient Rome.* London, Routledge (1993).

Beard, M., *The Roman Triumph.* Cambridge MA, Harvard University Press (2007).

Beard, M., *Twelve Caesars: Images of Power from the Ancient World to the Modern.* Princeton and Oxford, Princeton University Press (2021).

De la Bedoyère, G., *Domina: The Women who made Imperial Rome.* New Haven & London, Yale University Press (2018).

Bodel, J. 'Chronology and Succession 2: Notes on Some Consular Lists on Stone', *Zeitschrift für Papyrologie und Epigraphik, bd. 105* (1995), pp. 279–296.

Bowe, P., *Gardens of the Roman World.* Los Angeles, J. Paul Getty Museum (2004).

Bowman, A., Champlin, E. and Lintott, A. (eds.) *The Cambridge Ancient History Vol. 10: The Augustan Empire, 43 BC – AD 69.* Cambridge, Cambridge University Press (1996).

Bradley, M., 'Colour and marble in early imperial Rome', *The Cambridge Classical Journal, vol. 52* (2006), pp. 1–22.

Brunn, C. 'The Name and Possessions of Nero's Freedman Phaon', *ARCTOS vol. 23* (1989), pp. 41–53.

Brunn, C. and Edmondson, J. (eds.), *The Oxford Handbook of Roman Epigraphy*. Oxford, Oxford University Press (2014).

Brunt, P. A. 'Evidence given under Torture in the Principate', *Zeitschrift der Savigny-Stiftung für Rechtsgeschichte. Romanistische Abtheilung, vol 97* (1980), pp. 256–265.

Butler, M., *Theatre and Crisis 1632–1642*. Cambridge, Cambridge University Press (1984).

Carlson, D. 'Caligula's Floating Palaces', *Archaeology vol. 55, no. 3* (2002), pp. 26–31.

Carney, E. D. and Müller, S. (eds.) *The Routledge Companion to Women and Monarchy in the Ancient Mediterranean World*. London, Routledge (2020).

Lo Cascio, E., 'The Population', in Claridge, A. & Holleran, C. (eds.) *A Companion to the City of Rome*. Hoboken & Chichester, John Wiley & Sons (2018).

Champlin, E. 'The Testament of Augustus', *Rheinisches Museum für Philologie* (1989), pp. 154–165.

Chausson, F. and Galliano, G. (eds.), *Claude: Un Empereur au Destin Singulier*. Lyon, Musée des Beaux-Arts (2018).

Chrystal, P., *Women in Ancient Rome*. Stroud, Amberley Publishing (2013).

Claridge, A. & Holleran, C. (eds.) *A Companion to the City of Rome*. Hoboken & Chicester, John Wiley & Sons (2018).

Clarke, J. R., *Art in the Lives of Ordinary Romans*. Oakland, University of California Press (2003).

Clarke, J. R. *Looking at Lovemaking*. Berkeley, Los Angeles and London, University of California Press (1998).

Clarke, J. R. and Muntasser N. K. (eds.), *Oplontis: Villa A (Of Poppaea) at Torren Annunziata, Italy*. ACLS Humanities (2019).

Coarelli, F., *Rome and Environs: an archeological guide*. Berkeley, Los Angeles and London, University of California Press (2009).

Colin, J., 'Les vendanges dionysiaques et la légende de Messaline', *Les Etudes Classiques, vol. 24, no. 1* (1956), pp. 25–39.

Colls, D., Domergue C., Laubenheimer F., Liou B. 'Les lingot d'étains de l'épave Port-Vendres II', *Gallia* (1975), pp. 61–94.

Courtney, E. 'The Interpolations in Juvenal', *Bulletin of the Institute of Classical Studies vol. 22* (1975), pp. 147–162.

Cryle, P. M., *The Telling of the Act: Sexuality as narrator in eighteenth and nineteenth century France*. Delaware, University of Delaware Press (2001).

Cursi, G. M., 'Roman Horti: a topographical view in the Imperial age', in Bartz. J., (ed.), *Public | Private*. Berlin, Winkleman Institute, (2019).

Delia, D., 'Fulvia Reconsidered' in Pomeroy, S. B. (ed.) *Women's History and Ancient History*, Chapel Hill, University of North Carolina Press (1991).

Dunning, S. B., 'The transformation of the saeculum and its rhetoric in the construction and rejection of roman imperial power' in Faure, R., Valli, S-P. and Zucker, A. (eds.) *Conceptions of Time in Greek and Roman Antiquity*. Berlin and Boston, De Grutyer (2022).

Dunning, S. B., *Roman Ludi Saeculares from the Republic to Empire*. Thesis, University of Toronto (2016).

Eder, W. 'Augustus and the Power of Tradition' in K. Galinsky (ed.) *The Cambridge Companion to the Age of Augustus*, pp. 13–32, Cambridge, Cambridge University Press. (2005).

Edmondson, J. and Keith, A. (eds) *Roman Dress and the Fabrics of Roman Culture*. Toronto, University of Toronto Press (2009).

Edwards, C. *The Politics of Immorality in Ancient Rome*. Cambridge, Cambridge University Press (1993).

Fagan, G., 'Messalina's Folly', *The Classical Quarterly vol. 52, no. 2* (2002), pp. 566–579.

Fant, M. and Lefkowitz, M., *Women's Life in Greece and Rome: A Source Book in Translation*. London, Bloomsbury Publishing (2016).

Fantham, E., *Julia Augusti: the Emperor's Daughter*. New York, Routledge (2006).

Farrone, C. A. and McClure, L. K. (eds) *Prostitutes and Courtesans in the Ancient World*. Madison, University of Wisconsin Press (2006).

Ferrill, A., *Caligula, Emperor of Rome*. London, Thames and Hudson (1991).

Flory, M. B. 'Sic Exempla Parantur: Livia's Shrine to Concordia and the Porticus Liviae', *Historia: Zeitschrift für Alte Geschichte vol. 33, no. 3* (1984), pp. 309–330.

Flory, M. B., 'Livia and the History of Public Honorific Statues for Women in Rome', *Transactions on the American Philological Association, vol. 123* (1993), pp. 287–308.

Flory, M. B., 'Dynastic Ideology, the Domus, Augusta, and Imperial Women: A Lost Statuary Group in the Circus Flaminius', *Transactions of the American Philological Association, vol. 126* (1996), pp. 287–306.

Flory, M. B., 'The Integration of Women into the Roman Triumph', *Historia: Zeitschrift für Alte Geschichte* (1998), pp. 489–494.

Flower, H., *Ancestor Masks and Aristocratic Power in Roman Culture*. Oxford, Oxford University Press (1996).

Foubert, L. L., 'The Palatine dwelling of the "mater familias". Houses as symbolic space in the Julio-Claudian period', *Klio: Beiträge zur Alten Geschichte, vol. 92, no. 1* (2010), pp. 65–82.

Gallivan, P., 'The Fasti for the Reign of Gaius', *Antichthon vol. 13* (1979), pp. 66–69. Cambridge, University of Cambridge Press.

Gardner, J. F., *The Roman Household: A Sourcebook*. London & New York, Routledge (1991).

Ginsburg, J., *Representing Agrippina: Constructions of Female Power in the Early Roman Empire*. Oxford, Oxford University Press (2006).

Gorski, G. and Packer, J., *The Roman Forum: A Reconstruction and Architectural Guide*. Cambridge, Cambridge University Press (2015).

Griffin, M., *Nero: The End of a Dynasty*. London, Batsford (1984).

Groneman, C., *Nymphomania, a history*. New York, Norton & Co (2001).

Grubbs, J. E., *Women and the Law in the Roman Empire*. London and New York, Routledge (2002).

Grubbs, J. E., 'Making the Private Public: illegitimacy and incest in Roman law' in Ando C. and Rupke J. (eds) *Public and Private in Ancient Mediterranean Law and Religion*. Berlin, De Gruyter (2015).

Hallett, J. P., *Fathers and Daughters in Roman Society: Women and the Elite Family*. Princeton, Princeton University Press (1984).

Harris, C., *Queenship and Revolution in early modern Europe: Henrietta Maria and Marie Antionette*. Hampshire, Palgrave Macmillan (2016).

Haselberger, L. et. al. (eds) *Mapping Augustan Rome, Journal of Roman Archaeology, supplementary series 50*. Rhode Island (2002).

Hekster, O. and Rich, J., 'Octavian and the Thunderbolt: The Temple of Apollo Palatinus and Roman Traditions of Temple Building'. *The Classical Quaterly vol. 56* (2006), pp. 149–168.

Heller, W., *Emblems of Eloquence: Opera and Women's Voices in Seventeenth Century Venice*. Berkeley, Los Angeles and London, University of California Press (2003).

Hemelrijk, E., *Matrona Docta: Educated Women in the Roman Elite from Cornelia to Julia Domma*. London & New York, Routledge (2004).

Hersch, K., *The Roman Wedding: Ritual and Meaning in Antiquity*. Cambridge, Cambridge University Press (2010).

Höbenreich, E. and Rizzelli, G., 'Poisoning in Ancient Rome: The Legal Framework, The Nature of Poisons and Gender Stereotypes' in Wexler P., *History of Toxicology and Environmental Health: Toxicology in Antiquity, Volume II*. Amsterdam, Academic Press (2015).

Holleman, A. W. J., 'The "Wig" of Messalina and the Origin of Rome', *Museum Helveticum, vol. 32, no. 4* (1975), pp. 251–253.

Jakab, E., 'Financial Transactions by Women in Puteoli' in du Pleissis (ed.), *New Frontiers: Law and Society in the Roman World*. Edinburgh, Edinburgh University Press (2014).

Joshel, S. R., *Work, Identity and Legal Status at Rome. A Study of the Occupational Inscriptions*. Norman and London, University of Oklahoma Press (1992).

Joshel, S. R., 'Female Desire and the Discourse of Empire: Tacitus's Messalina', *Signs vol. 21, no. 1* (1995), pp. 50–82.

Kehoe, D., 'Production in Rome', in Claridge, A. & Holleran, C. (eds) *A Companion to the City of Rome*. Hoboken & Chichester, John Wiley & Sons (2018).

Kerkeslager, A., 'Agrippa and the Mourning Rites for Drusilla in Alexandria', *Journal for the Study of Judaism, vol. 37* (2006), pp. 367–400.

Kokkinos, N., *Antonia Augusta: Portrait of a Great Roman Lady*. London and New York, Routledge (1992).

Langlands, R., *Sexual Morality in Ancient Rome*. Cambridge, Cambridge University Press (2006).

Laurence, R., *Roman Pompeii: Space and Society*. Oxford, Routledge (1994).

Leiva, A. D., *Messaline, impératrice et putain: Généalogie d'un mythe sexuel de Pline au pornopéplum*. Nice, Du Murmure (2014).

Levick, B., *Claudius*. New Haven and London, Yale University Press (1990).

Levick, B., *The Government of the Roman Empire*. New York, Routledge (2000).

Levin-Richardson, S., *The Brothel of Pompeii: Sex, Class and Gender at the margins of Roman Society*. Cambridge, Cambridge University Press (2019).

Lindsay, H., 'The "Laudatio Murdiae": Its Content and Significance', *Latomus: Revue d'Études Latines vol. 63* (2004), pp. 88–97.

Ling, R., *Roman Painting*. Cambridge, Cambridge University Press (1991).

Machado, C., 'Building the Past: Monuments and Memory in the Forum Romanum', in Bowden, W., Gutteridge, A. and Machado, C. (eds) *Social and Political Life in Late Antiquity, vol. 3.1*. Leiden, Brill (2006).

MacMullen, R., 'Women in Public in the Roman Empire' in *Historia: Zeitschrift für alte Geschichte vol. 29 no. 2* (1980), pp. 208–218.

Marshall, A. J., 'Tacitus and the Govenor's Lady: A Note on Annals III.33–4' in *Greece and Rome, vol. 22, no. 1.* (1975), pp. 11–18.

Marshall, A. J., 'Roman Women and the Provinces', *Ancient Society vol. 6*, (1975), pp. 109–127.

McGinn, A. J., *Prostitution, Sexuality and the Law in Ancient Rome*. Oxford, Oxford University Press (1998).

McGinn, A. J., *The Economy of Prostitution in the Roman World*. Ann Arbor, University of Michigan Press (2004).

McGinn, A. J., 'Zoning Shame in the Roman City', in Faraone C. A. and McClure L. K. (eds) *Prostitutes & Courtesans in the Ancient World*. Madison, University of Wisconsin Press (2006).

MacMullen, R., 'Woman in Public in the Roman Empire', *Historia: Zeitschrift Für Alte Geschichte vol. 29, no. 2*. (1980), pp. 208–218.

Millar, F., 'The Emperor, the Senate and the Provinces', *The Journal of Roman Studies vol. 56* (1966), pp. 156–166.

Millar, F., 'State and Subject: The Impact of Monarchy' in Millar F. and Segal, E. (eds) *Caesar Augsutus. Seven Aspects*. Oxford, Clarendon Press (1984).

Moore, K., ' Octavia Minor and Patronage' in Carney, E. D. and Müller, S. (eds) *The Routledge Companion to Women and Monarchy in the Ancient Mediterranean World*. London, Routledge (2020).

Mouritsen, H., *The Freedman in the Roman World*. Cambridge, Cambridge University Press (2011).

Myers, K. S., 'The Poet and the Procuress: The Lena in Latin Love Elegy', *Journal of Roman Studies, vol. 86* (1996), pp. 1–21.

Nappa, C., *Making Men Ridiculous: Juvenal and the Anxieties of the Individual*. Ann Arbor, University of Michigan Press (2018).

O'Neill, J. R., 'Claudius the Censor and the Rhetoric of Re-Foundation', *Classical Journal vol. 116, no. 2* (2020), pp. 216–240.

Olsen, K., 'Matrona and Whore: Clothing and Definition in Roman Antiquity', in Faraone C. A. and McClure L. K. (eds) *Prostitutes & Courtesans in the Ancient World*. Madison, University of Wisconsin Press. (2006).

Osgood, J., *Claudius Caesar: Image and Power in the Early Roman Empire*. Cambridge, Cambridge University Press (2011).

Pagán, V. E., 'Horticulture and the Roman Shaping of Nature', in *Oxford Handbook Topics in Classical Studies*. Oxford, Oxford University Press (2016).

Pappalardo, U., *The Splendor of Roman Wall Painting*. Los Angeles, J. Paul Getty Museum (2009).

Patterson, J., 'Friends in high places: the creation of the court of the Roman emperor', in Spawforth, A. J. S. (ed.) *The Court and Court Society in Ancient Monarchies*. Cambridge, Cambridge University Press (2007).

Plescia, J., 'Judicial Accountability and Immunity in Roman Law.' *The American Journal of Legal History, vol. 45, no. 1* (2001), pp. 51–70.

Pomeroy, S. B. (ed.), *Women's History and Ancient History.* Chapel Hill, University of North Carolina Press (1991).

Purcell, N., 'Livia and the Womanhood of Rome', *Proceedings of the Cambridge Philological Society, no. 32* (1986), pp. 78–105.

Rich, J. W., 'Drusus and the spolia optima' in *The Classical Quarterly vol. 49, Issue 2* (1999), pp. 544–555.

Richardson, L., 'The Evolution of the Porticus Octaviae', *American Journal of Archaeology vol. 80, no. 1* (1976), pp. 57–64.

Richardson, L., *A New Topographical Dictionary of Ancient Rome.* Baltimore, Johns Hopkins University Press (1992).

Richlin, A., *The Garden of Priapus: Sexuality and Aggression in Roman Humor.* New York and Oxford, Oxford University Press (1992).

Richlin, A., *Arguments with Silence: Writing the History of Roman Women.* Ann Arbor, University of Michigan Press (2014).

Rose, C. B. *Dynastic Commemoration and Imperial Portraiture in the Julio-Claudian Period.* Cambridge, Cambridge University Press (1997).

Rounding, V., *Grandes Horizontales.* London. Bloomsbury Publishing (2004).

Salas, L. A. 'Why Lovesickness is Not a Disease: Galen's Diagnosis and Classification of Psychological Distress', *TAPA, vol. 152, no. 2* (2022), pp. 507–539.

Santoro, L'Hoir, F., 'Tacitus and Women's Usurpation of Power', *The Classical World vol. 88, no. 1* (1994), pp. 5–25.

Schaps, D., 'The Woman Least Mentioned: Etiquette and Women's Names', *The Classical Quarterly vol. 27, no. 2* (1977), pp. 323–330.

Shapiro, A-L., 'Love Stories: Female Crimes of Passion in Fin-de-Siècle Paris', *Differences: A Journal of Feminist Cultural Studies, vol. 3. no. 3* (1991), pp. 45–68.

Shapiro, A-L., *Breaking the Codes: Female Criminality in Fin-de-Siècle Paris.* Stanford, Stanford University Press (1996).

Sherk, R. K. (ed. and trans.), *The Roman Empire: Augustus to Hadrian: Vol. 6 Translated Documents of Greece and Rome.* Cambridge, Cambridge University Press (1988).

Sijpesteijn, P. J., 'Another οὐσία of D. Valerius Asiaticus in Egypt' for papyrus' relating to Valerius Asiaticus' holdings', *Zeitschrift für Papyrologie und Epigraphik* (1989), pp. 194–196.

Simpson, C. J., 'The Date of Dedication of the Temple of Mars Ultor', *The Journal of Roman Studies vol. 67* (1977), pp. 91–94.

Simpson, C. J., 'The Birth of Claudius and the Date of Dedication of the Altar of "Romae et Augusto" at Lyon', *Latomus: Revue d'Études Latines vol. 46* (1987), pp. 586–592.

Smallwood, E. M., *Documents Illustrating the Principates of Gaius Claudius and Nero*. Cambridge University Press, Cambridge (1967).

Spawforth, A. J. S. (ed) *The Court and Court Society in Ancient Monarchies*. Cambridge, Cambridge University Press (2007).

Von Stackelberg, K. T., 'Performative Space and Garden Transgressions in Tacitus' Death of Messalina' in *The American Journal of Philology vol. 130, no. 4* (2009) pp. 595–624.

Steintrager, J. A., *The Autonomy of Pleasure: Libertines, License and Sexual Revolution*. New York, Columbia University Press (2016).

Stern, G., *Women, Children, and Senators on the Ara Pacis Augustae: a study of Augustus' vision of a New World Order in 13 BC*. Berkeley, University of California (2006).

Strong, A. K., *Labelled Women: Roman Prostitutes and Persistent Stereotypes*. New York, Columbia University Press (2005).

Strong, A. K., *Can You Tell Me How to Get to the Roman Brothel? Public Prominence of Prostitutes in the Roman World*. Social Science Research Network (2010).

Strong, A. K., *Prostitutes and Matrons in the Roman World*. Cambridge, Cambridge University Press (2016).

Swetnam-Burland, M. 'Aegyptus Redacta: The Egyptian Obelisk in the Augustan Campus Martius', *The Art Bulletin vol. 92, no. 3* (2010), pp. 135–153.

Syme, R., 'The Marriage of Rubellius Blandus', *The American Journal of Philology vol. 103, no. 1* (1982), pp. 62–85.

Syme, R., 'Neglected Children on the Ara Pacis', *American Journal of Archeology, vol. 88, no. 4* (1984), pp. 583-589.

Syme, R. *The Augustan Aristocracy*. Oxford, Oxford University Press (1986).

Talvacchia, B. 'Classical Paradigms and Renaissance Antiquarianism in Giulio Romano's "I Modi"', *I Tatti Studies in the Italian Renaissance vol. 7* (1997), pp. 81–118.

Treggiari, S., 'Domestic Staff at Rome in the Julio-Claudian Period, 27 B.C. to A.D. 68', *Histoire sociale/Social history, vol. 6, no. 12* (1973), pp. 241–255.

Treggiari, S., 'Jobs in the household of Livia', *Papers of the British School at Rome vol. 43* (1975), pp. 48–77.

Treggiari, S., *Roman Marriage: Iusti Coniuges From the Time of Cicero to the Time of Ulpian*. Oxford, Clarendon Press (1991).

Turner, J., 'Marcantonio's Lost Modi and their Copies', *Print Quarterly vol. 21, no.* 4 (2004), pp. 363–384.

Varner, E. R., 'Portraits, Plots, and Politics: "Damnatio Memoriae" and the images of imperial women', *Memoirs of the American Academy in Rome, vol.* 46 (2001), pp. 41-93.

Varner, E. R., *Mutilation and Transformation, damnatio memoriae and Roman imperial portraiture.* Leiden, Brill (2004).

Wallace-Hadrill, A., *Houses and Society in Pompeii and Herculaneum.* Princeton, Princeton University Press (1994).

Wallace-Hadrill, A., 'Public honour and private shame: the urban texture of Pompeii', in Cornell T. J., and Lomas K. (eds) *Urban Society in Roman Italy.* London, Routledge (1995).

Wallace-Hadrill, A., *Rome's Cultural Revolution.* Cambridge, Cambridge University Press (2008).

Wardle, J. 'Valerius Maximus on the Domus Augusta, Augustus and Tiberius', *The Classical Quarterly vol. 50, no.* 2 (2000), pp. 479–493.

Watson, L. and Watson P. (eds) *Juvenal Satire 6. Text and Commentary.* Cambridge, Cambridge University Press (2014).

Weaver, P. R. C., 'Slave and Freedman "Cursus" in the Imperial Administration', *Proceedings of the Cambridge Philological Society* (1964), pp. 74-92.

Weaver, P. R. C., *Familia Caesaris: A Social Study of the Emperor's Freedmen and Slaves.* Cambridge, Cambridge University Press (1972).

Winterling, A., *Politics and Society in Imperial Rome.* Chichester, Wiley-Blackwell (2009).

Wiseman, T. P., *The Death of Caligula: Josephus Ant. Iud. XIX 1-273, translation and commentary.* Liverpool, Liverpool University Press (2013).

Wood, S., 'Diva Drusilla Panthea and the Sisters of Caligula', *American Journal of Archaeology vol. 99, no.* 3 (1995), pp. 457–482.

Wood, S., 'Messalina, wife of Claudius: propaganda successes and failures of his reign', *Journal of Roman Archaeology* 5 (2015), pp. 219–234.

Woodhull, M., 'Engendering space: Octavia's Portico in Rome', in *Aurora: The Journal of the History of Art, vol.* 4 (2003), pp. 13–33.

Woodhull, M. L., *Building Power: Women as Architectural Patrons During the Early Roman Empire, 30 BC – 54 CE.* Austin, University of Texas Press (1999).

Woods, D., 'The Role of Lucius Vitellius in the Death of Messalina', *Mnemosyne, vol.* 70 (2017), pp. 996–1007.

Wyke, M., *The Roman mistress: ancient and modern representations.* Oxford, Oxford University Press (2002).

Zanker, P., *The Power of Images in the Age of Augustus.* Ann Arbor, Michigan University Press (1988).

Endnotes

Abbreviations

CIL – *Corpus Inscriptionum Latinarum*
ILS – *Inscriptiones Latinae Selectae*
PLondon – *Greek Papyri in the British Museum*
RIC – *Roman Imperial Coinage*
RPC – *Roman Provincial Coinage*

Introduction

1. On the *I Modi* see Talvacchia, *Taking Positions: On the Erotic in Renaissance Culture*. On the surviving evidence for Marcantonio Raimondi's original prints see Turner, 'Marcantonio's Lost Modi and their Copies'.
2. Juvenal, *Satires*, 6.114–132.
3. Didot, *L'Arétin d'Augustin Carrache, ou recueil de postures érotiques*, 53–56.
4. Gorani, *Mémoires secrets et critiques*, vol. 1, p. 98.
5. For Medea's speech see Euripides, *Medea*, 214–267. Lines 230–231 are quoted here: translation, P. Roche, *Three Plays of Euripides: Alcestis, Medea, The Bacchae* (New York, 1974). For Boudicca's speech see Tacitus, *Annals*, 14.35.
6. The best example of the use of a woman's name to cast aspersions on her character is perhaps Apollodorus' speech 'Against Neaera' (included in the Demosthenic corpus, speech 59). See also Schaps, 'The Woman Least Mentioned: Etiquette and Women's Names'.
7. *Laudatio Murdiae*, lines 20–29: CIL VI 10230 = ILS 8394. For a discussion of this inscription see Lindsay, 'The "Laudatio Murdiae": Its Content and Significance'.

Prelude

1. The exact find spot of the pipe (Science Museum A635516) is unknown; it was acquired by the Wellcome Collection from the Italian opera singer and collector Evangelista Gorga in 1936.
2. Tacitus, *Annals*, 1.1.
3. Tacitus, *Annals*, 11.27.

I

1. Tacitus' narrative of these events can be found at Tacitus, *Annals*, 11.26–11.38. See also Dio's much briefer account at 60.31 and Suetonius, *Life of Claudius*, 26.2, 29.3, 36.
2. Tacitus, *Annals*, 11.27.

II

1. For an overview of the architecture, design, decoration and use of the forum see Richardson, *A New Topographical Dictionary of Ancient Rome*, 160–162. For a visual reconstruction of how the project developed see Gorski & Packer, *The Roman Forum*.
2. On this vow see Suetonius, *Life of Augustus*, 29.2, and Ovid, *Fasti*, 5.569–578. The forum was not dedicated until 2 BC: Cassius Dio, 55.10.1–8; Velleius Paterculus, 2.100.2; see also Simpson, 'The Date of Dedication of the Temple of Mars Ultor'.
3. For a comprehensive overview of the archaeology of the Forum Romanum see Coarelli, *Rome and Environs: An Archaeological Guide*, 74–161. Also Richardson, *A New Topographical Dictionary of Ancient Rome*, 170–174.
4. For Augustus' statue on the Rostra see Velleius Paterculus, 2.61.3.
5. On the temple's dedication see Cassius Dio, 51.22.
6. For the Forum Romanum as a site of communal memory creation and preservation see Machado, 'Building the Past: Monuments and Memory in the Forum Romanum'. For an example of the rhetorical use of Rome's memory-laden landscape see Livy's imagining of the speech of Camillus: *History of Rome*, 5.51.
7. On the imperial connotations of polychrome marble see Bradley, 'Colour and marble in early imperial Rome'. For a summary of the materials used in the Augustan forum see Gorski & Packer, *The Roman Forum*, 15–16.
8. Lo Cascio, 'The Population', 139–153; see also Kehoe, 'Production in Rome', 443–444.

9. Pliny, *Natural History*, 36.24.
10. On Marcus Lepidus' thresholds see Pliny, *Natural History*, 36.8. On Scaurus' columns (which were reused from a remarkably extravagant temporary theatre that he had erected) see Pliny, *Natural History*, 36.2.
11. Pliny, *Natural History*, 36.7.
12. Polybius, *Histories*, 38.21.
13. On the definition and development of this office see Badian and Lintott, "pro consule, pro praetore" in *The Oxford Classical Dictionary*.
14. On the pro-magistrate's powers and judicial immunity see Plescia, 'Judicial Accountability and Immunity in Roman Law' esp. pp. 51–56, in *American Journal of Legal History*, vol. 45, no. 1. For a famous example of a pro-magistrate held to account after his return from his province see Cicero's *In Verrem*.
15. Augustus, *Res Gestae*, 1.
16. Cassius Dio, 51.20.4.
17. Suetonius, *Life of Augustus*, 22; Augustus, *Res Gestae*, 13.
18. Augustus, *Res Gestae*, 12.
19. On the obelisk see Swetnam-Burland, 'Aegyptus Redacta: The Egyptian Obelisk in the Augustan Campus Martius'; for an overview of the Ara Pacis see Richardson, *A New Topographical Dictionary of Ancient Rome*, 287–289.
20. The identification of individual figures on the Ara Pacis is notoriously tricky: see, for example, Syme, 'Neglected Children on the Ara Pacis', and Stern, *Women, Children, and Senators on the Ara Pacis Augustae* for alternative versions both involving numerous members of Messalina's immediate family.
21. Augustus, *Res Gestae*, 34; Cassius Dio, 53.2–11.
22. Cassius Dio, 53.12. See also Millar, 'The Emperor, the Senate and the Provinces'.
23. For a summary of the settlements of 27 and 23 BC see Crook, 'Political history 30 BC to AD 14' esp. pp. 78–80 (27 BC) and 85–87 (23 BC), in *The Cambridge Ancient History Vol. 10*.
24. Suetonius, *Life of Augustus*, 99.

III

1. For his role in the revolution see Livy, *History of Rome*, 1.58; for his consulship see Livy, *History of Rome*, 2.2.
2. Syme, *The Augustan Aristocracy*, 147, 164–166.
3. On family *imagines* see Flower, 'Ancestor Masks and Aristocratic Power in Roman Culture'.

4. Syme, *The Augustan Aristocracy*, 147, 164.
5. On Faustus Sulla Felix' consulship see Syme, *The Augustan Aristocracy*, 164; a five-year dispensation had been granted to Claudia Antonia's previous husband; see Cassius Dio, 60.5.8.
6. Syme, *The Augustan Aristocracy*, 178–179.
7. Syme places Lepida's first marriage to Messalina's father in AD 15 and her birth some dozen years before this: Syme, *The Augustan Aristocracy*, 165–166.
8. Cassius Dio, 60.30.6; Suetonius, *Life of Claudius*, 27.2.
9. Tacitus, *Annals*, 11.37.
10. Ibid. 12.64.
11. Ibid. 12.64; Suetonius paints a somewhat different picture in his *Life of Nero*, 6.3.
12. For evidence of Domitia Lepida's possessions at Fundi see Brunn, 'The Name and Possessions of Nero's Freedman Phaon'. On the quality of the wine grown at Fundi see Athenaeus, *Deipnosophistae*, 27a, and Pliny, *Natural History*, 14.8.
13. Tacitus, *Annals*, 12.65.
14. On Domitia Lepida's holdings at Puteoli see Jakab E., 'Financial Transactions by Women in Puteoli', 123–150.
15. Vitruvius, *de architectura*, 6.5.
16. Cassius Dio, 61.17.1-2; Suetonius, *Life of Nero*, 34.5.
17. For an example of these luxurious villas on the bay see Clarke and Muntasser, *Oplontis: Villa A ('Of Poppaea') at Torre Annunziata, Italy*.
18. Martial, *Epigrams*, 1.62.
19. See, for example, the perhaps anachronistic tale of Verginia: Livy, *History of Rome*, 3.44.4, and Dionysus of Halicarnassus, *Roman Antiquities*, 11.28.3.
20. See Hemelrijk, *Matrona Docta: Educated Women in the Roman Élite from Cornelia to Julia Domna*, for a study of the education of elite girls.
21. Plutarch, *Life of Pompey*, 55.
22. Ibid.

IV

1. Pliny, *Epistles*, 5.16.
2. Suetonius, *Life of Tiberius*, 7.
3. Ibid. 11.4.
4. For the deaths of Gaius and Lucius see Cassius Dio, 55.10, and Suetonius, *Life of Augustus*, 64–65.

5. Suetonius, *Life of Tiberius*, 27.

6. Tacitus, *Annals*, 4.6.2–4. See also Suetonius, *Life of Tiberius*, 30–32.

7. Tacitus, *Annals*, 3.60–63.

8. Ibid. 3.65.3.

9. For a narrative of Germanicus' death and its allegedly suspicious circumstances see Tacitus, *Annals*, 2.69-2.73.

10. Tacitus, *Annals*, 3.2–3.6.

11. Ibid. 4.8.

12. Tacitus, *Annals*. 4.67. Suetonius, *Life of Tiberius*, 40 also emphasises the appeal of Capri's seclusion.

13. On Tiberius' journey to Capri and the excuse of the dedication of the temples see Suetonius, *Life of Tiberius*, 39–41.

14. Tacitus, *Annals*, 4.74.

15. Ibid. 4.74; Cassius Dio 58.5.

16. Cassius Dio, 58.5.

17. Tacitus, *Annals*, 4.68–70. On the Sabinus affair see also Cassius Dio 58.1.

18. Tacitus, *Annals*, 5.3–5,6.23, 6.25; Suetonius, *Life of Tiberius*, 53–54.

19. Tacitus, *Annals*. 4.18–19.

20. Ibid. 4.18–20.

21. Suetonius, *Life of Tiberius*, 65.

22. Josephus, *Jewish Antiquities*, 18.181–182.

23. For the whole narrative of Sejanus' decline and death see Cassius Dio, 58.3–12; Suetonius, *Life of Tiberius*, 65.

24. For the date of Faustus Sulla's consulship see Bodel, 'Chronology and Succession 2: Notes on Some Consular Lists on Stone', 296; see also Syme, *The Augustan Aristocracy*, 267. Bodel gives Sulla two colleagues in the consulship: Sextus Tedius Catullus (who served from May to July) and Lucius Fulcinius Trio (who served from July to October).

25. On her betrothal see Tacitus, *Annals*, 3.29; Cassius Dio, 58.11.5. On her death see Cassius Dio, 58.11.5–6.

26. Tacitus, *Annals*, 4.3.

27. Tacitus, *Annals*, 4.3, 7–11.

28. Tacitus, *Annals*, 4.3.

29. Cassius Dio, 58.11.7.

30. Tacitus, *Annals*, 4.2.3.

31. Suetonius, *Life of Tiberius*, 67.

32. Tacitus, *Annals*, 4.57.3.

33. For a collection of these rumours see Suetonius, *Life of Tiberius*, 43–44. For the accusations of sex with noble boys see Tacitus, *Annals* 6.1.

34. Tacitus, *Annals*, 6.1.

V

1. Cassius Dio, 59.9.
2. It is Lucan who refers to the hairstyle of the Roman bride as a 'towered crown': Lucan, *The Civil War (Pharsalia)*, 2.358.
3. Herschl, *The Roman Wedding*, 65–68.
4. Catullus, 61.75–81.
5. Suetonius, *Life of Claudius*, 5.
6. For an in-depth discussion of the evidence for Roman nuptial dress and rituals see Hersch, *The Roman Wedding*.
7. Suetonius, *Life of Claudius*, 1. The epigram is in Greek, trans. Loeb.
8. Simpson, 'The Birth of Claudius and the Date of the Dedication of the Altar of "Romae et Augusto" at Lyon', 586–592.
9. Cassius Dio, 55.1.
10. Livy, *Periochae*, 142.
11. For a collection and discussion of these fragments see Kokkinos, *Antonia Augusta: Portrait of a Great Roman Lady*, 68–86.
12. Ibid.
13. Pliny, *Natural History*, 9.81.
14. For this change in dress and the ceremonies that accompanied it see Edmondson and Keith (eds), *Roman Dress and the Fabrics of Roman Culture*, 48–59.
15. Suetonius, *Life of Claudius*, 2.2.
16. Ibid. 2.1.
17. On Claudius' various physical infirmities see Suetonius, *Life of Claudius*, 30; Pseudo-Seneca, *Apocolocyntosis*, 1, 5; Cassius Dio, 60.2.
18. Suetonius, *Life of Claudius*, 3.2.
19. Ibid. 3.4.
20. Ibid. 3.5.
21. Ibid. 2.2.
22. Tacitus, *Annals*, 13.3.
23. Suetonius, *Life of Claudius*, 31.
24. Ibid. 38.3.
25. Ibid. 4.5, 5.1, 33, 40.1; Tacitus, *Annals*, 12.49.
26. Suetonius, Life of Claudius, 26.
27. Tacitus, *Annals*, 4.22.
28. Suetonius, *Life of Claudius*, 27.
29. Ibid. 27.
30. For Claudius' marriage to, and divorce from, Aelia Paetina see Suetonius, *Life of Claudius*, 26. For the proposition of remarriage, floated by Narcissus, see Tacitus, *Annals*, 12.1.
31. Juvenal, *Satires*, 10.331–333.
32. On the right of a girl *sui iuris* to contract her own marriage see, for

example, Paulus, *Digest*, 23.2.20, cf. Grubbs, *Women and the Law in the Roman Empire*, 23–24. On the requirement of the consent of all parties for any marriage see Paulus, *Digest*, 23.2.2; Julian, *Digest*, 23.1.11.
33. Suetonius, *Life of Claudius*, 30.
34. For an introduction to this phenomenon in Roman visual culture see Clarke, *Looking at Lovemaking*.

VI

1. Translation, M. Staniforth, *Meditations* (London, 2006).
2. Suetonius, *Life of Caligula*, 13.
3. Ibid. 14.1.
4. Tacitus, *Annals*, 1.41, 1.69; Suetonius, *Life of Caligula*, 9.1; Cassius Dio., 57.5.6.
5. Suetonius, *Life of Caligula*, 15; Cassius Dio., 59.3.5.
6. Suetonius, *Life of Caligula*, 15.2; Cassius Dio., 59.6.5. These accounts are confirmed by epigraphic evidence: see Gallivan, 'The Fasti for the Reign of Gaius', 66.
7. Cassius Dio., 59.7.1.
8. For the emperor's behaviour as one of the crowd see Suetonius, *Life of Caligula*, 54, and Cassius Dio, 59.5.
9. Suetonius, *Life of Caligula*, 17.2.
10. On the honours paid to Caligula's sisters see Ferrill, *Caligula: Emperor of Rome*, 97. For their inclusion in senatorial oaths see Suetonius, *Life of Caligula*, 15.3.
11. There are a number examples of this coin type in the British Museum: see, for example, R.6432.
12. Suetonius, *Life of Caligula*, 24.1. For Aemilius Lepidus' position in Caligula's plans see Barrett, *Caligula*, 115–116 and Winterling, *Caligula*, 63.
13. Suetonius, *Life of Caligula*, 24.1.
14. Suetonius, *Life of Caligula*, 23.2; Cassius Dio, 59.3.6.
15. On incest in roman law and culture see Grubbs, 'Making the Private Public: illegitimacy and incest in Roman law'.
16. Philo, *On the Embassy to Gaius*, 31.
17. Ibid., 58.
18. Suetonius, *Life of Caligula*, 23.3.
19. Drusilla's death is recorded in an inscribed calendar found in Ostia: Fasti Ostiensis, Smallwood, no 31. lines 29–30, p. 28.
20. On the public mourning after Drusilla's death see Cassius Dio, 59.11; Suetonius, *Life of Caligula*, 24.2.

21. On honours paid to Drusilla after her death see Cassius Dio, 59.11, and Wood, 'Diva Drusilla Panthea and the Sisters of Caligula'.
22. Kerkeslager, 'Agrippa and the Mourning Rites for Drusilla in Alexandria'.
23. Suetonius, *Life of Caligula*, 24.2. Seneca decries Caligula's grieving process as undignified and un-Roman: *Consolation to Polybius*, 17.
24. Suetonius, *Life of Caligula*, 21.
25. Ibid., 37.1.
26. Seneca, *Consolation to Helvia*, 10.
27. Pliny, *Natural History*, 9.58.
28. Suetonius, *Life of Caligula*, 52.1; Philo, *On the Embassy to Gaius*, 79; Cassius Dio, 59.26.6–8.
29. Suetonius, *Life of Caligula*, 37; Cassius Dio, 59.2.6.
30. For Augustus' bequest see Suetonius, who judges the amount to have been a humiliating snub: *Life of Claudius*, 4.7; see also Champlin, 'The Testament of Augustus', 162. For Tiberius' bequest see Suetonius, *Life of Claudius*, 6.
31. On Claudius' bankruptcy see Suetonius, *Life of Claudius*, 9. Cassius Dio 59.28.5, puts the entrance fee at 10 million sesterces.
32. On married women's rights to own and administer their own property if their fathers were dead see Ulpian, *Digest*, 23.3.9.3; and Grubbs, *Women and the Law in the Roman Empire*, 101–102. On *sine manu* marriage see Grubbs, *Women and the Law in the Roman Empire*, 21–22. On *Tutela Mulierum* and its limits see Grubbs, *Women and the Law in the Roman Empire*, 25–34. On the dowry and the husband's responsibility not to dispose of it see Grubbs, *Women and the Law in the Roman Empire*, 91–98.
33. Suetonius, *Life of Caligula*, 32.3.
34. Ibid. *Life of Claudius*. 8.
35. All three of these affairs are mentioned by Suetonius, *Life of Caligula*, 36.1. On Caligula's alleged affair with Aemilius Lepidus see also Cassius Dio, 59.11.1; 59.22.6. Suetonius claims Caligula would kiss Mnester in public: *Life of Caligula*, 55.1.
36. Cassius Dio 59.3.6, 59.11.1, 59.22.6; Josephus, *Jewish Antiquities*, 19.204. The *Suda*, a tenth-century AD Byzantine historical encyclopaedia, even makes the implausible claim (in its entry on 'Gaius') that Caligula fathered a child with one of his sisters.
37. Suetonius, *Life of Caligula*, 33.
38. Ibid. 36.
39. Ibid. 25.1.
40. Ibid. 25.2.
41. Cassius Dio makes her eight months pregnant at the time of their wedding: 59.23.7. Suetonius claims the child had already been born

and was legitimised on the day of the wedding: *Life of Caligula* 25.3.

42. Suetonius, *Life of Caligula*, 25.3.
43. Ibid. 37.2.
44. On the archaeology of these boats see Carlson, 'Caligula's Floating Palaces'.
45. Accounts of Caligula's bridge are found at: Suetonius, *Life of Caligula*, 19, 32.1; Cassius Dio, 59.17; Josephus, *Jewish Antiquities*, 19.5–7; Seneca, *De Brevitate*, 17.5–6.
46. Suetonius, *Life of Caligula*, 19.3.

VII

1. Cassius Dio, 59.20.
2. Cassius Dio, 59.21.2; Suetonius, *Life of Caligula*, 43.
3. For accounts of the alleged conspiracy and its discovery see Cassius Dio, 59.21–23; Suetonius, *Life of Caligula*, 24.3.
4. This notice, dated 27 October AD 39, comes from an inscribed record of the acts of the Arval Brethren, an ancient priesthood revived by Augustus and dedicated to the worship of a native Italian fertility goddess: *Acta Fratrum Arvalium*, Gaius. fr. 9.19–21, Smallwood, p. 14.
5. Tacitus, *Annals*, 6.30.
6. Suetonius, *Life of Caligula*, 24.3; Cassius Dio, 59.22.7–8.
7. Suetonius, *Life of Caligula*, 25.4; Josephus, *Jewish Antiquities*, 19.11.
8. Suetonius Life of Nero, 6.2.
9. Cassius Dio, 59.23.
10. The following details of the care given to elite Roman women in labour are taken from the eminent second-century AD physician Soranus' treatise, *Gynaecology*.
11. Juvenal, *Satires*, 6.594.
12. Suetonius, *Life of Claudius*, 9.
13. Ibid. 9.1.
14. Cassius Dio, 59.22.9.
15. Hilaria's funerary inscription survives: CIL VI.8943.
16. For Domitia Lepida's care of Nero see Suetonius, *Life of Nero*, 6.3; Tacitus, *Annals*, 12.64.
17. For reports of Caligula's strange behaviour on the front see Suetonius, *Life of Caligula*, 44–48, and Cassius Dio, 59.21, 22, 25.
18. Suetonius, *Life of Caligula*, 49.
19. Philo, *On the Embassy to Gaius*, 181.

20. Philo, *On the Embassy to Gaius*, 185; Suetonius, *Life of Caligula*, 49.
21. For rumours that the capital would be moved see Suetonius, *Life of Caligula*, 49.2, see also 8.5. For Caligula's hit-lists see Suetonius, *Life of Caligula*, 49.3; Cassius Dio, 59.26.1, 60.3.2.
22. Suetonius, *Life of Caligula*, 40; Cassius Dio, 59.28.8, 59.28.11.
23. For anti-tax protests and Caligula's reaction see Cassius Dio, 59.28.11; Josephus, *Jewish Antiquities*, 19.24–19.26. For the story about the awning see Suetonius, *Life of Caligula*, 26.5.
24. Suetonius, *Life of Caligula*, 49.2.
25. Josephus, *Jewish Antiquities*, 19.86; Suetonius, *Life of Caligula*, 26.
26. For Caligula's belief in his own divinity see Cassius Dio, 26–27; Suetonius, *Life of Caligula*, 22; Philo, *On the Embassy to Gaius*, 74–80, 93–97; Josephus, *Jewish Antiquities*, 18.306, 19.4–6.
27. Cassius Dio 59.27.6.
28. Seneca, *On Anger*, 3.18.
29. For a discussion of this spate of senatorial executions see Barrett, *Caligula*, 249–251.
30. Cassius Dio, 59.16.
31. Ibid. 59.26.
32. Josephus, *Jewish Antiquities*, 19.12–13; see also Suetonius, *Life of Claudius*, 9.2.
33. Suetonius, *Life of Caligula*, 57.3; Cassius Dio, 59.29.3.
34. Cassius Dio, 59.29, Josephus, *Jewish Antiquities*, 19.17–69.
35. Suetonius, *Life of Caligula*, 56.2; Cassius Dio, 59.29.2; Josephus, *Jewish Antiquities*, 19.29.
36. On this widespread approval for the plot see Josephus, *Jewish Antiquities*, 19.62–63 and Cassius Dio, 59.29.1.
37. Suetonius, *Life of Caligula*, 57.
38. For accounts of the day of the assassination see Josephus, *Jewish Antiquities*, 19. 103–111; the quotations in the passages that follow are taken from T.P. Wiseman's translation, *The Death of Caligula* (Liverpool, 2013). Suetonius, *Life of Caligula*, 57–58; Cassius Dio, 59.29.
39. For the debate on the issue see Josephus, *Jewish Antiquities*, 19.190–194.
40. Josephus, *Jewish Antiquities*, 19.193; translation, Wiseman.
41. Ibid. 19.199.
42. For the deaths of Caesonia and Drusilla see Josephus, *Jewish Antiquities*, 19.196–200, translation, Wiseman; Suetonius, *Life of Caligula*, 59; Cassius Dio, 59.29.
43. For full accounts of Claudius' accession see Suetonius, *Life of Claudius*, 10; Cassius Dio, 60.1; Josephus, *Jewish Antiquities*, 19.158–273.

44. Ibid. Suetonius, *Life of Claudius*, 10.2.
45. Josephus, *Jewish Antiquities*, 19.159, translation, Wiseman; see also Tacitus, *Annals*, 11.1.
46. Suetonius, *Life of Claudius*, 10.3.

VIII

1. For this epitaph see: CIL VI.15346.
2. For this epitaph see: CIL VI.11602. Emphasis author's own.
3. For a general discussion of Fulvia see Delia, 'Fulvia Reconsidered', especially pp. 203–206 for her role in the Perusine War and its later mythologisation.
4. Cassius Dio, 49.38.1.
5. For a discussion of the emergence of the concept of the '*Domus Augusta*' as a public entity see Wardle, 'Valerius Maximus on the Domus Augusta, Augustus, and Tiberius', 479–483.
6. Suetonius, *Life of Augustus*, 58. Emphasis author's own.
7. This statue group was erected in the *Circus Flaminius*. See Flory, 'Dynastic Ideology, the Domus Augusta, and Imperial Women: A Lost Statuary Group in the Circus Flaminius', 287–306.
8. On Octavia's contributions to the image of Augustus' regime see Moore, 'Octavia Minor and Patronage'.
9. On the Porticus Octaviae and its significance see Richardson, 'The Evolution of the Porticus Octaviae'; Woodhull, 'Engendering Space: Octavia's Portico in Rome'.
10. Suetonius, *Life of Caligula*, 23.2.
11. On Livia's household generally see Treggiari, 'Jobs in the Household of Livia', 48–77. For the pearl-setter see ibid. 54–55.
12. Marcellus Empiricus, *On Medicines*, 15.6, 35.6–9.
13. See Flory, 'Sic Exempla Parantur: Livia's Shrine to Concordia and the Porticus Liviae'.
14. On Livia's rebuilding of the sanctuary of Bona Dea see Ovid, *Fasti*, 5.157–158. On her restoration of the cult of Feminine Fortune see Valerius Maximus, *Memorable Doings and Sayings*, 1.8.4, a passage confirmed by an inscription: CIL VI.883. On her possible involvement in rebuilding shrines to Chastity see Flory, 'Sic Exempla Parantur: Livia's Shrine to Concordia and the Porticus Liviae', 318–319.
15. Ovid, *Fasti*, 1.649–650.
16. Ovid, *Ex Ponto*, 3.1.115–118.
17. Tacitus, *Annals*, 5.1.
18. For this inscription, from Anticaria in the province of Hispania Baetica, see CIL 2.2038.

19. On Livia's combination of innovation and tradition in the construction of her power see Purcell, 'Livia and the Womanhood of Rome'.
20. Tacitus, *Annals*, 5.1.
21. Seneca, *On Clemency*, 1.9.
22. Pseudo-Ovid, *Consolation to Livia*, 349–356.
23. Ovid, *Ex Ponto*, 3.1114–144.
24. For a discussion of the use, development and connotations of this term see Balsdon and Griffin, 'princeps' in *The Oxford Classical Dictionary*.
25. For a summary of the terms of Augustus' will see Barrett, *Livia*, 74–75.
26. On the significance of Livia's adoption see Barrett, *Livia*, 147–155.
27. Cassius Dio, 56.46.
28. Cassius Dio, 57.12.
29. Tacitus, *Annals*, 1.4.
30. Ibid. 1.5.
31. For the story of Tanaquil's role in Servius Tullius' accession see Livy, *History of Rome*, 1.41; Cassius Dio, 2. fr. 9–10.

IX

1. Suetonius, *Life of Claudius*, 27.2.
2. Valerius Maximus, *Memorable Doings and Sayings*, 4.4.
3. Juvenal, *Satires*, 6.594–597.
4. Tacitus, *Annals*, 2.43.
5. Macrobius, *Saturnalia*, 2.5.3–4. Emphasis author's own.
6. Cassius Dio, 60.12.5.
7. Ibid. 60.12.5.
8. These games were held on Antonia's birthday, 31 January: Cassius Dio, 60.5.1. For an in-depth discussion of the honours granted to Antonia see Kokkinos, *Antonia Augusta: Portrait of a Great Roman Lady*. This work also collects a number of inscriptions and coins from across the empire that refer to Antonia using the title 'Augusta' evidencing both the granting and the widespread dissemination of the honour.
9. Suetonius, *Life of Claudius*, 11.2; Cassius Dio, 60.5.2. Livia's deification is also celebrated on Claudius' coinage e.g. RIC I2 Claudius 101.
10. A copy of this letter from Claudius to the city of Alexandria survives on a fragment of Papyrus now in the British Library: P.London, 1912.
11. On the identification of Messalina's portrait type see Wood,

'Messalina, wife of Claudius: propaganda successes and failures of his reign', 222–225; 227–234.

12. On this divine iconography see Wood, 'Messalina, wife of Claudius: propaganda successes and failures of his reign', 225–226.

13. On the nature and likely cause of the condition of the portrait see Wood, 'Messalina, wife of Claudius: propaganda successes and failures of his reign', 219–222, 226.

14. Tacitus, *Annals*, 13.45.

15. For a discussion of this iconography, see Wood, 'Messalina, wife of Claudius: propaganda successes and failures of his reign'.

X

1. Suetonius, *Life of Augustus*, 72–73 provides the fullest description of Augustus' house. He emphasises the modesty of the house's fabric and furnishing. For a summary of the house's archaeological remains see Varinlioğlu's entry 'Domus: Augustus' in *Mapping Augustan Rome*, 104–106.

2. Suetonius, *Life of Augustus*, 72.1.

3. None of the sources explicitly mentions Tiberius building a new residence on the Palatine, but the main imperial residence is continually referred to as the '*Domus Tiberiana*', suggesting that it was laid out by Tiberius and added to by later emperors. For a summary of its archaeology see Richardson, *A New Topographical Dictionary of Ancient Rome*, 136–137.

4. On these rooms in the so-called 'House of Livia' on the Palatine and their artistic context see Ling, *Roman Painting*, 37–38. For further description and vivid illustration see Pappalardo, *The Splendor of Roman Wall Painting*, 100–103.

5. See, for example, Philo, *On the Embassy to Gaius*, 363–365 and Pliny, *Natural History*, 36.24.

6. Rooms decorated by Caligula would have been finished in the then fashionable Fourth Style.

7. Augustus, *Res Gestae*, 21; Cassius Dio, 49.15.5. On the symbolic significance of this project and its link with the palace see Hekster and Rich, 'Octavian and the Thunderbolt: The Temple of Apollo Palatinus and Roman Traditions of Temple Building'.

8. Cassius Dio, 59.28.5.

9. Seneca, *On Anger*, 2.33.2. See also Osgood, *Claudius Caesar*, 39.

10. Levick, *Claudius*, 53. On the nature of the Julio-Claudian court see Paterson, 'Friends in high places: the creation of the court of the Roman emperor'.

11. Cassius Dio, 60.3.2.
12. Josephus, *Jewish Antiquities*, 19.272, translation, Wiseman.
13. Suetonius, *Life of Claudius*, 11.1; Cassius Dio, 60.3. For Sabinus' position and suicide see Josephus, *Jewish Antiquities*, 19.273. For Claudius' protection of the consul Quintus Pomponius see Josephus, *Jewish Antiquities*, 19.263.
14. Suetonius, *Life of Caligula*, 49.
15. For Claudius' treatment of the Senate see Suetonius, *Life of Claudius*, 12.
16. See the example in the British Museum: R1874,0715.4.
17. Suetonius, *Life of Claudius*, 27.
18. Ibid. 12.
19. Ibid. 35-37.
20. Ibid. 35.
21. For the marriage of Claudia Antonia and the betrothal of Claudia Octavia see Cassius Dio, 60.5.7-9. For the marriage of Domitia Lepida see Cassius Dio. 60.14.2-3.
22. For Pompeius Magnus' lineage see Syme, *The Augustan Aristocracy*, 277.
23. For a discussion of these roles and their hierarchy see Weaver, 'Slave and Freedman "Cursus" in the Imperial Administration'; for a more comprehensive study see Weaver, *Familia Caesaris. A Social Study of the Emperor's Freedmen and Slaves*.
24. Suetonius, *Life of Claudius*, 28.
25. Pliny, *Epistles*, 7.29. See also Suetonius, *Life of Claudius*, 28 on the wealth and honours granted to the freedmen.
26. Pliny, *Epistles*, 7.29.
27. Pliny the Elder, *Natural History*, 36.12.
28. For Valeria Cleopatra see CIL VI.4468. For Amoenus see CIL VI.8952. On the role of the *ab ornamentibus* see Treggiari, 'Jobs in the Household of Livia', 53; 'Domestic Staff at Rome in the Julio-Claudian Period, 27 BC to AD 68', 244-245.
29. For Valeria Hilaria see CIL VI.8943. For Philocrates see CIL VI.4459.
30. For Iudaeus see CIL VI.44. Lucius Valerius was probably a freedman of Messalina's who was later recorded working as an archivist attached to the financial office of a provincial procurator. Colls, Domergue, Laubenheimer, Liou, 'Les Lingots D'Etain De L'Épave Port-Vendres II', 70-74.
31. For Sabbio see CIL VI 8840. On the role of the *dispensator* see Treggiari, 'Jobs in the Household of Livia', 49-50; cf. Verboven, 'Dispensator' in *The Encyclopedia of Ancient History*.
32. For a comprehensive reconstruction of Livia's household on the

basis of epigraphic evidence see Treggiari, 'Jobs in the Household of Livia', 48–77.

33. Macrobius, *Saturnalia*, 2.5.6.
34. Cassius Dio, 60.2.7.
35. Seneca, *Natural Questions*, preface to *Book IV: The Nile*, 15.
36. Suetonius, *Life of Claudius*, 33.2.
37. Ibid. 28–29.
38. Tacitus, *Annals*, 11.3.
39. Ibid. 13.43.
40. Suetonius, *Life of Vitellius*, 2.5.
41. Cassius Dio, 60.12.4–5.
42. Cassius Dio, 60.8.5.
43. Accounts of Julia Livilla's fall, exile and death are found at Cassius Dio, 60.8.4–5, Suetonius, *Life of Claudius*, 29.1.
44. Tacitus, *Annals*, 13.42; Cassius Dio, 61.10.1; Pseudo-Seneca, *Apocolocyntosis* 10.
45. Tacitus, *Annals*, 13.42.
46. Seneca, *Consolation to Polybius*, 13.
47. Seneca, *Natural Questions*, preface to *Book IV: The Nile*, 15.
48. Cassius Dio, 61.10.
49. Tacitus, *Annals*, 6.15; Cassius Dio, 60.27.4.
50. See also Levick, *Claudius*, 56, 61.
51. Pseudo-Seneca, *Apocolocyntosis*, 14; Suetonius, *Life of Claudius*, 29. See also Baldwin, 'Executions under Claudius: Seneca's "Ludus de Morte Claudii"'.

XI

1. On the revolt and the fear it inspired in Claudius see Suetonius, *Life of Claudius*, 35–36; Cassius Dio, 60.15–16.
2. The main sources on the British invasion are Cassius Dio 60.19–23 and Suetonius, *Life of Claudius*, 17. See also Levick, *Claudius*, 137–148, for a convincing summary and reconstruction of events.
3. *Historia Augusta*, Hadrian, 16.
4. Cassius Dio, 60.21.5.
5. Ibid. 60.21.2.
6. On the possible presence of the imperial party at the dedication of this monument see Levick, *Claudius*, 168. On the celebrations at the mouth of the Po see Pliny, *Natural History*, 3.16.
7. Cassius Dio 60.22.1–3.
8. Ibid. 60.22.2.
9. Ibid. 60.22.1. Suetonius, *Life of Claudius*, 17.1 argues that the desire

for a triumph was the main motivation for Claudius' invasion of Britain.

10. See, for example, the descriptions of Pompey's famous triple triumph in 61 BC found in Plutarch, *Life of Pompey*, 45.
11. For accounts of Claudius' triumph see Cassius Dio 60.23.1; Suetonius, *Life of Claudius*, 17.2–3.
12. Persius, *Satires*, 6.43–47.
13. Pliny the Elder, *Natural History*, 15.39–40.
14. On the role of women in the Roman triumph see Flory, 'The Integration of Women into the Roman Triumph'.

XII

1. Tacitus, *Annals*, 11.26.
2. Augustus, *Res Gestae*, 34.
3. Suetonius, *Life of Claudius*, 29.
4. Cassius Dio, 60.2.
5. Accounts of Silanus' downfall are found at Cassius Dio, 60.14; Suetonius, *Life of Claudius*, 37.2. Narcissus' part in the affair is also referenced at Tacitus, *Annals*, 11.29.
6. Cassius Dio, 60.15.1.
7. Suetonius, *Life of Claudius*, 37.
8. Cassius Dio, 60.14.3.
9. On his consulship see Syme, *The Augustan Aristocracy*, 164. On the *maiestas* charge see Tacitus, *Annals*, 6.9.
10. For his account of Messalina and the freedmen's behaviour following the rebellion see Cassius Dio, 60.15–16.
11. On Arria and Messalina's friendship see Cassius Dio, 60.16.6. For accounts of Arria's devotion and bravery following her husband's indictment, and for her death, see Pliny, *Epistles*, 3.16 and Cassius Dio 60.16.6.
12. Pliny, *Epistles*, 3.16.
13. This quote is recorded by both Pliny and Cassius Dio: Pliny, *Epistles*, 3.16 and Cassius Dio, 60.16.
14. Cassius Dio, 60.16.7; Levick, *Claudius*, 60.
15. Tacitus, *Annals*, 1.29.
16. For the fall of Catonius see Cassius Dio, 60.18.3.
17. Cassius Dio, 60.18.3.
18. Pseudo-Seneca, *Apocolocyntosis*, 13.
19. On Pollio's appointment see Josephus, *Jewish Antiquities*, 19.267-268; Wiseman argues that Catonius Justus was probably appointed at the same time: *The Death of Caligula*, 97.

20. For the fall of Julia see Cassius Dio, 60.18.4; Suetonius, *Life of Claudius*, 29.1; Tacitus, *Annals*, 13.32, 13.43.
21. For this first marriage see Tacitus, *Annals*, 3.29.
22. For Julia's second marriage see ibid. 6.27.
23. Syme, 'The Marriage of Rubellius Blandus', 75.
24. These slaves gave evidence under torture. Only treason cases carried the same loophole. See Brunt, 'Evidence given under Torture in the Principate'.
25. For Suillius' part in the affair see Tacitus, *Annals*, 13.43.
26. For Pomponia's protest see Tacitus, *Annals*, 13.32.
27. For the marriage see Barrett, *Agrippina*, 84–85.
28. Barrett, *Agrippina*, 222, inscription no. 22.

XIII

1. Translation, Staniforth, 1964, 14.
2. Tacitus, *Annals*, 11.35–11.36.
3. Tacitus, *Annals*, 11.36; a further reference to Plautius Lateranus' affair with Messalina is found at Tacitus Annals 13.11.
4. Pliny, *Natural History*, 10.83.
5. For an introduction to Augustus' laws on adultery, and their political connotations, see Edwards, *The Politics of Immorality in Ancient Rome*, 34–62.
6. Paulus, *Sententiae*, 2.26.14.
7. Ulpian, *Digest*, 48.5.13.
8. See Olsen, 'Matrona and whore: clothing and definition'.
9. Ulpian, *Digest*, 48.5.30.
10. Suetonius, *Life of Augustus*, 65.
11. The letter does not survive but was well known in antiquity; see, for example, Pliny's mention of it: *Natural History*, 21.6.
12. Seneca, *De Beneficiis*, 6.32. See also Tacitus, *Annals*, 1.53.3 for less lurid claims of more run-of-the-mill adulteries.
13. Suetonius, *Life of Augustus*, 65; see also Tacitus' mention of the affair: *Annals*, 3.24.
14. On Polybius' role in Claudius' household see Suetonius, *Life of Claudius*, 28. On Polybius' own intellectual pursuits, including the translation of Homer into Latin and Virgil into Greek, see Seneca, *Consolation to Polybius*, 7–8.
15. For Polybius' influence and his appearance with the consuls see Suetonius, *Life of Claudius*, 28. For the incident in the theatre see Cassius Dio, 60.29.
16. Seneca, *Consolation to Polybius*.
17. Cassius Dio, 60.31.2.

XIV

1. Ovid, *Amores*, 1.4.
2. Ibid. 2.19.
3. On Claudius' spectacles see Suetonius, *Life of Claudius*, 21 and Cassius Dio, 60.6–7, 13, 23, 27.
4. Suetonius, *Life of Claudius*, 21; Cassius Dio, 60.7.
5. Ovid, *Ars Amatoria*, 1.89–228.
6. Suetonius, *Life of Claudius*, 32.
7. Suetonius, *Life of Claudius*, 5, 40.1. Suetonius quotes a letter in which Augustus expresses disapproval of Claudius' choice of friends: Suetonius, *Life of Claudius*, 4.5.
8. On the continuation of Claudius' old habits until the very end of his life see Cassius Dio, 60.34.2.
9. Cassius Dio, 60.18.
10. Ovid, *Ars Amatoria*, 1.281–341.
11. Catullus, 2.
12. Ibid. 68a.
13. Tibullus, 1.2 and 1.6.
14. Sulpicia, 6 (preserved in the Tibullan corpus).
15. Sulpicia, 13 (preserved in the Tibullan corpus).
16. On Messalina's brief affair with Traulus see Tacitus, *Annals*, 11.36.
17. Ovid, *Amores*, 3.4.
18. Ovid, *Tristia*, 2.207.
19. For Ovid's complaint about feminine grooming standards on the Black Sea see *Ars Amatoria*, 3.193–196.
20. Juvenal, *Satires*, 6.60–113.
21. Cassius Dio, 60.18.
22. Tacitus, *Annals*, 1.77.
23. On ancient pantomime and its performers see the second-century AD writer Lucian of Samosata's treatise, *On Dance*.
24. Galen, *On Prognosis*, 6. For a translation of this passage and a discussion of the case study in its context see Salas, 'Why Lovesickness is Not a Disease: Galen's Diagnosis and Classification of Psychological Distress'.
25. Lucian, *On Dance*, 3, translation, H. W. Fowler and R. G. Fowler, *The Works of Lucian of Samosata*, vol. 2 (Oxford, 1905).
26. Suetonius, *Life of Caligula*, 55.
27. Cassius Dio 60.28.5.
28. For accounts of Messalina and Mnester's affair see Cassius Dio 60.22, 60.28 and Tacitus, *Annals*, 11.35.
29. Tacitus, *Annals*, 13.45.
30. Cassius Dio, 60.22,3–5.

31. Tacitus, *Annals*, 11.36.
32. Cassius Dio, 60.22.3–4.
33. Ibid. 60.28.
34. Ibid. 60.28.5.

XV

1. On the symbolism attached to Claudius' assumption of this role see O'Neill, 'Claudius the Censor and the Rhetoric of Re-Foundation'.
2. Suetonius, *Life of Claudius*, 16.
3. Ibid. 29.2.
4. Cassius Dio, 61.29.6.
5. Pseudo-Seneca, *Apocolocyntosis*, 11.
6. A papyrus dated to 50–51 survives relating to lands previously owned by Valerius Asiaticus near Philadelphia and Euhemeria: Ann Arbor University of Michigan Library P.Mich.876v. Cited by Cogitore, in *Claude: un empereur au destin singulier*, 126–127. See also Sijpesteijn, 'Another οὐσία of D. Valerius Asiaticus in Egypt' for papyrus relating to Valerius Asiaticus' holdings.
7. For a summary of Asiaticus' career and success see Tacitus, *Annals*, 11.1. Seneca refers to Asiaticus as 'ferocem virum' which might be translated as 'bold', 'proud', 'arrogant' or even 'fierce'; *On Constancy*, 18.2. Claudius himself referred to Asiaticus as an athletic 'prodigy' whilst castigating him in an AD 52 speech which survives in an inscription found in Gaul: ILS 212, col. 2.14–17, Smallwood, no. 369, 98.
8. Seneca, *On Constancy*, 18.2.
9. On Asiaticus' presence in Britain see Tacitus, *Annals*, 11.3. On his second consulship see Cassius Dio, 60.27.1.
10. Tacitus, *Annals*, 11.1.
11. Ibid. 11.1.
12. Cursi, 'Roman Horti: a topographical view in the Imperial era', 125, fig. 1.
13. Bowe, *Gardens of the Roman World*, 7.
14. For a poetic description of an ideal Roman garden see Virgil, *Georgics*, 4.130–146.
15. Pagán, *Horticulture and the Roman Shaping of Nature*. For saffron see Virgil, *Georgics*, 4.109. For verbena see ibid. 4.130–146.
16. Pliny, *Natural History*, 15.30.
17. Tacitus, *Annals*, 11.1.
18. Plutarch, *Life of Lucullus*, 39.2.
19. Cassius Dio, 60.31.

20. Tacitus, *Annals*, 11.1.
21. On the political symbolism of the Saecular Games see Dunning, 'The transformation of the saeculum and its rhetoric in the construction and rejection of roman imperial power'. For the Saecular Games' association with the *gens Valeria* see Dunning, *Roman Ludi Saeculares from the Republic to Empire*, esp. 26–36, 46–47.
22. Tacitus, *Annals*, 11.11; Suetonius, *Life of Nero*, 7.
23. Suetonius, *Life of Nero*, 6; see also Tacitus, *Annals*, 11.11.
24. Accounts of the fall of Asiaticus are found at Tacitus, *Annals*, 11.1–3 and Cassius Dio, 60,29.4–5.
25. Tacitus, *Annals*, 11.1.
26. Ibid. 11.2.
27. For this episode see Cassius Dio, 60.29.5–6.
28. For the fall of Poppaea the Elder see Tacitus, *Annals*, 11.2.
29. Ibid. 11.4.
30. Cassius Dio, 60.27.4.
31. Woods, 'The Role of Lucius Vitellius in the Death of Messalina'.

XVI

1. See Candy, "lex Cincia on gifts" in *Oxford Research Encyclopaedia of Classics*.
2. Tacitus, *Annals*, 11.5.
3. For an account of this debate see Tacitus, *Annals*, 11.5–7.
4. Ibid. 11.6.
5. On Gaius Silius' good looks see Tacitus, *Annals*, 11.12; Juvenal, *Satires*, 10.331–332.
6. The fullest account of Messalina's affair with Gaius Silius is found at Tacitus, *Annals*, 11.12, 11.26. Juvenal also emphasises Messalina's desire for Silius, *Satires*, 10.329–333.
7. Tacitus, *Annals*, 11.12.
8. Ibid. 11.12.
9. Ibid. 11.12.
10. For Junia Silana's friendship with Agrippina see Tacitus, *Annals*, 13.19.
11. Ibid. 11.12.
12. Ibid. 11.12.
13. Cassius Dio, 60.31.
14. For Gaius Silius' proposal and Messalina's consideration of it see Tacitus, *Annals*, 11.26.
15. Tacitus, *Annals*, 11.26.
16. Ibid. 11.26.
17. Ibid. 11.26.

18. Ibid. 11.26.
19. The accounts of Messalina's bigamous marriage and fall are found at Tacitus, *Annals*, 11.26–38; Cassius Dio, 61; Suetonius, *Life of Claudius*, 26.2, 36.
20. Tacitus, *Annals*, 11.27.
21. Ibid. 11.28.
22. Ibid. 11.27
23. Suetonius, *Life of Claudius*, 29.3. The story is picked up by Robert Graves in *Claudius the God and His Wife Messalina*.
24. Colin, 'Les vendanges dionysiaques et la légende de Messaline'.
25. Tacitus, *Annals*, 11.30. Suetonius also stresses that it was Claudius' fear of a coup rather than anger at his wife that motivated his reaction: *Life of Claudius*, 36.
26. Tacitus, *Annals*, 11.32.
27. Ibid. 11.34.
28. Ibid. 11.37.
29. Ibid. 11.37
30. Ibid. 11.37.

XVII

1. Tacitus, *Annals*, 11.38.
2. Ibid. 11.38.
3. The first official senatorial decree also had been directed against a woman, Livilla. The destruction of images also occurred more informally, without a decree from the Senate, for example in the cases of Caligula and Caesonia. Varner, 'Portraits, Plots, and Politics: "Damnatio memoriae" and the Images of Imperial Women', 41–42.
4. On the removed statue at Lepcis Magna see Varner, 'Portraits, Plots, and Politics: *Damnatio Memoriae* and the images of imperial women', 64–65.
5. On the reused statues at Velleia and Naples see ibid. 65–67.
6. CIL 4474.
7. Varner, *Mutilation and Transformation*, 95–96. See an example in the Ashmolean: RPC 2654.
8. Juvenal, *Satires*, 6.114–132.
9. On the archaeology of the Lupanar see Levin-Richardson, *The Brothel of Pompeii*.
10. Juvenal, *Satires*, 6.15–16.
11. On the use of 'stage-names' see Levin-Richardson, *The Brothel of Pompeii*, 118–119.

12. On Latin terms for prostitution see Adams J. 'Words for Prostitute in Latin'.
13. For Dio's tale about Messalina see 60.31.1. For a suspiciously similar story told about Caligula see Cassius Dio, 59. 28.8–9; Suetonius, *Caligula*, 41.
14. Pseudo-Aurelius Victor, *Epitome of the Lives of the Caesars*, 4.5. On this text see Baldwin, 'The "Epitome de Caesaribus", from Augustus to Domitian'; see also Barnes, 'Review: Epitome de Ceasaribus', especially pp. 26–27.
15. Propertius, *Elegies*, 3.11.39.
16. Suetonius, *Life of Claudius*, 26.2.
17. On the significance of the grant of this title see Barrett, *Agrippina*, 108–109.
18. Tacitus, *Annals*, 12.1–2.
19. Narcissus was awarded only the ornaments of the quaestorship: Tacitus, *Annals*, 11.38; see also Levick, *Claudius*, 69.
20. Tacitus, *Annals*, 12.22; Cassius Dio 60.32.4.
21. For the rumours of incest see Tacitus, *Annals*, 12.3–4; Pseudo-Seneca, *Apocolocyntosis*, 8. For Silanus' suicide see Tacitus, *Annals*, 12.8; Cassius Dio, 60.31.8; Pseudo-Seneca, *Apocolocyntosis*, 10–11.
22. Tacitus, *Annals*, 4.53; Pliny, *Natural History*, 7.8.
23. On the praetorian password see Tacitus, *Annals*, 13.2. For these coins see an example in the British Museum: R6509. For Agrippina's appearance in a military cloak see Tacitus, *Annals*, 12.56; Cassius Dio 60.33. For Agrippina's attempt to receive foreign ambassadors see Tacitus, *Annals*, 13.5.
24. Tacitus, *Annals*, 12.7
25. Pliny, *Natural History*, 10.83.

XVIII

1. Accounts of the murder of Claudius and succession of Nero are found at Tacitus, *Annals*, 12.66–69; Cassius Dio 60.34–61.1; Suetonius, *Life of Claudius*, 43–46, *Life of Nero*, 8.
2. Accounts of Britannicus' death are found at Tacitus, *Annals*, 13.15–17; Cassius Dio, 61.7.4–5; Suetonius, *Life of Nero*, 33; *Life of Titus*, 2.
3. Tacitus, *Annals*, 13.17.
4. Barrett, *Agrippina*, 170–172.
5. For Lucius Silanus' involvement in the British campaign see Cassius Dio 60.21.5. For his triumphal ornaments see Cassius Dio, 60.23.2, 60.31.7. For his praetorship and gladiatorial games see Cassius Dio 60.31.7.

6. Tacitus, *Annals*, 12.3–4, 12.8; Pseudo-Seneca, *Apocolocyntosis*, 8, 10–11. Cassius Dio, 60.31.8.
7. On Junia Calvina's beauty and character see Tacitus, *Annals*, 12.4; Pseudo-Seneca, *Apocolocyntosis* 8.
8. Suetonius, *Life of Nero*, 7.
9. Tacitus, *Annals*, 13.16.
10. Ibid. 13.12.
11. Ibid. 13.12.
12. On Acte see Tacitus, *Annals*, 13.12. On the attributes of Poppaea the Younger see Tacitus, *Annals*, 13.46.
13. Suetonius, *Life of Nero*, 35.
14. Tacitus, *Annals*, 13.18–19.
15. Accounts of the fall of Agrippina are found at Tacitus, *Annals*, 14.3–9; Cassius Dio 61.12–14; Suetonius, *Life of Nero*
16. Tacitus, *Annals,* 14.59.
17. Suetonius, *Life of Nero*, 35.2.
18. Accounts of Octavia's divorce and death are found at Tacitus, *Annals*, 14.60–64; Cassius Dio 62.13; Suetonius, *Life of Nero*, 35.
19. Tacitus, *Annals*, 14.63.
20. Ibid. 14.64.
21. Ibid. 12.53.
22. Tacitus, *Annals*, 12.57; Cassius Dio, 60.33.
23. Tacitus, *Annals*, 12.65.
24. Ibid. 13.1; Cassius Dio, 60.34.
25. For the fall of Domitia Lepida see Tacitus, *Annals*, 12.64–65.
26. For Vitellius' public funeral and the statue see Suetonius, *Life of Vitellius*, 3.
27. For Publius Suillius' fall see Tacitus, *Annals*, 13.42–43.
28. Ibid. 13.42.
29. Ibid. 13.43. Emphasis added by the author.

XIX

1. For the first review see *The New York Times,* Thursday 23 January 1902, 8. The reviewer returned a second time and his report appeared on Saturday 8 February 1902, 8.
2. Honorius of Autun, quoted in Leiva, *Messaline, impératrice et putain,* 42.
3. Anon. *Vingt Ans de la vie d'un jeune homme,* 61.
4. Nerciat, *Les Aphrodites*; quote found on p. 94 in the 1864 edition. Translation, A. Winckler.
5. Restsif, *L'Anti-Justine,* 1798, 374; quoted in Cryle, *The Telling of the*

Act, 283. De Sade, *Juliette*, 9.44; quoted in Cryle, *The Telling of the Act*, 283.

6. Wilmot, *Rochester's Farewell*, 144–145. Emphasis added by author.
7. One 1790 French text refers to prostitutes as 'all Messalinas givers of sweetness': *Ordonnance de police sur les filles de joie*, 1790, 6:400, quoted in Cryle, *The Telling of the Act*, 285–286. In Britain, advertisements for the memoirs of the Dublin courtesan 'Kitty Cut-A-Dash' in the 1780s bill her as 'the Hibernian Messalina': for example, the one printed in *The World*, London, Thursday 11 October 1787.
8. See, for example, the 1771 print 'The Stable-Yard Messalina; The Hostile Scribe' in Yale's Lewis Walpole Library: 771.01.01.06.
9. *An epistle from L-y W-y to S-r R-d W-y, Bart*, published by P. Wright, 1782, 2. *The answer of S-r R-d W-y, Bart. to the epistle of L-y W-y*, published by T. Lewis, 1782, 1.
10. *The London Courant*, Tuesday 23 October 1781.
11. Letter one appears in the *Morning Post* on Monday 19 July 1779, letter two appears in the same paper on Monday 26 July 1779.
12. Charlotte Brontë, *Jane Eyre*, vol. 3, ch. 1.
13. For a comprehensive survey of Messalina's reception post-antiquity see Leiva, *Messaline, impératrice et putain: Généalogie d'un mythe sexuel de Pline au pornopéplum*.
14. Pseudo-Seneca, *Octavia*, 10–20.
15. Ibid. 270–272.
16. Boccaccio, *On the Fates of Famous Men*, 7.3.
17. Getty: Ms. 63 (96.MR.17), fol. 218v.
18. Bibliothèque de l'Arsenal, Paris: Ms 5193.
19. This painting is now in the Statens Museum for Kunst, Copenhagen.
20. *Reynolds Newspaper*, Sunday 16 March 1851, 9.
21. Nathanael Richards, *The Tragedy of Messalina*, act 5, scene 2.
22. Ibid. act 2, scene 1.
23. Ibid. act 4, scene 3.
24. Ibid. act 1, scene 2.
25. Ibid. act 1, scene 2.
26. Ibid. act 2, scene 2.
27. Ibid. scene 2.
28. Ibid. act 2, scene 2.
29. Leonard Gallois (ed.), *Réimpression de L'Ancien Moniteur*, Volume 18 (Paris: Au Bureau Centrale, 1841), 122: quoted and translated in Harris, *Queenship and Revolution in early modern Europe*, 39.
30. On Maria Carolina of Naples see Gorani, *Mémoires secrets et critiques*, vol. 1, 98, On Adélaïde d'Orleans see Aali, *French Royal Women during the Restoration and July Monarchy*, 185–191. For the James

Gilray print relating to Empress Josephine: BM 1851,0901.1162.
31. This painting is now in the Rjiksmuseum, Amsterdam: SK-A-4779.
32. This sculpture is now in the Musée des Beaux-Arts, Rennes.
33. This sculpture is now in the Musée d'Orsay, Paris: RF A16.
34. Quoted and translated in Rounding, *Grandes Horizontales*, 107.
35. Pona, *La Messaline*, translated into French by Lattarico, 53.
36. Ibid. 54.
37. Ibid. 57.
38. Ibid. 71.
39. Ibid. 55.
40. For an account of the 'Affair Du Bourg' see Gildea, *Children of the Revolution*, chapter 13.
41. Shapiro, 'Love Stories: Female Crimes of Passion in Fin-de-siècle Paris', 60–61.
42. Dumas, *L'Homme-Femme*, 187, edited and translated by G. Vandenhoff (New York, 1873).
43. Ibid.
44. Ibid.
45. Dumas, *La Femme de Claude*, act 1, translation, C. A. Byrne (New York, 1905).
46. Ibid.
47. Ibid. act 2.
48. Ibid. act 1 and 2.
49. Ibid. act 1.
50. Krafft-Ebing, *Psychopathia Sexualis*, 4.i, translation, Klaf, F., (New York, 1965).
51. Wyke, *The Roman Mistress: Ancient and Modern Representations*, 328–330.
52. Baudelaire, *Les Fleurs du Mal*. Translation, W. Aggeler (Fresno, 1954).
53. Quoted in Leiva, *Messaline, impératrice et putain*, 202.
54. Translation, Friedman, *An Anthology of Belgian Symbolist Poets* (New York, 2003).
55. Graves, *I, Claudius*, 378.

Image Credits

1. The Picture Art Collection / Alamy Stock Photo
2. Miguel Hermoso Cuesta, Wikimedia Commons
3. DEA / G. DAGLI ORTI / Contributor / Getty Images
4. Marie-Lan Nguyen / Wikimedia Commons
5. Marie-Lan Nguyen (2011), Wikimedia Commons
6. Art Collection 3 / Alamy Stock Photo
7. The Picture Art Collection / Alamy Stock Photo
8. DEA / G. DAGLI ORTI / Contributor / Getty Images
9. © Staatliche Kunstsammlungen Dresden / Elke Estel / Hans-Peter Klut
10. Robert Kawka / Alamy Stock Photo
11. Artefact / Alamy Stock Photo
12. The Picture Art Collection / Alamy Stock Photo
13. incamerastock / Alamy Stock Photo
14. Alessandra Benedetti - Corbis / Contributor / Getty Images
15. Universal History Archive / Contributor / Getty Images
16. Historical image collection by Bildagentur-online / Alamy Stock Photo
17. Heritage Images / Contributor / Getty Images
18. © Isabella Stewart Gardner Museum / Bridgeman Images
19. User:Bibi Saint-Pol, own work, 2007-02-10 / Wikimedia Commons
20. DEA / A. DAGLI ORTI / Contributor / Getty Images
21. Giorgio Cosulich de Pecine / Contributor / Getty Images
22. Photo Josse/Leemage / Contributor / Getty Images
23. Sepia Times / Contributor / Getty Images
24. Sepia Times / Contributor / Getty Images
25. Hansrad Collection / Alamy Stock Photo
26. Heritage Images / Contributor / Getty Images
27. © Marie-Lan Nguyen / Wikimedia Commons / CC-BY 2.5 / Wikimedia Commons
28. Everett Collection, Inc. / Alamy Stock Photo
29. © Aubrey Beardsley, 1895. Photo Tate Britain
30. © Peter Willi / Bridgeman Images

INDEX

Page references followed by fn indicate a footnote